Sharing HEARTS

Love & Surprises

NANCY ASHWORTH

authorHOUSE®

AuthorHouse™
1663 Liberty Drive
Bloomington, IN 47403
www.authorhouse.com
Phone: 1-800-839-8640

Published by AuthorHouse   10/23/2014

ISBN: 978-1-4969-3306-5 (sc)
ISBN: 978-1-4969-3367-6 (e)

Library of Congress Control Number: 2014914274

Cover artist is Robert Seely III.

This book is printed on acid-free paper.

SHARING HEARTS
Love & Surprises

By Nancy Ashworth

With Love to my sister, Bonnie Wheeler,
who always inspires me with her sharing heart,
And family: Garry, Brad, Kevin and Lonna.

To my sister of the soul
who has helped me become
the woman I am.

To our heroes who have and are sharing their
lives for our freedom:
Garry, Brad and grandsons:
Branden and Matthew

To Kevin with his loving, caring, sharing
and kind heart.

To Lonna with her open heart filled with
God's gracious spirit.

The Lord is my light and my salvation....
Psalms 27:1

2nd in the Heart Series

THANK YOU

Thank you to Rob Seely III for drawing and painting my book cover. Rob is like a son to me as he has been my son's best friend since they were small. You did a great job Rob!

Thank you to my friends Sharon, Elizabeth, Marilyn, Carolyn, Lori, Kirk, Linda and Steve who have encouraged me to continue this series. I hope that you enjoy it as their stories continue. Go with God Always…it is the only way to go.

SHARING HEARTS CHARACTERS

GRAY'S
JOSEPH (JOE) AUGUST - 35 – 6'2" white blonde hair, green eyes, muscular, husband of Elizabeth
ELIZABETH (LIZBETH) JAMES/HAWKINS/GRAY- 32 –5'7"- red hair, brown eyes, beautiful, wife of Joe.
GLORIA (GLORY) LEANN - 15 – 5'6" – long white blonde hair, green eyes, willowy figure, country talking and raised.
BETH ANN - 12 – 5'3" – red hair and brown eyes – Looks like a younger version of her mother – Elizabeth – very smart and kind hearted.
SAMUEL (SAMMY) JOSEPH- 8- 4'9"- white blonde hair and green eyes – curious and bright, sweet and caring child.
NONA JAMES - 52 – 5'6" – Brown hair and eyes- sturdily built – Owns Nona's Café in City of Roy, wonderful cook. Very good hearted and plain speaking. Mother of Elizabeth.
SAMUEL (SKINNY) JOHN GATES - 76 – 6' –Gray eyes and thick gray hair, very thin and wiry, Rancher, father of Lora, brother of Pokey – Elizabeth's grandfather.
ERNEST (POKEY) CHARLES WHITE -75 -5'10"- Faded blue eyes and balding gray hair. Retired Marshal, cocky and stern, man of few words, second father to Lora, brother to Skinny and adopted grandfather of Elizabeth.
REVEREND MAX ROY – 74 - 6'- Bushy red beard with red and gray hair. Preacher in Cities of John, Roy and Ernest. Talks loud, outspoken but tenderhearted. Cousin of Skinny and Pokey.

EWING'S:
ZAKARIAH (ZAK) EDWARD – 36 – 6' – Black hair and brown eyes, Muscular and good looking, husband of Stephie, best friend of Joe.
STEPHANIE (STEPHIE) CAROLYN - 35 -5'5"- Blonde and blue eyes – Lovely and soft spoken wife of Zak and best friend of Elizabeth.
JACOB (JAKE) MARK - 18 - 6'3", Black hair and brown eyes like dad –Very big and muscular and extremely good looking. Charming personality - Loves Glory.
WESLEY RAY (SHORTY) - 15 - 5'8" – Light brown hair and blue eyes – Slim and tough. Good hearted and sees only black and white no in-betweens.

CAROLYN (CARRIE LYNN) SUSAN - 12 – 5'3" – Lovely dark blonde hair and blue eyes- Refreshingly smart and sensible – Best friend of Beth Ann.

PAYTON YVONNE – 8 – 4'5" – Brown hair and blue eyes – small, impish and hard headed.

DON EWING – 56 – 5'10" – Balding gray hair and blue eyes – Father of Zak – A Cowboy who can fix anything.

JOYANN (GRANNY JO) EWING – 54 – 5'3" – Graying brown hair and brown eyes – Great cook, dry sense of humor. Mother of Zak.

FREED'S (EX-SERVANTS OF ELIZABETH'S)

BENNY - 30 – 5'9" – Beautiful dark eyes – Slender and very muscular – Kindhearted – Loves Sammy – Husband of Minnie.

MINNIE – 28 – 5'5" – Happy, sassy, honest to a fault – kindhearted –Loves Sammy like her own as she raised him – wife of Benny.

ARTY – 11 – 4'8" – Small and very thin – insecure – raised with Sammy so loves him like a brother – son of Minnie and Benny.

CONNIE AND CATIE – Twins born to Minnie and Benny.

JOE'S INDIAN FRIENDS- GOOD HEART'S FAMILY

GOOD HEART – 30 – 6'2" – Big muscular man, great tracker, honest and loving, great with horses, great friend to Joe.

YELLOW MOON – 26 – 5'2"- Large brown eyes and long black hair, long long eyelashes – very beautiful with a heart shaped face–a healer.

RUNNING BEAR – 11 -5'5" – Young brave almost a man by Indian standards, slender and a good hunter.

JUMPING RABBIT – 9 – 5' – Very fast runner and good tracker.

SMOOTH WATERS -6 – 4'4" – Beautiful like her mother – small, delicate and slender. Good hearted – smiles all the time.

MORNING SUN – 4– 3'9" – Lovely like mother and sister – very tiny boned – brave and not afraid of anything – sees the good in all things.

BRIGHT STAR – Baby boy – just born.

THE BAXTER'S - CITY OF JOHN FRIENDS

BOBBY JOE – 36 – 6'2" - big and muscular. Brown hair and eyes. Wonderful sense of humor. Loves his family most of all.

HANNAH GAYLE – 28 – 5'3"- small and lovely – kind hearted – Blonde and blue eyed. Very lovely.

ROBERT – 18 – 6' 3" brawny – Brown eyes and hair. Son of Bobby Joe and Jane. Tall and good looking. Very patient and kind.

JANA LEE – 7 – 4'6" Sun streaked brown hair with brown eyes. Looks like Hannah…very motherly to younger siblings.

GRACIE ROSE – 5 – 4'2" -Brown hair and blue eyed…little spitfire.

MARYANN – 3 – Red hair and brown eyes – shy & quiet- easily distracted

CHARLEY – 1- brown hair and eyes – into everything – follows Jana Lee everywhere she goes.

JOE'S COWBOYS

OLD PETE RYAN – 62 – 5'5" – Bald and very witty – Thin and scrawny but strong as an ox. Cooks for Joe's cowboys.

GEOFF RIOS - 19 – 5'10" - black hair and brown eyes – exceptionally good looking. Been with Joe since he was 15 and an orphan. Joe is like a father to him.

KEVIN TEE – 20 - 5'9" – blonde hair and blue eyed- trustworthy and loyal Breaking horses is his favorite thing to do

RANDY MCDEE– 34 – 5'10"- black hair and blue eyed- extremely handsome Best cowboy on the ranch with doctoring cattle and horses

DAVID SUNDAY – 45- 6'2" –brown hair and brown eyes –weathered cowboy Great with cattle and breaking horses.

EARL COE – 40 – 5'8" – brown hair and blue eyed – Slim and tough. Best friend of Joe's since they cowboyed together.

CITY OF ROY FOLKS

HANK BOGGS - 56 – 6'7" – Huge man – totally bald – Huge bear like arms –softhearted and kind-Loves young'uns and animals – Owns Boggs Livery Stable. Married to Ella.

ELLA BOGGS - 55 – 5'8"- Tall and very thin with wiry gray hair – Plain speaking but loving and kind hearted – Gifted Seamstress – Married to Hank.

FRANK OWENS – 35 – 5'10" – Slim and muscular – Brown hair and eyes – fair in business and kind hearted. Owns Owen's Mercantile.

MARILYNN OWENS – 32 – 5'5" -blonde and blue eyed - slim, beautiful and knows it. Spirited and good hearted.

ST. LOUIS FOLKS

EDGAR HAWKINS - 62 – 5'8" -Thin and crafty, bossy, small eyes and sharp nose. Father of Elizabeth and married to Lora. Dies in gun fight after kidnapping Glory in Loving Hearts.

LORA HAWKINS - 60 – 5'5"-Tall and homely looking, bony and sharp tongued. Mother to Elizabeth. Daughter of Skinny. Was killed by Edgar after they kidnapped Glory in Loving Hearts.

FRANKLIN POTTER - 60 – 5'5" – Short, fat and balding with the manners of a pig. Mean spirited. Owner of Potter's Bank in St. Louis. Killed in Loving Hearts after kidnapping Glory.

JUDGE DEAN BURNFIN –62 6' -Brown hair and blue eyes -Tall, slim and dignified. Good natured and fair.

MRS. LESLIE BURNFIN – 55 – 5'5"-Brown hair and brown eyes -wife of "The Judge" –Lovely and kind hearted.

SHERIFF GARTH WHEELER – 39 – 5'11" Sandy blonde hair and blue eyes – Fair and honest to a fault. Kind hearted but goes by the law.

CHARLES SLOAN – 24 – 5'10" – Brown hair and long eyes lashes with brown eyes – Kind hearted and honest – nephew of Franklin Potter and works at the bank.

FRANCIS RONVO- 22 – 5'5" – Beautiful brown hair and blue eyed lady who is engaged to Charles Sloan.

DONNA SLOAN – 20 – 5'2" – Brown hair and blue eyed – Small and delicate looking. Sister of Charles and niece of Franklin Potter.

JAMES (JIM) ALBERT – 24 – 5'10" – Big shouldered good natured young man engaged to Donna Sloan.

RANDY FORD – 25 – 5'9" – Black hair and blue eyed – works at Hawkin's Mercantile honest with a wonderful, kind personality.

CHRIS BALL – 20 – 5'8" – Blonde and blue eyed – Works at Hawkin's Mercantile stocking shelves and delivering goods.

CATHERINE FORD – 16 -5'5" – Beautiful blonde haired blue eyed young lady.

JOHANNA LIGHT – 23 – 5'6" – Long black hair, brown eyes, very white skin, beautiful beyond words, Smart and kind hearted. Owns Johanna's Café.

BILL COLLIER – 28 – 5'10" – Blonde and blue eyed handsome man who is a waiter at Johanna's Café.

STEVEN CULLY – 42 – 5'8" – Rancher who holds a grudge against Pokey and keeps trying to shoot him.

JANETTE MASTERS– 22 – 5'8" – Beautiful young lady who is a gifted horseback rider.

ERNESTEEN MASTERS– 50 – 5'6" – Loving mother of Janette.

MRS. ANITA MARKS – 35 – 5'4" – Friend of Lora's – who loves her daughter a lot.

JACI MARKS –9 – 4'5" – very small and delicate girl with a loving heart.

MRS. MARY LOUISE– 42 – 5' – Black hair and brown eyes – small and slender she is a seamstress with a heart of gold.

HOWARD AND CINDY PEABODY – Young couple with five children that are helped by Glory and Beth Ann.

BALDINGER HOTEL IN ST. LOUIS

CHRISTINA BALDINGER – 22 – 5'5" – Beautiful brown hair and eyes – Spirited and lovely to be around. Owns the Baldinger Hotel in St. Louis.

ETTA MAY – 14 – 5'3" – Young colored maid. Stout and strong young lady with a generous smile and attitude. Has a large gap in her front teeth.

BESSIE – 13 – 5'2" – Young colored maid – Has an overabundance of hair tied in little pig tails all over her head.

SADIE – 14 – 5'4" – young colored maid – very thin and slender but strong. Has a large scar on her arm.

BRIAN RAYMOND– 25 – 5'6" – Dark brown hair and brown eyes – Bell Hop and all around help at the hotel.

STEPHEN GREER– 40 – 5'10" - Owner of Greer's Fine Food inside the Baldinger Hotel. Blonde and blue eyed with a wonderful personality.

ADAMS BATHING HOUSE

LEE ADAMS – 46 – 6' – Older Cowboy who owns the Adams Bath House – walks with a limp due to an accident at Skinny and Pokey's ranch. Great friend of theirs.

GAY ARTHUR – 25 – 5'2" – Black hair and blue eyes – lovely lady – slender and curvy – works in the Adams Bath House.

POTTER'S ST LOUIS SERVANTS

LUCIEN – Butler – 45 -5' 8" – Very dark colored servant – Very thin and regal.

ILA KAY – 40 – 5'7" – Beautiful light skinned colored servant – A little outspoken but kind hearted.

DOTTIE – 38 – 5'5" – Lovely golden skinned colored servant – beautiful to see.

CHESTER – 23 – 5'8" – Dark black colored servant – very muscular – works in the stable – a little slow in learning.

MOLLY – 12 - 4'8" – Very small dark skinned colored servant – cute and sweet.

BETH ANN'S ST LOUIS SCHOOL FRIENDS

DENNIS – 13 – 5'5" - Light brown hair and green eyes – slender and competitive.

KATHY – 12 – 5'5"-Lovely blonde haired and blue eyed girl. Kindhearted and friendly.

GINA – 12 – 4'10" - Tiny blonde and blue eyed girl who seems to float on air as she walks.

RODNEY – 12 – 5'4" – Brown hair & eyes – Ruggedly built – always competing with Dennis.

MARKUS – 13 – 5'6" – Black hair & brown eyes – Full of fun…loves telling jokes.

DENISA – 12 – 5'2" – Brown hair and eyes – Full of mischief – always teasing everyone.

LEA – 12 – 5'3" – Brown hair & blue eyes –shy & quiet with a wonderful sense of humor.

EDGAR'S ST LOUIS SERVANTS

JASPER – Butler –38 – 6' – Wiry build dark skinned colored servant – kind hearted. Married to Bootsy and Mertie is their daughter.

BOOTSY – Cook & Housekeeper – 36 – 5'5" – Light skinned colored servant – sassy and kind hearted. Married to Jasper and Mertie is her daughter.

OLD MARTA – 50 – 5'2" – Dark black colored servant – Wonderful cook – a little overweight. States the obvious and has been a slave all her life.

MERTIE – 11 – 4'8" – Colored servant child – cute as can be and always willing to help- loving and happy.

SKINNY & POKEY'S COWBOYS

BRADFORD RAY – 20 - 6'2" -Muscular – Black hair and Blue eyes. Orphan that Skinny & Pokey found on the streets in St. Louis and took in. Bodyguard for Pokey and Skinny quite often fast with a gun.

JAY JAMES - INDIAN - 20 – 6'1" - Very muscular and slim. Watched solders kill his parents and they left him to die at 10 years old and badly injured. Skinny found him and nursed him back to health. Bodyguards for Skinny and Pokey quite often…fast with a gun or knife.

JOSH BECK – 19 – 6' – muscular cowboy – Brown hair and eyes -Orphan that Skinny and Pokey rescued after his family is killed in a fire.

KEVIN DANIELS – 19 – 5'11" – Blonde hair and blue eyes – Parents killed by outlaws when he was 6 years old…raised by Skinny and Pokey.

DAVEY RAYMOND – 24 – 6' – Brown hair and eyes – tough young man with a great sense of humor and is a big kidder. Orphan after mother dies…she begs Pokey to take him and raise him. He loves to pull jokes on the other cowboys.

MATT JACKSON – 27 – 5'10" – Brown hair and blue eyes – orphan who family dies in a fire. Is dramatic with his joking and jokes as often as he can.

MIKE ADAMS – 25 -5'8" – Blonde haired and blue eyed –Serious young man – takes care of everyone around him. Saw his pa gunned down in front of him at 12 years old and no other family so raised by Skinny and Pokey. Very thoughtful and caring young man.

BRANDEN BARNS – 26 – 5'9" – Brown hair and eyes –great musician plays drums and other instruments. Full of fun but tends to be serious – always reliable. Family dies when he is 12 years old and he is ill for a long time so Pokey and Skinny took him home with them.

GREG WILEY – 21 – 5'10" – Brown hair and brown eyes –Tall and lanky built. Works with the cattle the most. At 5 years old the riverboat he is on sinks and he is the only survivor on it. No one claimed him so Pokey took him home with him.

BIG JOHN SWEENEY – 44 – 6' - Light brown hair and blue eyes – Big heavy set man. Cooks and watches over the ranch while Skinny and Pokey are gone. Great sense of humor…kids around a lot with everyone. Was shot in the back by outlaws who killed his wife and child when he was 25 years old. Skinny took him in and nursed him back to health so he stays on as cook and doctors the cowboys for them.

RON (DOC) ARTHUR – Doc – 32 – 6' - Brown hair and blue eyes – was orphaned at 14 when outlaws kill his ma and pa who was a doctor because his outlaw patient died. So he and Big John doctor the cowboys when needed.

JC (PREACHER) PATTON – 30 - 5'10 - Brown hair and blue eyes - 16 years old when outlaws ambush him and his pa and kill his pa then are torturing him to find out where they hid their money when Skinny stops it. He has burn marks on his chest. Father was a preacher and he knows the bible and lives by it.

JESSE (CHARMER) CARY – 30 – 6'3"- Black hair and blue eyes - Been with Skinny since he was 14 years old and his ma died after being shot in a bank robbery in St. Louis and he has no other family. Skinny brought him home with him. Good with a fiddle and sings beautifully.

NORMAN (TRACKER) LIGHTFOOT – 35 - 6'1"-Kiowa Indian –Black hair and brown eyes. When he was 7 years old – left for dead after soldiers kill his family. Skinny and Pokey found him and keep him as they can't find any other family of his. Scar on shoulder where he was stabbed by soldier with a bayonet. Great tracker like Jay.

TOM SNELL – Papa Tom – Gray hair and faded blue eyes - older than dirt he says – in his 60's plus – Small bow legged cowboy who has been with Skinny and Pokey most all his life. Too old to ride much so helps out at the ranch everywhere he is needed. Wonderful sense of humor. Like a grandfather to the cowboys.

SKINNY & POKEY'S INDIAN FRIENDS- Tribe of Cherokee Indians that live close to Skinny and Pokey's Ranch. All have dark brown eyes and black hair.

RED SUN – CHIEF – 42 - 5'10" – slim and tough – Good leader and good sense of humor. Wise man.

GRAY BEAR – 18 – 5'10" – Slender and muscular and very good looking – Son of Red Sun

MORNING LARK – 16 – 5'3" – small boned..lovely girl with large brown eyes and long lashes. An orphan who loves Gray Bear.

BROKEN ARROW – 17 – 5'9" – muscular and good looking.

RISING MOON – 23 – 5'11" – tough and hardened young man.

WILLOW – 15 – 5'3" – young beautiful Indian girl.

SPRINGING LION – 20 -5'8" – Small, muscular and kind hearted.

RACE AND HIS OUTLAW FRIENDS FROM ST. LOUIS

RACE JACKS – 35 – 5'6" – Ferret looking small man with shifty eyes and a wiry frame, greedy – Son of Edgar Hawkins.

GOLDEN EAGLE – 35 – Big broad shoulders golden colored skin instead of red...wide nose with long scar across his chest. Mean and follows all orders.

PATCH FLYNN - 34 – Large muscular man with long blonde hair and one blue eye with a mean temper. Has lost an eye so wears a patch.

ALBERT BROTT – 28 – Tall and thin with brown hair and blue eyes. Card shark who takes what he wants when he wants it.

Outlaw who is talked about from Loving Hearts

PATRICK SULLY – 38- Outlaw who worked for Edgar Hawkins and Franklin Potter who kidnapped Glory and was sent to prison.

1850 GRIEVING FOR LORA
Chapter 1

"Do the best you can and leave the rest to God."

"Well, brother, our girl is gone. She redeemed herself at the end. Wish I'd done things differently. God, Pokey, she suffered at his hands. I never thought that would happen," Skinny sadly admits as tears run down his weathered cheeks.

"Yeah, I wish I'd done some thangs different, too. I could have been kinder and tried to understand more. Naw, I never thought Edgar was that mean either," Pokey replies as he also wipes tears from his eyes.

"What's done is done though, brother. We cain't change it and we tried to do what was right by Lora. I know we did. I don't know now.... maybe we should have understood...," Skinny says looking through tear filled eyes at the sky then continues humbly, *"Lord, oh Lord, my dear Lord, were we cruel to Lora? Were we unreasonable to expect so much? We gave her more than we thought was good for her and yet she always wanted more. Sweet God in Heaven what could we have done differently?"*

"I just don't know, Skinny," Pokey answers sadly.

Joe is standing silently behind the two old gents. He was on his way to the pasture to check on the runaway milk cow when he came upon the two men sitting behind the big lilac bush. Joe sighs at their pain at losing their only child, Lora. Lora wasn't a child when she died; she was a grown woman who had chosen the wrong man to marry, a wicked greedy man, who only wanted more and more money. Poor Edgar, he chose the wrong path in life. Bowing his head Joe silently prays, *"Lord, what can we do to hep Grandpas Pokey and Skinny? How can we lessen their grief? I know it was just yesterday that Lora died and was buried and that time heals but Lord cain't we do somethan' now to hep'em? Please Lord give me an idea of how to do it?"*

"I shorely hate leaving her out there all by herself," Pokey sadly admits, "Think we otta make a better restin' place for our girl."

Lifting his gray head Skinny answers, "Yeah, we should do that. We could take her home to the ranch, couldn't we?"

"Guess so," Pokey slowly agrees shaking his head yes.

Suddenly Joe knows what he needs to do. Silently he turns around walking back to the ranch house to his wife, Elizabeth.

Elizabeth is standing at the sink washing the breakfast dishes when Joe walks back into the kitchen. Smiling he puts his arms around her slim waist asking as he kisses her smooth neck, "Lizbeth, come and sit down for a minute, honey. I need to talk to ya."

Smiling wanly Elizabeth dries her hands asking, "Do you want some more coffee, Joe?"

"No, not right now. I have an idea and need to see what ya think about it," Joe replies as they walk over to the large kitchen table and sit down.

"Not more bad news?" Elizabeth asks suddenly as her face whitens at the thought.

"Oh, no, honey. I didn't mean for ya to think that. I think it will be good news. I want to know what ya think about it," Joe replies quickly as he looks at her red rimmed eyes and tired face then asks, "Are all the young'uns still asleep?"

"They are lying down, if nothing else. I told Nona, I mean, Mother, to lie down on our bed and I'd finish the dishes. I wanted to be alone a little while," Elizabeth answers smiling slightly.

"I was out lookin' for Bessie; she chewed through the rope again. I was walkin' behind the lilac bushes and heard our grandpas talkin'. They are grievin' somethan' terrible and talkin' about Lora and how they hate she is buried out thar by herself. It started me athinkin', how about makin' a buryin' plot here and movin' her body here. What'cha think?" Joe explains smiling hopefully at her.

"Oh Joe, that is a wonderful idea. I was just thinking the same thing a little while ago and shedding a few tears that I'd never know where her grave is because it doesn't take long for all traces to be gone. Where could we make it though?" Elizabeth asks smiling happily at her adored husband.

"I haven't thought on it much but how about close to that row of lilacs ya like so much. It is a restful spot. That is where they are sittin' right now." Joe replies smiling happily.

They both cock their heads to the side as they hear a noise outside.

"Is that a horse coming up the road?" Elizabeth asks as she rises and walking over to the door looks out saying, "It is Reverend Roy, Joe."

Smiling and nodding yes, Joe answers, "God works in wonderful ways, honey. I just asked him to hep us out and he sends Rev Roy. God is good. Hey, Reverend Roy, step down and come on in."

Now Reverend Maxwell Roy is a tall thin man with a bush of white hair hanging down to his shoulders and a beard of red bright enough to make you blink and then those blazingly blue eyes make him a sight to behold. His wide smile and booming voice follow right along with his boisterous laughter.

Dismounting he smiles sweetly at Elizabeth as he gently asks, "Little lady what is going on that has caused you such sorrow?"

Elizabeth bursts into tears at his kindness so Joe pulls her close to his chest as he welcomes, "Come in Rev Roy we have a sad story to tell ya."

Max Roy follows them into the kitchen as Elizabeth asks, "Would you like some pie with your coffee, Rev Roy, or would you like breakfast?"

"Wouldn't mind a piece a pie a bit, thank you, Elizabeth. Now tell me what has happened. I rode into Roy last night and heard Nona had rushed out here after ole Pete came and told her she was needed. Somebody sick?"

Joe explains, "Yes, Beth Ann and Sammy were both very sick but are all right now. Let me start at the first so ya'll understand it all. Well first Glory was kidnapped in the dead of the night by men hired by Edgar Hawkins and Franklin Potter."

"Glory KIDNAPPED!" Rev Roy states aghast.

Nodding yes Joe continues, "Yep, she knew better than to go outside by herself. We were being real careful; at least, we thought we were. Beth Ann got bad sick to her stomach and couldn't keep anythan' down so we were tendin' her all day and into the night. Glory wanted to empty the chamber pots and needed to go to the outhouse herself so she went. Can't rightly say why she didn't wake us up but know we were all tuckered out from the ordeal with Beth Ann. Glory's alright just bruised up some. Anyway we didn't find out till morning that she was gone until the guards changed and found my cowboys were knocked out and trussed up. Good Heart had been watchin' the house so he followed the outlaws and left markers for us to follow. They took us a long around way of going ten miles from here. Bless Glory's heart she did her best to mark the trail. God was with her as they didn't catch her leave her shoes and a ribbon behind. We found Good Heart's trail and slipped in about dusk last night. Lordy, was it only last night? It seems ole Edgar and Mr. Potter wanted to do away with me and take my family back to St. Louie with them, Rev Roy. My cowboys, Skinny and Pokey's cowboys, me and, of course, Jake, all slid down the hills into a natural valley they had camped out in. Good

Heart was in one of the trees and whistled to us tellin' us he was thar. Glory knows his calls so she was relieved to know he was watchin' out for her also."

"My gracious what happened next?" Rev Roy inquires anxiously as Joe stops for a breath.

"We were awatchin' and awaitin' ta git a good shot at rescuin' her when Edgar and ole Potter, who were all lickered up, decided they were gonna have some fun with our Glory," Joe explains with a snarl.

"Betcha Glory didn't let that happen," Rev Roy replies as he leans back in his chair sipping his hot coffee.

"Not for a minute. Her hands were tied to a wagon wheel and she couldn't git loose at first but she worked the ropes until she loosened 'em up. I think Lora heped. Lickered up they decided they were man enough to mess with our Glory then Lora jumped to her defense. She fought like a tiger for Glory and Reverend they killed her," Joe explains sadly.

"Glory said she tried to make amends for going along with them. She never thought they would hurt Glory. I'm sure she didn't know that. They beat her Rev Roy and Edgar – who isn't my father by the way – kicked her in the head and she died," Elizabeth explains on a sob. She lowers her head to her hands crying out her pain.

Max Roy leans over patting Elizabeth's quaking shoulders saying, "She redeemed herself, didn't she? She had a change of heart and knew she had done wrong and was sorry for it. I'm sure God knows that, honey."

Elizabeth smiles weakly shaking her head yes adding, "I hope so."

"Okay, what is going on and why is Elizabeth crying again!" asks an exasperated Nona from the doorway, "Max Roy if you make my girl cry again I will never bake you another pie!"

"Oh, don't threaten me with such a dire fate, Nona. I'm finding out what has been happening here the past couple of days. It's a sad tale," Max Roy states meekly.

Nona's face clouds as she walks over laying her callused hands on Elizabeth's shoulders agreeing, "Yes, some goin' ons that is for sure."

"Sit down Nona and let Joe finish telling me the tale," Rev Roy begs while he pulls the pie pan closer to him taking another slice of apple pie out.

Nona picks up the coffee pot refilling their coffee cups then sits down to listen.

"Glory baited'em with questions. She demanded to know why Edgar would even think immoral thoughts about her so he tells her she weren't no relations to him. It made him no difference. So she asked him what he meant cause Elizabeth was his daughter and he bragged and told her a story about stealin' Lizbeth when she was a little girl from a woman named Nona who was travelin' in a wagon train through St. Louie," Joe explains then sits back as Max Roy stares first at Elizabeth then Nona.

He sputters, "Well I'll be danged why didn't I see it! They are alike in many ways but Elizabeth looks more like her pa than Nona. Well, I'll be hung by my toes, I never saw it before."

"We didn't either," Nona replies tearfully as she gently caresses Elizabeth's arm, "I knew I loved this girl but I never realized she was my own. I never imagined that she was kidnapped. I thought she'd been killed by some animal. We searched all over the area for days looking for her. It broke our hearts to lose her."

Elizabeth smiles lovingly at her mother Nona, saying, "I was taken in revenge for Nona…Mother refusing to become my fath…uh Edgar's mistress. It is so confusing! How could he steal a child from her mother! I can't understand his thinking!" Tears run rivers down her lovely flushed face as she stares at Rev Roy waiting for an answer.

Patting her hand he gently answers, "Oh, honey, humans are capable of inhuman deeds all the time. He just acted on his need for revenge. If I remember correctly he weren't a good looking fellow and he probably was awed by Nona's beauty."

"Oh, get on with you, Max Roy. I ain't never been beautiful," Nona spouts blushing wildly.

"You know better than that Nona. You've always been beautiful and you have a beautiful spirit inside of you. You've been fighting off men ever since I knowd you and you cain't deny it," Max Roy states firmly raising up one bushy eye brow.

"Weren't none that compared to my husband and I weren't interested in none of them! Including you! You'd run a woman ragged doing all this trasping around you do. So I just feed you when you come home to Roy to stay a bit. So don't be givin' me any grief about any man wantin' me," Nona states firmly.

Joe, Elizabeth and Max all roar with laughter at Nona's statement. "Well don't call me a liar MOTHER but I say yar full of a bushel of beans on that statement," Joe replies laughing then jumps out her way as she reaches over to slap his hand.

Laughing Max replies, "I'm too close to you to say another word about it."

Nona arches her eye brows then looking over at Elizabeth is pleased to see she isn't crying anymore so asks, "And you, young lady, what do you have to say?"

Smiling Elizabeth replies, "Nothing, Mother," then giggles.

"Well that's a first," Joe states flatly then moves farther back in his chair as Elizabeth slaps at his hand.

With the mood much lighter Joe continues his story, "Edgar sent Lora away for a while then they brought Elizabeth, who Nona had named Lizzy, back as their child."

"Well, I'll be hanged by my toes," Rev Roy exclaims again.

"Well then thangs got out of control. They made my girl real mad and that ain't a good thang," Joe explains chuckling.

"No, I wouldn't say so. She's got the temper of a wildcat when stirred up. I saw it a couple of times but it was injustices she avenged not for herself," Rev Max Roy explains with another chuckle.

Nodding yes with his crooked smile Joe continues, "Yep, she inherited her ma's temper alright," then chuckling again jumps out of his chair as Elizabeth leans menacingly towards him.

"Enough wisecracking, Joe, finish the story," Nona demands with a reluctant grin.

Serious now Joe continues, "Well they tried to hurt her. Tore the front of her dress and she was furious. So she got ready to fight'em all."

"What do you really mean she fought them? How?" questions Rev Max Roy startled.

"Fighting'em as she was one mad girl. She fought like Good Heart had taught her. We couldn't hep her – she was right in front of us. If we'd come out they coulda killed her before we got to her so we didn't have any choice but to watch and wait for our chance to out number'em. It was an amazin' sight somethan' I'll always remember. When one of those tough guys tried to grab her she went down on one knee and tossed him over her shoulder. When three came at her she went down on her knee and swung out her right leg and tripped'em all. When another one came at her she grabbed him and threw him into two other men. It was only when they joined together that they were able to take her to the ground. I'm real proud of her. She did a fine job of protectin' herself, didn't leave much for the rest of us to do. Oh yeah, Jake got to fight the leader, Patrick Sully, is his name. He bullied Glory and bruised her up on the way out thar; I do believe the boy enjoyed it."

"Did you hang'em out there?" Rev Roy asks concerned.

"They wanted to but I wouldn't let'em. Don't want no hangings on my conscience. We sent'em to the sheriff in the City of Roy, he will take care of them legally. Boys should be gettin' back tomorra. I told'em to take their time, they deserved it," Joe answers thoughtfully.

"What about Skinny and Pokey, where are they?" Rev Roy asks looking around into the other rooms from his seat.

"Out in the pasture mournin' Lora?" Joe answers sadly then continues, "That is why I came back into the house, Lizabeth, to talk to ya about a thought I had when I saw how much they are grievin'."

"What Joe?" Elizabeth asks puzzled.

"They are worried they won't be able to find Lora's grave ta visit it, ya know, later. I think we should make us a buryin' plot and bring her here and bury her proper like. It's the right thang to do. Don'tcha think?" Joe asks looking around.

Tears start again as Elizabeth jumps up grabbing Joe; she hugs him saying, "Oh, yes, please Joe. It would mean the world to all of us. I know it sounds mean but I don't want Him here but I do want my Mother Lora. She did her best by me and the children."

Elizabeth looks over at Nona beseechingly for her to understand why Lora was so important to her and is rewarded when Nona says, "Elizabeth it would be unusual if you didn't love her. She raised you and she did a fine job of it too."

Elizabeth moves over and hugs her real mother saying, "Thank you for understanding, Mother."

Nona hugs her back explaining, "Elizabeth, I wish you'd call me Ma like you did as a little girl. Mother is too dignified to me and, well, that was Lora's name. I'm just a ma or mama. What'cha think?"

"I think I can force myself to do that if it would please you," Elizabeth answers truthfully smiling happily at her.

"Me, too, MAAAA," Joe jokingly adds.

"Let's go find my old brothers," Rev Roy advises standing up and heading for the door.

"I'll stay here and start some dinner. Elizabeth, you go with them," Nona orders briskly.

"Yes, madam," Elizabeth quietly murmurs so taking Joe's outstretched hand, she follows him out the door.

The three of them walk over to the row of lilac bushes (which Elizabeth had planted so many years ago). They rise majestically high to the blue sky in lush colors and heavenly smells. Pokey and Skinny are still sitting on the ground on the far side talking to each other and remembering Lora.

Rev Max Roy and Joe talk on the way over of non important things so that the two old gents won't be startled when they walk up.

Hearing them coming they both wipe their eyes starting to stand up when the three join them.

"Sit down for a few minutes with me, please," Elizabeth begs.

Patting her hand, Skinny replies, "Sure honey. Everything okay?"

Looking down at the sparse grass Elizabeth answers, "Well, not really grandpas."

"Then tell us and let us help ya with whatever problem ya have, honey," Pokey replies seriously.

Looking up at them she states plainly, "I want Mother to be buried here at the ranch and not out there all by herself!"

Both old gents glance at Joe with a glimmer of hope in their eyes but without saying a word. They remember the danger and heartache that Joe has gone through due in part by Lora's determination to take his family back to St. Louis and they also know Lora and Edgar wanted Joe dead.

Joe and Rev Roy sit down on the grass as well when Joe replies, "I think that would be a good idea. She shouldn't be out thar all by herself. We could make a buryin' plot right here where the lilacs smell so good and sweet. What'cha think?"

Skinny and Pokey look at each other as Pokey quietly says, "This be a fine place."

Skinny looks up at the sky blinking away tears muttering, "A real fine place."

Smiling Max Roy says, "Well then we need to get busy don't we. We need a nice box, a wagon to get Lora in, a grave dug and some words spoken."

"We can make the box. Do you have some wood, Joe?" asks Skinny smiling for the first time.

"Sure, in the barn. Use what ya need. I'll get the wagon and ask Zak to go with me and we will git her and bring her home," Joe agrees nodding yes.

"I'll go, too," Elizabeth states taking a deep breath.

"No, honey, ya need to be here ready to put her in one of her prettiest dresses to be buried in. I think Nona and Stephie will help ya. I'll ask when I go over to Zak's," Joe explains softly.

"Oh yes, that is right. I've never done this before," Elizabeth admits then thinks about dressing her dead mother and doesn't quite know how to go about doing it, so smiling sadly adds, "I'm sure they won't mind helping me."

Patting her shoulder Rev Roy answers, "No, honey, they won't mind helping you." He nods at Joe and motions for them to leave so he can talk to his two old friends.

"Come, Elizabeth, we have work to do," Joe states as he stands then pulls her to her feet.

"Okay," Elizabeth replies as she looks back to the three older gents talking softly as they leave.

Putting his arm around her shoulders Joe explains, "I think they need some time together, don't ya?"

"I guess so. I don't want my grandpa's to leave for awhile Joe. They need us and we need them," Elizabeth replies emphatically.

"We will do what we can to keep them here for as long as we can," Joe solemnly promises then continues, "I'm goin' to get two of the men to dig a grave. I'll go put some markers out for where I want'em to dig then I'll get the wagon and go over to Zak's. I'll see ya later." Joe kisses her cheek as he leaves.

Thoughtfully Elizabeth walks back towards the house. Sniffing she smells food cooking thinking, "How lucky I am. *Thank you, God, for blessing me with Nona. Thank you that I had Lora and Edgar. They were good to me and even though they manipulated me they did love me and I loved them. It will take some time, Lord, but I will be okay with your help. Thank you so much for keeping Glory safe and for taking care of Joe and keeping him from harm. I'm going to be the best wife in the world, Lord. Please help me to be that. I want to be really really bad. Amen.*"

Standing silently at the door Nona watches Elizabeth standing in the middle of the yard praying and prays a prayer too: *"Lord, I don't know why this happened to us. Why you allowed her to be taken from me and why you have allowed her to be returned to me. Maybe it is so we will appreciate each other. You gave me Joe and Glory for many years and I thank you for that, Lord, more than I can ever say. I feel so blessed to have Elizabeth back in my life…daughter or not…just to be around her makes me happy. I love Sammy and Beth Ann already. Thank you, God for blessing me so. Amen."*

Raising her head Elizabeth looks directly into her mother's kind eyes and smiling brightly she walks closer saying, "I'm so blessed Non… Mothe…Ma. I'm so blessed to have you in my life. I don't think I deserve all this happiness though. I'm going to be a better person. I promise you that."

"Just be the loving woman God meant for you to be and everything will be fine, my dear girl. Don't worry about calling me Ma or Mother or Nona. Whatever is natural will be fine, honey," Nona explains as she throws her arm around Elizabeth's shoulder hugging her then adds, "What do you want to fix for supper to go with stew and cornbread? I was thinking about a pie or two. Want to help me out, daughter?"

"Yes, Ma, I'd love to. Beth Ann would love to have a little pudding, too. Let's make cream pies, what'cha think?" Elizabeth requests with twinkling eyes again.

"Sounds good to me," Nona smilingly replies.

"Ma, Joe is going to get Mother…Lora's body and bring it home and we are going to bury her out by the lilac bushes," Elizabeth hesitantly explains then continues, "Humm, I'd like to put a nice dress on her and clean her up. I've never done it before. Humm…. would you help me? Is it too much to ask?"

Looking at her lovely daughter Nona replies, "There is never anything you cain't ask me. I won't always say yes but you can always ask. I'd be honored to help you lay out your other mother decently."

Elizabeth really smiles and grabbing her birth mother around the neck hugs her tightly whispering, "Thanks for always being here to help me. I missed you so much when I was gone. It was one of my punishments that I didn't get to be with you."

Hugging her hard right back Nona whispered softly, "Ever try to leave me again girl and you'll find out what a mean ole ma I can be!"

Leaning back and looking directly into her eyes Elizabeth promises, "Never will I leave you all...not until death takes me."

Laughing Nona gives her a smacking kiss on the cheek saying, "Well that will be a long time a comin' then. Let's get busy we have some work to do later this afternoon. Do you have any sorghum Lizbeth? It goes right fine with my cornbread."

"Yes and freshly churned butter, too. Oh, that sounds good," Elizabeth smiles again and Nona keeps her busy all afternoon.

Rev Max Roy sits on the feeble attempt of grass and moves around to find a more comfortable spot for his skinny behind to sit on. He chuckles which brings both sets of eyes on him stating, "I think I need a little more paddin' for sitting on the hard ground."

"Ya otta remember that on Sunday mornin's Rev," Pokey replies smiling for the first time.

"Yep, those pews get real hard after a while," Skinny grins also and pokes Max Roy in the ribs.

Max Roy gives a loud laugh and their tensions seem to lower considerably.

"What brought you out here today Max?" Skinny questions wonderingly.

"Heard there was some trouble out here when I rode into Roy yesterday so headed out here to see if I could help," Max answers truthfully.

"Powerful trouble," Pokey answers sadly.

"Sorry to hear about Lora," Max sadly replies then continues, "Heard she did right by Glory though."

Pokey smiles and shaking his head answers, "Yep, she did right by Glory. She knew right from wrong, Max. Would like to think she was forced to do some of the things she did bad but she were a grown woman and had a say in what was happening. Maybe not a big say but she was a part of the bad things that were going on."

Skinny added, "We saw she tried to stop them from hurtin' Glory girl. That's when they killed her!"

"I wonder what would have happened if she hadn't stopped them?" Max asks solemnly.

Grinning suddenly Skinny proudly says, "That Glory she was a sight to see when she was fightin' those outlaws. She stood straight and tall and faced 'em down like a man in a duel. She threw back that beautiful silver hair of hers and proudly stood before'em. Yep, ole Franklin ripped her dress down to her waist and she got mad. Man, she was so mad it was amazin'. She looked like an avenging angel standing there. The wind was blowing, down into that little hollow we were in, and it lifted up her hair and blew it in a circle around her. I'd swear there were angels around her when it happened cause there weren't any other wind ablowin'. She egged'em on to come and grab her and she was ready for 'em. Most amazin' fightin' I've seen in a long time. She whorled around like a twister, knocking down one and then another, faster than we could almost see. Amazing! Good Heart taught her how to take care of herself that's for sure. She did right good til three or four of them "gents" grabbed her at once. Then we took action and took care of our girl."

"Joe said it was somethin' special seein' her take on those rattle snakes who called themselves men," Pokey agreed then explained, "I wanted to go. Better shot than Skinny but he talked me outta it. I shoulda gone!"

Patting his arm Skinny sadly says, "Nothin' ya coulda done, Brother. If so, I'da done it. We couldn't save our girl but we saved Glory and that is what we gotta look at as the best thin' that coulda happened. We needed ya here taking care of the rest of the family. That was your job and you did a good job there."

Lowering his head Pokey's tears trickle down his weathered face as he mutters, "Yeah, I knowd it."

Max Roy softly explains, "You know Lora was saved and where she is going brothers. I baptized her myself. She made mistakes but we all do. Joe said she helped Glory and stopped what she could. Sounds like she repented of her mistakes to me, you know, God is a forgivin' man. He takes that into consideration. We cain't judge her, no man has the right to do that but God, so let God take care of it. We can mourn her but we cain't judge her for anything she did on earth. Yep, we can be sorry she sinned but just give it over to our Lord. He is merciful and mighty and He will take care of her for us. We can do what we need to bury her in dignity and honor her and that is all we can do."

Raising his head Pokey advises, "We can remember the good times, too. There were lots of them, right Skinny!"

"Yep, remembering will keep her alive in our hearts and memories and as long as we remember her....well, that is enough for me," Skinny replies with faith.

"Good memories will sustain us all and forgettin' the bad ones that bring us pain. God is merciful and kind. Let us pray: *"Dear Lord, we ask for your help today. We all loved our Lora. She brought us great joy. She was such a sweet little girl and we thank you for bringing her to us. She brightened up our lives when we needed it the most. We are sad that she is gone now but know she is with you and, Lord, we ask of you, please allow Lora to be beautiful in Heaven. She wanted to be beautiful so badly. Thank you for the honor and grace you gave us by allowing us to share her. In Jesus' name I pray. Amen."* Ya know we should tell Lora's story to the family. They need to know it. I know we said we wouldn't ever tell it but they need to know it now," Max prays softly then states firmly.

"Yep, no reason to keep the secret any longer," Pokey replies nodding yes.

"Yeah, won't hurt her anymore to know and the family should know. Maybe it will help'em understand her a little," Skinny agrees then adds, "After she's buried we'll tell'em."

All three nod yes. Then hearing a wagon pulling up into the yard they all look over in that direction.

"Guess that is Lora's wagon. Probably should go through it and see what's in it," Pokey states with distaste.

"Let's go back to the house and sneak some pie and coffee and think about what we need to do. We gotta fix us up a nice box for Lora and think about a few things. The wagon can sit awhile," Max replies positively.

"Shore could use a cup of hot coffee, Elizabeth makes a good cup now," Pokey agrees so they all three stand up and walk slowly towards the house.

BURYING LORA
Chapter 2

"The end can also be the beginning of something wonderful."

The cowboys drive the wagon into the yard then stop by the barn. The horses look tired and thin from the trip.

Opening the kitchen door, Elizabeth and Nona stand looking at the covered wagon. "Elizabeth? What do you want to do?" Nona asks her waiting to see what she will say and do.

"I'm not sure what should I do?" Elizabeth answers as she looks out.

"What would Joe do? Do that." Nona advises waiting.

Elizabeth shakes her head yes then walks towards the two cowboys (that she knows are her Grandpa Skinny's men) she says, "You can leave the wagon right there. The horses look like they could use some good feed. Please put them in the corral and give them some grain. Ask ole Pete to fix you something to eat at the bunk house when you are done."

Both tip their hats at her and smile saying, "Yes, madam."

"That was easily done," Elizabeth says as she walks back to Nona's side.

"Good job now what are you goin' to do about what's in the wagon? We will need some clothes for Lora and to get all the food stuff out and put away," Nona asks matter of factly.

Elizabeth nibbles on her thumb nail as she warily looked at the wagon before replying, "Yes, I know. Humm… not really something I want to do."

"Who is gonna do it then?" Nona asks looking Elizabeth squarely in the eye then continues, "Are you gonna make your grandpas do it or Joe or maybe the young'uns?"

Elizabeth stares at the wagon rubbing her chin then replies, "No, they don't have to go through that. I'll do it; in fact, I'll do it right now."

"Good girl. I see your grandpas and Max are walkin' up. Probably need some coffee and pie by now. I'll get it for'em and you git on over to the wagon and sort through the stuff and decide what you are gonna do with it," Nona agrees then states firmly.

Elizabeth slowly walks over to the wagon then struggles to get the tail gate down and the little ladder set up so she can climb into the covered wagon. Everything is a mess. Food, gun belts, coffee pot and cups all lay scattered around the trunks and the big feather bed. Elizabeth starts picking up everything and stacking them on the tail gate to be taken out. She gives a little chuckle as she thinks about the past when she would have yelled for Minnie to do this while she sat with a cup of coffee or tea inside the house. She smiles again at her change of thinking and the ideas that Joe has forced on her to make her grow up. "Well, Elizabeth

Hawkins"…abruptly she stands up thinking…"I was never actually a Hawkins, was I. No, I was a humm…James. Nona and Harvey James. Elizabeth James…now Gray. Something new to think about…well…I'll think on that later." Shrugging her shoulders she smiles as she cleans and even starts humming to herself as she remembers some good times. So involved is she in the cleaning she doesn't notice when Skinny, Pokey and Rev Roy stroll by the wagon. They sadly look up at it then hear her humming by a united vote walk on into the house.

"Did I just hear Elizabeth in the wagon out front?" Pokey asks Nona astonished.

"Reckon you did," Nona answers as she starts pouring hot coffee into the heavy mugs on the table.

"What's she doing?" asks Skinny puzzled.

"Why cleaning it out, of course," Nona answers secretly pleased but acting surprised they would ask.

"Who told her to?" Pokey asks starting to rise, "We can do it."

Nona firmly pushes him back down and gently replies, "She decided it was her job to do and she wants to and is doing it. You men have to allow her to grow up and quit jumping to do every little thing for her. You haven't helped her out by doing it for her. SO STOP! Life can be tough and she doesn't need to be protected anymore."

Pokey stares up at her belligerently then looking down thoughtfully replies, "Yep, your right."

Nona pats his shoulder kindly saying, "She wants to do this for you. She wants to show you in a small way how much she loves you, let her do it. If there is anything you want out of the wagon just say so when it comes out. It will do her good to do this for Lora and maybe, Edgar, too. They were a big part of her life and she has to accept them for who they were and what they did and understand it all. It will take time and patience but she will do it."

"You are right, Nona. She will have some rough times accepting all these changes in her life. The life she has lived and the one she would have had if they had taken her back. She will come through it all well though, she is your daughter after all, Nona," Max Roy explains smiling.

"She said she wasn't going to give us up either. That is some woman we all love," Pokey adds nodding sadly but smiling some, too.

"Yes, she is a woman now. Every day she becomes more of one due to having to do things she never did before or for a long time. It is a pleasure to see," Nona replies smiling as she stands in the doorway looking at the covered wagon sitting by the barn.

"I'm right glad for Joe and Elizabeth. It ain't easy tamin' a hard headed woman," Max announces with a wink at Pokey and Skinny.

Riled now Nona swings around saying, "Now listen here…" when all three men burst into laughter. Smiling she says, "Oh, get on with you, ole goats, I got things to do." She sails out of the room like a ship sailing through the ocean with her chin held high and a sparkle in her beautiful brown eyes.

"What a woman!" Max Roy states softly chuckling.

"She is some woman!" Skinny replies still smiling.

"Yep, a rose among the thorns," Pokey nods yes smiling also.

Meanwhile Joe drives up to Zak and Stephie Ewing's home just north of his ranch about six miles as the crow flies.

Zak and Stephie hear the wagon so walk out the front door to meet him just as he pulls up.

Stephie looks at Joe with his silver blonde hair and startling green eyes then at her beloved husband, Zak, with his coal black hair and brown eyes and can't decide who is the best looking. "Zak is only a year older at thirty six years and both are tall, slim and very muscular. But their coloring is totally opposite and they would die for each other she concludes with a smile. Both have been there for each other numerous times. When Joe was almost killed by that mountain lion to when Joe saved Zak in the blizzard, they have such a strong bond. *Praise the Lord they have each other!*" "Welcome Joe. How is everyone at the ranch? Jake's told us all about the kidnapping," Stephie asks, "Want some hot coffee?"

"Howdy! Everyone's doin' pretty good. Takin' Elizabeth's… well…we got a lot of things goin' on right now, I guess," Joe stops suddenly then continues, "Turns out that the Hawkin's kidnapped Elizabeth when she was just a baby and raised her as their own."

"Elizabeth was kidnapped! Oh my," Stephie gasps horrified.

"Yep, and you'll never guess who her real parents are?" Joe asks smiling.

"They are still alive? You act like we know'em," Zak exclaims amazed at this information.

"We know her mother – Nona James," Joe explains leaning back on the seat smiling broadly.

"Elizabeth is Nona's daughter? I heard she had a little girl but she died when she was just a baby," Stephie replies shocked then walking over to a rocking chair on the porch she plops down thinking.

"That is a mighty big surprise," Zak answers then starts laughing, "She is your mother-in-law. Oh, POOR JOE, you'll never be able to live this down!" He laughs so hard he has to sit down and wipe the tears from his eyes.

Joe smiles and laughs some then humbly says, "Nona has been my mother for most of my adult life and I'm proud to call her Ma now."

"Yes, it's been noticeable that you and Glory love her and she loves you right back," Stephie agrees smiling happily then adds, "Is that what you came to tell us? Does Elizabeth need me to come over and help out right now?"

"Well, I mainly came to ask for Zak's help in a little unpleasant job. Nona, Pokey, Skinny and Rev Roy are all at the house right now but yar welcome to come over anytime ya want," Joe explains.

"Sounds like you have a house full, I'll wait a while before I go over," Stephie replies smiling at Joe.

"Well there is somethang Lizbeth and I are hopin' ya might help us do with burying Lora? I'm on my way to get her body and Lizbeth needs help in dressin' and gettin' her ready to be buried at the ranch. I know this is a big favor to ask but would ya hep Lizbeth do this, Stephie?" Joe asks hesitantly.

"Oh, yes, certainly. When do you need me to ride over?" Stephie asks nodding yes.

"Guess after Zak gets back if he will go with me?" Joe answers after scratching his head thinking.

"What do you need my help with Joe?" Zak asks smiling.

"I can do it myself but would appreciate it if'n ya could go with me to get Elizabeth's ma from her grave and just talk a spell," Joe answers hopefully.

"Sounds like you have some thinkin' to do," Zak answers looking Joe in the eyes.

"Yeah, I'd like to ask yar opinion on some thangs I have to figure out," Joe explains with a thoughtful frown.

"Move over, brother, and I'll get in. You got two shovels? Yep, I see you do," Zak answers himself then calls out, "Be back in a few hours, Stephie."

Joe scoots over saying, "Thanks."

"What's on your mind, Joe?" Zak asks as they start on the rough ride in the wagon.

"I've got some choices to make and I wondered if ya'd give me some council on'em?" Joe asks seriously.

"Shore enough, what?" Zak answers truthfully.

"Well, the first thing is I got my family back. No one will be leavin'. I'm happy to say they want to stay with me. Second is now that the Hawkins's are dead and that is all over....Elizabeth has some adjustin' to do with findin' out all this about her being kidnapped and Nona bein' her ma and all. Then Beth Ann and Sammy bein' troubled about what the Hawkins's were to'em, you know, grand folks like they were and how they formed their minds about life. Some good but mostly bad stuff I don't like atoll. I don't wanna come down harder on'em but I don't want'em to think life is easy and just a bowl of peaches to take what ya want anytime and not have any responsibilities or penalties to pay when things don't go thar way. I don't like feelin' mean and punishin'em – any of them – but I want'em to be law abidin' – carin' people too," Joe admits confused.

"Ain't nothin' bad with that, Joe. You have already made them realize a lot even Lizbeth. It will just take time and patience to see it through and man you got plenty of both," Zak replies as he slaps Joe on the back.

"I've got the patience and love to help'em through anythan'," Joe admits smiling a little then adds, "There's such a big difference in Beth Ann in a short amount of time. She looks at me so eager to please me in all she does, but because she's insecure of my love. How do I get her to understand that I'll always love her no matter what she does, it's unconditional?"

"Joe, you are being hard on yarself. You didn't raise those young'uns so it's natural it will take some time to get acquainted and for you to teach'em what you want'em to know. You just gotta be patient. They are both trying so hard to belong to you....really be YAR young'uns...not Lizbeth's so much as YARS. You just need to tell'em often you love'em and praise their efforts when you see 'em trying hard to do what you are teachin'em. Give'em a good sense of worth like you have Glory," Zak advises earnestly.

"I'm tryin' to do that but I just want to make sure I'm doin' it right," Joe replies as he stares at the hard red dirt then continues explaining,

"Zak, I had a wonderful ma, she was beautiful, loving and real kind. But my pa was a drinker and a bully. He enjoyed hurtin' my ma and me. I don't enjoy seein' others in pain and I don't like correctin'em either. But I shorely DO want'em to be fine upstandin' grownups and that is what I'm aimin' at."

"From what I'm seein' Joe, you are doin' a good job of that," Zak replies then looking out the corner of his eye asks, "Sounds like Glory did a fine job of takin' care of herself out thar from what Jake told us. She get that temper from you, ole son?"

Smiling happily Joe laughs loudly with Zak saying, "No, I believe she got that from her mother! She certainly was a sight to see. Jake got his eyes full, that is for sure, about rilin' her up. She is a feisty little thing. Jake got to take some of his anger out on that cowboy, Patrick Sully, and it's a good thin' or else he'd have given Glory a spankin' she'd never forget. Actually I don't think she will forget the one he gave her anytime soon."

"Jake spanked Glory? He didn't tell us that," Zak replies shocked then continues, "Honestly I figured she'd always get her way in everythin' the way he moons over her. Why did he paddle her?"

"For disobeyin' the rule of not goin' anywhere by herself, he was there watchin' over'em for quite awhile and knew as well as she did she was never to leave the house alone. Which, ya know, she did in the middle of the night. I was thinkin' about it on the way home of how to handle it when all the sudden Glory starts yelling NO Jake and he flips her over and whops her fanny good and hard. She will think twice about crossin' him again that's for sure. I'm glad he showed her he means what he says," Joe explains with a raised eyebrow and a grin.

"He said he punched that Patrick Sully for being rough with Glory," Zak proudly admits.

"He pounded him in the ground. Ya shoulda seen him, Zak. He saw the bruises on Glory's face and arms and he was ready to take on a mountain lion. When she said, "Patrick did it," well this evil little grin came over his face and he quietly says, "Let me take care of this for ya, Glory. Please let me." She stuttered, "Okay." I don't think she was capable to sayin' anythin' then he walked over to Sully and softly said, "So ya like to hit young girls, huh," and punched him til he couldn't get up. It looked like a good fight for a few minutes but Patrick Sully was no match for our Jake."

"Glad that he taught a bully a lesson, I dislike bullies. Men who beat up on women leave a bad taste in my mouth. I'll have to ask him about this though. He didn't explain it as well as you have," Zak replies chuckling.

"I'm gonna have to build onto my house. With two more young'uns there just ain't enough room now. Knew when the young'uns got bigger I'd have to do it but didn't need to until now. Also Nona is gonna need a room cause I have a feeling she is gonna want to be around Lizbeth as much as possible and then there the grandpas. They are alone now only family they have is us'n so they need to have a place they feel comfortable in so I'm gonna build on some more rooms and make our bedroom a little separated from the other ones, if you get my meanin'," Joe explains laughing a little.

"Yep, I understand. Now my house is getting emptied out with Jake goin' and gettin' married then Shorty's gonna leave first chance he gets. He has the wanderin', see the world, desire that is a fire under him. He feels he is in Jake's shadow cause he is younger and smaller than Jake. But he is one tough nut, so quiet sometimes it purely amazes me. I sees him sizin' up every little than' afore he does it. Stubborn as a mule, too. I tried to break him of it when he was a little'un but weren't never able to. He gets an idea and he'll burst before he changes his mind. Course he takes after his ma's side of the family," Zak explains laughing and slapping his knee.

"I've always admired Shorty for his integrity. He only sees black and white, no gray in between. It is right or wrong. He would make a good sheriff with his ideals and he handles a gun real good like now. He and Glory are the same age. I kinda thought at one time that they'd make a match of it but Glory never had eyes for anyone but Jake," Joe answers smiling again.

"Nah, Shorty is like a brother to Glory. Jake never had eyes for any other girl but Glory. I've never seen any man with as much passion and love for a woman or girl in this case. I've told him for the past year he had to contain it and he has done a good job of it," Zak explains smiling. He is proud as he can be of his young giant of a son.

"Jake has a heart of gold, black hair and dark brown eyes of his father and a carin' and givin' personality as well is full of fun and loves pulling jokes on everyone. Shorty or Wesley Ray Ewing is two years younger, not as tall, not as good looking as Jake and very quiet. He has brown hair and blue eyes like his mother but plenty of spunk when he needs it. A right good man to have at your side anytime," Joe thinks as they ride along the bumpy pasture.

They talk about how and where to build onto Joe's ranch house all the way to the grave.

Hearing a horse they turn around looking behind them as a horse gallops up to them and they see it is Good Heart.

"Howdy!" Good Hearts says with a smile then asks, "Where ya goin'?"

Joe explains about moving Lora's body to a grave at the ranch and tells him all about the grieving that Skinny and Pokey are going through as well as all about Elizabeth's kidnapping.

Good Heart listens and is amazed at hearing that Elizabeth was kidnapped as a child from Nona.

"I see woman named Nona many times. She seems full of fire," Good Heart replies smiling then adds, "Good woman. She saved yar life, Joe!"

"Yes, she did. She and Glory gave me the will to live after the mountain lion attacked me," Joe answers truthfully.

Reaching the canyon Joe drives the wagon over to the place where Lora is buried and they all step down to her grave. Joe asks, "Let's say a quick prayer before we move her, okay?" The other two men agree and they all say a quick private prayer before digging up Lora's body. They lift her blanketed body into the back of the wagon then tie it down so her body won't bounce around on the rough trip back to the ranch house. They refill the grave then turn and head back home without even looking at Edgar and Franklin's graves.

Riding back Good Heart asks, "When Glory and Jake get married?"

"Sooner than we like," Joe replies smiling faintly.

"They love each other, plain to see," Good Heart agrees firmly.

"Yes, they do. Glory turns sixteen this summer. Not very long now. I told her she has to wait til then," Joe explains wonderingly then asks, "Where have all the years gone to."

"Yeah, wasn't so long ago that Jake was interested in frogs and tadpoles and now he'll be a husband," Zak mutters almost to himself.

"Where they live?" Good Heart asks.

Smiling Joe and Zak look at each other as Joe replies, "We were thinkin' about that acreage at the base of the mountains northeast of my place. It has those hot springs near it and those caves for storing feed for the livestock. With Jake's horses that could come in handy. Right, Zak?"

"I agree that is a nice piece of land especially since Jake plans to raise horses more so than cattle. Remember it has that natural corral for horses on my land. Jake has been using it for the last couple of years and knows his way around there. He has about twenty horses that he has broke and he knows a good horse when he sees one," Zak agrees thoughtfully.

"That be true. He knows horses good, real good. I know where ya talk about and it is a good place," Good Heart agrees nodding yes.

"Young Robert is looking for a stud at their ranch. He's comin' over this week to look Jake's horses over," Zak explains thoughtfully then continues, "Jake will make a good living on those horses. He will have to do some travelin' but he and Glory can go together and do that. Be good for both of them."

"No one will be able to pull the wool over Jake's eyes when it comes to a horse and Glory knows horses and cattle real well. She's been tendin' to'em most of her life," Joe replies proudly.

"Shore enough. Drop me off right here, Joe, and I'll walk up the hill to the house. No reason to go the extra half mile. I want to do some thinkin' and figurin' on this land and cattle," Zak requests then jumps down when Joe stops.

"Look out for rattlers. They are mean right now," Good Heart advises then rides on with Joe.

"Big changes comin' Joe. Glory, be wife soon. She is one fine girl, Joe. I be real proud of her. She learned well. Take good care of herself. I remember always seein' her knock those bad men down with tricks I taught her. Right proud," Good Heart exclaims smiling.

Smiling Joe answers, "Yes, me, too, old friend. I cain't thank ya enough for watchin' out for her and markin' the trail for us. It would've taken us some time to find it without ya. I can tell ya I was vastly relieved when we saw yar trail and knew ya were followin' and watchin' over our girl. I owe ya a bigger debt, Good Heart, what can I do to repay ya?"

"No debt to repay, Joe. Yar my blood brother. No debt. Git me some tobaccy when ya go to store that be payment enough," Good Heart replies with a deep chuckle.

"Will do," Joe answers nodding yes thinking, "And a few other things."

Good Heart leaves Joe and heads over to his home as Joe turns towards his ranch house. Smiling he looks at what God has blessed him with and what his own sweat has been spent building. "A big barn, a bunk house for the cowboys, sheds full of tools, meat, pigs and chickens, corrals full of good horses and more cattle than I can count, well almost, and a small house." He frowns as he concentrates on the house and how he will change it. "I believe I'd better get Hank and his boys out here ta hep me build this addition. Hank....Uncle Hank now....my uncle by marriage ....Nona's aunt and uncle...Aunt Ella and Uncle Hank...wow...I have more family than I knew I did and a great family they are. *Thank you, God, for blessin' us all with family. Thanks for Nona and her loving heart and now we have Aunt Ella and Uncle Hank and all their young'uns. I feel so privileged to have them in my life and my young'uns, yar so gracious and kind to me. Thank ya very much Lord. Thank ya very much and thank ya for watchin' over us all and takin' care of us'ns durin' this bad time. It soothes my soul knowin' yar walkin' beside me. Amen.*"

Pokey and Skinny pick out some lumber from the barn, sawing and hammering the pieces into a coffin. They know Lora's height so it isn't a problem getting the right size. When they have it all finished. Pokey looks at Skinny saying, "I never thought I'd be making a casket for her. It needs something special on it!"

"Yep, it does," Skinny replies then smiling, says, "Words of love."

"She always wanted to be beautiful let's think of somethin' like that," Pokey states thinking out loud.

"That's it: She is beautiful in Heaven!" Skinny agrees smiling then adds, "I'm sure she is."

"Me, too," replies Pokey. So they carve "She is beautiful in Heaven" on the top of the casket and when Joe brings in the wooden grave marker they carve it on it too. They stand looking at the casket and cross then smiling at each other say, "*Amen.*"

Joe notices the covered wagon as he pulls up to the house then sees his children and Randy and Earl carrying things to the bunk house and barn. Slowing he pulls up beside the barn and stops.

Elizabeth pops her head out of the front of the wagon smilingly saying, "Hi Joe. I'll be right out." She disappears then climbs out of the back of the wagon as Joe walks towards it.

"I thought I'd better get this unloaded and see where to put everything they have in the wagon. No use wasting the food stuff, you know," Elizabeth explains smiling.

Joe is definitely surprised seeing the dirt streaks on his lovely wife's face and every day dress makes him wonder. "What made ya decide to go through the wagon? I'da thought you'd have avoided it," Joe questions seriously.

"That would have meant you or my grandpas would have had to do it and you are all three very tired and you didn't need to have something else to do so I did it. I put Fath…Edgar's trunk with his clothes and such with Franklin's in the barn. I don't want them in the house. Ole Pete and Randy carried them out for me. Then I temporarily put Moth… Lora's trunk in there until we choose her clothing for burial. The food stuff that we don't need in the house, I asked the cowboys to carry to the bunkhouse. They were right proud of it. They told me so," Elizabeth explains as she counts it off her fingers.

"Right proud? You said "Right Proud"! That ain't proper English Mrs. Saint Louie lady?" Joe jokes.

"Well I ain't no Mrs. Saint Louie lady No More Sirahhh. I'm a Mrs. Joe Gray lady now and forever," Elizabeth drawls right back at him.

Hugging her Joe kisses her with love and passion as she clings to him.

Releasing her he humbly says, "Sorry, Elizabeth, forgot how dirty and probably smelly I am."

"NEVER apologize for kissing me, husband, because I want everyone I can get. I have a lot to catch up on," Elizabeth tartly advises as she grabs his shirt pulling him closer and kisses him again.

Chuckling Joe willingly kisses her back.

"Hummpppp!" sounds right beside them so they slowly break apart and there stands Rev Roy smiling at them as he says, "Think you can wait until tonight young'uns. I think we'd better get this burial done before the sun goes down. Then the tensions around here will be lessened a whole passel."

"Yes, sir! Sounds good to me. I was ..uhhh …just telling Lizabeth that is what we need to do," Joe jokes as he kisses his lovely wife once more.

Elizabeth smiles then walks back to the big wagon to finish up.

"Yeah, I believe that. Lying to a preacher now Joe you know where that will land you," Max Roy replies as he follows Joe into the barn helping to carry Lora's body. They clear off a work table then tenderly lay Lora's body upon it. "Joe, you think it is a good idea for Elizabeth to do this. She probably ain't never done it before."

"Yep, I think she needs to do this to repay Lora for takin' good care of her all those years. Stephie and Nona will be here to help her. I think I hear horses comin' now. That's probably Zak and Stephie," Joe answers so they walk back outside the barn. Sure enough it is Stephie and Zak along with Carrie Lynn and Payton.

"Howdy, everyone's in the house right now why don'tcha put yar horses in the corral and head on over. We will be right thar," Joe requests.

"We cain't stay but awhile so we will leave the saddles on them," Zak advises his family. He opens the corral and leads all four horses inside.

Elizabeth climbs down from the wagon again saying, "Welcome. Come on into the house. Are you hungry? Nona, has…Ma has…oh; it is a long story, come on in. I'm going to wash all this dirt off of me before I come in,"

"Lizbeth, we need to finish this today. Before we eat supper, honey, let's don't put it off. Okay?" Joe reminds her sympathetically.

Grimacing Elizabeth takes a long breath replying, "Yes, Joe. I know.

Joe asks Earl to put the small wagon away and take care of the horse while he cleans up then he walks into his house. Elizabeth enters about the same time with a clean face and hands. She smiles and hugs Stephie whispering, "Thank you for coming to help. It isn't going to be easy is it?"

Stephie hugs her back replying, "It's never easy but a job of love to do it."

Blinking back tears Elizabeth states, "Yes, a labor of love."

They drink a cup of coffee then the three ladies walk out to the barn to prepare Lora for burial.

Elizabeth takes a deep breath when she sees the blanketed form on the table. She is carrying a bucket of warm water and some rags as Stephie carries a second bucket and Nona carries some towels for drying the body.

Elizabeth takes a deep breath before explaining, "I picked out a dress and underwear today. It's in her trunk and a really pretty blanket. I'll get them before we start." She rushes out as the other ladies pull the blanket back and gasp as they see how bruised Lora is.

"Poor thing she took a beatin'," Nona states sadly then thinks, "You stole my baby from me, Lora. I will be able to forgive you in time. Time is what you stole from me with my lovely girl. It hurts right now to know this but that will lessen in time."

Stephie looks at Nona seeing the anger and sorrow in her face as she looks down at the woman who had stolen her child and Stephie thinks, "I don't know what I would do if it had been me." Closing her eyes she prays for Nona and Elizabeth and also for the soul of Lora, *"Most gracious Father in Heaven...I know you don't give us more than we can bear but sometimes it seems like it. Help Nona to accept what has happened and to be able to forgive the ones who did her harm....Lord, I know it won't be easy.... it certainly wouldn't be for me....please Lord grant her grace and thank you so much dear Savior for saving Glory and keeping her alive and well. In Jesus Name I pray. Amen."*

Nona turns (when Elizabeth walks back in) advising, "Elizabeth take a deep breath and know she died protecting Glory."

Walking forward hesitantly Elizabeth answers, "Yes, they said she di..... Oh, my God, look at her face!" tears run streams down her face as she looks in horror at the mother who raised her. Her face is black and blue and she is dirty. Elizabeth lays down the dress, comb and brush, lacy cap and the pink blanket sniffing she states, "Mother hated being dirty. Let's get her cleaned up."

Nona pulls a pair of scissors out of her apron pocket and starts cutting away the filthy dress and underwear. Thinking, "Fortunately her arms are down at her side and her legs are straight so getting her clothes on her will be easier". They quickly wash her body then slide on her underwear as well as they can then they slide on the silk dress that was one of Lora's favorites. Her shoes won't fit so they just pull her dress down to cover her feet. Lora was a tall woman but not a heavy one so after draping the blanket in the coffin they quickly lift her and lay her in it wrapping the lovely pink blanket around her feet and lower body.

"She looks lovely, Elizabeth." Nona states as she pats Elizabeth's hand then asks, "Do you want the children to see her this way?"

Elizabeth stares at Lora's battered face before saying, "Just Gloria and my grandpas. I want them to see her looking nice."

"We will get them, Elizabeth, you take a few minutes alone," Stephie advises as she carries the empty buckets and rags away taking Nona's arm as they leave the barn.

Elizabeth's tears come again as she looks at the woman who raised her whispering, "Mother, I don't know why you did what you did. I know you loved me and the children. It was a hard life you chose to live. I'm sorry that I disappointed you at times. I never stopped loving Joe and I never will. I'm sorry they hurt you so bad, Mother. I'll always love you."

"Ma??" Glory questions behind her.

Elizabeth holds out her hand and Glory takes it and steps up beside Lora's wooden coffin, "She tried to save me, Mama. She stopped'em from hurtin' me. She didn't agree with what they were doin' but she couldn't stop'em. She did try," Glory explains softly.

"She was good to me most of my life. So was Fath….Edgar… most of my life. They were greedy, honey, that is all … pure greed. She could have gone and lived with your grandpas but she loved the city life. She wanted to be Someone – that was the most important thing… being Someone. She didn't realize she always was Someone to the ones who loved her. I won't make the same mistakes, Glory. Money means nothing to me if I don't have all of you to love," Elizabeth explains then adds, "I want you to see that she is decently buried. In a nice dress and cleaned up – not in a dirty blanket – she never liked being dirty that I can remember. She would change clothes three or four times a day if she had any dirt on her. I never understood it but it was just the way she was."

"I'll tell you why later, Elizabeth," Skinny answers as he and Pokey walk up behind them.

Tears run freely down their faces as they look at their daughter, Lora, "She looks really fine," Skinny admits smiling faintly.

"Her favorite color is pink," Pokey replies sniffing.

"Yes, she always liked pink. She said she was too old to wear pink but she loved it and wore it often, saying she didn't care if the other ladies liked it or not," Elizabeth explains smiling lovingly at Lora.

"The coffin is really nice grandpas," Glory adds as she hugs Pokey's skinny body.

"Yes, it is lovely. Who carved the saying: "She is beautiful in Heaven" on the lid?" Elizabeth asks as she runs her fingers over the words.

"Both of us did, we are carpenter's sons after all," Skinny replies faintly smiling at Elizabeth.

Looking at them Elizabeth takes Glory's hand saying, "We will give you a few minutes." As they walk out Elizabeth continues, "I'm going to put some clean clothes on before we bury her," and into the house they walk.

Looking around the kitchen table, Elizabeth states to all as she walks in, "I'm filthy I'm going to wash up. I'll be back in a few minutes." She hurries over to their bedroom and slips in. She takes her dirty dress off, lays it in the dirty clothes pile then looking at her dirty hands she walks over to the wash basin, pours water in and starting soaping her hands. She looks down at her hands saying, "Not so pretty anymore are you. You work now when you never did anything before. Didn't do anything but lift a tea cup or fork. She looks into the mirror noticing the weight she has lost. I'm no longer plump around the hips and thighs but slender and supple from the work I've been doing. Well isn't that something. I walked quite a bit in St. Louis and that helped keep some weight off but nothing like this. She stares into her own eyes softly asking her reflection, "Why did I allow them to control me? Why?"

"Because you were used to it and it was easy," Joe answers from the doorway, continuing, "You were used to takin' the easy way out, honey. They wanted to control you and they knew that."

"Shows a weakness of character, doesn't it!" Elizabeth replies sadly looking down again at her hands.

"Only if ya allow it to make ya weak, it can make ya strong if ya want to be. You were strong today. Ya tackled the wagon and ya just did a very hard but loving thang – gettin' Lora ready for buryin'. I'll say ya've had a change of mind and will be strong and yar own person now," Joe advises.

Smiling slyly Elizabeth looks at him out of the corners of her eyes saying, "Maybe, just maybe."

Joe laughs heartily and picking her up swings her around in a circle while kissing her flushed cheeks.

KNOCK KNOCK sounds on the door then Nona calls, "No foolin' round in there. We got a funeral to go to."

Elizabeth and Joe look at each other then say at the same time, "Yes, MA!" and giggle happily.

Nona can't keep a straight face either so chuckles all the way back to the kitchen saying, "They'll be right out."

Joe helps Elizabeth dress so soon they re-enter the kitchen holding hands. Everyone is talking and joking around with each other so as one they stand up and walk out the door.

Joe, Zak, Skinny and Pokey pick up the coffin and walk to the newly made cemetery plot. Rev Max Roy leads the way with everyone following. As they walk Nona starts singing *Amazing Grace* and everyone joins in. Then they sing *In the Garden* as Lora's coffin is lowered into the ground. The younger children hand out wild flowers they have gathered to each person.

Rev Roy with Bible in hand starts: "No one is without sin! Let no one throw rocks of guilt upon the guiltless and harbor grudges against the living or dead. God knows all and sees all and He is a loving God. He is our Father and cares about our every need. Know, my loved ones, that God is with you every moment of your life and he knows the trials and temptations that you go through each and every day. Lora Lea Ann Gates Hawkins was a good woman. She was a human and with human weaknesses she sinned as we all do. Lora turned sixty years this year or there abouts. She was the lovin' daughter of Samuel "Skinny" Gates and Ernest "Pokey" White. Lora was mother of Elizabeth James Gray and grandmother to Glory, Beth Ann and Samuel Gray. She worked hard striving for every womanly accomplishment she could. She enjoyed her family and loved them. She grew up on a ranch, lived in the city of St. Louis most of her adult life and came back to a ranch to be buried. Lora, we love you and will continue to love you, all the days of our lives. *We pray you have peace and joy in Heaven and beauty that is awesome to behold. Amen.*"

Skinny steps closer to the grave saying, "You were our treasure, Lora, we did everythin' we could to make you happy. *God's blessin's on you now, my girl, may you be eternally happy. Amen.*"

Standing next to Skinny, Pokey says, *"Loved ya since ya were a baby, Lora, we will miss ya. Amen."*

Walking up behind them Elizabeth lays her hands upon their shoulders saying, *"Mother, you were good to me. Thank you for taking such good care of me. I know you loved me and that you only wanted what was best for me. I'm sorry I couldn't do all that you wanted me to do, but my heart belongs to Joe and no other man. Forgive me for letting you down and please Mother, be happy. Amen."*

Stepping forward Joe says, *"Thank ya for lovin' Elizabeth and raisin' her to be the fine woman she is. Thank ya for heping to raise Beth Ann and Sammy. Thank ya for takin' care of Glory when she needed ya. Amen"*

Glory, Beth Ann and Sammy step closer with Sammy holding one of Pokey's hand as Beth Ann is holding Skinny's hand.

Glory smiles softly at the lovely box saying, *"Thank ya, Grandma, for takin' care of me and keepin' me safe from harm. I really didn't know ya until then. May God give ya a glorious crown in Heaven. Amen."*

Sammy frowns down at the box saying, *"Grandmother …uh…I'll try harder to eat the food I'm given and I'll remember you told me to always be a good boy and mind my manners. Amen."* He turns around putting his arms around Elizabeth's waist as he squeezes her tightly. Not crying just sad.

Sniffling Beth Ann says, *"Grandmother you were always good to me. You spoiled me a lot but you made me study hard. Thank you for teaching me to learn on my own and that just because you are smart, you don't have to be a know-it-all. I'll always remember some of your teachings and your ways of being a lady. I'll try to always be one, Grandmother. I love you. Amen."*

Rev Roy smiles then pats Beth Ann's bent head as she holds tightly to Skinny's callused hand. *"God gives us people in our lives that we never expect. People who help us grow into better people or people who we can learn lessons from, good ones and bad ones. Lora lightened up all three of our lives when she came into it. Thank you, dear Lord, for the blessing of her life with us. Praise God for all the blessings of this day and the ones to come. Amen."*

"Please join me in Psalms 23," Rev Roy requests then leads with everyone joining in: *The Lord is my shepherd; I shall not want. He maketh me to lie down in green pastures: He leadeth me beside the still waters. He restoreth my soul: He leadeth me in the paths of righteousness for his name's sake. Yea, though I walk through the valley of the shadow of death, I will fear* no evil: for thou art with me; thy rod and thy staff they comfort me. Thou preparest a table before me in the presence of mine enemies: thou annointest my head with oil; my cup runneth over. Surely goodness and mercy shall follow me all the days of my life: and I will dwell in the house of the Lord forever."

Everyone says, "Amen."

Each one who wants to scoops a shovel full of dirt tossing it onto the wooden casket along with some of the wild flowers they are holding. Then Joe and Zak fill in the grave from the mound of dirt on the side and everyone lays the remaining flowers across the top of the grave.

"Nice marker," Zak states as he looks at it and reads the words. He doesn't know what to say about, "She is beautiful in Heaven." So he says nothing.

"Thank ya," Pokey answers smiling sadly.

Reaching over Ole Pete takes Joe's shovel saying, "I'll put them up for ya, Joe."

"Appreciate that," Joe answers as he hands it to him, then turns and follows the family back to the ranch house.

THE TRUTH ABOUT LORA
Chapter 3

*"Hidden truths cannot hurt the dead and
the living will deal with them."*

Zak and family leave soon after the funeral and the rest walk back into the house to eat some stew and cornbread and, of course, pies. After eating and having dessert Max Roy nudges Skinny and Pokey with, "We have a story to tell ya'll about Lora."

Clearing his voice Skinny starts the story, "I'll start off. Lora was not really our daughter except we found her and kept her. Lora was a prairie child."

Putting her hands up to her face in horror Elizabeth states, "A prairie child. A lost child, oh, Lord, how terrible."

Smiling faintly Skinny continues, "I found her when she was about two years old. Never knew what happened to her folks. She was covered in mud and red dirt from head to toe in the blistering hot summer fifty eight years ago. I was out checking on some cattle at the far end of the ranch when I heard her crying. Poor baby was half starved and scratched up all over. She was a poor looking little thing. All skin and bones and tangled brown hair. I fed her and wrapped my extra shirt around her and searched the area all around there for her folks but couldn't find anyone. When I got back to the ranch Pokey rode out and searched for anyone who had lost a little girl. He heard that some Indians had captured a white family so he sought out Lumbering Bear, our friend Red Sun's father, and asked him. He said the white family was dead. So we just kept her. She was a happy little girl and Ma was thrilled to have her. She raised her while we worked the ranch."

Here Pokey joins in, "I'll never forget how she hated to be dirty. Any dirt on her clothes made her cry. Ma made her a number of little dresses because she just couldn't be dirty at all. She wouldn't learn to ride because she would get dirty. She couldn't do any house cleaning if she would get dirty, course that didn't work with Ma. She smacked her bottom and made her learn how to cook and clean but Lora never liked it. Then when Lora was sixteen years old Ma died right after Pa died. They just couldn't stand to be apart. We always told Lora that her ma died and was married to Skinny cause Skinny was there all the time while I was out huntin' down outlaws all over the country."

Then Max chimes in, "Skinny, Pokey and I all grew up close together and have been like brothers all our lives. Skinny and Pokey's Ma, Ruby, was my Ma's sister and my Ma, Connie, was sickly so we stayed at Uncle Michael and then Uncle Ralph's ranch quite a bit.

"I'm confused. Who are Ralph and Michael?" Joe asks trying to concentrate but is confused.

Smiling Skinny explains, "My pa was Michael Gates and my ma was Ruby Lee Gates. My pa was killed in an Indian attack when I was just a wee baby but they didn't kill my ma. Ruby was a little thing just a tad over 5 feet tall but she had a backbone of iron. She stood up to the Indians after they killed my pa and they respected her for it."

"Then my pa, Ralph White, married my ma, Ruby Gates, cause Lumbering Bear, the Indian chief, liked our ma so well he wanted to marry her and she weren't gonna have that atoll. Pa was a bachelor and he lived by his self on the ranch right next to the Gates ranch. So they married and had me within a year. That's why we have different last names," Pokey explains.

Max added, "Uncle Ralph was a carpenter and a very quiet man. That's why Pokey don't talk much, it hurts his voice box." Everyone laughs at this truth because Pokey doesn't talk much.

"My pa he talked when he had somethin' important to say and I do the same," Pokey states with dignity, "No use yapping the tongue if'n ya don't have somethin' worthy of sayin'"

Max just laughs saying, "That is cause I never shut my mouth. Skinny is a big talker compared to Pokey. Pokey is just too stubborn to talk. Hey, I'm tellin' ya the truth!"

Everyone relaxes listening to the cousins as they explain many things they have wondered about.

"Did either of you ever marry?" Nona asks curiously.

"Yep, I did. Once. She was a beauteous girl named, Molly Fay," Pokey replies sadly then continues, "She died cause of me. Bushwhacker couldn't find me to shoot so he killed my Molly. I never wanted to put another woman in danger again."

"I married once and it was to Donna Sue. She was a tiny little thing with sparking eyes and a beautiful face. She died in childbirth with our first baby. I never looked around after that. Didn't think I could live through that again," Pokey explains sadly still seeing his lovely young wife in his mind's eye.

"What about you, Reverend Max?" Nona asks when Max just sits there looking into space.

"Bonnie Jean Adams was her name. She had the voice of an angel. I was just a young'un myself. Pa died and Ma had been gone a long while so I traveled around seeing the world. I rode all through the East. Worked when I had to and left when I wanted to then walking down the street in Topsham, Maine, I heard the voice of an angel. She was singing a song about God with the sweetest voice I'd ever heard. They were having a church meeting inside so I slid into a pew and listened and fell in love with Bonnie Jean. She was singing *Amazing Grace*. Her pa was the preacher. He preached and I listened and listened some more. I went back every night and listened and found Jesus. I believed and went forward and was baptized in the cold water of the ocean that next Saturday. In salty and very very cold ocean water, I can tell you. I followed them around while he preached for six months and Bonnie Jean fell in love with me. Bonnie Jean's pa wouldn't let me marry her even though we both fell in love until I proved I was a good man. Then one night God spoke to me saying,

"*Maxwell Roy, you will preach my word everywhere you go. You will bring many people to me. Go forth and tell the world about me.*" And I've tried to do that ever since."

"What happened to Bonnie Jean?" Glory asks in the quiet when he stops speaking.

Taking a deep breath Max sadly replies, "Well, my lovely Bonnie Jean died of consumption three years after we wed. We were in the Ozark Mountains around the hot springs at the time and a sickness came along. She took care of the sick ones then took it. We never had any young'uns……so I sorta gave my love to Lora also. She was all of us'ns own little girl and she needed so much love."

Beth Ann turns to Nona asking her, "Grandma, what about you and Grandpa Harvey?"

Smiling Nona explains, "He was the love of my life. We lived on a farm next to Aunt Ella and Uncle Hank's in Ohio. We'd only been married a few years and Elizabeth was just a walkin' when he got gored by a bull and bled to death. We couldn't stop it. Doc said the bull tore into his kidneys. He lived for a couple of days and he told me to stay close to Aunt Ella and Uncle Hank that they would take care of me. I told him I didn't need anyone to take care of me that I'd take care of them. It's been a pretty even swap all these years. So I gave all my love to my little girl, Lizzy. She was the prettiest little girl and she looks to this day so much like her pa. I don't know why I never saw it before. I was with child when Harvey got gored and I grieved so much for him that I lost that baby. Soon after that Max came through and offered us some good land down here so we followed him here. I bemoaned the leavin' for years cause I lost Elizabeth and thought she'd died through my neglect. We thought an animal had dragged her out of the wagon and killed her. I've relived that day a thousand times." Nona takes a deep breath looking at her hands as she smiles saying, "God does work in ways we will never understand. Who but God could have led Joe to St. Louie and to Elizabeth and back here where we are?"

"Yes, God does amazing things in our lives that we never really understand or even realize. If we will trust His hand and follow His lead we will never have to go it alone," Max Roy answers firmly.

Everyone is exhausted so at dusk they all say good night and head for their beds.

Max, Skinny and Pokey walk down to the bunk house after a short walk back to Lora's grave and a few minutes of prayer there.

Nona insist on sleeping in the parlor on the sofa (instead of in Joe and Elizabeth's room) so soon the house is quiet.

Joe wakes up early as usual and Elizabeth awakes as well as he moves around in the bed. "Time to get up? Already?" Elizabeth sleepily asks.

"Yep, gotta milk the cow and git out and check my cattle. Get up lazy bones and fix yar man some breakfast," Joe teases as he gives her a light smack on her bottom.

"Oh, men! Bet my grandpas are up, too. Rev Max is my cousin, how amazing life is. I'm sure they are hungry. What do you think about some ham this morning and maybe some beans and ham for supper?" Elizabeth asks as she stretches her arms high above her head then looking slyly at Joe asks, "Maybe we could wait another thirty minutes before getting out of bed?"

Wigglying his eye brows at her, Joe replies, "Not today, my darlin'. Got too many people in the house and Ma will be knocking on the door afore we know it."

"Yes, you are right, as usual," Elizabeth sighs then picking up her everyday dress she is quickly ready for the day.

As she reaches the bedroom door Joe grabs her in a big hug whispering, "Tonight we will sneak out and go to the hot springs for an hour or so, what'cha think, darlin'." Then he kisses her with passion.

"You have a date, my dear," Elizabeth answers as she gives him another quick kiss before slipping through the door and out the back door to the out house then to the smoke house for ham.

Returning quickly she washes her hands again, makes a pot of coffee, starts cutting the ham for breakfast and for the red beans, then starts making a mountain of biscuits for her hungry brood.

Walking in yawning Nona asks, "What'cha need me to do honey?"

"Why don't you pour a cup of coffee for both of us and as soon as these biscuits are in the pan I'll join you," Elizabeth asks as she finishes the biscuits then adds, "Do you think this will be enough biscuits, Ma? They seem to eat them until they are gone."

"Those ole goats love biskuts with jelly after they eat biskuts and gravy and before that they eat one with butter on it. I never know how many it will take to fill'em up. You'd think they'd be fat as pigs the way the three of them eat and I out weigh two of 'em. Ain't fair…just ain't fair," Nona grumbles as she sits down with a hot cup of coffee.

"I thought you were a morning person, Ma," Elizabeth asks with a small smile.

"Usually am. Couldn't go to sleep athinkin' about all the hard times the old gents have had. Really sad losin' their wives like that," Nona replies with feeling.

"Just like it was sad when Harvey…uh pa died," Elizabeth responds looking at Nona's sad face.

"Yep, that was a hard time. But, honey, hard times come to all of us. We have to be tougher than the situation is then we will survive it. You've had some hard times lately but you seem to be handlin' it pretty good," Nona explains smiling at her lovely daughter.

"Having Joe and the children safe and sound means the world to me and knowing you are my mother makes me feel so blessed. I'll miss my mother Lora and I'll grieve for her but not so much since I have you. I'm amazed that I didn't realize you were my mother. I was thinking about it last night remembering how close I've always felt towards you. The first time I met you all those years ago; it was like I knew you. I remember how you taught me how to cook and clean and to be a good wife. I should have listened better," Elizabeth explains with a laugh.

"I felt the same way. I knew you were close in age to my Lizzie but didn't know exactly how old you were. I bet you don't know your actual birth date do you?" Nona asks with a happy smile.

Surprised Elizabeth's mouth drops open as she replies, "I've always celebrated July 8th. Is that correct?"

"Nope your birthday is June 7th. They took you on July 8th so guess that tells us why they said it was your birthday," Nona frowns into her coffee cup.

Elizabeth plops down in a chair staring at the floor thinking, "Everything I think to be true is false. How do I deal with this?" She looks up with a troubled frown stating, "It is sad not to know your own birthday. I wonder about everything now….what is true and what is false, how many lies have I been told all my life?"

"The sad thing is that when lies start they don't get smaller they get bigger and bigger and tryin' to remember 'em gets harder and harder. You always get caught out in them so it is best not do any in the first place," Nona advises looking sternly at Elizabeth.

"Yes, I've learned lies always come out and there is always a price to pay," Elizabeth mutters remembering the spanking she'd received from Joe then another from both her grandpas for all the lies she'd told them. She cringes at the memory so quickly pushes those memories to the back of her brain thinking, "I don't ever want to think about the pain and embarrassment I went through because I was so hard headed. I have learned that lesson very well."

Nona can tell by Elizabeth's flushed face she is remembering the hard spankings she'd received for her lies so she doesn't add anything else to it instead she advises, "Best get the next batch of biscuits in, sweetie, those should be about done by now."

Standing up Elizabeth can't help rubbing her bottom in memory of how sore she had been for so long after those spankings. She reaches for the pot holders checking the biscuits and indeed they are ready to be taken out of the oven. She sets another pan in then standing up she shakes off those painful memories again then walks to the back door standing and looking out.

"Anyone comin' in yet?" Nona asks puzzled.

"Joe will be soon. There is smoke coming from the cookhouse so guess they are eating breakfast, too," Elizabeth answers then turning around asks, "I think I'll let the children sleep a little late. Would you mind fixing eggs for everyone when they come in? There is something I'd like to do."

"Sure thing, honey, I'll be here if you need me," Nona answers rather puzzled.

Elizabeth walks to the barn, picks up a pair of her work gloves, a shovel and a small spade then walks towards Lora's grave. Humming she takes the shovel making a big square the size of four graves by dipping the shovel into the ground every six inches or so around the grave. She looks around and finds some sticks so sticks them in all four corners of her square. Standing up she looks all around her, smiles then walks back towards the house. At the back of the house she digs up one of her rose bushes and carries it back to the grave site, digging another hole she plants it outside of the line she has outlined. She repeats this with three other rose bushes until all four sides have a rose bush on it. Wiping the dirt off her hands she sits down looking at her handiwork. "It's not good enough yet," she thinks as she looks it over. "It needs something else. What? Honeysuckle? The lilacs smell so good. Do I need honeysuckle or would something else look better? What?" She sits thinking of all the plants she has in the area around the homestead. "Morning glories would be nice but I've been saving them for Glory's house. Glory loves them so much and they always make her smile, so not them. Okay, nothing that spreads out. That just won't work. Oh, yes, I can take some of the roots from the peonies – they always look beautiful. I'll just have to water these plants quite a bit til their roots take." Smiling she stands up just as Joe walks over.

"I wondered where ya went to then figured it must be here. Looks like ya've been workin' hard. It looks really nice, honey," he says proudly as he looks at her design and the rose bushes she has planted. "Kinda big ain't it?" he questions.

"There is a reason for that, Joe. I want my grandpas and Uncle Max to be buried here, too. So I made room for them on each side of Mother. I guess I should have asked you about it but it just seemed to jump out of my mind and I had to work it out in the soil. I hope it is okay with you," Elizabeth asks looking concerned into Joe's handsome face.

"It's a good idea, honey. A very good idea. We ain't gonna lose'em or let'em be alone or Uncle Max neither. Do ya want a fence in that line ya made?" Joe asks looking down at her handiwork again.

"Yes, please. I'd like it to be about waist high. Uhhh…my waist high, if you will," Elizabeth requests with a light shining in her eyes.

"I believe I can manage that, my darlin', but it will be after I return from the pasture. I've gotta check my cattle right now," Joe explains as he kisses her cheek.

"Oh, that will be fine, Joe. Joe, uhh, thanks for everything. You have been so gracious through all this. I know …well…I know…," Elizabeth tries to explain looking sad and forlorn.

Putting his finger under her chin and lifting her face up and seeing her teary eyes Joe explains, "It is over and done with my love. Don't worry or think about what if or what coulda happened. God made it happen as it did for a reason. I'm just happy Glory is safe, you and the young'uns are here with me and I have a mother in Nona, two grandpas in Skinny and Pokey, and an Uncle in Rev Max and we have Hank and Ella and all their young'uns. We are mightily blessed, honey. I just feel blessed right now."

Hugging Joe hard Elizabeth cries tears of joy now instead of sadness. They stand this way for a few minutes then Joe asks, "Have ya done everythang ya want to do for now?"

Elizabeth looks back at the rose bushes and the line in the ground then answers, "Yes, I feel at peace with it now."

"Good, walk me back to the barn and kiss me again afore I leave," Joe requests with a squeeze.

Picking up her gloves Elizabeth reaches for the shovel and spade but Joe has already picked them up so they turn back towards the barn.

"I was thinking about putting honeysuckle on the fence but then the lilac smells so good I decided that it wouldn't work so I thought I might plant some peonies there. What'cha think?" Elizabeth explains then asks his opinion.

"Peonies smell good, too. You could put grapes on the fence. The grape vines need to be replanted and I just haven't gotten to it yet or you can tell me where you'd like another fence to be built for the grapes," Joe explains then asks.

"Humm….grapes? I hadn't thought about them. I did see they are really over grown. Let me think about it, okay?" Elizabeth answers as they reach the barn. She gives Joe a sweet kiss before walking into the house.

Everyone sitting at the kitchen table is very surprised when Elizabeth walks in drying her hands off with the rag by the wash basin at the back door.

"I was wonderin' when you'd be back," Nona states as she looks into Elizabeth's smiling face.

"Where have you been Mother?" Beth Ann wonderingly asks.

"That is a surprise, Beth Ann. One that isn't completed yet, I'm hoping you children will help me finish it," Elizabeth answers smiling at them then adds, "Anyone hungry? I'm going to fry me an egg or two. Grandpa's did you save me any biscuits?"

Everyone looks around the table as Pokey states, "Well maybe just one. Nona made us a bunch of 'em and we ett most of 'em already."

Smiling Nona answers, "Lizbeth made them, not me."

"Well I'll be dipped in butter; they tasted just like yours," Skinny states laughing, "Well like mother and daughter, ehhhh."

"Ma taught me how to make them so that is a good one," Elizabeth explains then looking over at Glory asks, "Did you eat anything honey?"

Glory squirms on the pillow she is sitting on answering, "I'm not real hungry, Mama."

Elizabeth nods remembering very well the soreness of having a well spanked bottom so asks, "Gloria, come here a minute."

Glory almost groans but sustains it, then walks over to her mother looking at her inquiringly.

Elizabeth whispers "Go into my bedroom and get that big jar of cold cream and put in all over your bottom, honey. It helps."

Glory smiles sadly then kissing Elizabeth's cheek says, "Thanks, Mama."

"What'cha whisperin' about, Ma," Sammy asks nosily.

"I was just asking Gloria if you young'uns have finished your chores and she said she's not sure if you have or not? Also young man, I believe you know better English than you are speaking," Elizabeth answers looking at both Beth Ann and Sammy.

Beth Ann guiltily looks down as Sammy frowns as he lowers his head muttering, "Yes, Mother."

Elizabeth grins impishly replying, "What'cha think yar papa will say about yar slurrin' of the good English ya learned in St. Louie?"

Both Beth Ann and Sammy jerk their heads up looking at their mother (who is standing with her eye brows raised and arms folded across her chest looking at them) questioningly.

They look at each other then Glory pips in, "I believe papa will say we need to larn better English, what'cha think Mama."

Now Sammy and Beth Ann look at each other again as if what are Elizabeth and Glory doing when Elizabeth and Glory burst out laughing. Then they realize their MOTHER was joking with them. "She never used to do that," Sammy thinks shaking his head (as if to clear it) saying, "You were joking... you NEVER joke!"

Putting her hand under his chin Elizabeth replies, "I do now," then gives him a smacking kiss on the cheek. He grins happily at her as she asks again, "Are your chores done?" looking at both children.

Beth Ann looks uncomfortable replying, "Mostly."

Sammy puffs out his small chest proudly stating, "I'm done. Come on, Beth Ann, and I'll help you finish yours."

They jump up and rush outside. Looking inquiringly at her younger brother Beth Ann asks, "Why do you want to help me finish mine?"

"Cause I'm gonna need help one of these days and you are gonna owe me and then I'll collect," Sammy giggles happily.

Smiling back Beth Ann answers, "Oh dear, how we weave the web of life we live in."

Frowning at her Sammy says, "Huh?"

Beth Ann gives a smug smile saying, "I understand, Sammy. I owe you and I'll repay you when you need it. Now help me clean out the chicken coop."

"Yuk! I didn't know that was your chore," Sammy replies wrinkling his nose in distaste then looking slyly at her states, "Okay, but you really owe me now."

"I know," Beth Ann replies smiling happily.

The children work hard so soon the chicken coop is cleaned out and the manure is taken to the garden. Nona is hoeing in the garden so asks for them to shovel it in several sections that need it as she works it into the soil. The garden patch is doing very well. Due to all the tensions around the ranch everyone goes out and works in the garden area to relieve their stress.

Nona looks at the tomato plants saying to Beth Ann, "With the lettuce and tomatoes almost ready soon we can have us some good salads. I know your papa likes the wilted lettuce with bacon grease on it with boiled eggs. Want me to teach you how to make it? It is really easy and you can show off your cookin' ability."

"Does Glory know how to make it?" Beth Ann asks thoughtfully.

"Reckon she does. I've had years to teach her how to cook but not much with you, YET," Nona replies as she hugs her granddaughter.

"You want to teach me how to cook?" Beth Ann asks looking amazed at Nona.

Stepping back Nona looks into Beth Ann's baffled face before replying seriously, "Well, of course, I want to teach you all I know and that's a lot, beside, honey, you are like one of those sponges I've had. You just soak up knowledge and then you use it. You know what I see in you?"

Wincing and hunching her shoulders Beth Ann looks down at the ground muttering, "No, I don't know," just waiting for the criticism she always received from her other grandparents.

Nona lifts Beth Ann's chin up softly saying, "Look at me, Beth Ann."

Hesitantly Beth Ann glances up into her grandmother's brown eyes so like her own that she can't help but smile.

"Honey, you use your brain and you are very smart. You learn by reading. Most people can't read a book and learn how to do things but you can. That is a big blessing, honey. God has given you a brain...a very smart brain. I heard you say your Grandma Lora said for you not to be a know-it-all. It can be hard when you are smart not to throw it in other's faces," Nona explains kindly.

"I used to correct people when they didn't use good English, it just irritated me that they wouldn't or couldn't use it," Beth Ann admits before adding, "Grandmother Lora said it was rude to do that."

"If people don't know better then it is rude, I agree with her. If you are teachin' someone something then that is different. I figure you know a whole lot about thangs you've read in books that I've never heard of and I'd like to hear about them and I believe a lot of people, like your papa, would enjoy hearing about them too. You could just say, I've read about England or Paris would you like to hear about it? Or somethin' like that and it will start a good conversation," Nona advises.

"But isn't that being a know-it-all?" Beth Ann questions wonderingly.

"Not in my book. I think that is a conversational piece. Somethin' interestin' to talk about, I'd like to hear about things and places I ain't never been to and won't ever see," Nona answers smiling at her smart young granddaughter.

"Okay, Grandma. I'd like to learn to cook. Actually, I do need to learn to cook. Papa has told me that when I have a husband he will want a good cook because everyone wants good food and in exchange I'll tell you about the books I've read and Grandma I'll write down your recipes so I won't forget them," Beth Ann agrees and promises with a smile.

Nona hugs her adorable granddaughter again saying, "I'd be right proud for you to do that. You never know Sammy might marry a girl who cain't cook and will need them."

"As much as he eats now he better find a girl who LOVES to cook," Beth Ann replies with a laugh.

"Amen to that," Nona states chuckling.

"Know what grandma. In St. Louis Sammy was hit over and over at every meal because he wouldn't eat all the food they gave him. Now he eats all his food and as much more as he can get. It is strange when I think about it," Beth Ann explains frowning.

"Maybe he wasn't happy there and that is why?" Nona answers thinking sadly of that happening to Sammy all the time.

"Only Minnie and Benny treated Sammy nice in St. Louis, grandma. I was mean to him too," Beth Ann sadly confesses and explains.

"Why did everyone treat him mean?" Nona asks frowning.

"I didn't know then everyone just did but now I know it was because he looks so much like papa and they hated papa. They talked bad about him all the time," Beth Ann explains as she thinks back.

Sadly Nona nods yes saying, "Glad that is over then. We can only do our best now and try to undo the bad memories we've made."

"I'm working on undoing the mean things I did," Beth Ann states looking sadly down at the ground.

They talk for a while then Elizabeth walks out asking Beth Ann, "Isn't it your turn to help fix lunch?"

"Yes, Mother. I'm coming," Beth Ann answers winking at her grandmother.

"You sound willing. What have I missed?" Elizabeth asks them.

"Nothing at all, my dear," Nona replies winking back at Beth Ann.

"What are we having for DINNER, Mother," Beth Ann asks smiling.

"Hummp...dinner is still in the evening to me....but YOUR father insists we call it dinner here and supper at night. Hump...I have some ham and red beans for SUPPER cooking but we need something for lunch uh...dinner. I am thinking about some ham and mashed potatoes with fresh peas. It looks like there is enough for a good mess. We have an hour so we'd better get started and, honey, after lun....dinner you and Samuel can go down to the hot springs then this evening we will work on my surprise," Elizabeth thinks it out as she decides how to do it.

Smiling Beth Ann states, "Yes, madam, I love surprises!"

"We'd better make a big batch of biscuits and if we have time we could make a batch or two of cookies, what'cha think?" Elizabeth asks innocently.

"Yes, please, Mother, and will you teach me how to make them. I really like the oatmeal cookies you made last time," Beth Ann pleads then thinks, "Remember to write down the recipe so I can make them next time."

"Certainly, I thought you might like to have them again. By the way, I'm really proud of you with your eating. You have such good manners and you eat slower now and my, oh my, you look so nice and healthy now," Elizabeth explains happily smiling down at her look alike.

Beth Ann beams at the praise thinking, "I'm going to work even harder at being pleasant and easy to get along with as it seems to make everyone happier especially me."

They walk towards the house and start dinner for the large number of people eating.

Riding in for dinner and after rubbing down his horse Joe looks at his pile of planks of wood stacked in one of the empty stalls then starts pulling out a number of them and laying them on the now empty saw horses and starts counting off how many he will need for the fence around the cemetery plot.

Sammy runs in asking, "Howdy Papa, what'cha doin'?"

Smiling and rumpling his hair Joe explains, "Your mama and I are plannin' a surprise, want to hep me?"

Sammy's eyes light up as he enthusiastically replies, "Yes, sir. I certainly do!"

"Good boy. I'm counting the wood we have here cause I'm gonna be cuttin' it after dinner and makin' a fence. I'm gonna have to go measure the place first and see how long to make the fence. Then cut the wood and white wash it and make it look real nice. Do ya wanta go with me and hep me?" Joe explains looking down at his adorable son.

"I can help. I'm eight years old. I'm not a baby anymore," Sammy quickly qualifies.

"Yes, you are a big boy now and it's gonna take a big boy to help cut and tote the wood for the fence. The white washin' is a fun thing to do…to see the wood turn white, course gotta put on a couple of coats of it so it takes some time to do it right," Joe praises then explains.

"I can do it right, Papa, I can do it," Sammy states jumping up and down excitedly.

"Course ya can. YOU are just the man for the job. Course ya gotta remember this is a surprise and ya cain't tell anyone til it's finished," Joe advises seriously then thoughtfully continues, "Course it IS a big job this white washin', might need hep from Beth Ann with it. She might like to do a surprise, too. What'cha think?"

Lowering his head Sammy thinks, "Beth Ann is really smart so she might like it but she don't like to work much so she might not but she likes surprises really well so maybe I'll ask her." He looks up at his pa answering, "I could do it all by myself but don't guess it'd hurt to ask her."

Patting Sammy's white blonde head Joe replies, "Know ya could but it is always more fun to have hep. Why don't cha ask her after we eat dinner?"

"Okay, Papa." Sammy replies with a big smile then adds, "We finished our chores today and I helped Beth Ann clean the chicken coops."

"Ya did, well that was right nice of ya," Joe answers as he picks Sammy up and tosses him in the air.

Sammy's laughter rings through the barn as he enjoys this time with his beloved papa.

Elizabeth and Beth Ann hear his laughter in the kitchen. Beth Ann looks longingly at the back door but keeps working. Elizabeth notices so asks, "Would you like to go tell your father dinner is about ready, honey?"

Looking up quickly Beth Ann looks around the room before deciding, "I'd like to Mother but I'd better finish what I'm doing first." She quickly finishes setting the table and putting the cooled cookies on a plate. She takes her precious notebook of recipes and sets it on a high shelf so it won't get dirty and doesn't notice her mother's raised eye brows as she watches her young daughter systematically clean up what needs to be done.

Quickly the table is finished then Beth Ann asks, "Mother, may I run get some flowers for the table now?"

"Certainly, all I have to do is finish the gravy. Call everyone in to eat please," Elizabeth replies with a warm smile.

"Ma? Uhhh...I really enjoy being around you," Beth Ann stammers as she runs out the back door.

Looking at the door as it quietly closes Elizabeth ashamedly murmurs, "Yes, honey, me, too."

A few minutes later, after telling her great grandpas and her Grandma Nona that it is time to eat, Beth Ann runs into the barn with a handful of flowers calling out, "Papa, Sammy, come in and eat!"

She starts to turn around and go back towards the kitchen when Joe calls out, "We'll be right there. Hey, honey, will ya come here a minute."

Turning around she walks into the darkened barn and it takes a minute for her eyes to adjust. She sees her papa and Sammy with a large pile of planks of wood stacked together. "Yes, Papa?" she asks.

"I'm workin' on a surprise with yar ma and wondered if ya'd like to hep out. Sammy boy is gonna hep me make a fence around yar

Grandma Lora's grave and we were thinkin' maybe ya'd like to help. Sammy has somethin' to ask ya," Joe whispers as he kisses her flushed face then walks towards the house.

"Yeah, I get to white wash the whole fence and Papa and I were talkin' and thinkin' maybe you'd like to help me make it extra special like?" Sammy asks puffing out his chest.

"How could I make it extra special?" Beth Ann questions then states, "Sounds like you just want me to help you paint it."

"I don't need any help with it! Papa said it would be nice if I asked you IF you WANT to help me," Sammy answers belligerently.

"Oh, I see. I'll think about it over dinner. Okay?" Beth Ann replies thoughtfully then turning she walks back to the house.

"Girls! Can't say yes or no without thinking about it a long time," Sammy mutters as he follows her.

Lunch or dinner as Joe calls it is a big success. Everyone praises the food and loves the oatmeal cookies that Elizabeth and Beth Ann baked for them.

"It seems anything sweet is a big success with men and boys," Beth Ann thinks as she watches them eat them and drink more coffee. Of course, they love pie, too. "Men eat so much! It isn't fair that all of them are as skinny as a board and I can't eat half that much and I get fat!" Thoughtfully she watches as the men eat a large plate full of food then more biscuits and gravy and cookies then pie and coffee. "My goodness my grandpas and Rev Roy eat more than two people." She stares wide eyed as they eat. They don't gulp down their food like Mr. Potter did, they eat slowly as if each forkful is a piece of Heaven and they enjoy every bite.

Nona notices Beth Ann watching the men so leaning over whispers, "It ain't fair they can eat so much and be so skinny. I just look at food and I gain weight!"

Beth Ann looks over at her nodding yes, you are right.

"Great meal, Elizabeth and Beth Ann," Skinny announces patting his full stomach.

"Indeed! Thank you," Pokey adds sipping his hot coffee.

"Best mashed tators and gravy I've had in a long time," Max Roy groans as he eyes the last bit of potatoes in the bowl.

"Help yourself to the rest," Elizabeth requests with a smile.

"Don't mind if I do. Pass that last biskut too," Max asks Skinny.

"Oh, there ain't no biskuts left. This one just jumped into my plate," Skinny advises as he bites into the last one.

"Ya could have given me half!" Pokey whines with a menacing leer.

"Ya ate six already, Pokey. Learn to share," Skinny states as he licks his finger adding, "I shoulda put jelly on it. You rushed me!"

"Lizbeth just outta curiosity how many biskuts did ya make?" Joe asks with a chuckle and a smile.

"Thirty-six," Elizabeth replies smiling adding, "Each pan holds a dozen."

"Sammy, how many is a dozen?" Joe quizzes.

"Twelve, Papa," Sammy answers quickly.

"Glory, how many people are eating the biskuts this meal?" Joe asks.

Glory looks around the table counting: ma, papa, Grandma Nona, Grandpa's Pokey and Skinny, Rev Roy, Beth Ann, Sammy and me, "Nine, Papa."

Joe nods then asks, "If we have an equal amount how many biscuits would each of us have eaten, Beth Ann?"

Beth Ann looks at him questioningly for a minute then answers, "Thirty-six divided by nine is four, Papa."

"I believe some people ate more than their share and some people ate less than their share, don'tcha think?" Joe inquires looking at the old gents.

"Uhhh…yep, yar right," Pokey stutters embarrassed.

"Guess, maybe …uh…we ate more than our share," Skinny mutters also embarrassed.

"Not really cause some didn't want four biscuits and to some six ain't enough so it works out good with no left overs," Joe replies smiling at them.

"Point taken," Max admits then whispers to Elizabeth loudly, "Please make four dozen next time."

Everyone laughs at the comedy of the disappearing biscuits as Elizabeth dutifully shakes her head yes.

"Or maybe bigger ones?" Pokey asks innocently.

"Man, they are three inches wide and three inches thick. How big do you want'em?" Nona asks amazed.

"Good biskuts cain't ever be too big!" Pokey immediately states looking at her in amazement.

All of the men nod yes. The ladies just shake their heads and laugh.

Nona and Glory have clean up duty so Elizabeth takes Beth Ann's hand and they slip away.

"Where are we going, Mother?" Beth Ann asks as they walk toward the back pasture behind the smokehouse.

"I want to see the grape vines, honey, and see how we can transplant some," Elizabeth explains as they quickly walk towards the long fence Joe had built years ago explaining, 'Your papa says some need to be moved and I know of a good place to put them. I've brought my shears with me so I can cut the dead ones away and have it ready to dig up when we need them."

Beth Ann blinks in surprise asking, "You know how to prune grapes?"

"Yes, I learned when Glory was a baby. Remember the grape vines back in St. Louis against the back wall? You ate jelly from them most of your life. I took care of them and the flowers. Your grandparents didn't have the time or patience to do it. Remember your grandmother didn't like to get her hands dirty," Elizabeth explains frowning slightly.

"Yes, I remember. Show me how please," Beth Ann begs.

They prune the grapevines for an hour or so then carry the dead vines away stacking them in a spot for burning later.

Beth Ann looks with appreciation at her mother saying, "Mother, I've lived with you all my life and I never knew you. I didn't really think you liked me or wanted to be around me. Why didn't we talk like this and do things together in St. Louis?"

Elizabeth blushes then putting her hand on her daughters shoulder and looking her in the eyes truthfully replies, "Beth Ann, you look like me but you have your father's brains. He is very smart just not school smart. I'm school smart but I don't have his intelligence. I saw this in you and it angered me that you are like him and I missed him dreadfully. It was just hard headedness that I didn't come back. Pride is a terrible thing when it stops you doing what you want and need to do. I'm sorry I wasn't a very good mother to you. It was just so much easier to buy you things than feel the pain of seeing Joe in you every time I talked to you. I encouraged you to be haughty and arrogant so I wouldn't feel guilty about not spending time with you. I'm basically a lazy person and a very spoiled one."

"You are not so spoiled now, Mother," Beth Ann states smiling.

"I found out being spoiled isn't such a nice way to be. Being spoiled caused me to lie, cheat and treat others with disrespect and in the end my pride took a heavy toll on my bottom." Elizabeth explains giggling.

"Papa spanked me hard that first time, too. He told me things I had never thought about before then. He asked me how I wanted to be when I grew up and I was hateful and sarcastic and he spanked me harder," Beth Ann says looking down at the ground then adding, "I didn't think he'd ever stop then afterwards he asked me to spend the afternoon with him and Mama we had a wonderful afternoon. Remember I turned my ankle and Papa carried me home and you were waiting at the back door mad."

Grimacing Elizabeth nods yes then explains, "Yes, very well. I was angry because you were getting Joe's attention and I wasn't. I was shocked when he spanked you. Really shocked. I never considered that Joe would do that to you or me. I just thought he would let me walk all over him like I always did. Then I thought about all the things I'd done to him, all the lies I'd told and how I'd run off with you and especially about not telling him about Sammy. I was terrified he would spank me. I cringed every time I heard him give you a spank because I knew that if he spanked me I'd never be able to sit down again. But I grew up and I told Joe I was ready for that spanking because I knew I deserved it. I never want to get another one like that one, it is not something I ever want to think about or remember."

Nodding yes Beth Ann replies, "I'll never forget that one either. Papa has smacked my bottom a time or two but I'm not giving him any reason to paddle me so hard again."

Laughing softly Elizabeth replies emphatically, "Me, neither!"

They giggle as they work and talk girl talk so soon their job is completed. Beth Ann explains to her mother how she is going to help Sammy paint the fence before she walks over to do that and Elizabeth walks back to the ranch house.

Nona is working in the garden along with the three old gents. They all hoe the weeds and when the birds keep trying to eat the blooms off the vegetables the men declare a scarecrow is needed. Pokey and

Skinny find some old clothes of theirs while Max Roy takes a long tree limb and cut it to the right size and digs a hole and sets the tall pole in it. After they put the pants on the scarecrow, they add a good size limb for the arms and fit the shirt over it then tie it to the body. They take some dead grass from the compose pile and stuff the scarecrow into a more human shape. Proudly they stand back looking at their handiwork.

"Looks right fine to me," Pokey admits looking at his old red flannel shirt.

"Yep, my pants look better on him than me," Skinny replies with a chuckle.

"Well, I think my hat looks right fine on him," Max proudly states.

"Yep, it does. But it took a whole lotta grass to fill that pumpkin size head to keep that hat on," Skinny laughs as he pokes Max in the ribs.

"Men, they are all the same," Nona thinks smiling to herself as she watches them admiring their handiwork.

Elizabeth is pleased to see them ribbing each other and having some fun so she joins in saying, "Ma, you'd better get Grandpa Pokey outta that tree over there. I'd recognize his shirt anywhere."

Smiling Nona joins in, "Well he donated that shirt to a good cause. That there skinny fellow ain't your grandpa it's a scarecrow." She chuckles at the looks of outrage that follows her statement.

"Oh, you are right! Hi Grandpas and Uncle Max," Elizabeth says laughing as she walks over to admire the scarecrow.

"Can't get no respect around here," fumes Pokey.

"None atoll," Skinny replies smothering a grin.

"No appreciatin' the old ones," Max grumbles also hiding his smile.

"Well, I'll just have to say this here is the bestest scarecrow this woman's ever seen," Elizabeth drawls out dramatically.

They all guffaw at her outrageous accent.

"Let's have some coffee and cookies," Elizabeth requests smiling then adds, "I've worked hard enough that I deserve it."

They all agree they have too and are finished so they walk into the kitchen. Nona checks the red beans for supper as Elizabeth starts another pot of coffee and opens the crock of cookies.

Joe with Sammy tagging along measures the length of the fence that will be needed and also to the height Elizabeth has requested then they walk back to the barn and Joe saws the wood to the right sizes. He shows Sammy how to sand down the sharp edges then they carry the boards outside and lay them on the grass. Joe shows Sammy how to mix the paint just as Beth Ann walks up so he goes over the instructions for the paint mixing again. Both say they understand it so Joe goes back to checking on his cattle.

With a bucket of powered white wash and a bucket of water beside it they take turns stirring it to the right consistency. It takes a while until they get it correct.

"This looks right, Sammy. Take your brush and see if it stays on the board," Beth Ann briskly requests.

Sammy stands up belligerently stating, "Beth Ann, I am the boss here remember! I asked you if you wanted to help me, not BOSS me around!"

Beth Ann's mouth drops open and she frowns at him then shrugging agrees, "You are right, sorry. Do you want me to brush on the white wash and see if it is thick enough?"

Sammy blinks at her in surprise then quietly says, "I'd like to."

It is perfect so they begin to paint each board which takes a little while since the fence is going to surround a good size piece of land.

"Sorry, I yelled at you, Beth Ann," Sammy contritely says.

"No, I was wrong and you were right," Beth Ann readily admits.

"Thanks for helping me do this. I might not have gotten the paint right if you hadn't helped me. It was hard stirring it, too," Sammy also admits.

Beth Ann smiles at her temporarily humble little brother saying, "I'm enjoying it and it will be so nice to give them a surprise."

"They are gonna be really surprised, Bethy." Sammy states with a sparkle in his eyes. "Papa said to let these dry then turn them over and paint the other side."

"Okay. These are all done what do you want to do now?" Beth Ann asks a little bit tired.

"We could go take a swim?" Sammy suggests hopefully.

"We will just get paint on us again," Beth Ann answers frowning.

"We could go get some cookies and milk?" Sammy suggests again.

"How are we going to explain the paint on us?" Beth Ann asks.

"You are too smart! What can we do?" Sammy demands pertly.

"We can get a drink of cold water from the well then do a chore or two so we won't have to do them later then finish this and go have cookies and milk," Beth Ann explains as she counts the ideas off her fingers.

"I thought you'd come up with some more work to do," Sammy mumbles adding, "I suppose to put hay in the stalls for the horses."

"I've got to gather the eggs. Want me to help you then you can help me?" Beth Ann asks surprising even herself.

"Those chickens are mean! They spur me when I go get the eggs!" Sammy admits frowning.

"Glory said she kicked one across the yard once when it spurred her and it never did it again. I am real careful when I'm getting them. I do not like being pecked or spurred either," Beth Ann answers wonderingly.

Sammy sticks out his paint covered grimy hand saying, "Okay, it's a deal!"

Looking down at his filthy hand Beth Ann looks at her own hands, which are almost as dirty, then shrugging and giggling says, "Deal!" and shakes his hand adding, "Let's do the hay first cause we can't go into the house with the eggs until we clean up."

"Okay, wanna race!" Sammy asks laughing.

"Yeah!" Beth Ann agrees then lifting her skirt starts running back into the barn.

"Wait! I didn't say go," Sammy yells as he races after her.

GLORY'S REALIZATION
Chapter 4

"Seeing the truth is sometimes harder than knowing the truth."

Glory is lying on her stomach on her pallet bed in the loft thinking about all that has happened to her. She remembers her shock as she'd been grabbed outside the out house, being hit on the jaw and knocked out and feeling sick to her stomach when she woke up face down across the saddle of Patrick Sully. "Oh, Glory, why did you go outside when you knew better? Papa told me …Jake told me…well …everyone told me not to leave the house by myself. But I had to go to the outhouse. I had to. I couldn't wait anymore. I did try to. But if they had killed papa because I disobeyed…oh, what would I be feelin' now." Tears run down her drawn little face at the thought. "I was too headstrong, as usual. If I hadn't carried on so Patrick wouldn't have spanked me. I know he enjoyed it and it hurt so bad. My temper got away from me again. Larry was kind. I hope they don't …well…I don't know what is right. They wanted to hang'em all but papa said no. I wonder what they will do to'em? Then Grandma Lora tried to save me. I don't remember her before then except when they came into Roy and would have stopped Mama and Papa's second weddin'. Oh, it was so nice. We all looked so pretty in our new dresses and mama and papa were so happy until we turned around and saw them. Poor grandma she couldn't hep she weren't pretty. I bet having a pretty daughter made up for that some. I acted like a wild girl when they attacked me. They acted like seein' my bosom was a rare sight. They wanted to touch me! Jake said they wanted to do more than touch me…ohhhhh…*thank you, God, they didn't do that.*"

She moans slightly as she shifts her position and her bottom throbs from the two spankings she'd received. "Jake sure walloped my fanny. Oh, it hurts. Papa never spanked me so hard. Papa??? Oh, no!" She leans up and groans again at the throbbing pain in her poor bottom thinking, "Papa woulda spanked me for disobeyin' him! He let Jake do it instead! Oh, my goodness, why did he do that?" Her face flushes with embarrassment as she remembers Jake sternly saying, "I'm gonna spank yar bottom till ya cry, Glory, for disobeyin' the rules and gettin' yourself kidnapped!" "And he did! Jake really did and he walloped my fanny terrible! I never thought that he would ever spank me even after our talk in Roy when I asked him if he would if I was bad. I was thinkin' of ma though …not me. Jake said if'n ya love someone ya want'em to be the best they can be. Papa says that, too. I was sorry I disobeyed Papa but not nearly as sorry as I am now." Tears fall freely down her flushed face as she remembers the humiliation of Jake forcing her across his lap on Comfort then giving her lick after lick on her already sore bottom. Then looking up and seeing Papa's face and Grandpa Skinny's sorrowful looks as they watched. Glory puts her hands over her red face remembering the sound of each whack as Jake smacked her bottom. "Then he sat me down again on his lap and comforted me and told me, "Never make me have to do that again." Then he told me horrible things they wanted to do to me. Put their hands on my body and …ohhhh… I don't wanta think about that!" She quietly sobs as she tries to lie completely still.

Everyone walking in from the garden hears her sobs.

Sighing sadly Nona says, "I'll go up and talk to her."

Laying her hand on her mother's arm Elizabeth says, "No, Mama, let me." Walking into her bedroom Elizabeth picks up the jar of cold cream then awkwardly climbs up the ladder to the loft. She knocks softly on the door and Glory quietly says, "I'd like to be alone please."

Elizabeth knocks again asking, "Please, Glory, may I come in?"

"Mama? Yes, I guess so," Glory answers surprised. She starts wiping her tears away as her mother walks in.

Walking over to the pallet Elizabeth sits on the floor beside Glory saying, "My poor baby, you understand what could have happened to you and now it has scared you."

Tears flow freely as Glory starts crying harder, "Yes, Mama, why didn't I listen?"

"Because you are my daughter and I have a bad habit of not listening. I am going to put some cold cream on your fanny as I am sure it is hurting quite a bit," Elizabeth explains raising Glory's skirt she sees Glory isn't wearing any bloomers.

Glory's face turns redder as she admits, "It hurts to have anythang touch me."

"I remember," Elizabeth sadly replies as she gently applies the cold cream all over Glory's sore bottom.

Glory moans then lays her head in her mother's lap asking, "Why do men want to hurt women like those men wanted to hurt me? I don't understand."

Elizabeth remembers Franklin Potter and how often he had lusted after her as other men had but doesn't know quite how to explain it. "Oh Glory, it is a part of being a woman and of God's plan that men and women are attracted to each other romantically. Do you feel anything romantically for Jake?"

"I like when he kisses me," Glory smiles wonderingly, "It makes me feel good."

"When you love someone you want to kiss them and hold them and it brings pleasure to each of you. That is desire and it is good for a husband and wife to have desire for each other. Humm... I'm not sure how to explain it exactly, honey. I don't think you will really understand it until after you and Jake are married on your wedding night. I know I didn't. Men and women shouldn't do it without marriage. God says not to in the Bible and we should listen to God's teachings. But lots of people don't listen to the rights and wrongs of loving they just mate. Mating is like horses doing it or cattle doing it or any animal, it isn't love. Some men and women don't care how many they mate with but with your wedding vows you promise to love just one man and to keep faith with that one man or woman. You love just them and don't just mate with anyone around. It is something special then," Elizabeth explains as best she can.

"I know how animals do it, ma. Is it like that with men and women, too?" Glory asks blinking in surprise.

"Similar to, yes," Elizabeth answers honestly.

"Oh, my goodness," Glory states wide-eyed.

"Gloria, look at me. It can be the most wonderful feelings you will ever feel in your life when you areloving the man you are married to and knowing he loves you right back. Sharing yourself with him and giving him what he needs and wants as he gives it to you is the closest to Heaven you will get on earth," Elizabeth explains brushing Glory's hair softly with her fingers.

"Better than kissing?" Glory asks innocently.

"One hundred million times better," Elizabeth answers truthfully.

"Oh, my," Glory replies amazed, then asks, "Mama, how should I act with Jake. I'm a little mad he spanked me. I understand why he did and I know papa probably would have if Jake hadn't but…I'm mad he hurt me."

"Oh, I know that feeling very well and I can tell you what I said to myself: Did I deserve this? Only you can answer that, Glory. I know your papa said Jake was frantic for you. That he was wild to find you and mad at you for going outside by yourself. If anything had happened to you, I don't know what Jake would be doing right now. He loves you and with loving someone you want what is best for them even when they can't see it," Elizabeth explains as best she can.

"Jake near crushed me with a bear hug when they rescued me. He nearly beat Patrick Sully to death for hurtin' me. I think he shot Mr. Potter when he was tryin' to hurt me," Glory shudders at the memory then continues, "I know he was worried and scared for me. He talked to me all the way back and he wouldn't let me ride with Papa or Grandpa Skinny. He just put me on his horse and I was happy to ride with him until he spanked me. I didn't believe he would ever do THAT to me and he did. I tried to jump down after he did and he said no and if I tried again he'd paddle me again. He meant it, too. I saw it in his eyes. Then he told me all those bad things about men…I didn't know," Glory eyes fill with tears again and they roll swiftly down her pale face.

"I know it is hard to understand Glory. I think you'll know how to act towards Jake the next time you see him. You love him and that will win out over it all," Elizabeth explains then asks, "Want me to bring you up some cookies and milk?"

Smiling faintly Glory replies, "Papa wouldn't like it. He made me sit at the table yesterday and he will today, too, so I'll wait until supper then come down. Thank you, mama, for talkin' with me."

"My pleasure, my little darling," Elizabeth replies as she kisses Glory's forehead then returns downstairs.

Jake is working like a mad man all through the day and is soaked with sweat and he still has energy to burn. "I don't know what to feel," he angrily thinks as he works. "She asked for that paddlin'. She asked for it. I was fair in doin' it. But I can't forget that look she gave me. She looked so shocked and, oh, my God, I made her cry. I told her I'd make her cry and I did. Her sobbing echoes in my ears. I hurt her. I smacked her bottom so hard my hand hurt. These big ole hands!" He pounds his fists into each other as tears run down his dirt streaked face as he cries out with the pain of his memories. Finally he kneels down sobbing and prays, *"Lord, I feel I done wrong by Glory. I was so worked up about her. So scared! I shook in my boots, God Almighty, I shook in my boots I was so scared. NEVER been scared like that afore. NEVER. I spanked her. Oh, Lord, I spanked her and not once but probably a dozen times. I know my strength. How could I have done that?"*

Zak silently watches his handsome son all day and knows he will soon hit rock bottom with his emotions as they have always run strong in him."I know Jake will feel guilt over his treatment of Glory and that he will be very sorry (as he always is) when he feels he's done wrong." So when Jake goes down on his knees, Zak can see he is praying so he patiently waits until Jake just kneels there crying out his anger and hurt. Zak smiles knowing his son so well, "My tender hearted son, who never wants to hurt anyone, and who will always try to joke his way out of an awkward situation." So he patiently waits until it is time to talk to him. Thirty minutes pass while Jake prays and Zak works, waits and prays also, *"Dear Lord please give me the wisdom and the words to help my son.*

He is so tender hearted and loves Glory so much but he needs to learn how to handle her, too. She could have got herself killed and he needs to handle this really well so there won't be another time…thank ya Lord. I appreciate your help. Amen."

Jake wearily stands up totally exhausted and spent of emotion then turns to walks to his horse.

"Jake are you ready to talk, son?" Zak asks quietly.

Jake's head is bowed as he tiredly replies, "Nothing to talk about Pa I done her wrong. She probably hates me right now if'n she feels anything for me."

"Oh, I reckon she has powerful feelin's about you right now. She's got a powerful hurtin' in her fanny to remind her you spanked her," Zak replies smiling slightly.

Startled Jake raises his head turning bright red as his shoulders droop again then he states, "Joe told ya, huh."

"Yep, he was proud of you for doing it. Son, I never figured you had it in you," Zak answers truthfully.

"I hope to God I never have it in me again. I hurt her! I smacked her bottom so hard my hand hurt!" Jake roars at his father. Now Jake has never raised his voice to his father before and they both know it. Taking a deep breath Jake lowers his head sadly admitting, "Sorry, Pa. I ain't fit to talk to right now."

Slapping him on the shoulder Zak explains, "Jake, you proved you were a man goin' out there huntin' for Glory. I was worried for you. I can truthfully say I was REAL worried what ya'd do when you found those scoundrels. I was afraid ya'd tear'em limb from limb cause I know you have the muscle to do it but not the soul for it. You mastered yar temper a long time ago and I'm proud of you for it. It takes a man to know his limits and when to say yes and when to say no. You have learned that. I'm real proud of ya. Son, look at me."

Jake raises tormented eyes to his father and Zak realizes how much it bothers him to have hurt Glory, so he asks, "Could you have killed those men, son?"

Jake raises his head up higher, clenches his jaw tightly and with a steely look in his eyes shakes his head yes, "Yes, sir, and I did shoot Mr. Potter – three times and I ain't sorry for it. He was a mean low down human bein'. He was fixin' to hurt my Glory. I saw it with my own eyes."

"Was Glory there because she'd disobeyed everyone's orders to not go anywhere by herself?" Zak asks quietly.

Jake tiredly lowers his head admitting, "Yes, sir, she was."

"Wasn't she lucky to have Good Heart there watchin' over her?" Zak asks again.

Frowning slightly Jake takes a deep breath before replying, "Yes, she was."

"What do you think would have happened if ya'll hadn't gotten there when ya did?" Zak questions thoughtfully.

Taking deep breath Jake replies, "Potter and her supposed grandpa woulda hurt her if'n they could."

"Would the other cowboys have hurt her if'n they could?" Zak asks sadly closing his eyes and looking down at the ground.

Closing his eyes Jake holds his breath ten seconds then groans, "Yep, they would have." His eyes are full of grief at the thought of what she would have endured.

"So what did she deserve for puttin' herself in that situation, son?" Zak asks looking Jake steadily in the eye.

Jake sadly smiles his crooked smile for the first time replying, "A hard spankin' just like she got."

"Right son. She deserved the licks you gave her and let me tell you somethin', she won't forget it for a long time and when she acts up again all ya'll have to do is remind her you will do it again and to my thinkin' she will think hard before she disobeys you again," Zak advises smiling at him.

"I'm worried about her not forgivin' me," Jake answers looking towards Joe's place.

"Maybe she should be aworrin' about YOU not forgivin' her for doin' what she did. Maybe if she thinks you are still upset with her it will make her think about her actions in the future," Zak drawls out thoughtfully.

"So you think I shouldn't go see her for a day or so?" Jake asks not liking the thought. "I want to hold her and comfort her and just know she is alive and well," he thinks sadly.

"That's up to you, son. But I think I'd give her a couple of days to think about what coulda happened and how lucky she is," Zak advises sagely.

"Maybe I will. I'll think on it and pray about it Pa," Jake acknowledges humbly then does a rare thing. He hugs his pa then kisses his check mumbling, "Much obliged, Pa." He turns and walks away deep in thought.

Zak wipes a tear away praying: "*Dear Lord, thank you for the words and the wisdom. I'm in your debt. Amen.*"

Minnie and Benny's wagon pulls up at the Gray's ranch house bright and early the next day. Benny jumps down and walks around to the other side of the wagon to help the heavily pregnant Minnie down.

"Lordy, Lordy it's gettin' harder to climb up and down the wagon," Minnie states breathing hard.

"I tole ya we didn't need to come over so early," Benny states impatiently, "You'da thought ya coulda waited til later but no ya had to git up and rush through the chores and git over here and check on thangs here."

"I'ze worried about'em, Benny. I cain't stands to worry no more," Minnie replies with tears beginning again.

"No more bawlin', Minnie, ya bawl all the time now. Yar drivin' me to distraction!" Benny states impatiently.

"Then why don'tcha go back home and let ME have some peace and quiet today, old man. YOU are driving me to distraction," Minnie replies tearfully.

Looking at the love of his life Benny wearily placates her, "Now Minnie ya know I don't really mean what I'ze said. I'll sure be glad when ya has these twins. Yar not so sweet tempered now."

Minnie looks him in the eyes saying, "HUMPPPP!!!" then turning around walks over to the door where Joe is standing waiting.

"Sorry to be so early Joe, I couldn't keep'er away any longer," Benny explains with a shrug.

"Always happy to see ya. Minnie, yar cryin'. No cause for that," Joe says as he puts his arm around her shoulders and walks back into the house with her.

Startled for a minute at a white man touching her, Minnie thinks, "Wasn't so long ago, I'da fainted at the thought of it. But now it feels right cause we couldna found better friends than Big Joe and Elizabeth."

"I be's alright, Big Joe. Just couldn't settle down til I found out everythan' is alright over here," Minnie explains smiling through the tears that seem to come all the time.

"Good Heart said he rode over and told ya'll we got Glory back and she is unhurt," Joe asks inquiringly.

"He did, yes, he did. But Minnie has to see with her own eyes that yar all doin' fine," Benny replies aggravated then continues, "She has been drivin' me to distraction with her demands to come over here and pester ya'll."

Minnie bursts into tears again so Joe pats her shoulder saying, "Well, we need some help right now, Minnie and yar just the one we need it from."

Minnie's large brown eyes look hopefully up at Joe as she asks, "What Joe?" then she turns those same beautiful brown eyes towards her husband, Benny, and sniffs at him as if saying, "You don't know everythang".

Smiling at Benny over Minnie's head Joe replies, "Everyone's grievin' and we are all keepin' so busy we ain't had time to think about the future. Maybe ya could get Lizbeth and Nona plannin' Glory's weddin' and maybe ya could talk to Glory about cookin' or somethin' and take her mind off of herself for awhile."

"Yes, sir, I could do that," Minnie exclaims smiling again.

"Come in and have some coffee and rest a spell. Have ya ett yet? We have some oatmeal cookies that Beth Ann and Lizbeth made yesterday to have with the coffee," Joe invites Benny and Minnie.

"If'n ya don't need me, Joe, I'm gonna head back home. I'ze got a lot of work to do today. I'll come back for Minnie this afternoon, if'n that be okay," Benny replies then gives Minnie a kiss on the cheek and leaves as Joe nods that will be fine.

"What'cha need done now, Joe?" Minnie asks as she looks around the clean kitchen.

Joe sits back down at the table as he thoughtfully replies, "Glory's feelin' bad about gettin' kidnapped and she knows now what they coulda done to her and it has scared her. Lizbeth is keepin' real busy like so she won't have to think about Lora dying. Nona is Lizbeth's real ma. Old Edgar Hawkins stole her from Nona when Lizbeth was about two years old and they raised her as their own. He bragged about it afore he died when he tried to…uh…hurt Glory."

"Lordy, Lordy, how terrible," Minnie states (looking down at her callused hands) in horror, "How's she doin' with her grievin'."

"She's cried over Lora but she won't even think about Edgar at all," Joe explains sadly shaking his head no.

"He weren't a good man, Big Joe. He was always mean and ornery but thinkin' about it….he was always purdy good to Elizabeth. He watched her like a hawk and questioned everythan' she did and where she went," Minnie musingly explains.

"Yeah, he wanted to keep her for himself or ole man Potter and not give her a chance to come back to me," Joe thinks as he sits drinking coffee. He looks over at Minnie with her caring heart and smiles thinking to himself, "I remember when Minnie, Benny and their son, Arty, arrived with Lizbeth and my young'uns a few months ago. How they have changed since we gave them their freedom in writing and I'll never forget them choosin' a last name as they didn't have one before and didn't want their old master's last name. Freed! It is a good name. Slaves ain't treated very nice it seems in a lot of places. No one should own another human being."

"Where is everyone?" Minnie asks looking around.

"Come with me and I'll show ya," Joe requests then picking up a chair from the table carries it as they leave the house and walk towards the newly built cemetery plot. Joe takes Minnie's hand (much to her surprise) when they leave the hard packed ground of the yard to walk on the sparsely covered grass area to where Elizabeth and the children are. Smiling Joe explains, "It is rough in places and I don't want'cha to trip and fall."

Smiling Minnie agrees gratefully, "Thank ya, Big Joe."

Elizabeth is softly singing as she plants the grape vines around the fence of the newly made cemetery plot.

Minnie stops to take a breath while listening and looking about her. All three children are helping Elizabeth with the vines, tying some here and some there. Sammy is pouring water over the newly planted ones and Beth Ann is, oh, my Lord, she is down in the dirt planting them. Minnie raises her eye brows in shock at seeing Beth Ann working happily with the other children and Elizabeth. "My, oh, my how thangs has changed, Big Joe," Minnie admits quietly.

Joe smiles happily at his family until he looks over at Glory who is raking discarded leaves, grass and dirt to the side. There is no expression on her face at all…just dully working. So unlike her usual demeanor that he frowns worried again then calls out, "Look who came to visit us."

Everyone looks up and smiles seeing Sammy and Beth Ann's ex-nanny, Minnie, who Joe had forced Elizabeth to free after they moved down here a few months ago.

"Good Morning, Minnie. It is good to see you. How are you feeling?" Elizabeth asks smiling up at the black woman who she has learned so much from and has become her confidant in a lot of ways.

"Purdy good just seem to be bawlin' all the time. I'ze been drivin' Benny crazy so I made him bring me over so I could see ya'll," Minnie replies then smiles up at Joe as he sits the chair in the shade and she thankfully sits down then continues, "I'ze cain't believe how big I'm gettin'. These babies are sure gettin' big fast. Lordy, I tire easily and I still have months to go afore they be born."

"Just rest a spell, Minnie. I've got to go check the cattle so I'll see ya'll at dinner time," Joe says turning towards the barn.

"This looks really purdy. Yous doin' a fine job of makin' it a purdy place," Minnie exclaims seeing the sweat on each of their faces. "This be Missy Lora's grave? We's sorry that she died. She…uh…she shore loved ya'll." Minnie can't say she was a nice person because she usually wasn't very nice, she was very demanding and critical of everything.

Sitting back Elizabeth smiles saying, "Thank you, Minnie, it has been rather a shock. Too many shocks right now… to understand their reasoning." She lowers her head and bends back down over the grape vines arranging them just so.

Sammy walks over proudly explaining, "I helped Papa make the fence and Beth Ann helped me white wash it. It is a surprise for our grandpas."

"Where are they, ain't seen'em or Nona since I gots here," Minnie asks looking around.

"Grandma needed to go back to town and so our grandpas and Uncle Max went with her," Beth Ann explains then adds, "They haven't seen this yet so it is our big surprise."

Minnie smiles then looks inquiringly at Glory as she just listlessly rakes the ground over and over in the same place. "Glory, don'tcha think we otta start plannin' yar weddin'?" Minnie asks pleasantly.

Opening her eyes wide Glory stammers, "Don't know if there'll be a weddin'," then dropping her rake she runs back to the house sobbing.

"Jake hasn't been over since the morning he brought her home and she is upset by what could have happened. She is very emotional right now. We can let her cry for awhile then check on her," Elizabeth advises as Minnie rises and stands looking helplessly after Glory's flying figure.

Glory reaches the house and goes inside.

"Jake ain't been over to check on her? That sounds odd?" Minnie replies musingly.

"He may be mad at her. It is probably the first time ever. He spanked her on the way back home for leaving the house after she had been repeatedly told not to. So she is mad at him and scared he won't come over ….doesn't love her …well, you know…and he probably is mad at her for doing it and giving her time to get over being mad at him. I'm just guessing," Elizabeth explains shaking her head sadly.

"Sounds logical to me. Young'uns have a hard time of it sometimes gettin' their problems figured out. Me and Benny we'uns had some humdinger of arguments a time or two. But they all came out well and fine in the end," Minnie explains fondly smiling then mischievously adds, "He's put out with me right now cause I cain't stop bawlin' all the time. Everything makes me bawl and he just hates it but I cain't stops it."

"It will pass. I know mine did," Elizabeth assures her then teases, "Sure you only have two babies in there, Minnie?"

"Two's all I'ze be able to handle, better not be more than that," she chuckles then adds, *Sorry, Lord, I be very obliged to any young'uns ya gives me.*"

"Do you want boys or girls, Minnie?" Beth Ann inquires smiling at her.

"Don't care either way…well…would surely like a little girl again. I luved my little Patty a whole passel before she died and ain't never forgot her either," Minnie declares wiping away a tear.

"Maybe God will remember that and give you a girl this time Minnie," Sammy adds happily as he strokes Minnie's arm lovingly. He adores Minnie and Benny as they are the only ones in St. Louis who ever gave him any attention. Minnie was more his mother than Elizabeth was his first eight years. She fed him, bathed him, dressed him, loved him, comforted him and rocked him to sleep most every night of his life until they arrived at Joe's ranch. Sammy had thought his father didn't love him since he'd never seen him then found out his mother, Elizabeth, had run away from Joe when she was pregnant with Sammy and stayed in St. Louis with her parents for almost eight years and Joe didn't know Sammy existed or that Elizabeth had been pregnant when she ran away. So Minnie, Benny and Arty were family to Sammy more than anyone else those first eight years. So their love goes deep.

Minnie hugs her precious little boy saying, "God blessed me with a beautiful little blonde haired boy a long time ago. I knows he will bless us with what we needs and we'uns be overjoyed to be havin'em."

"What'cha gonna name them?" Sammy asks interested.

"We's been thinkin' about that, Sammy boy. What do ya think of Catie, Katherine, Connie, Carl, Frankie or Francie?" Minnie asks as she can't keep from touching his back with a caressing hand.

Sammy pouts as he thinks a minute saying, "Girls...humm... Catie and Connie are pretty. Boys...humm... could name one Sammy? Nope, I'm the only Sammy...humm...I like Frankie and Carl or Kevin ain't...uhh...isn't bad." He gives his mother a sorry for the bad English look.

"What do ya think Beth Ann?" Minnie asks looking at the thoughtful girl.

Smiling happily at being asked, Beth Ann replies, "Connie and Catie are really pretty names and Catherine can be Catie or Cathy. Francie is nice but Francie Freed doesn't...oh...sorry. I like Catie and Connie best, too."

"Sounds beautiful to me also," Elizabeth agrees smiling fondly at Minnie.

"How are the plans going for Arty's birthday? We are going to have it back at your home now, right?" Elizabeth asks.

"Yes, now that the excitement is over that is what we'uns will do," Minnie explains then adds, "He's never had a party that's more than us'ns and Sammy here. We'uns are real excited about havin' ya'll comin' over."

"Thank you for inviting us, Minnie. We can hardly wait," Beth Ann answers also thinking, "Minnie makes the best cakes ever."

JAKE'S TERMS
Chapter 5

*"Sometimes ya cain't bend when the
bendin' will break yar back."*

Elizabeth turns at the sound of a horse riding in seeing Jake riding towards the ranch house so says, "Fireworks are going to be going off any time now. Why don't we stay out here and let them battle it out. I don't think we need to be in the blast of their tempers right now."

Looking at Jake Minnie can see he is mad by the set of his face as he lets his horse, Comfort, loose in the corral and heads straight for the house. He takes off his hat smacking it against his leg to knock the dust off of it before knocking on the door.

Glory doesn't answer.

Looking around he notices the group sitting by the lilac bushes and starts walking towards them when he notices Glory isn't there. Elizabeth points back towards the house. Slapping his hat back on his head, Jake strides purposefully into the house. He starts looking into each room for Glory. The kitchen is empty. The parlor is empty. Walking to the back door he looks into the garden area and it is empty. Taking a deep breath Jake looks up to the loft area where Glory's bedroom is calling out, "Glory, come down and talk to me."

No answer.

Gritting his teeth he bellows, "Glory, git down here!"

"I ain't got nothin' to say to you....you... BRUTE! Go away!" Glory shouts down to him. Glory is lying on her pallet bed feeling sorry for herself when she heard Jake ride up so decides she isn't about to jump up and run to him.

Walking to the bottom of the ladder (that climbs up the wall to the loft) and talking in a normal voice Jake demands, "Gloria if ya don't come down right now. I will come up there and you don't want me to have to do that in my frame of mind!"

"His frame of mind! I don't care about his frame of mind. Who does he think he is to order me around," Glory muttered to herself then she hears Jake counting. "Papa counted to five before he spanked Beth Ann. Darn him!" She rises painfully then opening the door stands at the top of the loft hatefully asking, "What do ya want?"

Jake bristles at her defiance then smiling coolly replies, "I believe we have some unfinished business to attend to, Glory."

"None that I know of," Glory answers sarcastically.

"Now ....now love...you don't wanta be that way right now. I'm still angry enough to paddle ya again for scaring ten years offa my life so don't be giving me any grief right now," Jake states firmly.

Looking down at him, Glory's anger and frustration reach the lowest ebb as she meekly asks, "Why didn't ya come see me yesterday? I waited all day to see ya."

"Because I couldn't be sure that I wouldn't spank you again," Jake replies flatly, "I've been so riled up since you were kidnapped that I still cain't think straight. Come down and talk to me, honey."

Glory starts down then realizes she has taken her bloomers off again so says, "Just a minute I forgot somethang." Turning she walks back into her bedroom putting back on the silk ones that her mama had brought her from St. Louie. Returning she slowly climbs down the ladder gritting her teeth to keep from groaning out loud as she does. At the bottom she turns around looking at Jake (who is standing across the room) watching her.

Jake's eyes never leave her as she climbs down the loft ladder when she turns around he is astounded, she has dark circles under her eyes, her dress is very wrinkled and she appears dead in a living person with her chalk white face.

Raising her head up she really looks at him. "He has dark circles under both eyes and oh, my lord, I've never seen that look in his eyes before," Glory realizes then before she can stop herself she runs to him and he opens his arms and they hug. Bursting into tears Glory can't seem to stop crying.

Jake takes a couple of steps back and sits down in a kitchen chair pulling her onto his lap.

Glory sits then gasping stands immediately back up and furiously starts rubbing her throbbing bottom as more tears run down her pale face. "Oh, Jake, ya hurt me so bad!" she wails sorrowfully.

"I know I did, Glory, but you done a bad thing and you coulda... uh....bad things coulda happened cause you didn't obey yar pa. You scared the life outta me, girl! I almost went crazy trying to find you! You deserved that spankin' I gave you and don't say you didn't!" Jake replies sternly to her as she stands between his legs looking down sorrowfully.

"I know I done bad, Jake, and I am sorry. Was sorry when they grabbed me and sorry all the time. But I didn't want no spankin' at fifteen years old and not from YOU!" she declares testily.

Taking a deep breath Jake sits back in the chair laying his hands on his thighs as he looks at her steadily explaining, "Well you acted like a child so I treated you like a child. Besides you woulda got a lot worse from yar pa. I figure he'd a taken you to the woodshed and given you a worse spankin' than I did. Are you forgettin' that Patrick gave you the first spanking? You were already sore from it....so it wasn't just the spankin' from me that's made you sore."

Glory's green eyes blaze at his words and she starts to slap him for them then thoughtfully sits down gently on his thigh and lowering her head thinks, "He is right. I didn't think at all. Patrick did spank me first when I tried to slow them down and it really did hurt but Jake's hurt more. I did act like a child and I reacted to the situation. I am totally to blame for all of it." Looking up at Jake and seeing his stern look she is sadden by it. Tears start again as she starts to move off his thigh when Jake softly asks, "Tell me what yar thinking?"

With her head down she answers, "Yar right, Jake, it was my fault. I cain't blame anyone else for it. If'n I'd done what I shoulda, they couldna got me and we wouldna had this bad scare. I guess...I deserved the spankin'." She lets out a large breath then continues, "Maybe Papa was right and I'm too young to git married now. I was really lookin' forward to bein' yar wife though. I'd really set my heart on it."

Jake almost gasps at the thought of them not getting married then narrowing his eyes he thinks, "Is she trying to get me to beg her to marry me? Does she think she will always get around me by crying? I think not Glory." So he answers, "Well, I hope not, too. I've got my heart set to marryin' you when you turn sixteen, which ain't long now. How long do you figure it will take ya to decide to grow up so yar pa will let'cha marry me? Do you still want to marry me?"

Glory's back stiffens at Jake saying she is too young to marry then when he asks if she still wants to marry him her anger burns bright again and she leaps off his knee and starts pacing. "I thought I did until ya manhandled me and now a sayin' I'm still a baby and don't know my own mind then comin' back to this spankin' business. I want yar word ya'll never do that to me again!"

Jake takes a deep breath then looking at her steadily replies, "I cain't give ya my word on that. Cause if'n I had to do it again, I would." Leaning back in the chair he folds his arms across his broad chest.

Glory paces back and forth thinking, "Now what do I do. He won't promise never to spank me again. This hurts terrible. I don't wanna another one. I don't know what to think…he has always done what I want him to do and now that it is real important he won't do it." "I cain't think now Jake. Just go home and let me think!" she demands.

"Nope! Decide now if'n ya wanta be my wife or not!" Jake replies firmly but his insides are shaking. "What if she says no, what will I do then?" But he gives not a glimmer of his thoughts.

Glory stomps around the room twice thinking furiously trying to make him agree mentally to her wishes. When he remains quiet just watching her she plops down hard in a kitchen chair, lets out a little scream of pain then runs out of the room rubbing her throbbing fanny while fresh tears run down her angry and confused face.

Jake's stern voice follows her, "Glory! Come right back here! Now!"

Amazingly she stops still rubbing her sore fanny she takes some deep breaths before shakily replying, "What do ya want?"

"An answer. Now," Jake sternly demands as he quietly swallows to moisten his dry throat.

Glory turns around defeated then walks back to his chair to stand beside him replying, "Jake, ya know I love ya. I always have. Yes, I do wanna marry ya."

"Are you gonna grow up and stop actin' like a baby now? I don't want NO baby to marry but a woman!" Jake demands firmly.

Glory's eyes widen at his words as she looks searchingly into his handsome face then smiling softly agrees, "I'll be grown up, Jake. I won't be a baby to ya anymore. Will ya forgive me for what I did?"

"Will you forgive me for spankin' ya?" Jake asks softly back.

Smiling sadly herself Glory replies, "In a week or so I'll probably forget all about it."

"Oh, no, ya won't Glory. You ain't never gonna forget it cause I don't wanna ever do that again. You hear me," Jake states firmly as he pulls her closer to him.

"Don't reckon ya'll let me forget, now will ya," she saucily answers.

"Nope, I won't and Glory, if'n I have to do it again…well, darlin'… you won't sit yar fanny down for a month after I'm through with ya and that is a promise!" Jake firmly promises then demands, "Tell me ya understand."

Looking into his dear but stern face Glory replies, "I understand, Jake."

"Good, now give me a kiss! I'm starvin' for one," Jake declares smiling at her, with his good humor returning, his eyes lighting up with happiness. *"Thank you, God! I was so worried she'd never forgive me and I'd lose her. Thank you, Lord, for the words and the strength to carry them through."*

Glory hugs Jake after kissing him saying her own little prayer, *"Father, I was so afraid he'd say he doesn't love me anymore. I know he does now. Help me to grow up and be a good wife to Jake. I do love him so. Thank you soooo much, dear Lord."*

Riding in while they are talking, Joe and Elizabeth slip over and are standing outside the back door listening to Jake and Glory talking. Joe gently pulls Elizabeth away from the door as they whisper, "Guess Glory gettin' kidnapped grew Jake up a bunch. I'll be real proud to call him my son and Glory is seein' Jake as a man now, well, I think that is all to the good."

"I agree. Jake handled that very well. Glory will need to grow up a little more, before she is really a woman, but she has made a good start," Elizabeth replies smiling at her handsome husband.

Kissing her Joe asks, "Remind me tell ya how beautiful ya are, my lovely wife!"

"I will never let you forget it," she answers back laughing softly.

The old gents ride in late in the afternoon with Nona. They are more relaxed now and pleasantly tired. It was a nice ride with enjoyable conversation on the way home. Nona is pleased thinking, "Glad there weren't any problems with the café, Aunt Ella and Rosie are doing a fine job."

"I cain't wait to see Elizabeth's face when she sees what I bought Sammy boy at the mercantile," Pokey states laughing.

"You'd better get ready to run when you show her," Nona advises, shaking her head no at him, but laughing with them.

"I think Bethy will be pleased with the candy I bought her," Rev Max states loftily.

"I bet she shares it with everyone," Skinny states chuckling.

"Wonder if Glory is feelin' any better, maybe the candy I bought her will cheer her up a bunch," Skinny asks worriedly, "She has been really wan and upset the last day or so."

"Well, I'm glad to say court worked out real well, them scoundrels got what they deserved. Ten years in prison. Shoulda hung'em," Pokey declares angrily.

"I'm not into hangin', as you both know, so I'm glad they got sent to prison, oughta make them sorry for a long time. They didn't kill anyone so hanging wasn't the best for'em," Max states positively.

"Seems odd to me that Patrick Sully was so angry at Glory, don't understand why when he kidnapped her, maybe it is the whippin' he got for layin' hands on her that has him all riled up," Skinny adds thoughtfully.

"They shoulda beat'em to death," Pokey states angrily, "No one should treat females like that especially not young girls. Glory is lucky that is all he did."

They ride into the yard noticing everyone is sitting outside in the wooden chairs made by Jake under a large shade tree.

"Have a good ride?" Joe asks smiling at them.

"Weren't bad atoll," Pokey answers smiling back at them.

"Those varmints got ten years for kidnapping Glory," Nona states looking around for Glory, "Where is she?"

"Glory and Jake are walkin' down by the hot springs, Ma. They have some talkin' to finish up on. They have made up and bless Jake's heart he's become a man over this kidnappin' and he told her what he expects of her IF she is gonna marry him. She had her little temper fit and he faced her down and said it would be his way or no way. I was so proud I coulda whooped with joy, course Lizbeth stopped me as we were listenin' when we shouldna," Joe explains smiling proudly.

"He was very stern with her and after awhile she agreed to everything he said. He did a fine job of it, too," Elizabeth replies happily.

"Yep they are talkin' weddin' stuff now," Sammy states with a grimace.

"Wanna see what I found for you in town, Sammy boy?" Grandpa Pokey asks holding up a wrapped present.

"Yes, sir!" Sammy eagerly replies. He jumps up and runs over to take the package. Excited he rips it open seeing a wooden sling shot.

"Wow lookee at this!" he declares smiling happily, "It's a sling shot! I had one in St. Louis."

"Which you continually got in trouble with," Elizabeth replies raising her eye brows and shaking her head no at him.

"But Mother I learned how to use it right, didn't I. I'll be more careful," pleads Sammy.

"Two lamps and two windows were broken with one of those," Elizabeth states pointing at the sling shot and looking at him through narrowed eyes.

"Just cause you wouldn't let me go outside and play with it," Sammy challenges her angrily.

"Samuel?" Joe says softly frowning at him.

Sammy sticks his chin out stubbornly then looking at his pa knows he'll have to apologize so answers sourly, "I wouldn't have broken anything if you had let me practice outside like Benny asked you to, Mother."

Elizabeth studies Sammy thoughtfully before answering, "Alright I'll make you a deal. YOU don't use that around the house at all. You don't hit cattle or horses with anything you throw from that and if you do there will be consequences to pay, you understand, young man?"

Smiling happily Sammy answers, "Yes, Madam."

"Sammy, I believe the consequences should come from me," Joe quietly continues.

Sammy opens his eyes wider then gulping replies, "Yes, sir."

"Okay, you may play with it," Joe replies after looking at Elizabeth for confirmation. She nods yes shrugging her shoulders.

"Grandpa, you may have opened a can of worms you won't like with this," Elizabeth points out with a raised eyebrow and a sigh.

"Let the boy be a boy, Elizabeth. Young'uns are only young once," Pokey answers rather defiantly.

Watchfully Skinny asks, "Sammy, come over here a minute, son."

Walking over Sammy looks up at him saying, "Yes, sir?"

"Just to keep you honest me and Pokey will teach you how to use it and that will keep us ALL outta trouble," Skinny insists with a small smile.

"Oh, thank you, Grandpa Skinny. I'd love that," Sammy answers smiling happily again.

"Beth Ann, this is for you," Max Roy announces holding out a bag to her.

"Me, you brought me something?" Beth Ann exclaims excitedly and quickly walks over taking the bag from his hand. Opening it she sees four large sticks of peppermint candy. She looks up at Rev Roy asking, "This is all for me?"

"Yes, all for you," he replies smiling at her.

"Then I can share it if I want to?" she happily asks with a beautiful smile on her face.

"Shorely, you can," Max replies laughing then turning to his cousins he gives them a look that says told ya so.

Beth Ann looks at the candy again then runs into the house. They hear her moving about then she walks back out with a tin plate with broken pieces of the candy in it. She offers everyone a piece then she sits down and slowly eats hers.

Sammy eats his quickly then asks, "Can I have another piece Beth Ann?"

"I'm saving the last two for Jake and Glory but I'll give you a piece of mine," Beth Ann replies starting to break a piece off of her small piece.

Shaking his head no Joe says, "No, honey, he gobbled his down that is all he needs."

"Aww, Papa, it is so good," Sammy complains with a frown.

"Ya shoulda savored it like we are. Next time maybe ya will," Joe states firmly.

Sammy turns to Elizabeth requesting, "Can we do it now?"

Smiling Elizabeth replies, "Yes, now would be a good time." Turning to the old gents she requests, "We'd like to show you something. Please come with us."

All the old gents look askance but stand up and follow behind Sammy and Beth Ann as they run off into the trees.

Joe and Elizabeth manage to get in between the old gents and Nona and talk to them on the short walk to the burial plot.

The older people's eyes widened as they behold a lovely sight in front of them. A white picket fence surrounds Lora's grave along with rose bushes and green grape vines strung along the fence.

"That is really purdy," Grandpa Pokey says looking at all the hard work they had put into making it a nice place.

"You made it big," Skinny declares looking at all the space around it.

"There is a reason for that. Grandpa's Pokey and Skinny you have the places on each side of Mother and Uncle Max you have a place on the other side of my grandpas. Not that we are ready for you to go but so that you know you have a beautiful spot to be laid in peace at," Elizabeth smilingly explains as a tear or two rolls down her pink cheeks.

"That's right kind of you, honey, but we don't know where we'll die at. It might be at the ranch or somewheres else," Pokey adds seriously.

"It makes no difference we will bury you here," Elizabeth firmly states.

"Well I'll be what a nice thought and idea you have given us. We are mightily pleased at your thoughtfulness," Rev Max states as he kisses Elizabeth's cheek and hugs her then does the same to all the rest.

Skinny and Pokey seem frozen as they look at the grave sites then back at Elizabeth and Joe then Skinny says, "Guess you meant it when you said we'd always have a home here and a place to stay."

Smiling Joe nods his head yes replying, "Yes, always and forever."

Looking at Elizabeth Pokey says, "Lora would be so pleased at your thoughtfulness, honey. Thank you." Then the grandpas hug and kiss each one of them.

Sammy and Beth Ann immediately go into all the details telling them what they had done and that it was their mother's idea and how they had all jumped in to help.

OUR GRANDPAS DECISION
Chapter 6

"When there is work to be done, don't hesitate, just git it done!"

Early the next afternoon while drinking coffee Skinny states, "Pokey, we gotta go to St. Louis and close down the house and mercantile."

Smiling sadly Pokey replies, "It's gotta be done. We need to inform Marshal Garth of Franklin Potter's death as well as Edgar and Lora's."

Sitting around the kitchen table that evening Skinny advises the family of their plans. "I hate to end a nice time but we gotta go to St. Louis and close down the house and Edgar's store. We are planning to leave in a couple of days," Skinny states solemnly.

"Ain't gonna be any fun," Pokey adds looking down at the ground, "But we gotta do it."

"I can't go with ya'll even though I'd like to," Max Roy replies sadly, "I've got to be over west of here next week."

Glory, Sammy and Beth Ann look at each other as they hadn't thought about this coming so soon.

"I don't want'cha to go," Glory says solemnly, "I've just got to know ya'll."

"I don't want you to leave us, grandpas," Sammy exclaims looking concerned at them then adds, "I don't know how to use my sling shot yet."

Skinny pats his arm replying, "We'll teach you how to do that afore we leave Sammy boy, we don't break our promises."

Elizabeth pleadingly looks at Joe shaking her head no slightly to him that she doesn't want to go back to St. Louis for any reason.

Joe sits quietly thinking for a few minutes before saying, "I could go with ya and hep ya do this."

"No, Joe. You've got too much to do here and beside we don't need anyone to go with us. We can do it," Skinny explains smiling slightly.

Beth Ann is sitting quietly thinking then states, "I'd like to go back and get my clothes.....I have some things I'd really like to have. I know the people there, too, and I could help you," she explains looking at Joe then continues, "Papa, it is unfinished business."

Joe stares at the pleading look in his young daughter's eyes knowing she does need to go back and do this so smiling he answers, "Then I will definitely go with ya, honey. If'n ya need to go and if'n our grandpas don't mind, we will go and do what ya need to do."

"Papa, I'd like to go, too. I've never been to any cities but Roy, Ernest and John and I'd like to see what St. Louie looks like," Glory explains with her beautiful green eyes beginning to sparkle.

Looking at her Joe nods then agrees, "Yes, it would be good for ya to go and see a big city like St. Louie. That will be all right. Sammy, what about ya? Do ya want to go back to St. Louie and see yar friends and get yar things?"

"I don't have any friends there, Arty is the only boy I ever played with and he is here. No, Papa, I want to stay here with you," Sammy quickly exclaims looking confused at Joe and Elizabeth.

"I know Sammy needs stability in his life right now that only I can give him and it will take some time but I'll willingly give it," Joe muses smiling at his young son.

"Joe, I could go and look after Glory and Beth Ann and hep out where I'm needed. Pa won't mind if I go," Jake states suddenly as he has been thinking about how he could go since the conversation started with Glory saying she wants to go.

Smiling Joe replies, "That would be wonderful, Jake. I know ya can keep the girls in line and not let'em cause our grandpas any trouble."

Both girls say, "PAPA!" as Joe chuckles at their indignant faces.

"Jake, we'd be proud for you to come, if'n you want to, but we'll have plenty of cowboys around to watch over the girls, if'n it's their safety, that's causin' you to worry," Skinny advises.

"Oh, no, sir! I'm not a worried about that atoll. I know Beth Ann will do just what you tell her to but, well, with Glory....," he trails off as she socks him in the arm and they all laugh.

Smiling Sammy blurts out, "You just don't want her to see any other fellas and like one of them," and they all laugh and it breaks the tension some.

"Sirs..." biting his bottom lip Jake starts to say.

When Pokey interrupts him saying, "No more sirs here, son, soon you're gonna be our great grandson so just call us Grandpa like the rest do."

"Thank you...uh grandpa. I was just a thinkin' my sister, Carrie Lynn, she ain't never been any farther than Glory has. Would it be askin' too much for her to come, too?" Jake inquires smiling slightly.

"You'll be there to watch over her, son, so don't make no difference to us," Pokey replies, "She mind ya?"

"Yes, she will! I'll make sure of it," Jake states firmly.

"Yes, I bet'cha she will," Pokey answers chuckling a little.

Glory elbows him in the ribs and he grunts then whispers to her, "You will behave, my love. I'll make sure of it," as he kisses her cheek then added, "We will find out if we can tolerate each other afore we get hitched."

"Oh, really, Mr. Tough Man," Glory declares with raised eye brows.

Smiling Jake notices she calls him a man now and not a boy, which is a first for her, so he whispers back to her, "I will only be as tough as I need to be so it will be up to you, as it always will be, my love."

"I love ya dearly, Jake. I'll be good, ya can count on it," Glory answers patting his cheek, then thinks, "Leave in a day or so! I cain't sit down now how can I ride that soon."

As if reading her mind, Elizabeth asks, "When do you want to leave?"

Skinny and Pokey glance over at Glory then back to Elizabeth as Pokey thoughtfully replies, "One week from now will be just fine."

Elizabeth and Glory let out a long sigh but for different reasons.

"I can ride in a week, surely, I will be able to," Glory thinks relieved.

"I will tell Joe tonight and that will help him understand one of the main reasons I don't want to go and Sammy needs him here now," Elizabeth thinks looking at Joe through the sides of her eyes.

Beth Ann sits looking out the door as she thoughtfully mumbles, "I wonder…." then anxiously asks, "Papa, I have a lot of books I'd like to bring back. Where can I put them? I like to read and learn more than anything."

Joe knows this and realizes he is going to have to build onto his house so he says, "I've been thinkin' on that Bethy and I'm gonna have to build a couple rooms on the house. I can get this done in the time ya'll are gone so it will be ready when ya get back."

Elizabeth grins at him happily because she wants a lot of the furniture from her parent's house in St. Louis and knows there isn't enough room for them without an addition.

"Do you think we could have bedrooms downstairs, Papa?" Beth Ann asks hesitantly.

"Ya really hate climbin' into the loft, don't ya?" Joe adds teasingly.

"It's not easy," Beth Ann answers adding to herself, "And the memories of that spanking you gave me up there will be left there."

"Let us think on this and plan it out some with your grandpas now, young'uns. Why don'tcha go swimming in the hot springs for awhile." Joe advises so the young'uns leave to do so.

"Grandpas it will be a hard trip on ya and takin' the young'uns with ya? Seems like a rough trip," Joe asks thinking of their comfort.

"Aw, Joe, it's gonna be a rough trip anyway, the young'uns will keep us goin' as long as we're around them," Skinny answers slightly smiling.

"I think the young'uns will learn a lot on this trip. It'll give Glory, Carrie Lynn and Jake a good look at the big city. Beth Ann can say good bye to her friends and pick up her beloved books and if'n ya are plannin' on gettin' rid of the furniture then I'm sure Lizbeth wants some of it," Joe replies thoughtfully.

"I'm gonna empty that house out! That house has nothin' but bad memories for me. I bought'em that house when they got married and I cain't say there ever was any love in it except for Elizabeth and the young'uns," Skinny states firmly then adds, "Everything is goin', Joe, ever pot and pan is goin' somewhere."

Looking over at Elizabeth, Joe nods adding, "Well we'd be obliged to have some of that furniture here if it makes Elizabeth and the young'uns happy."

"It all belongs to Elizabeth, Joe. It don't belong to us," Pokey replies confused.

"What?" Elizabeth stammers.

"Yep, I made Edgar pay me back the price of the house years ago," Skinny explains while looking at Elizabeth then adds, "Everything they have belongs to you and your family."

"No grandpas that is not right. You owned the store, Grandpa Pokey?" Elizabeth asks amazed.

"Made him pay me back for it, too, and he did. It's been his for the past fifteen years now. I don't own none of it except the land it's on," Pokey replies firmly.

"But…I never thought or expected this," Elizabeth stammers starting to shake.

"You would have inherited it any way Elizabeth," Pokey quietly replies looking at her shocked face.

"But…but…they weren't my real parents," Elizabeth exclaims as tears start running down her face, "It doesn't belong to me."

Pokey's eyes light up angrily as he replies, "Then yar goin' back on yar word to us, huh!"

"What?" Elizabeth asks again bewildered.

"You said we was still your grandpas," Skinny explains quietly laying his hand upon Pokey's arm to calm him down.

"Yes, always and forever!" Elizabeth answers quickly.

"Then that means Lora was yar ma, too. Even if'n she stole ya she was still yar ma and she is leavin' this to ya because she loved ya more than anything," Pokey states angrily.

Elizabeth's mouth opens and closes but nothing comes out as she looks at Joe questioningly so he replies, "Do ya want the thangs in St. Louie Lizbeth?"

She can't talk her voice is so clouded with emotions so she just nods yes.

Turning to the grandpas Joe replies, "We'd be obliged for the furniture and what nots ya bring us from St. Louie, grandpas. Let's talk about it more in the morning."

They all nod yes as the three old gents stand up as one and leave for the bunk house to go to bed.

Elizabeth has tears running streams down her face as she sits looking at the kitchen table as memories fly fast and furious through her head. So many good memories and so many tainted by untruths.

Joe walks to the door with the older gents and kisses Nona's cheek as she walks into the parlor then sits back down beside Elizabeth softly asking, "Do ya really want to go back to St. Louie and help empty it out?"

Shaking her head no Elizabeth quietly but firmly says, "No, I don't ever want to go back there. There is nothing but bad memories there."

"What's wrong then, honey?" Joe inquires looking at her distress.

"Let's go into the bedroom, Joe. I have something to tell you," Elizabeth requests smiling shyly at him.

Puzzled Joe rises and they walk into their bedroom where Elizabeth immediately starts taking her clothes off. Joe stands watching with his crooked smile in place when she turns around to him and pats her naked stomach asking, "How soon do you think I'll be showing?"

"Showing?" Joe's eyes jump up to her face (which is blushing beautifully) as she smiles then continues asking, "Yar havin' a babe?"

"Believe so. Are you happy, Joe?" Elizabeth hopefully asks smiling shyly.

"YAHOO!" Joe's voice echoes all over the house as he picks up his lovely wife and swings her around after kissing her cheek.

Of course, Nona being just a little ways down the hallway hears and laughing softly says, "I thought you were pregnant, you have all the signs. *Thank you, Lord!*"

ELIZABETH'S NEWS
Chapter 7

"A new life and a new beginning helps the
heart heal and the soul sing."

The air is filled with music when everyone comes in to eat breakfast on this fine sunny day. Elizabeth and Joe are humming and singing as has become a habit with them and they are full of joy today.

Smiling smugly Nona pretends she doesn't know a thing and the children don't know because they were outside when Elizabeth told Joe she was pregnant the night before. Joe and Elizabeth are overjoyed with the news and can't wait to share it with everyone.

The older gents arrive to the sizzling of bacon and baking biscuits and it brings a smile to their worn faces seeing Elizabeth scurrying around the kitchen so happy. It makes their hearts sing with joy. Joe is in and out of the kitchen helping Elizabeth and can't keep from touching his lovely wife continually as she returns the loving caresses.

When everyone sits down at the table Joe asks, "I'd like to say the blessing this morning." Everyone nods okay lowering their heads. Winking at Elizabeth, Joe prays, "*Lord, we are so humbly grateful for all that ya have given us. We are mightily blessed, Lord. We thank ya for our grandpas, Uncle Max Roy and Mama Nona and, Lord, the way ya saved our Glory! We are so very grateful she is alright. We thank ya for the bounty of the land, the peace ya have given us on the hard days past and the beauty of yar love shining through Elizabeth as she brings forth a new babe into the world. Amen.*"

"Babe? Elizabeth is going to have a baby?" Pokey stutters astonished.

"Well, I'll be," smiling Max Roy stands up and kisses Elizabeth's blushing face.

Slapping Joe on the back Skinny says, "Good job!" and all the adults laugh.

Sammy sits looking at them with shock on his face then looks over at Beth Ann, who is sitting quietly watching everyone congratulate their parents. Glory is laughing and hugging their mother also, but they just sit and watch.

Joe notices their concerned faces so kneeling down between their chairs asks, "Ain'tcha happy for us? Ya'll will be gettin' a baby brother or sister."

Sammy looks down thinking, "Now I won't get any attention from my papa all he will want to do is play with the baby." Looking over at Beth Ann, he sees she has a tear running down her pale face.

Beth Ann thoughts are the same thing, "I only get to spend a little time with papa now and I am just getting to really know mother and now there will be a baby and it will take up all their time and attention." Tears flow and she can't stop them.

Sammy slips his hand over to hers and they clasp hands in mutual dismay.

Happily Elizabeth glances over and notices the shocked look on both of her younger children's faces and sobers immediately. *"Oh, dear Lord, I didn't think about how this will change their lives. We are working on becoming a family and here a new baby comes into it and they probably feel left out again and think they will be neglected again. Lord, I won't ever do that again. Please help me to always give them the attention they need. Amen."*

"Dear Lord, how can I explain to them that they are more precious than gold and that I won't love the baby more than them," Joe silently prays for the right words to say.

"Young'uns we are gonna need a lot of help from ya'll," Joe starts out when Sammy quietly and flatly replies, "We do our chores, papa."

"I wasn't thinkin' of chores, Sammy boy. I was thinkin' of hep with the ranchin'. I was wonderin' if'n you two would like to start ridin' out with me in the mornings and afternoons while I check on the cattle and horses so I can teach ya more about ranchin'," Joe explains earnestly.

Both hopefully look up at him blinking and thinking the same thing, "He wants to spend time with me, just me." Then Beth Ann sadly replies, "Papa, I will need to help Mother, too. I won't be able to go with you every day."

Elizabeth knows an answered prayer when she hears it so says, "Oh, Beth Ann and Glory, I will need more help cooking. If you would do that and help around the house, I would definitely appreciate it."

Smiling wanly Beth Ann dryly states, "I guess that means washing clothes also?"

Everyone laughs as they know this is what Elizabeth and Beth Ann hate to do and it breaks the tension of the children's unhappiness and they smile.

Laughing Nona explains, "Don'tcha worry about havin' to do it all, honey, Grandma is here to help out as much as needed. I have three young'uns to love and I want every minute the Lord gives me with you all." Then she looks over at Joe hesitantly asking, "Joe....uh.."

"Ma?" Joe replies smiling at this mother of his heart.

"I was just wondering if you might consider building a little house close by so that I could come over and help Elizabeth out more as her time nears," Nona requests watching Joe's face closely as she asks.

"No need for that, Ma. Yar always wanted, needed and loved here so ya will be here at the house with us," Joe answers smiling happily at her.

Nona's face clears immediately and smiling happily she replies, "Thank you, Joe. Thank you!"

"There will be plenty of room as soon as we get some rooms built on. When we go to Roy tomorra and Sunday for Uncle Max's sermon I'll catch hold of Hank and his boys and we'll see about them a comin' out and hepin' us git it built. It shouldn't take long to add on a room or two." He winks at Elizabeth again as they share a private joke.

"Papa, I won't have to share my room with a crying baby will I?" Sammy asks with horror in his eyes.

"No, son, ya won't have to do that and neither will Beth Ann," Joe answers seriously.

"It might be fun to have a little girl in my room when she gets older," Beth Ann adds thoughtfully, "It will be like having a doll around again."

"A loud and wet doll!" Sammy states wrinkling his nose in disgust before explaining, "Remember Melinda next door and when she got a baby brother, Timmy cried all the time and he didn't smell good either."

"Sammy, he had the croup. I remember very well. He couldn't help it that he had diarrhea a lot," Elizabeth admonishes her young son.

Beth Ann wrinkles her nose distastefully then suddenly she smiles saying, "I was allowed to play with Timmy some and he was a sweet baby. Sammy, he did outgrow the croup and you played with him at our house remember?"

"Yeah, Timmy slobbered all over my toys and Minnie had to wash them after his mama left," Sammy replies again with disgust.

The adults can't help smiling over what both children remember about a baby and see they are reconciling to the fact of having a new baby in the family.

Smiling at her papa Glory states, "I kinda thought the next baby would be mine!" then laughs at his shocked look continuing, "I've heard tell that babies do come when ya get married looks like its true."

All the adults burst into laughter as Joe and Elizabeth look at each other and mouth the words, "Grandma and grandpa?" Their eyes widen as they burst out laughing.

Everyone is amazed at the happiness in Glory now that she and Jake have made up and all is right with them again. It is as different as the sun and the rain. After the ordeal Glory went through, the spanking from Jake and their mutual disagreement Jake and Glory have a new understanding of each other and of the responsibilities of life.

As soon as the children leave to do their chores Joe sends out his cowboys to check the cattle for him. Elizabeth makes a fresh pot of coffee then they all sit down with paper and pencils. Elizabeth mentally goes through every room in her parent's home in St. Louis and makes a list of what she wants. Joe and the men draw plans for how much wood will be needed for Joe's addition. Of course, Joe doesn't tell them he is getting twice as much as they think he will need. It will be their surprise when it is completed. After Elizabeth's lists are made she gives them to Joe then walks out to find the children and ask them what they want from St. Louis. She helps them with their chores and soon all three children are sitting around the table writing down what they all want.

"Papa and grandpas will I be able to bring my bedroom suite back with us?" Beth Ann asks hopefully.

"Anything ya want ya can bring back here," Joe answers knowing he will make room for anything to make her happy.

"I uh…uh…have a desk; too," she admits sheepishly, "I'd like to keep it also."

Walking around the table Joe lays his arm around her shoulders hugging her saying, "Beth Ann anything ya want to bring home, ya can, anything that ya treasure we will find a place for it. Ya don't have to ask about every little thang ya want. Yar room will be big enough for it."

"But, Pa, I have...uh...had a large room in St. Louis and it is full of furniture," she admits faintly.

"Do ya want all the furniture in that room?" Joe inquires.

"I don't know yet, Papa?" Beth Ann answers truthfully.

"Bring whatever ya want and need, honey," Joe answers again kissing her cheek.

Beth Ann sits thinking a long time then starts writing down her list.

On his piece of paper Sammy writes, "Toys, NO SHORT PANTS, bed and dresser," then hands it to Joe.

Raising his eye brows Joe asks, "That's all?"

"Yep, got everything else I need here," Sammy states positively then looking at his mother winks so like his father she can't help but laugh and lean over and ruffle his hair.

Their lists finished Joe asks Elizabeth, "Honey, why don't we take Beth Ann and go visit Minnie and Benny and see if they would like to go back to St. Louie for anything."

Sammy pipes in, "They won't leave. They are as happy as two peas in a pod. Minnie told me so saying, "I ain't NEVA leavin' here!" His mimic is so well done that everyone laughs at his expression and tone of voice which are so like Minnie's.

"Well, we will ask anyway," Joe answers patting his son's head then asks, "Ya wanna go with us?"

"Nah, I wanna stay with Glory. She said she knows how to use a sling shot and I gotta practice some more, right Grandpas?" Sammy asks shaking his little head positively.

"Doin' good but could use some more practice," Pokey agrees grabbing him and tickling him.

Elizabeth and Beth Ann leave the room to change into their riding skirts as Joe walks out to saddle the horses with Sammy's giggling echoing in their ears.

Glory mumbles to herself, "No, thank ye, don't believe I'll take that ride with ya today. I know why I wasn't asked to go but soon very soon I'll be out there ridin' my horse. I'll appreciate him more too. Bet he would like some company." So she slips out the door and strides into the barn.

"Wanna go ridin' Glory?" Joe asks without sympathy when she walks into the barn.

"No, Papa, not yet," Glory grumbles.

"Whose fault is it that ya cain't?" Joe asks seriously.

"Mine, Papa," sighs Glory then asks, "Why did ya let Jake do that to me? I never thought he would."

Leaning against his horse's side Joe replies, "First thing is he didn't ask me for permission he just did it. Second, ya deserved it. Third, I was just as scared that they had hurt ya bad that I'da probably spanked ya worse than he did. It was gonna be the woodshed for ya, my girl. So just figure ya got off real light by Jake paddlin' ya instead of me, Glory."

Hanging her head and thinking Glory raises it stating, "Papa, I'm real sorry that I worried ya so. Real sorry. I've learned my lesson about this. I'll be more careful in the future; ya can take my word for it."

Smiling his crooked smile Joe answers, "Good, I'll take it. I was real proud of Jake when he did that cause he showed me he is a man and he will take care of ya in all ways."

Glory smiles back saying, "Yeah, he showed me a side of him I'd never seen before and don't wanna see again. He looked like ya do when ya get real aggravated at me and I know I'd better be real good. Papa, he said…uh…he said he'd do it again if'n I deserve it." She looks concerned for a minute then shakes it off with, "I've learned my lesson, there won't be no next time."

"Good for him. He is a man who knows how to be a good husband and he will be a good pa someday," Joe replies winking at his lovely young daughter then grabbing the reins of the three horses he starts walking out of the barn. When he passes Glory he gives her a sharp smack on her sore fanny and she lets out a shriek as he says, "Remember that one and be glad it is only one."

Tears spring instantly to Glory's eyes as she tries to rub the sting out of her now throbbing bottom, she sighs whispering, "Yep, I'm real glad ya let Jake take care of me." She gives a low chuckle and turning to her horse she talks to Midnight about all her troubles as she always does.

Joe, Elizabeth and Beth Ann ride into the yard at Minnie and Benny's home admiring how nice it looks. Everyone had jumped in and helped by planting flowers and especially the honeysuckle that Minnie likes so well all over the fences and around the house so the bright colors of flowers and their wonderful smell and their beauty is appreciated by all who ride in.

Elizabeth smiles as she dismounts (with Joe's help) thinking, "He seems to think I'm breakable now," and gives a little giggle.

Joe looks at her questioningly so she says, "I'm very happy, that's all."

"Me, too," Joe answers kissing her cheek.

Benny walks out of the barn and over to them in time to help Beth Ann down from her horse.

Smiling she says, "Thank you, Benny."

Benny remembers and smiles thinking, "She has changed so much in just a couple of months away from St. Louis. She was such a mean little girl there and here she is like a little angel. She is thoughtful and kind and has such a nice ways about her now." "It is good to see ya'll," Benny states smiling at them as Minnie walks out of the house.

"Well hows ya'll doin' this fine morning?" Minnie asks pleasantly.

"Fine! We have a few things we need to ask ya," Joe replies walking with Elizabeth to the door.

"Well come right in then," Benny motions them forward.

"My grandfathers are going to St. Louis to close down the store and the house," Elizabeth starts explaining and notices that Benny moves closer to Minnie putting a protective arm around her, "We wondered if there is anything from the house you'd like for them to bring back to you or would you like to ride back with them to get anything from St. Louis?"

"No place in St. Louie I wanna ever see again," Minnie states positively.

Benny thinks a minute before answering, "Cain't rightly think of anythang we left there that be worth the bringin' back. I thank ye for askin' about goin' but we cain't leave our fields and farm and Minnie cain't travel no where but close by til the babies be born."

Joe and Elizabeth nod then she asks, "Is there anything that you need that you'd like to have brought back to you?"

Minnie looks over at Benny then at the tin dishes on the table then shaking her head no replies, "Nothin' I'ze can think of."

Benny turns and walks to the window looking over towards the barn thinking of the leather for harnesses and tools he could use but knows he doesn't have the money for anything so turning he smiles saying, "No, madam, cain't think of anything that we's needin'. It's shorely nice of ya'll to come over and ask. We greatly appreciate yar kindness."

"Are ya comin' over Tuesday for Arty's birthday?" Benny asks to change the subject.

Winking at Arty, Joe replies "Wouldn't miss it for the world."

Excited with having a birthday party for the first time Arty almost vibrates with excitement.

Joe, Elizabeth and Beth Ann sit down to talk for a little while.

"How are ya feelin' Minnie?" Joe asks looking at her glowing face.

"Right fine, Big Joe. Keepin' busy as can be and that makes the time fly by so fast," Minnie states happily.

"Benny how is the fencin' comin'? Need any hep finishin' it up?" Joe asks a little worried about Benny's cattle straying.

"Jest got one more row to git up and it will be done," Benny states happily as he pats Arty's shoulder then continues, "Couldn't do it without my son hepin' me. He is a big hep!"

Smiling happily Arty nods yes answering, "It is right hard to do but we got it almost done now."

Beth Ann looks at her mother asking, "May I tell them, Mother?"

Smiling happily Elizabeth nods yes.

"Mother is going to have a baby!" Beth Ann announces smiling.

Minnie and Benny jump up and hug Elizabeth and Joe as they celebrate with them.

Arty looks over at Beth Ann quietly asking, "Sammy happy about this?"

"Yes, but it was a shock to us. We thought papa wouldn't have any time for us when the baby comes but he says he needs our help ranching. We are going to ride out with him most every day and learn about how to take care of a ranch," Beth Ann quietly explains.

Minnie brings out a small cake she had baked for supper and they all enjoy a small piece in celebration of the good news.

Half way home Beth Ann asks, "I know there are things they need. What about new dishes and silverware? Minnie needs sewing needles, thread and material for clothes for them and the babies? Why didn't they say they could use it?"

"It costs money, honey, and they don't have any," Elizabeth answers flatly.

"That's the truth of it. Yes, they could use a lot of thangs like leather for harnesses and tools but they need a good crop or two before they can afford to buy it," Joe answers sadly.

"Hummm....maybe there is something I can do about that," Beth Ann thinks as she silently makes a list in her head of things she knows they can use. "It will be one way of making up to them for all the hard times I gave them while we lived in St. Louis and (guiltily) even on the way here."

Bright and early on Tuesday morning Arty sits up in bed, "Today is my birthday and I'm eleven years old! I'm gonna have my first birthday party with cake and maybe lots of presents. Ha ha I cain't believe these good thangs keep happenin' to us."

Minnie and Benny are already up and getting dressed. They are as excited as Arty is as they have never had a birthday party either. Of course Minnie helped with all of Beth Ann's and Sammy's birthday parties so knows what usually happens but never has her son had one before.

"Rise and shine birthday boy, I'm gonna fix ya flapjacks with maple syrup," Minnie calls out to her birthday boy.

Arty giggles in happiness at this special morning wakeup call so answers, "I'm ready, Ma. Maybe since I'm older I could eat five big flap jacks!"

They all laugh at this joke (which is said quite often) because they all know that Arty still can't eat five large flap jacks like he once asked Joe to cook for him. Everyone was astounded when Joe asked Arty how many flap jacks he wanted and Arty said five. Joe just said okay then he cooked him five small ones which was all that he could have eaten anyway. He had treated him with respect as he always does; it was one of the first lessons on being treated with respect they received since they arrived here.

Soon after a wonderful breakfast with real maple syrup with the beautifully cooked flapjacks and their chores done, the males help Minnie straighten up the house as they wait for everyone to come over in the early afternoon.

Joe and his family ride in first in a buckboard. A large canvas covers something large in the back of it along with a couple baskets of food.

Grandpas Skinny and Pokey are riding beside the wagon each carrying a small bundle.

Zak and family ride in on their horses laughing and talking with Zak carrying a large package in his arms.

Looking all around Arty rather disappointedly asks his pa, "Where's Jake and Shorty? I thought they'd come."

"Give'em some time, son, it's early yet," Benny responds smiling and waving at everyone.

Soon everyone is climbing down from their wagons and the ladies are carrying in the baskets of food as they all laugh and enjoy visiting with each other.

Arty looks down the driveway but still can't see Jake and Shorty but obeys when Benny calls him inside to eat dinner. Grudgingly he takes one last look wanting to see these two special friends of his then shrugging walks into the house. He doesn't see Joe wave his arms wide behind him so is surprised when he hears horses coming in. Turning back around he sees Jake and Shorty galloping in a cloud of red dirt. Smiling happily he waves at his two friends then notices they are leading a gray horse behind them. Puzzled he watches the beautiful young horse as they ride on in coming to an abrupt halt in front of the house. Jake and Shorty are both smiling broadly as they jump down from their horses and walk towards Arty.

"Sorry we're late but it took a little while to catch this horse and bring him to his new home," Shorty announce as he notices Arty hasn't taken his eyes off the beautiful horse yet.

"He is real purdy. What's his name?" Arty asks as he slowly walks toward the gray horse.

Holding back his smile, Jake scratches his head saying, "I don't know…what are you going to name him?"

"Ya'll let me name him?" Arty asks surprised.

"Well, shorely, Arty. A man names his own horse," Jake adds with a chuckle.

Arty's eyes grow larger and larger as he looks first at Jake and then Shorty as he stutters, "Heeeee is mine? Ya'll ain't kiddin' me, are ya?"

Going down on one knee Jake looks him in the eyes promising, "No, Arty, we ain't jossin' ya. This here beauty is yours."

Tear spring to Arty's eyes as he looks back at the beautiful horse so he quickly wipes them away and walks closer to him talking softly he says, "We are gonna be the bestest friends ever. I'm gonna name you. Somethang nice…uh…Silver…no…Gray Boy…no, that don't sound right. You are the color of the sky right after the sun goes down…how about Dusty? You like that name, boy?" Arty quietly says as he rubs his horse's sensitive nose.

Dusty must have decided he likes that name because he nods his regal head yes and everyone laughs.

Nothing else matters at this moment to Arty but this beautiful animal so he stands patting him and rubbing his hands down his neck and back. Dusty must have liked it because he nuzzles Arty right back.

In a few minutes, Benny clears his throat saying, "Son, ain'tcha got somethan' to say to Shorty and Jake?"

Jake softly replies, "He already has Benny. He already has." Smiling happily Jake and Shorty walk closer as an embarrassed Arty takes his eyes off of the horse and turns to them. He opens his mouth but no words come out he is so choked up.

Shorty opens his arms for a hug so Arty runs to him hugging him hard enough to knock him down. Laughing loudly Shorty states, "This is the best thank you I ever got!"

Jake rubs Arty's head as Arty grabs him around the waist and hugs him, too. Arty is so full of emotion he can't talk or he will cry and the young men understand this.

"Hey, Arty, wanna see what Lizbeth and I gotcha?" Joe calls out to him.

Taking a deep steadying breath, Arty hugs each of the young men again then turns around saying, "Yes, Sir!" He smiles happily as he runs over to Joe waiting.

Joe lays his arm across Arty's shoulders leading him over to the wagon saying, "Here it is," pointing to the large wrapped bundle in the wagon.

Arty's eyes widen as he looks at the large object then he tentatively climbs into the wagon and looks it all over before he gently pulls the rope holding it together off and sees a saddle. Not decorated (yet) just a beautiful leather saddle ready to be decorated. Arty gulps as he takes another deep breath then turning to Joe leaps into his arms hugging him tightly.

Joe laughs delighted as he holds this thin young boy (who is growing up into such a fine young man) as he says, "Yar gettin' heavy, son. How much ya weigh now?"

Delighted Arty hugs him again saying, "More than a toe sack, Big Joe!" Everyone laughs at his joke of weighing a hundred pounds…when he weighs much less than that.

Joe whispers to him, "Better go thank Lizbeth or her feelin's will be hurt."

Nodding yes, Arty jumps down and runs toward Elizabeth who opens her arms to hug him. This is a first for both of them. Arty has never hugged Elizabeth nor in the past would she have hugged him but times change and people change for the better sometimes.

"I luvs it, Mrs. Elizabeth!" Arty states happily as he looks into her beautiful face.

"We are happy you like it, Arty. My grandpas want to tell you something," Elizabeth explains as they hug again.

"Yep, Arty we asked Joe to git you a plain saddle so we can teach ya how to make it real fancy like and so you and your pa can learn how to do it," Skinny explains to the astounded young man.

"We know ya like the saddle now but after ya make it extra special yourself…well you will treasure it always," Pokey adds.

Arty's eyes are dancing with happiness as he reaches out his hand to shake hands with the two older gents but instead grabs them and hugs them both tightly. He turns his eyes to his new horse and his new saddle and just stares wide eyed in disbelief at what he has received.

Hearing someone clear his voice, Arty turns to Zak as he holds out a large bundle to him, "Another present? Wow, I ain't never got so many presents afore." He rushes over to Zak's side as Zak sets the large bundle on the ground. Zak's eyes are dancing almost as much as Arty's are.

With trembling hands Arty unties the knot holding the canvas together and the insides just jump out at him. Startled he jumps back looking down at a roll of leather ready to be made into reins for his horse and saddle. Down inside the coil of leather is a small bag that draws Arty's attention, reaching down he picks it up and opening it finds a silver belt buckle. It is of a horse rearing on its hind legs engraved on the silver buckle.

Smiling happily Stephie kneels down beside him saying, "We thought you might like to make yourself a belt out of part of the leather and you will need a good belt buckle to hold it together."

"It's so shiny and purdy…thank ya Mrs. Stephie and Zak…thank ya so much. I'll always treasure it," Arty states with stars in his eyes even more so now.

"We thought ya'd enjoy them, son," Zak states wiping a tear from his eyes.

Arty looks at them with tears in his eyes not for sure what he should do when Zak opens his arms and Arty flies into them hugging him hard then turns and does the same thing to Stephie as they all wipe away happy tears.

Minnie and Benny are unashamed to be wiping tears from their eyes at the wonderful presents their son has received. Both are continually wiping them away as more flows. *"Oh Lord we'uns are so blessed. Everythang has been so good since we got here. Please bless these nice folks for all their kindnesses to us and hep us Lord to hep them when they needs it. Amen,"* Minnie prays from the heart.

Arty takes a deep breath as he stands up holding the leather and the buckle then walks over to show them to his mother and father. "I cain't believe I got these presents…nobody ever cared about my birthday afore except ma and pa." He looks stunned at everyone helping to celebrate his birthday and bringing him gifts.

"Like we's said afore Arty, people here much different than the ones we left. We can jest be us'ns and be happy ever day like we's been. God is so GOOD!" Benny states as more tears fall down his happy face.

"It don't seem real like sometimes," Arty softly states as he looks around at his friends. Frowning all the sudden he asks, "Where's Sammy? I just noticed he ain't here." Concerned he turns to Joe as he hears Sammy giggling. Turning swiftly he sees Sammy holding his hand over a puppy's mouth as it wiggles to get down.

"It is a good thing you finally missed me, Arty. I was having a hard time keeping this puppy quiet," Sammy states giggling happily.

"You got a puppy, Sammy. He is so purdy," Arty states walking closer to Sammy to pet the puppy when Sammy shoves the wiggly puppy into Arty's hands saying, "HE ain't mine…he is yours!"

"MINE? Ya got me a puppy? Where? How?" Arty stutters then hugging the puppy turns to his pa asking, "Pa????" He doesn't have to say Pa can I keep him…it is evident by the longing look.

"Yep, you can keep him. Big Joe already asked us afore Sammy brought it over for ya," Benny states beaming happily.

"Papa asked me to walk the last half mile so you wouldn't see him when they all rode in. The horse is your big present. The puppy is just a small one," Sammy explains adult like. Everyone smiles at the two young boys as they talk and pet the sweet puppy. "Good Heart found him for you and brought him over this morning," Sammy explains looking at the dog. "I want a dog, too, but I ain't got one yet," Sammy thinks longingly looking at the pup.

Good Heart rides in about this time with his sons (Jumping Rabbit and Running Bear) and they are all riding bareback. Good Heart is carrying a bundle in his arms, too. He smiles when he sees Arty holding the little pup then asks, "You like pup?"

"Yes, sir! I really do," Arty exclaims looking up into the handsome Indian's face.

"He be big dog…good watch dog for you. Part wolf so I will teach you how to train him to find his own food or he eat you out of home," Good Heart explains grinning broadly.

"Part Wolf? Wow, thank you Good Heart…he is beautiful," Arty states amazed.

Good Heart jumps down from his horse as Running Bear leads the stallion away from the people as he is very wary of all people since he was mistreated by a cowboy. Good Heart lays the bundle down then takes the pup and holding him says, "Yalla Moon make this for ya. Ya need it for yar horse or ya hurt his back with the saddle."

Arty unties the rope again opening the canvas to see a woven Indian blanket in blues and greens folded inside. "This is really nice. Thank ya Good Heart for the puppy and the blanket," Arty gratefully states as he manages to take the puppy back from Good Heart. Walking over to his parents he shows them the puppy and whispers, "Can ya believe this? I ain't never seen no one git so many presents afore."

"Yous is one lucky boy that is for sure," Minnie states as she happily looks around then announces, "Ready for some dinner and cake. I'ze made a big nice apple cake for today."

"Just got one or two more presents," Skinny states as he walks over and hands Arty and odd shaped paper wrapped package.

"I'ze so lucky…ain't nobody ever treated me so good exceptin' Big Joe, of course," Arty states smiling happily again. He takes the package and laughs out loud when he sees it is a sling shot just like Sammy received from his grandpas a week or so before. Looking up at them he promises,

"Thank you so much! I remember what Sammy said about using it and I will be real careful like just like he is."

"Just to keep ya honest, Skinny and I will teach ya how to use it," Pokey drawls as he rocks back and forth on the heels of his boots before continuing, "Nona sent ya this package." He hands Arty another bag and when Arty looks inside he gasps out loud. Inside is eleven pieces of candy that Nona has sent out to him.

"She couldn't come today but wanted ya to know she is celebratin' with you, too," Skinny advises as he sees the delight on Arty's face.

Rushing over to his ma and pa he shows them the bag of candy then says, "I will tell her thank you next time I see her."

"You are one lucky young man, Arty, see how many people love you already," Beth Ann states smiling happily at him.

"I neva thought I could be this happy...neva did," Arty states with eyes glowing in happiness.

GOING TO CHURCH
Chapter 8

"Refreshing the soul is as important as filling the stomach."

Saturday morning they all climb into the wagon and head to the City of Roy for the church service on Sunday and to visit with all their friends and neighbors.

Max, Skinny and Pokey all stop by Lora's grave before they leave and say a quiet prayer.

"I'll be back in about a month. Gotta go check on a couple of families and see they are doin' all right." Max explains as they walk back towards the waiting wagon.

"Then we'll see you when we get back from St. Louie then, brother," Skinny replies slapping him on the back.

Joe is driving the wagon with his family inside of it. The old gents ride their horses alongside (with Bradford and Jay who accompany them everywhere they go). After a few run ins with outlaws and rowdy cowboys (who want a showdown with ex-sheriff Pokey) the cowboys are a concession to this reoccurring problem. The happy group laughs and teases all the way into town.

Zak and family meet them on the way. Jake isn't with them so Glory asks, "Where's Jake?"

Shorty answers, "His turn to stay and take care of the animals, Glory."

"Oh, thanks, Shorty," she mumbles wishing she'd stayed home also.

"Glad you are alright Glory and they didn't hurt you like they could have," Shorty states looking sternly at her.

Raising her eyes to the Heavens Glory replies, "Not you, too, Shorty. Everyone is tellin' me over and over how lucky I am. I know it. I did a dumb thang. I've paid for it. Believe me I'm still payin' for it!"

"Don't get riled at me, Glory, you did it and you got what you deserved. So that is that," Shorty answers abruptly.

"You are really mean, Shorty," Glory states as she glares at him.

"Just telling you the truth, Miss Gloria," Shorty states then rides over to the grandpas and starts talking to them.

Beth Ann looks at Shorty in amazement saying, "He talks very well. He doesn't put all the slang in his speech as everyone else does."

"Probably just showing off, he doesn't do it often but he is really good at it," Carrie Lynn replies with a sniff of her nose and turning her back on Shorty she hugs Glory saying, "I'm so glad you are okay, Glory. You gave us an awful scare."

"I know and I'm real sorry that I did," Glory replies for the hundredth time and is getting really tired of saying it.

"Jake was in such a temper, we couldn't even talk to him. Did you know he worked two whole days, till he almost fell asleep on Comfort? He worked so hard that Ma was really worried about him. Pa watched over him and told Ma that he'd be there when Jake broke down and he was. I heard tell Jake cried and cried at the thought of losin' ya. He was so upset and I mean really upset and mad. Glory, I've never seen him like that before. I don't want to ever again so you take care of yourself, okay?" Carrie Lynn explains as she speaks from her heart.

Humbled Glory promises softly and sincerely, "I'll be much more careful in the future, I promise ya."

Thoughtfully she sits and goes over all she has heard from everyone about all that went on while she was kidnapped and she knows she will listen much better in the future. Looking up at the sky she prays,

"Lord, ya helped a lot of people save me. I don't know that I appreciated all ya did to keep me safe before. I'm sorry I was disobedient and I'll be more careful in the future. Thank ya so much, dear Savior, for watchin' over us all and takin' care of us. I appreciate yar kindness. In Jesus Name I pray. Amen."

Driving into the City of Roy Joe stops at the livery stable as usual. Hank (a giant of a man) lumbers out laughing good naturedly walks towards them with open arms. Joe is the closest so Hank lifts Joe off of the wagon seat hugging him saying, "So, nephew, how are ya doin' today?"

Joe hugs him back saying, "Doin' fine, Uncle Hank."

Tears came to Hank's blue eyes as he looks at everyone in the wagon and unashamedly he wipes them away saying, "Knew ya'll was always special to me didn't know ya'll was my family except from the heart."

Walking around the wagon to Elizabeth he says, "Our little Lizzie, my God, our little Lizzie is alive. We thought ya was dead and gone a lifetime ago. *Thank ya, GOD, for the blessin' of having Elizabeth back. Amen."*

Tearfully Elizabeth hugs her newly found Uncle back (as he lifts her down from the wagon with one arm) saying, "It is still a shock to learn that I was kidnapped and how….it all happened. Does everyone know?"

"Purdy much. Nona, she's as proud as a peacock and tellin' the world. Ya have no idea of how pleased we are cause Nona she blamed herself all these years cause ya disappeared like that. She felt she shouldna never left ya for a minute back then. It's healin' some wounds I can tell ya," Hank explains as he gives her another big smacking kiss on the cheek then he sets her on the ground. Hank is a gentle giant. He is almost seven foot tall (and about as wide) and tough as nails with the tender heart of a lamb. Beloved by everyone and awed by many, he has the gentleness of a lamb with animals and loves them as much as people. Sniffing he helps each of the children down hugging them as he sets them on their feet. He gives Glory and extra hard hug saying quietly, *"Thank ye, God in Heaven, for watchin' over our little gal. Amen."*

A tear drops onto her cheek as he lowers her to her feet and she kisses his weathered cheek saying, "Thank ya, Uncle Hank."

"Take care little one, don't let that happen again. Ya was real lucky the men got thar in time," Hank replies with his heart in his eyes.

"I will," Glory promises as she pats his cheek lovingly.

"Go see Ella so she's assured of yar good health," Hank advises solemnly.

"I plan to," Glory promises smiling up at him again.

Zak, Stephie and Payton wait by their wagon until the greetings have been given then leave their wagon at the livery also.

Zak and Stephie walk directly to the hotel to get their rooms for the night while Payton stays talking with Hank.

Joe and family walk straight to Miss Ella's (Hank's wife) dress shop to see her next. It is just down the street from the livery and on the way to Nona's Café.

Elizabeth walks in first hesitantly calling out, "Aunt Ella?"

"Lord a Mercy!" Ella cries out as she rushes over grabbing Elizabeth with her long bony arms. She hugs her crying, "We shoulda known. We shoulda known. Heres we had you all these years and didn't know it. NOW Lizbeth I'm mad you went to St. Louie and left us."

"I am, too, Aunt Ella. I lost so many years with all of you and was miserable there," Elizabeth replies tearfully smiling at her blood aunt.

Both hug and kiss again as they continue talking, "I didn't know I had any relatives except my grandpas all my life and now I am lucky enough to have a big family. I'm so delighted having you all," Elizabeth exclaims happily.

"More than ya'll want at times but a big lovin' one any ways," Ella answers as she puts both hands on Elizabeth's cheeks looking into her beautiful face. Then she continues saying, "Ya do have the look of your pa. I cain't think why we never saw it before. Ya got yar ma's red hair but yar pa's eyes. Guess we just never thought to look close enough to see it. Shame on us!" Ella sees the smiling face of Joe as he leans his shoulder against the door frame behind Elizabeth. She gives him a wink and waves him closer saying, "Come give me a big hug, nephew, and make it a good one. Knew ya most of yar life and didn't know ya was my nephew, just knew I loved ya like my own."

Joe hugs her tightly lifting her off the floor giving her a smacking kiss on each cheek then one on the mouth saying, "I've loved ya right back too, Miss Ella...uh..Aunt Ella."

Ella notices the children so when Joe sets her feet back down on the floor she goes around giving them all a big hug and gives Glory an extra hard one whispering, "*Thank ye, God.*" She doesn't say a word of censure to her, which greatly relieves Glory.

They stop at the hotel and Joe reserves their rooms for the night then they walk into the mercantile to do their shopping.

Elizabeth meets Marilynn and Stephie talking at the counter and they all hug then walk off talking and laughing while Joe, Zak and Frank shake hands. Joe pulls his list out and starts requesting items they need. He chooses a large pouch of tobacco for Good Heart as well as a number of other items as a thank you gift for saving Glory.

Frank glances over at Glory as she looks at material saying, "Joe, it is such a blessing that those heathens didn't hurt Glory. Heard tell she did a good job of fighting them off, when they tried to…uh…hurt her. She is a beautiful girl, Joe. Thank God she was unharmed."

Smiling sadly Joe answers, "Yes, God was watchin' over her that is for sure. It was the most hepless moment of my life awatchin' as they all ganged up on her and tried to…hurt her. She did a good job of fighting them, thanks to Good Heart's teachin's, but they still took her down. Then we took our shots. Heard Patrick Sully was a cussin' us when he got that whippin'?"

Looking worried Frank answers, "Yeah, when the judge ordered he get ten stripes with the whip for manhandling Glory, well, he swore revenge, Joe."

"Shoulda hung'em, Joe, made an example of 'em," Zak states with heat.

"The men wanted to hang'em all for kidnappin' Glory but I couldn't do that, Zak. I ain't got no right to take anyone's life like that. I shorely hope I'm not proven wrong with that decision," Joe answers worriedly.

"They are off to prison now for ten years. So it should be over with," Frank advises shaking his head at the outlaw's greed.

"Hope they learn their lesson and go on with their lives when they get out," Zak replies solemnly.

Suddenly Marilynn and Stephie let out screams of joy and start hugging Elizabeth. Frank looks at Joe (who is beaming) asking, "What's the good news?"

"We're gonna have a baby," Joe answers as his eyes light up happily.

"A baby! Why that is wonderful. Need some cigars to celebrate. The first one is on me," Frank replies laughing then looks over at Marilynn and they share a trembling smile. They have been married for years now and not been blessed with children and would love to have some. Doc Martin told her after the last miscarriage she shouldn't get pregnant again.

Zak pounds Joe on the back saying, "Well done, son! When will it be born?"

"Early next year Lizbeth thinks," Joe replies smiling back at Elizabeth.

"Didn't waste much time, did ya?" Zak laughingly says then laughs more when Joe blushes.

Carrie Lynn and Beth Ann are wandering around the store talking about the new baby. "I'm not sure I'm happy with a baby coming, Carrie. I don't get to spend much time with papa now," Beth Ann whispers unhappily.

"I know it can be hard and sometimes there just ain't no time… oops …there is not enough time to do or say everything you want to," Carrie Lynn answers correcting her English as she goes along.

Beth Ann smiles at her and loves her even more because Carrie Lynn is trying to talk correctly now as she wants to be a teacher just like Beth Ann does.

"It is selfish of me not to be really happy about the baby but it is hard," Beth Ann admits to her best friend.

"I like Payton, most of the time, but she really gets on my last nerve quite often," Carrie Lynn answers thoughtfully then continues, "But she can be a bunch of fun, too. It is more fun doing the chores with someone else than doing them all by myself."

"That's true. Sammy and I have been sharing our chores a lot this past week and it goes faster and it is more fun," Beth Ann thoughtfully answers.

"Maybe the baby will be a sweet little one and you can enjoy playing with him or her and it won't take too much of your ma and pa's time," Carrie states positively.

"Yes, hopefully so," Beth Ann replies disbelievingly.

Jake is riding Comfort (his large stallion) looking over his herd of horses considering what he owns in regards to supporting Glory. "If'n I sell about six horses that should get us through the winter. We can plant a late garden and get a lot of food stuff stored for the winter. Humm… I'll talk to the folks and see if we can do that at home since I'll be goin' to St. Louie pretty soon. Maybe I should enlarge Ma's garden plot…that would be smarter. I think Nona and the grandpa's already planted more over at Joe's, they all like gardening. Getting married seemed so easy until Glory got kidnapped, I guess, I thought it would just be an easy life. Now I know it can be really hard." Jake's face tightens as he thinks again about what could have happened to Glory and how she could have been damaged physically and emotionally if she'd been harmed by those varmints. His eyes harden as he can't keep the images out of his mind of the men pulling her to the ground and tearing her dress. Shaking his head he closes that off in his mind and smiling remembers her valiant attempt at protecting herself. "She's got plenty of spine, my girl does." Smiling he looks up and decides he will ride over to the piece of land Joe and Zak have talked to him about them setting aside for him and Glory. Jake rides slowly around the horses then looks over the cattle as he canters over to their promised land.

He crosses the river thinking, "I'm glad it is low right now. It can be a wild one." Then about hundred yards south of the river, he stops and rising in his stirrups, he looks at the acres of their promised land feeling joy lift his spirits up higher and higher. "The soil here is good, not just red clay like it is in so many spots." He looks east seeing the hills becoming mountains and remembers the caves over there. "Joe said we could store feed in the caves during the winter." A smile crosses his face as he thinks about the small hot springs that are located in the mountains. Not a lake like Joe has just a small pond fed by a hot spring. "Just big enough for Glory and me and that is all we need. I think ma and pa sneak over there some evenin's," Jake smiles at the thought. Looking around he says to himself, "Where is a good place for a well. That is the first thing we have to figure out then we can build the house close by. I hope it is a good one with sweet water. Then Glory and I can plan out where the house will set and how many rooms we want. We gotta plan one room for our young'uns. I hope we have awhile afore we have any though. I want Glory all to myself for a good long time. We will have a good life. We will work together and make it so." Jake steps down walking around the land. He picks up soil feeling its texture smiling happily at their future.

Seeing a rider in the distance Jake walks over to the shade of an oak tree waiting to see who it is. Soon he smiles and remounting heads toward the rider waving his hat to stop him.

Robert sees him so turns his horse from going towards Zak's ranch, he meets Jake and they walk their horses under a big shade tree to talk.

"Came over to see those horses of yours, Jake, Pa said he wants to get two good ones for our ranch and wonders what ya have," Robert asks as they lift their left legs and cross them over the saddle horn relaxing together.

Jake smiles saying "Got a number of good horses. Ya want ridin' horses or wagon horses?"

"Need two good ones for pulling a wagon right now," Robert answers then continues, "Ma and pa are plannin' on a second honeymoon late this summer. Gonna take a trip over to Amarilla and pick out some new stock for the ranch. Pa is gonna get a new bull. One of pa's friends wired that he's got a real good one and Pa wants it. The bad part is they are gonna leave all the little ones with me while they are gone. Course Dave and Roxie will be out helpin' me as often as they can and Roxie works miracles with the young'uns. Heck, I offered to take care of them for a month so they could just have a relaxing time."

Jake looks at his best friend (next to Shorty) realizing Robert Baxter is a good looking man, "Any girl will be lucky to find such a good man."

"Glory and I are gettin' hitched this summer, Joe done give us his blessin'. We are gonna go to St. Louie and help Glory's grandpas first. Then get married. I came over here to look over this piece of land and see where the house, barn and sheds otta be," Jake explains smiling happily. They talk about it for a while as Jake points out places he thinks will be good for the house, sheds and barn then they turn and head back towards Jake's horses.

"Ain'tcha worried takin' on all those young'uns, Robert?" Jake asks seriously, "You got a bunch of 'em."

"Yep, they can be a handful but they are mine, too. I was there when everyone was born and they are like my own in lots of ways," Robert answers smiling. "Little Gracie Rose, gosh Jake, she is more mine than Pas. She follows me everywhere I go and I let her, kinda like it."

"How old are they now?" Jake asks as they ride through the low river.

Robert sits back a little answering, "Jana Lee is seven years old, Gracie Rose is five years old, MaryAnn is three and Charley is one. Ma don't want to leave'em but it will be like a second honeymoon for them."

"Bet ya got a racket in your house all the time," Jake asks with a grimace.

"Sometimes, but Ma keeps the young'uns in line. Pa just has to say a word and they calm down. They mind me real good, too," Robert replies smiling.

"Must be like havin' yar own with so many underfoot," Jake asks amazed at Robert's love and devotion to his younger sisters and brother.

"Naw, not really. I sleep at the back of the house in a room Pa built on when Jana Lee was born and it's a ways from everyone else. Course if one of them makes a big noise I hear it but not usually," Robert explains smiling then slapping Jake on the back says, "I've learned little ones come when a man and woman get hitched. You'll probably be a pa in the next year. What a thought! Jake a pa!" Robert laughs loudly at Jake's comical expression.

They ride into the canyon where Jake's horses are corralled then dismounting Robert looks over the ones Jake brings over for him to inspect.

After choosing the two he likes he requests, "Will you ride over with them and let Pa take a look next week?"

"Be glad to," Jake answers thinking, "Here's some money I can save for me and Glory and have some spending money in St. Louie. *Thank you Lord!*"

After Robert leaves Jake goes back to the cattle and after looking them over again decides it is getting dark so rides home to eat some soup with Granny JoyAnn and Grandpa Don wondering what Glory is doing in the City of Roy. "Won't be long Glory til we will be together every day. Cain't hardly wait to see you again," Jake whispers as he watches the stars come out and the night sky turn dark.

Later that evening as Marilynn and Frank sit at their supper table they are subdued to say the least. "I am happy that Elizabeth is going to have another baby," Marilynn states smiling slightly.

"Me, too, honey. Just kinda wish it was us having the baby. I know we can't and we know Doc Martin said no more pregnancies as it might kill you. We gotta look at it this way, honey. You are the love of my life.

I'd be lost without you, Marilynn. I can do without young'uns as long as I have you!" Frank states sincerely as he feels another crack in his heart knowing they can't have children.

Taking his hand Marilynn lifts it to her cheek kissing it she replies, "I love you more than you will ever know and I am SOOOOO sorry that I cannot carry a baby to be born. I don't know why God made me this way but I know God has a reason for everything he does so I'm going on faith that we will have some young'uns. I don't know how but I believe God knows we'd love them and care for them really well."

Wiping tears away Frank smiles at her saying, "You are right we have to keep faith in God and know He always takes good care of us. You are my treasure on earth, Marilynn, and I thank God every day for you."

"Same here, my love," Marilynn answers smiling brightly at her adored husband.

On Sunday mornings it is the normal routine of having breakfast at Nona's Café with everyone joining in to help. The top conversation is Elizabeth being Nona's daughter – the prodigal daughter so to speak. Glory is glad that after people say they are glad she is safe that they stop talking about her kidnapping because she is very tired of talking about it.

Rev Roy's sermon is about appreciating all the joys we have in life and not taking them for granted. Rev Max's voice thunders through the room with, "This is our Father's World! He made it for us. He gave us everything we need to live a happy contented life," his voice becomes softer, "He gave us the air we breath, the coolness and the warmth of it. He gave us trees, flowers, all plants and even tumbleweeds. He gave them to us for shelter, for beauty, for heavenly scents to inspire us and to feed us. He gave us rain to savor the sweetness of water, to cleanse our bodies as we should our minds, to feed us and sustain us all every day. This is Our Father's World – he created it and gave it to us as a gift and on loan. It is up to us to take care of what we are given and treat it as the treasure it is. People are treasures, too. Sometimes they get damaged and dented but they are still our treasure and we need to remind them that they are loved and wanted. Being wanted is very important to every soul on Earth. God is a mighty God! He born us and He can take us away at any time. Now do you know where you will go when your time on Earth ends? Are you takin' a chance that you'll be flying with the angels when you ain't made any plans for it yet? Believe that God loves you and wants to give you the

Living Water of eternal life. Breathe in the breath of God into your life and inhale the greatness of his love and enclose it in your heart forever more. Amen."

Everyone is smiling happily as they leave the church after such an uplifting sermon.

Dinner is at Nona's as usual is spent rehashing the sermon. Joe's family, Zak's family, the grandpas, Rev Max Roy and Nona all sit around one of the long plank tables discussing the trip to St. Louis.

"If'n we leave late this week we could be back in a month to six weeks, dependin' on how the weather is goin' and comin' back," Skinny advises.

"What'cha plannin' on doin' in St. Louie?" Zak asks interested.

"Well, we gotta close the mercantile and Lora's house," Pokey replies sadly.

"Jake says that he intends to go and that it will be okay if'n Carrie Lynn goes, too," Zak asks just to be sure.

Both gentlemen smile at the blushing hopeful look in Carrie Lynn's beautiful face so nod yes, "Yep, we could use Jake's help and Carrie Lynn will be welcome to come, too," Skinny replies smiling at the radiant young girl.

"It won't be an easy ride cause we wanna get there and get it done," Pokey states looking seriously at Carrie Lynn.

"I can ride real good, sirs. I won't be a problem. I promise you," Carrie Lynn states positively.

"We have told her that her brother will be there to see that she isn't a problem and that she is to do everything that you all say and also her brother," Stephie states positively.

"I will, I promise," Carrie agrees again smiling happily.

"So will I!" Beth Ann answers also smiling brightly at everyone.

"So be it," Skinny nods smiling then adds, "I'm looking forward to some good cookin' on the trail. Usually Pokey and I eat a lot of beans but I just bet these young ladies know how to make biskuts in a camp fire."

Leaning forward Glory replies, "If'n we don't now, we will before we leave. We wanna keep our grandpas happy."

Everyone laughs with her at the direct statement.

Nona advises, "It ain't hard I'll be sure and tell you how to make'em," then she looks at the older gents and cocking her eye brow up at them states, "Be sure you buy enough flour. We all know how much you like biskuts."

Laughing Joe asks, "How many pack horses are ya takin'?"

Sitting back in his chair Pokey thoughtfully says, "We thought two but maybe we'd better change that to three! We really like biskuts!"

After dinner is over and the washing up is completed everyone walks back towards the livery to pick up their loaded wagons.

The wagons aren't heavily loaded since not a whole lot of supplies are needed. Joe has a box for Good Heart and family and one for Minnie and Benny and a larger one for them so it does take up some of the space.

Beth Ann asks to ride with Carrie Lynn to the crossroads where the families split up so that helps give the others more room.

Sammy rides with one grandpa then the other one and talks their ears off. Nona is staying in town at the café and Rev Max Roy has already headed off in another direction so it is a well contented group heading for home.

Monday morning everyone starts working getting the group heading towards St. Louis ready by checking lists, deciding which clothes to take, pots, pans, tins dishes etc. Elizabeth and the girls gather everything together and set is aside then start gathering the food items.

Elizabeth repeatedly admonishes the girls, "Remember to take your hats and always wear your gloves. No reason for a young lady to have calluses on her hands from riding. Be sure your blouses are long sleeved so you don't get a sun burn. Take them and wear them every moment you are on those horses or in the sun."

Both dutifully answer, "Yes, Mother," giggling when they look at each other.

Elizabeth and Joe discuss what to bring home then agree upon the items Elizabeth wants and what the ranch can use then they pull Glory and Beth Ann to the side and talk to them.

Elizabeth starts out, "When you are at the house and the store girls you will see many new and wonderful things. If you think we need them or can use them then do bring them home but if you don't see any need for them then sell them or find a good home for them."

Leaning back in his chair as they all sit at the kitchen table Joe adds, "Girls we are givin' ya a lot of responsibility on this. Ya got the lists yar ma's made of thangs she wants. Jake's got some lists, too. Different thangs he can hep us with. Choose thang ya want also, this will probably be the only time in yar lives that anythang in a mercantile can ya have if'n ya want it. Remember it has to be brought back home and it won't be easy with as much is already a comin' but do use yar heart on this. We trust ya to do what is right and girls if'n ya find that yar grandparents caused hurt to others then try to fix it, if'n ya can. Grandpa Skinny is gonna keep an account of the money bein' spent and will give us an accountin' when ya'll get back."

"Will our grandpas let us have anythang we want?" Glory asks surprised.

Leaning forward Elizabeth explains, "Our grandpas insist that everything in St. Louis belongs to us. That Mother and Father...uh... Edgar would have wanted us to have it."

Both girls look at each other and after thinking a moment Beth Ann replies, "That is true, Mother. They ....she loved us a lot."

Joe and Glory look at each other but don't say anything as there really isn't anything to say about people who hate just because they can't control other people like the Hawkins had tried to do to Joe.

Smiling Glory admits, "I've got a twenty dollar gold piece that I'm gonna take so that I can buy somethin' special while we are thar."

Smiling back Elizabeth advises, "Then buy something not in the mercantile, something that will always remind you of your trip."

"Papa ...Mother...uh...remember that in St. Louis people tip others at cafés and restaurants. Can we have money for tips and little things we want?" Beth Ann requests hopefully.

"Certainly ya can and I want ya each to pick out a few toys for yar brother to bring back as a surprise. Will ya remember that?" Joe answers then requests smiling at his lovely girls.

"Sure. I'd planned on doin' that with my money anyway," Glory answers smiling at Joe and Elizabeth.

"Well then ya can spend that money on yarself and I'll give ya some for spending on what ya want to bring home as presents. How does that sound?" Joe answers chuckling at their good hearts.

When both girls nod yes, Joe rises from the table, walks into the bedroom, and picks up some money then returning hands each daughter some coins.

"Remember girls when ya see something that tugs at yar heart, pray about it and do what ya feel is right. Okay?" Joe requests again.

Both girls answer, "Yes, Papa!"

"Jest one more thang. We are gonna build on some rooms while ya'll are gone for you, Beth Ann, Grandma Nona, Sammy, yar grandpas and Uncle Max Roy. Bring anythang ya think will look real nice in thar. I'm gonna move yar beds in the loft down here for the grandpas beds but they will need other furniture in thar rooms. Chose a big bed for Rev Max for us," Joe whispers so if the old gents happen to be outside they won't hear their plans.

Smiling gleefully both girls reply again, "Yes, Sir!"

"Git to bed! It is gonna be a long day tomorra," Joe orders as his pretty daughters jump up obediently, kiss their parents then climb up to the loft for the last time.

Before the sun rises on Wednesday morning they have everything ready to leave. Carrie Lynn and Jake had spent the night so all are ready to leave. Elizabeth (with all the girls help) makes big batches of biscuits with meat in them for their noon meal and by nightfall they will be at their grandpa's ranch. So today there won't be any cooking done on the trail.

Canteens are filled with fresh sweet water, harnesses and saddles put on well rested horses. Excitement is in the air.

Pokey and Skinny visit Lora's grave once again before they leave and feel at peace when they ride out of Joe's driveway.

As everyone is mounting up Joe asks, "Let's pray for a safe trip. *Dear Lord, please watch over our family as they go on this trip. Keep'em safe from harm and hep'em in the tasks before'em. Show'em yar lovin' kindness and keep'em healthy and in good heart on the way to St. Louie and back. In yar Son's name, I pray. Amen.*"

Everyone answers, *"Amen".*

An hour after they leave Glory is beginning to feel the effects of sitting on a hard saddle. She shrugs and sits higher but by noon she is very glad to climb down and eat and especially happy when they walk their horses for an hour before getting back on them and riding on.

"I'm a little sore Beth Ann, are you?" Carrie Lynn admits at noon to Beth Ann.

"A little, but not much, I've been watching Glory and she seems to be doing okay too," Beth Ann advises.

"The grandpas seem to just jog along like they do this every day," Carrie Lynn states as she watches the way they ride. Not one peep of complaint comes out of the girl's mouths. The younger girls ride in the middle of the group with the grandpas out in front and Jake and Glory behind them and their grandpa's cowboys in the rear.

About 2pm Pokey and Skinny glance back then pulling their horses onto each side of the young riders explains, "We are on our land now. See those hills over there…that is the start."

"Where does it end?" Carrie Lynn asks as she sees the huge expanse of land in front of them with no houses or barns in sight.

"Quite a ways away, honey. We'll tell ya when we reach it," Pokey happily advises her as he scans the land with pride.

Two hours later Skinny calls out, "Josh!"

One of his young cowboys rides up saying, "Yes, sir?"

"Ride on to the ranch and tell Big John we are comin' and we are starvin', son," Skinny requests smiling at the handsome young man.

Smiling and nodding yes Josh rides off towards his home with a whoop and a holler.

As darkness approaches Skinny turns to Beth Ann saying, "We're almost there now, honey." He and Pokey know the girls don't usually ride this much and have been expecting to hear them complain after riding for almost eight hours but the girls haven't at all.

Beth Ann talked all afternoon about St. Louis and what to expect and what they will see. The shops, the people she knows, her school and the young people she knows. She doesn't mention the store or the house at all, which makes Skinny and Pokey wonder why.

Glory is very uncomfortable as she knew she would be…earlier in the day she had taken off her light jacket and folded it as a pillow and sat upon it and that seemed to help some but she never complains to Jake or her grandpas, "I am happy. So very happy," she repeatedly tells herself all day, "This is a dream trip. I'll be seein' places I've never been, talkin' to people in a big city and be with my grandpas and Jake all day. It couldn't git better than this."

Watching the girls Jake has been ready to cut off any complaining he hears from any of the girls so is very surprised when none comes. He smiles very happy about it, because it shows him they will do well on this long ride.

GRANDPA'S RANCH
Chapter 9

"A home can be any place your heart lives."

Soon they see lights in the distance and know they are close to the ranch. They pass close by a herd of cattle (more than they can count) and meet many of their grandpa's cowboys, fixing fences, and on watch for outlaws and wild animals. Skinny and Pokey talk to each one (calling them by name) asking how everything has gone on since they left. They find out they had a few problems but no big ones, which is good.

"Boss, good to see your back. Need any help with anything?" JC calls over from his horse as he herds some cattle around some cactus.

"Not right now, son, thanks for asking," Skinny calls back.

"Boss, we got twenty calves born while you were gone," Doc Ron calls out happily.

"Great news...thanks for the update," Pokey calls back.

"Boss, are you gonna stay for a while this time?" asks Branden curiously.

"Why? Do ya need somethan'?" Pokey calls back.

"Nope, just wanted to see if we could have a music night soon," Branden asks hopefully.

"Sorry, son, we have to head to St. Louis but you can have one anytime you want, you know that," Skinny calls back over to the young man.

"Yeah, I know. But it is more fun when ya'll are here when we have it," Branden states shaking his head sadly then rides back towards the cattle.

"Well that makes me feel good and bad," Pokey admits watching their young cowboys working the cattle.

"Yep, me too. Guess we have been gone quite a bit lately. We will just have to plan on having that music night soon. The boys really enjoy them and it is nice they like us old ones to join in with them," Skinny admits smiling.

"Well, brother, you do have a nice singing voice," Pokey admits with a sly look.

Jay and Bradford can't hide their chuckles because it is well known on the ranch that Skinny can't carry a tune.

"Then we will just have to endure your croaking, brother," Skinny states joking right back at him.

"I think we'd best let the boys do the singing unless we all do then no one will know how bad we both sing," Pokey advises with a chuckle.

When the young people see the ranch house they are very surprised as it is just a small house. The bunk houses for the cowboys are a lot bigger than the ranch house.

Surprised they look at each other and wonder why. Skinny and Pokey ride straight to the barn and dismount. Wanting to groan, the girls stop themselves as they also slowly dismount. Jake jumps down off Comfort and helps a very stiff Glory dismount from Midnight. She has held herself straight for so long that her back is really hurting her as well as farther down. She smiles wanly at him then stifling a groan follows everyone into the house.

Jake takes all the girls packs off their horses then asks the cowboys to bring in the supplies off the pack horses which they readily agree to do. More cowboys walk out to care for their horses so soon they are all taken care of. Each cowboy spends a few minutes with their bosses.

Beth Ann and Carrie Lynn stop in surprise when they walk into the kitchen and see the bareness of the small house. All that is in the kitchen/living area is: a large plank table with many mismatched chairs around it and two old rickety rocking chairs (sitting by a window which would probably have good light). Three doors open off the kitchen which they guess is three bedrooms. The kitchen takes up one half of the house with the three bedrooms on the other side. The dishes are covered in dust and the shelves are almost bare of food items. The only thing that looks used is the large coffee pot and coffee bean grinder with old mugs sitting beside them.

"Guess we shoulda had one of the boys clean up a little in here," Pokey states looking around a little embarrassed.

"Why Grandpa? It looks fine to me," Glory replies smiling warmly at them.

"Surely does," Beth Ann replies positively and Carrie Lynn nods yes.

"Our cook, Big John, will bring us some grub in a little while so rest yourself, if'n ya want. We're gonna check out our horses," Skinny advises.

"Would it be alright if'n I look at yar horses too?" Jake asks very interested.

"Surely, come on," Pokey answers glad they are interested.

The men walk out and the girls follow farther behind as they are very tired.

"Don't guess Grandpa has a hot springs we can bathe in," Glory asks wistfully.

"They didn't mention it," Beth Ann answers looking around.

"I think they would have, if there was one," Carrie Lynn states flatly.

"Yeah, me too. I was just hopin'. Wonder if Jake would carry in some water for us to take hot baths in?" Glory asks aloud.

"You know Jake will do anything you ask of him," Carrie Lynn answers positively.

Shaking her head no Glory replies, "Not anymore. He …well… he has changed. He has become much sterner than he ever was. I miss the old Jake."

Looking closely at her sister Beth Ann asks, "Why? Because he was someone you bossed around and now he won't let you? He bosses you around."

Frowning at her Glory thinks a minute then truthfully answers, "Maybe."

"Men change Glory. Papa said everything we go through changes us, for good or for bad. Jake is a man now. He won't listen to a girl unless he wants to," Beth Ann advises sagely.

"He'd better listen to me. I'm gonna be married to him soon," Glory replies heatedly.

"Well, maybe, you should listen to him, too," Carrie Lynn advises softly.

"Ohhh, I have a lot lately. More than ever, actually. But I miss the best friend that I had in Jake. I seem to have lost him. He hasn't joked much at all since I was kidnapped," Glory explains sadly.

"He had a bad shock. It'll take him some time to get over it. Maybe this trip will help him," Carrie Lynn answers positively.

"I hope so," Glory agrees sadly.

Minnie and Benny lay in bed that night going over all the things they have accomplished this fine day and what needs to be done the next day when Benny sits straight up saying, "Bet Big Joe and Lizbeth would enjoy some time alone now that most everyones gone back to Roy or on the way to St. Louie except Sammy boy."

Minnie's eyes light up as she answers, "Yes, sir, that is a wonderful idea, Benny. Will ya ride over tomorra and ask if'n Sammy could come over here for awhile and hep us out."

"Yeah, I like that idea. Let's come up with some thangs that we need hep with if'n they ask," Benny replies smiling happily at doing this for Joe and Elizabeth plus the bonus of having Sammy with them for a time.

"Could say I'ze needs help with my chores since I'ze gettin' so big, which is true. Then we could say you an Arty got too much to do with plantin' and need some one to run and tote for ya," Minnie replies as she thinks about things a young boy could do to help out.

Smiling happily Benny says, "Sounds good, sugar plum. I'll go in the mornin'."

About noon Benny rides over to Joe's ranch (as Joe will be home to eat) asking, "Big Joe, we'uns was wonderin' if'n ya could spare Sammy boy for a couple of days. We's needin' some hep at the farm and surely could use him for a spell."

Joe blinks surprised at the request then smiles when Benny winks at him so turning to Sammy he asks, "Sammy, what do ya think? Wanna go over to Minnie and Benny's for a couple of days and hep'em out?"

Sammy had rushed over to hug Benny when he'd walked in the door with Joe so is standing close to Benny's side. His little beautiful face lights up in a smile and grown up like he asks, "I'ze be glad to, Benny. What'cha needin' help with?"

Benny bends over looking Sammy in the eyes explaining, "Wa'll, ya know, Minnie. She's gettin' real big with these babies and she needs some hep, ya know, totin' water and helpin' her out some."

"I can do that. I help Mother all the time, don't I?" Sammy replies smiling happily as he looks to Elizabeth for confirmation.

"Yes, you do a very good job of carrying water for me," Elizabeth states smiling at Benny and Sammy.

"Then's there the plantin', Sammy boy, it seems ever time I git to the field I finds I'ze forgot somethin' and I has to go back and git it or send Arty back and I'ze thinkin' maybe ya'd hep me out there for a while?" Benny explains trying to contain his smile.

Joe turns his back and walks over to his chair and sits down while controlling his mirth.

Biting her lips to keep from smiling Elizabeth also sees through this ploy thinking, "What a nice thing they are doing for us."

Sammy turns happily back to his parents begging, "Can I go and help them out? Can I?"

Joe seriously asks, "Does this mean ya want to be gone from here for a few days, kinda like a vacation, and hep Benny and Minnie for a spell?"

"Yes, sir! They need me!" Sammy replies happily.

Joe's smile falters for a moment at Sammy wanting to be needed then looking over at his beautiful wife asks, "Do ya think we can do without Sammy for a couple of days, darlin'?"

Elizabeth also understands that Sammy needs to be wanted so she pretends she is thinking it over saying, "I think that would be a really nice thing to do and it will be hard, but, yes, I think we could let him go for how long, Benny?"

Benny hadn't realized how much Sammy needed to be wanted and he wants to give him all the help and security he can so he says, "Wa'll, if'n ya can spare him for a whole week that would surely hep us out!"

"Can I go for a whole week? Please! Please!" Sammy begs earnestly.

"Sure you can. You will be good and do everything they tell you to do, won't you, Sammy?" Elizabeth asks as she watches joy fly across his small face.

"Oh, yes, madam, I will and I'll be a big help. Benny, just wait and see I'll be a big help to you," Sammy promises doing a little dance around the table.

Elizabeth and Joe hug Benny a little while later when he and Sammy are ready to leave and quietly thank him for their thoughtfulness.

After they ride out Joe looks at Elizabeth saying, "We have the whole house to ourselves, honey. What would ya like to do?"

Blinking her eyes lashes at him rapidly she coyly answers, "I guess the dishes. No one has asked me..."

In one long step Joe reaches her, picking her up, he carries her into the bedroom.

At the grandpa's ranch Jake stands at the rail of one of the corrals looking over the six horses that Skinny and Pokey are looking at then asks, "Had these ones long?"

"Naw, Matt said just coupla days. He says no one can ride'em especially that mustang over thar," Skinny replies pointing to a wild stallion in the corral next to the other five. "I'd shorely like to stud him out but only if'n we can control him."

"Can I try him?" eyes lighting up happily Jake asks watching the spirited horse dance around the corral.

Both of the old men glance over and see the look of glee and concentration on Jake's face so answer, "Sure, son. Go to it."

Taking off his gun belt he hangs it on a fence post then picking up a lariat runs it through a belt loop on his pants then with his hands empty he slides through the gate. Talking softly Jake slowly walks towards the stallion, who immediately dances away from him every time Jake gets close. Jake doesn't give up he just keeps on talking until he corners him and is able to touch the lovely animal. Touching the horse he feels the tension trembling through its great body so he keeps talking softly to the wild horse rubbing his large hands gently along its neck and down the length of his back. Slowly the stallion stops trembling and brings his head down until he is looking Jake in the eyes. It is as if they are hypnotized the way they stare into each other's eyes as Jake continues to talk in a quiet voice telling the stallion he has nothing to fear that he will be fine etc. After about fifteen minutes of this Jake is able to gently wrap the rope around the stallion's regal head and walk him around the corral.

Skinny and Pokey look at each other silently but their brains are working as they realize: He is a charmer. "I cain't believe he got that'un calmed down so quick like and now he docilely walks beside him. He shorely has a way with horses."

After spending about an hour with the horse and giving him an apple that Pokey hands him, Jake takes the rope off and slips through the gate again. The stallion walks over and lays his head over the side of the fence watching every move Jake makes.

When Pokey tries to touch him, the horse jumps back and snaps his sharp teeth at him.

"Give him some time and he will be a prize, grandpas, he just needs some soothin' for a while," Jake advises as he holds out his hand.

The large stallion comes right over allowing him to caress his jaw again. Jake feeds him another apple which he noisily munches.

Watching Skinny realizes that Jake has a love of animals and a caring that shows through when he is with the animals so says, "You have a way with animals, Jake, more like a charmer than a bronco buster."

"I learned a long time ago to treat every animal with respect and with gentleness and it will return the same treatment to me," Jake explains with the same gentleness of tone.

After watching Jake for a few minutes the girls return to the house and set to work cleaning it up. Soon the kitchen is sparkling and coffee is perking in the huge pot. They know men like their coffee so when the men come in they will have hot coffee waiting. They look for flour for biscuits (but none can be found) so they just dust and straighten up the house while they wait for Big John (the cook) to tell them their supper is ready.

Soon Big John comes in yelling in a loud voice for the men to come and eat as he brings over a huge pot with steaks on top and fried potatoes on the bottom then another pan full of big light biscuits. Danny (his helper) follows with a tray with butter, jelly and big pickles on it.

Big John smiles at the neatness of the room then starts laughing when Beth Ann sniffs hungrily stating, "Biscuits."

"Yep, gotta have biskuts or cornbread with every meal or I will lose my job! Bosses say ya fix'em or ya leave! So I fix plenty and keep my job!" he laughs loudly with good humor.

The girls have the table already set just waiting for the food so they are ready to eat very quickly. The girls have washed the trail dust off their hands and faces and combed their hair as well as they can, but long for a bath.

Big John quickly sets the food on the table and soon all three men walk in. As he is getting ready to leave he asks, "If'n the ladies would like a shower tonight, we can kick the men outta the shower house and they can have one."

"You have a shower house, grandpa?" Beth Ann asks amazed.

"It ain't much and ya have ta wash-up real fast. We don't allow long shower but it does clean ya off. You girls wanna go over thar after supper?" Pokey answers then asks.

All three girls heartily reply, "Yes, sir!"

Laughing Jake says, "I've heard about them but ain't ever seen one, reckon it wouldn't hurt me either."

"Might as well join ya then, no reason to waste precious water," Skinny states winking at the girls.

"Best put on some warm water to take with us to wash in. The shower is cold water and it can give ya chilly bumps," Skinny advises. So he and Jake set two big kettles of water on the hot stove to take with them then sit down to eat the wonderful food.

Skinny bows his head saying the prayer for the food, "*We thank you, Lord God, for gettin' us home safe and sound. Thank you also for takin' care of all around us and for all the blessin's of the day and this past month. Watch over us on our way to St. Louis and help us all to do the best we can on the way thar. Take care of our young'uns and keep'em safe. Bless the food we are about to eat and nourish our bodies with it. In your Son's holy name I pray.*"

They all hungrily eat all of the good food then the girls gather their clean clothes, towels and two buckets of warm water for their shower.

The men carry the buckets for them leading the way.

"Get yar hair soaped real good and rinsed before the water is poured on ya," Skinny advises as they cheerfully walk over to the shower house.

"How does it work?" Carrie Lynn asks when she first sees the small building then says, "Oh, I see the big barrel on top. It has water in it and it falls down on us. I understand."

"What'cha do is go in and thar sits a bench and ya hang yar clothes on the pegs on the wall in the first room. The floor is slanted a little so the water goes into a funnel underneath and we pump it back into a barrel to water the garden and other places that need water. We don't waste no water around here. In this room here (he opens the door and walks through to make sure no men are in it) you hang yar clothes like I just said and sit on the bench and wash your hair and all over with soap then all three at the same time walk into the shower room behind you. See this door?" Pokey explains opening the door to a small room. He points to a rope with a knot in it hanging from the ceiling in the middle of the room then continues, "When ya'll are all ready – hair washed and your bodies soaped then you come in here and stand in the middle of the room and raise yar heads up, pull the rope here and water falls down on you from the barrel above. Now it is only a small barrel but it will splash down on you with cold water. But it is mighty refreshin' especially after a hot day like today. When ya'll finish then you dry off and get dressed and come back to the ranch house."

All three girls nod they understand then Jake firmly replies, "I'll be outside the door waitin' to take you back to the house."

Again all three girls nod yes and walk in, closing the door they look at each other, as Beth Ann embarrassed says, "I've never undressed around anyone but Minnie before."

Carrie Lynn is already taking her clothes off so shrugging replies, "I've taken baths with Payton before and she is a girl and you are girls so ya ain't got nothin' I ain't got."

Glory isn't used to anyone seeing her naked either so she turns her back as she starts taking her clothes off also. When she turns around she notices both girls looking at her wide eyed so modestly she crosses her hands over her nakedness asking, "What's wrong?"

Blushing furiously Beth Ann says, "You are beautiful Glory."

Blushing even more, Glory replies, "I'm just older so I'm filled out more. It won't be long and ya'll will be, too."

Laughing Carrie Lynn replies, "I want a bosom like you have."

Glory's face is beet red by now.

Chuckling Beth Ann answers, "But I can do without the bruises on your bottom."

"I got bruises?" Glory asks trying to see her bottom.

"Just a few," Carrie Lynn replies giggling with Glory's comical actions.

Jake hears it all holding his breath when they mention Glory's lovely bosom. "I've never forgotten seeing her near naked at the hot springs and then when they ripped her dress and her lovely breasts were there for all those varmints to see…well…it took my breath away." When he hears Beth Ann mention bruises on Glory's fanny he feels about two inches tall but shaking his head he mutters, "She deserved what she got."

The girls use the buckets of warm water they had brought from the house and wash each other's hair then their bodies with the soap as they have been told to do. Laughing they tease each other and enjoy this shared bath time since neither of the Gray girls have ever experienced it before.

When they are finally ready (it seemed forever to Jake) the girls walk into the back room closing the door then Jake hears water splashing and shrieks as the cold water falls down on the girls. He can't help laughing as he hears their remarks.

"Oh, my, oh, my, it is like ice," Beth Ann stammers.

"Ohhhhh, ain't it grand," Carrie Lynn coos.

"I'm freezing. Let's get dried off and get to the house," Glory stutters through clenched teeth as she shivers.

When the girls walk back into the other little room, it seems much warmer than the shower room. They squeeze the water out of their hair and that is a chore as they all have very long hair. Drying off they put on clean clothes to wear back to the house.

Still shivering a little they open the door to a chuckling Jake who asks, "The water is cold, huh. I thought I heard a gaggle of geese in there then all of sudden it was like the squealing of little pigs."

All three look at him then at each other and stick their small noses in the air as Glory asks, "Who is this person ladies? He is dirty and smelly! Don't reckon he is anyone I know." She sniffs disdainfully and follows the younger girls back to the ranch house.

Jake is walking right behind her so grabbing her long silver hair he gently pulls her farther behind until she stops by necessity of him having a handful of her wet hair. "You smell like sunshine, Glory. I cain't wait until I get ya married and can see yar lovely body and have you all to myself." He leans down to kiss her ear then her cheek.

Glory's breathing stops as the wonderful sensations envelope her and she whispers back, "Soon, very soon, Jake. I cain't wait either."

Pokey walks to the back door asking, "Jake, did ya and Glory get lost?" then chuckles as he sees them standing in the moonlight talking. "Glad to see they are talkin' to each other again. Just cain't let it go any further than that." So he says loudly, "Skinny, are ya ready for our shower?"

Skinny is talking to the younger girls so turns around in amazement looking at his brother's almost order then Pokey nods outside to where Jake and Glory are. Nodding Skinny calls out, "Jake, are you ready?"

Jake and Glory are kissing with a sweetness beyond words and are jolted back to the present by Pokey then Skinny. Jake kisses Glory's chin saying, "Better get in the house the watch dogs are after us."

Dazed Glory looks into Jake's eyes mumbling, "Yes, ya'd better."

It isn't long before Jake stifles a yelp in the much needed cold shower as the water is indeed very cold. Briskly drying off he is rushing out the door when Skinny lays a hand on his shoulder asking, "Think ya'll need another cold shower tonight, Jake?"

Startled Jake turns around looking at both of the almost naked and scrawny older men so laughing replies, "If'n I do I'll let you know," then laughing he lopes back to the ranch house.

Pokey and Skinny chuckle all the way back then Pokey states, "We'll have to keep a close eye on those two."

"Yep, passions run high in those young'uns," Skinny admits and chuckling again they walk into their house to a sight they have never seen before. They join Jake (who seems frozen in place) in looking at the sight.

Sitting at the table are three beautiful young girls with long long hair and they are stretching their arms as far as they can to comb their hair dry.

Gulping the men stand as statues looking at the lovely hair on the girls, Glory's hair is a silver blonde that crackles with her brushing. Carrie Lynn's hair is a golden blonde color, which looks like sunlight shining in the small simple cabin. Then glancing at Beth Ann's hair it is as if lighting is running through her fingers as she sits detangling her long red tresses, as red as a brilliant sunset glowing across the plains. Glorious beauty is seen by the three men as they can't seem to stop staring at the girl's beautiful hair.

Looking up Glory asks, "What'cha doin' standin' in the doorway like that for?" Never suspecting the picture the three girls make combing their long thick hair.

"Need some help combin' your hair, Glory?" Jake asks as if drawn to her by a magnet.

"Sure could. I've got a world of tangles in it tonight," Glory replies as she works on another tangle in her silvery hair.

Walking over to Beth Ann Skinny asks, "I'd shorely like to comb your hair Bethy?"

Startled Beth Ann looks up seeing Jake combing Glory's hair so shyly replies, "If you want to."

Walking over to Carrie Lynn, Pokey asks, "Can I comb your hair, Carrie?"

Smiling brightly Carrie Lynn replies, "Oh yes, please, I always have a lot of tangles in it. They are so hard to get out."

"Men are funny creatures," the girls think as the men comb and detangle their hair.

But the men think, "This is heavenly to touch this silky hair and feel it trail through my fingers and see the way the light shines on it. How lucky can a man be?"

Memories flood Skinny as he remembers combing Lora's hair when she was a child and sadness overwhelmed him for a moment until he thinks, "She is in a much better place now. She is at peace," sighing he smiles at the memories of a sweet child calling, "Papa, help me climb up or Papa pick me up and especially Papa, I love you more than anyone in the whole wide world." A single tear runs down his weathered face as he smiles at the memories.

Pokey also remembers when Lora was a little girl and would cry when she got dirty (which was all the time). "She cried bucket of tears", he sadly thinks then prays, *"Lord we gave her everything we could I hope it was enough. If we hadn't found Lora she would have died and by Skinny finding her she gave us a life we hadn't expected nor asked for but it was a good life and we shared a lot of joy during those years."* Taking a deep breath he continues, *"Thank ya, Lord, for givin' us a little lost girl named Lora. She gave us more than we ever gave her. I'll never forget her runnin' to me with her arms outstretched everytime I came home. The feel of those little arms huggin' me tightly made me know there was some good left in the world after I'd seen thangs beyond horror and grief. Thank ya, Jesus! Havin' Lora was a miracle to us and we are grateful. Amen."*

Their sadness over losing Lora diminishes some and the old gents enjoy a simple task that fathers all over the world do for their daughters and granddaughters. The simple pleasure of brushing their hair is relaxing and refreshing.

Jake's thoughts are very different from the old gents. Looking at the silvery hair cascading down Glory's back and feeling the silkiness of it sliding through his big callused hands he prays, *"Lord, I see this miracle in Glory. Even her hair mesmerizes me with its beauty. I thank you, Lord, for making Glory the way she is and, Lord, I'm needin' help. Temptation is on me strong. Help me to be strong and resist it for I want what is best for Glory, too, and I know that is to wait until our weddin' night. Thank ya, Lord. Amen."*

Rising Skinny says, "Girls you can have the bedroom in the middle. It's the one Elizabeth always uses when she comes and it has two beds in it. We'll be on each side of you and Jake can bed down here in the kitchen.

Nodding yes everyone quickly walks to their rooms exhausted so quickly falls asleep.

The next morning Glory awakes early hearing the coffee perking and smelling freshly made coffee. She dresses quickly then slipping out of the bedroom she sees her grandpas sitting at the kitchen table.

"Don't reckon I noticed how clean everythan' is last night. Thank you, ya'll did a right fine job here," Skinny states as he rises and kisses her cheek.

Hugging them both she pours herself a cup of coffee then sits back down with them.

"Sure you don't wanna stay and cook and clean for two old men, Glory?" Pokey asks with a wink at his brother.

"Don'tcha let them old coots start givin' ya honey words, Glory! You are goin' home with me," Jake states with a smile as he walks into the room.

Smiling happily at him she walks back to the stove and pours another cup of hot coffee for him. "Don't worry Jake. I'm not lettin' ya outta of my sights either. I've heard about city girls," she teased him then turning asks, "Will we leave for St. Louie tomorrow grandpa's?"

"Yep, believe we can check out everythan' we need to today," Pokey replies as he makes a mental note of everything he needs to do.

Skinny nods then grinning says, "I've gotta talk to a couple of my men about gettin' some wood for a house to be built back in Roy." He ponders a moment before saying, "You know, your house is gonna be closer to the City of John than to the City of Roy."

Nodding yes Jake replies, "Yes, sir. Your right. It is closer but we've always liked Roy better course got some good friends around the city of John like Robert Baxter and his family. Robert's the best fellow around. He has helped me out a lot over the years and I do the same for him. It was really rough on him when his ma died a long time ago but now he's got Hannah and they are a real happy family. I don't know about all those young'un though."

"They are really nice people, Grandpas," Glory adds with a smile of affection for Jake.

"We can leave tomorra morning at daybreak," Pokey states as he thinks of all he needs to accomplish. "Sound good to ya'll?"

"Sure," Skinny answers then turning to Glory asks, "Better git the girls up. Big John will be here any time with breakfast."

"We could go down there and eat. He don't have to bring it to us," Glory asks thinking of the extra work it will be for the man.

"He don't mind and it gets him some exercise. I told'em I'm feedin' him too good," Pokey answers laughing.

Skinny walks to the door looking out to see if Big John is coming when Jake asks, "Would it be alright if'n I work with the mustang again?"

"Shore nuff. Appreciate it," Pokey replies thoughtfully.

All the girls are dressed when Big John brings in a huge breakfast. They enjoy a good breakfast then clean up the kitchen before asking, "What do you want us to do today?" Beth Ann asked her grandpas.

"Nothin' really," Pokey answers thoughtful again as he plans out his day.

"Grandpas we ain't used to sittin' around and doin' nothin'. Can we make some pies or some cookies to take with us? I can go huntin' and shoot us some meat and we can make some jerky outta it," Glory asks puzzled.

"We got plenty of that and I'll have Big John fix us up some biscuits tomorra morning afore we go," Skinny answers thoughtfully then adds, "Just do whatever you want girls." Pokey and Skinny leave and Jake follows a few minutes later leaving the girls to themselves.

"Well, I like that! They think we are hepless cause we're girls," Glory fumes.

"Glory don'tcha go gettin' any ideas of ridin' out somewhere. Jake won't like it and we'll be doing a lot riding tomorrow," Carrie Lynn admonishes the restless girl.

"Yeah, yar right," Glory answers thoughtfully as she remembers past events. Narrowing her eyes she says, "I'll find something to do. Why don'tcha ask Big John for supplies for cookies. We'd all like'em the next few days."

After she walks out the younger girls look at each other then Beth Ann says, "She's up to no good. I can tell by the look in her eyes."

"She had better be careful," Carrie Lynn replies looking at the empty doorway.

Walking out the door Glory decides, "I'll just watch Jake. I cain't afford to get in anymore trouble not with ridin' so much in the next weeks." So she climbs up into the loft of the barn, fluffs up some hay, lies down on her stomach and watches Jake soothing the huge stallion from the large open door in the second floor of the large barn. She lays looking down at him admiring how good he is with horses, relaxing she soon falls asleep.

Jake works with the stallion for an hour or two then decides it is time to check on the girls and get something cool to drink. Walking into the kitchen he sees the two younger girls baking cookies (so snitches a couple of them) then not seeing Glory asks, "Where's Glory?"

The girls look at each other shaking their heads no then Carrie answers, "Don't know, Jake, she left right after you did."

Frowning he returns outside looking all around calling her name. She doesn't awaken.

He calls again and vaguely she hears his voice so rolls over and her long braid falls out the opening of the loft. Walking into the barn Jake asks one of Skinny's cowboys (Dean), "Did you see Glory, the oldest of the girls – the one with the long silver hair lately?"

"Yep, saw her in here a long time ago. Don't know where she went though," old Dean answers chewing on a sliver of straw.

Worried now he looks for her horse and Midnight is in the corral with the other horses. Suddenly he hears a noise above him and slaps his hand down to his pistol. He listens but there isn't any other noise. Silently he creeps over to the ladder and climbs up ever alert for trouble of any kind. What meets his eyes startles him and rattles him considerably.

Glory is sleeping in the sunlight her beautiful hair is shining like a lamp in the semi darkness of the loft. She has turned over on her back (as the sun was shining in her face) so now lays half in the sun and half in the shade sleeping peacefully in the hay.

Jake's silently climbs up the rest of the steps on the ladder then sits down besides her waiting. "She looks like an angel lyin' there so innocently," Jake thinks as he sits looking at his beautiful young lady. "I'm happy to see the dark circles are gone from under her eyes now (as his are). It seems that while we were so unhappy we worried ourselves sick and didn't sleep good a toll. I'm totally rested," he thinks then smiling promises, "Soon, my little lady, you will be sleeping with me every night." Relaxing soon he, too, falls asleep leaning back against the wall.

Glory wakes up first and stretching she sees Jake sitting by the ladder. Smiling she watches him for a few minutes thinking, "I'm so lucky. He loves me. He said he always has. I'm gonna be his wife when we git back home and we will be happy forever." Smiling happily at the thought she sits up. Her movements wake Jake up abruptly and he looks around quickly to see what the danger is but there isn't any. Instead he looks into the beautiful green eyes of Glory. Frowning he states, "I had a hard time finding you, Glory. You gave me a scare."

Blushing Glory replies, "I didn't mean to. I watched ya for a long time then fell asleep. Seems like yar tireder than ya thought, too."

"I didn't know a worryin' about someone could be so tirin'," he replies truthfully.

"There won't be any more of that around us now. Things are gonna be right nice. We will make them that way," Glory states smiling as she crawls on her hands and knees over to Jake then sits on her heels in front of him.

"Oh, I imagine there will be some rough times, honey. But as long as I have you....well, we can handle anything together," Jake answers sincerely.

"Yes, we can," Glory states firmly then leaning up softly kisses him.

Lightning shoots through Jake as he closes his eyes and moans at the sweetness of her kiss then mumbles, "Glory, we cain't keep doin' this! It is too hard and we gotta long trip to go on. I have to be in control of my feelin's better than I am right now."

Leaning back Glory with her eyes still soft from sleep replies, "Anything ya say, Jake."

Then laughing she rolls over him and climbs down the ladder before he can even move. Giggling she looks up when she reaches the bottom then sees Jake is ready to drop down so quickly moves out of his way.

Jumping down instead of climbing down Jake playfully chases her out of the barn.

She runs around the back of the house and stops. When she doesn't hear him coming she creeps back looking around the corner then lets out a scream when he grabs her from behind and tosses her over his wide shoulder. Laughing they almost fall down from the motion of her kicking around. Jake carries her into the kitchen over his shoulder so the younger girls look alarmed for a minute until they see they are laughing so hard they can hardly catch their breath.

"So you found her," Carrie Lynn states as she starts pulling hay off of her brother, "In the barn?"

"Yep, she fell asleep," Jake replies bending over and setting Glory on her feet again.

"Why do YOU have straw all over you?" Beth Ann questions with a raised eye brow.

Looking at her in surprise Jake answers, "MY goodness YOU look just like your ma and sound just like her, too."

Beth Ann and Carrie Lynn look at each other then fold their arms across their breasts and start tapping their shoes on the floor in a manner their mothers often do.

Jake and Glory burst out laughing so hard they have to sit down.

Jake huffs, "I cain't believe it both of our ma's are in this room and I thought we'd left them back home!"

Laughing so hard tears are running down her face Glory adds, "I know, please, oh, please, tell me if I ever do that!"

Carrie Lynn and Beth Ann start laughing then Carrie advises, "You'd better get over here and let us get that straw off of you before the grandpas get here or they will think you've been kissing in the barn."

Glory and Jake look at each other again as Glory burst out laughing again saying, "We DID!"

Sobering up Jake replies, "Glory, git over here and let me get that straw off of you. I don't want anyone thinking bad about you."

"I just kissed ya once, Jake. I didn't do nothin' wrong," Glory answers sadly.

"I know and we were playin' around but they are right. We don't wanna give the grandpas any reason to be sorry we came," Jake advises as he tugs her long braid.

Walking closer they all start pulling straw out of her hair and clothes then do the same for Jake.

The two older gents are tired when they ride in. It has been a hard day of checking on the cattle and taking care of the problems involved in a large cattle ranch. They smile when they reach the wash-up table outside of the house seeing steam coming from the pitcher and the basin sparkling clean. Smiling they wash their hands and faces before entering the house.

They inhale the scent of sunshine on the clean towel as they dry off and wonder why they never re-married so they could have enjoyed these little luxuries.

Wearily Skinny and Pokey walk in then stop in the doorway and look at the clean kitchen and especially at the kitchen table with a bright cloth on it, wild flowers in an old cracked pitcher, tin plates full of cookies then the tin plates and cups regally set out perfectly aligned with the old tarnished silverware. The majority of their weariness vanishes amidst such lovely surroundings. Smiling they look at the three girls dressed so prettily as they stand behind the table awaiting their approval.

"Well dog goned if this don't beat the band. What a lovely surprise," Skinny states smiling at them.

"Too purdy to eat on," Pokey admits, as they both walk around the table and kiss the girl's cheeks.

Smiling happily Glory asks, "Ready for some hot coffee and maybe ya'll can sneak a warm oatmeal cookie afore Big John gets here." She sassily winks at them as she walks over for the coffee pot.

Pokey takes a sip of the hot coffee saying, "Thank you, for the warm water to wash up in that was a nice surprise."

Smiling Carrie Lynn replies, "That was Beth Ann's idea. We heated water then when we saw you coming, she filled up the pitcher for you.

"Appreciate yar thoughtfulness," Skinny states again smiling at her. He looks over at Pokey saying, "Think maybe we should just kidnap these girls and keep'em around all the time. It shorely is nice comin' home to this kind of welcome."

"Might better keep Jake around, too, he's good with horses," Pokey states hiding a smile as he snitches another cookie.

Glory pipes in, "No need to kidnap us, grandpas, at Mama and Papa's ya'll can have this every day."

"That is quite a thought," Pokey replies thoughtfully.

"But who will run the ranch if'n we are at your house all the time," Skinny asks wondering what they will say.

Beth Ann looks thoughtful for a minute then smiling says, "Papa would and Jake would help."

"Yep, I would," Jake states positively as he nods his head yes.

"Yep, they would and we appreciate it but for right now, the ranch needs us," Skinny admits with a raised eye brow and a rueful grin as he thinks of his cowboy sons.

Pokey asks, "Did ya talk to Big John about supper? When is he bringin' it? I could eat a bear! I'm starvin'."

Just then the door opens and in walks Big John with two helpers behind him all carrying platters. "I was a watchin' for ya'll to come in. Well, my, oh my, lookee boys how nice the young ladies fixed up the table. Be careful now not to spill anything on it," Big John Sweeney states admiring the neat table.

Carefully John, Danny and old Dean set the platters of pork chops, mashed potatoes and gravy, fresh tomatoes and two peach pies down on the table.

"Oh, it looks so good. Thank you, Big John," Beth Ann says smiling up at the big man with the beautiful blue eyes. He is the size of a giant but with the heart of a kitten.

"Thank you, Miss Gray. Wonder if I could have one of your oatmeal cookies and see if they are as good as mine?" John asks wiggling his bushy eye brows at Beth Ann.

"Certainly, would you each like to have a couple?" she asks the helpers.

Pokey mumbles, "Givin' away my cookies! Shame on you, girl!"

Everyone bursts out laughing as Carrie Lynn pats his thin shoulders saying, "We baked cookies all afternoon. There will be plenty for tonight and for the next couple of days."

Looking around at the table Beth Ann raises her eye brow looking at her grandpas and Jake (who have already eaten many cookies each) stating, "I think it will be a good idea if we divide the cookies up for each of us so SOME of us get some."

The girls all laugh as Jake grumbles good naturedly, "Bet you ate six each as they came out of the oven."

Smiling happily Glory replies, "We'll never tell."

Supper is a fun meal and the leftover meat is set aside for the trip in the morning. The girls wash the dishes and cleanup the kitchen again then everyone retires to bed as tomorrow will be a long day.

HEADING FOR ST. LOUIE
Chapter 10

"A trip can be fun when riding with those you love."

At daybreak the ten riders head out for St. Louis, four cowboys (Bradford, Jay, Josh & Kevin) riding along to help out where needed. The pack horses are fully loaded with enough food and needed items for the trip.

After the third hour they all walk their horses for a time and get some exercise. Pokey asks the girls (who are still as fresh as a daisy), "It woulda been easier on you girls if'n we'd brought a wagon for ya'll to ride in."

Beth Ann thoughtfully looks at him before saying, "It is so nice to be out in the sunshine and feel the wind on my face. I'd rather ride a horse," laughing suddenly she glances at Glory adding, "Thought you would never hear me say that did you?"

"That's true. Papa made ya learn to ride and ya do it beautifully," Glory answers sincerely.

Smiling Carrie Lynn shyly adds, "I've been around horses all my life and didn't really like them but when Beth Ann started riding then I decided I'd better learn really well so that we could visit more often and we do."

"I've been riding since I was two years old. I love the wind in my face and the sun on my head," Glory answers raising her lovely tanned face to the sun.

"Be sure you keep your hats on," Jake remarks with a smile, "Lizbeth and ma will pull my hair out if'n anything happens to your pretty skin."

"Yes, we were told over and over about keeping a hat on our heads," Carrie Lynn answers with a sigh.

At their dinner break Skinny advises, "We have plenty of food for today why don't we try to go as far as we can today then tomorra we will rest up some and cook up enough for the next day. We can keep doing this until we get to St. Louie. I've found it works purdy good. We will haveta rest two days after five days to give the horses some restin' up time and us washin' up time."

None are tired so eagerly agree but during the long afternoon the girls become very weary but never complain out loud. Every couple of hours they walk for a while letting their horses have a rest and also to keep their legs and backsides from getting too sore. When they stop for the night all are tired and ready to sleep so after eating the last of the pork chops and biscuits they quickly fall into an exhausted sleep.

Pokey wakes everyone up before daylight with a couple of rabbits from his snares. He quickly skins them and has them frying for breakfast before the girls have hardly opened their eyes. The roasted rabbit tastes good to the refreshed group. What is left over is wrapped in oil skin paper and laid in the saddle bags for lunch.

Later in the day, Pokey requests (as he sees some birds flying by), "Jake, it's gettin' close to dinner! What'cha think about looking for some game with me?"

"Shore enough," Jake happily answers so they ride off.

"Thars a nice place to stop and eat dinner not far from here, Pokey knows the place and they can find us by the fire. It isn't very far now," Skinny advises the girls.

The girls nod yes then Glory advises, "We aren't really tired but we are gettin' hungry." So all agree to do whatever is requested of them.

In about an hour they ride into the shade of some oak trees smiling at the coolness there. Skinny points to the back of the tree line explaining, "Thar's a spring just behind those trees. It has water all the time. Who wants to go with me to fetch some water to clean the game with?"

"I will, grandpa," Glory instantly says grabbing one of the buckets, she walks away with him.

Beth Ann and Carrie Lynn help the cowboys unload the needed dishes for their meal then gather wood for the fire.

Soon Jake and Pokey ride in with three ducks and another rabbit.

Jake hands the game to Beth Ann and Carrie Lynn saying, "It's your turn to skin and clean'em." He watches Beth Ann's shocked face knowing she will refuse but gulping she asks instead, "Wwiiill you show me how?"

Smiling he hugs her saying, "Shorely, I will." So he goes about showing her how to skin the rabbit.

Beth Ann barely keeps from gagging as she watches him clean the rabbit thinking, "I never knew this was how it was done."

He half skins it then hands it into her unwilling hands and watches her eyes go wide in fear. Then she lifts her head and taking a deep breath finishes skinning and cleaning the rabbit as Jake has shown her.

When it is done she smiles triumphantly when she looks up at Jake.

Smiling he admits, "You did that perfectly, Beth Ann. I'm real proud of you. It took Glory a lot longer to learn than it did you."

Of course, this makes Beth Ann feel wonderful that she can do something better than her sister or rather learn something faster. She knows Glory has skinned many rabbits so probably can do it better and quicker than she can.

Beth Ann helps with plucking the feathers off of the ducks and cleaning them ready for roasting. Both girls are delighted when Glory and Skinny return with the much wanted water. Both girls are happy when they can wash their hands of the blood and gore from the dead animals.

Leaning over as they finish their difficult job Carrie Lynn whispers, "Jake thought we'd say no. But we had already decided we'd do everything we are asked and we did. Ain'tcha proud of yourself, I shorely am."

Nodding yes happily Beth Ann replies, "Sometimes it is better to do as you are asked than be difficult about it when you know you have to do it anyway." They finish preparing the meat to be cooked then the cowboys bury the feathers, rabbit skin and entrails so that no wild animals will follow them for a food source.

Smiling happily Carrie Lynn states, "We did it!"

Smiling brightly at her best friend Beth Ann answers, "I didn't know if I could but when I looked at Jake's face I knew I had to prove to him that I could do it. It wasn't so terrible and it will taste sooooooo good. Oh, Carrie, I keep forgetting to tell you that I'm so proud of your good English. You make me feel so proud!"

Carrie Lynn hugs Beth Ann admitting, "Thank you. It is hard to remember but if I want to be a teacher like you then I have to speak good English so I'm really trying."

Soon they have a wonderful meal cooking. Glory works on making the biscuits just like Grandma Nona had taught her while the younger girls watch and learn. They are a little brown when they are brought out of the fire but taste very good anyway and are eaten with compliments. Beth Ann makes the second batch and watches them closely then Carrie Lynn does the third batch and all are thrilled with the results.

They do indeed have enough food for the next day's noon meal so after another hot day in the saddle the girls are happy to rest awhile before having to fix supper the next evening. This time all the men go hunting with the exception of young Josh (one of Skinny's cowboys) who has to go a little farther out to find some firewood.

So the girls are left to themselves for an hour at twilight to build the fire and fix cornbread to go with the red beans and whatever meat they kill this night. All are sore and tired so when Glory says, "Let's go to the stream and take a bath while they are gone." They eagerly agree. Glory leaves first walking towards the river to find a good place to swim where it's clearer and not the dirty red river water.

A few minutes later the younger girls starts to walk down the trail following Glory with their clean clothes, towels and soap when they hear the sharp crack of a twig close by. Expecting Josh (the young good looking cowboy) with firewood they turn smiling in that direction to tell him where they are going when they see four young Indian bucks in the tree line between them and Glory.

Screaming shrilly, "Glory!" they cling to each other in terror.

"What do we do?" Carrie Lynn asks as tears of fear run down her lovely face.

"Glory knows Indian language," Beth Ann replies (eyes wide in terror).

The young braves watch the girls carefully then walking around they see no men only a couple of horses and food items. They taste the cold beans saying, "Ugg!" One picks up the pieces of bacon for the beans with his knife and drops it into the pan the beans are in. The fire is very low as they don't have much firewood yet. He nods at the cold food then the girls and talks to his friends again. They seem to agree and before the girls know what is happening they start walking purposely towards them.

The girls scream again and when the young braves try to pull them apart and move them towards the horses Carrie Lynn cries out, "Drop down to the ground and leave a message for Jake."

Both girls kick and fight the young braves until they manage to get the words Indians scratched in the hard red earth with their fingernails. The young bucks finally pick them up and sit them on the girl's horses. The saddles are off so the girls can't even sit on them without falling off so two of the braves jump up behind the girls and off they ride.

Glory impatiently waits for the girls to arrive so when they don't she finally dives in for her bath. She swims around enjoying the clean water she was able to find. She is under water when the girls scream so doesn't hear them. Irritated at their tardiness she decides, "I'll have to go back and git them. They musta gotten lost." Drying off she redresses in clean clothes then quickly walks back to the campsite but no one is there. Amazed she sees their scattered clothing as well as soap and towels so calls out to them over and over but no one answers. She stomps around for a minute or two wondering where they have gone to then notices the letters scratched in the dirt. INDIANS! Glory panics for a minute then remembers that her grandpas had already told them they know some friendly Indians who live north of the ranch. "Okay, Glory, what do ya do? What can ya do?" Glory thinks a minute then picks up some green brush and all the wood she can find, she builds a big fire. Much larger than she would need to cook supper on and soon it is blazing high.

All the men are bragging about their hunting skills when suddenly Pokey points puzzled, "Look at that fire, surely, the girls know that is too big a fire."

Jake's head swings around seeing the big bond fire he states, "That means trouble," so he heads off at a gallop.

Glory hears them coming before she sees them. It is late in the afternoon but not yet dark so she sees them fairly quickly. She runs towards them and as soon as Jake sees her worried face he stops Comfort then jumping down runs to her asking, "What's wrong?"

"Indians were here and I think they took Beth Ann and Carrie Lynn. I can't find them anywhere. See the ground here," she takes him to where the girls scratched Indians in the red clay and looks up at him in despair.

Jake turns to the dismounting men as they ride up saying, "Indians took Beth Ann and Carrie Lynn!" He walks over to the pack horses hidden on the far side of the little treed area and starts getting more ammunition out.

Skinny looks at Pokey a little worried saying, "Red Sun's tribe is not too far away. I imagine the girls are thar. Jay and Bradford start looking for a trail. Kevin come with us. Josh stay here with Glory and Jake. We'll be back as soon as we can."

"No, sir! I'm not staying here while my sister is in danger and I'm to watch over Beth Ann, too. I'm coming!" Jake states stubbornly.

"What about me!" Glory storms before adding, "I'm as good a shot as ya'll are. I can ride as well as ya'll can and Beth Ann is my sister! I'm coming, too!"

"Glory, you are more beautiful than the younger girls are. If they want women they will want you even more than the girls. We WILL get the girls back. I promise you that," Skinny explains as he walks to the pack horse taking some supplies out and a few things they can trade.

"I showed ya I can take care of myself! I WILL NOT be left behind," Glory bellows angrily then adds pitifully, "I shoulda watched over'em better. They said they would follow me to the river. I shouldna have left them even for a few minutes."

Jake takes her into his arms saying, "Glory, don't blame yourself. You would just have been taken, too, if'n ya'd been here."

"But I could have talked to'em and I know how to take care of myself, I can track, I can ride and I AM COMING with ya'll," she states adamantly.

Both older men nod yes as Skinny agrees, "Okay, Glory, but you'll do what we tell ya to do and the same goes for you, Jake. We know these people and they are good people so don't start something we can't finish. Do we have your word on that?"

"I'll do whatever ya say, Grandpas, but I will go," Glory replies with her green eyes flashing danger signals.

"I'll follow orders," Jake agrees as he leaps into his saddle. He slaps his calf where he has strapped an extra knife onto his leg stating, "I'm ready."

Glory does the same. She has already changed from the riding skirt she was wearing into her favorite buck skin pants and vest. She helped Yellow Moon make them so she treasures them.

Jake looks at the tightness of the pants thinking, "I don't know if'n this a good idea but we gotta hurry." He notices she has her gun belt on and a knife in the belt also. "She is well prepared," he realizes so nods okay to her.

Pokey calls out to Kevin and Josh saying, "You two are to stay with Glory at all times. She is not to be out of your sight!"

Both answer, "Yes, sir!"

Glory grimly nods back and they all ride out.

They ride at a steady pace watching the hoof prints in the red clay. Jay is riding out ahead of the rest as he is the best tracker. As he is part Indian himself and has been well taught, he signals for everyone to follow him. He rides a little to the side following a set of shod horse prints as these two sets are more deeply etched into the soil so he and Brad know they are the ones the girls are probably on with the braves. They keep a steady pace the whole way then see the teepees in front of them.

In the darkness Pokey softly calls out for them to stop then he and Skinny talk a little bit. "We should leave Glory here. It ain't good to take a beautiful young woman in thar."

"She won't stay behind, Pokey, she'll follow us in. You know she will," Skinny answers flatly.

"Jake can stop her," Pokey states looking around at the teepees.

"Jake is worried about his sister. He will ride right in, too," Skinny explains flatly.

"Then we will all ride in together. Don't think we'll have anything to worry about with Red Sun," Pokey answers firmly but slides his gun loose ready for action.

Glory is riding beside Jake on her horse (Midnight) and looking at the teepees says, "I count ten that must mean this is a small band."

"Could be five men for each teepee, lots don't sleep inside unless they have to," Jake replies quietly looking around the camp site.

"Do you see the girls?" Bradford asks Jay.

"No, they are in a teepee. Girls pretty so....it maybe hard to get them back," Jay replies keenly watching and waiting.

Skinny and Pokey start their horses walking towards the teepees as they quietly whisper, "Keep alert."

Beth Ann and Carrie Lynn are tied together with a rawhide strip one around each of their wrists and another one tied to each of their legs so they can't run away. Both sit terrified inside a teepee listening to the Indians talk but not knowing what is being said. There have heard angry shouts from an older man and a lot of muttering from the young braves who took the girls.

Some young Indian maidens looked at Beth Ann and Carrie Lynn angrily when they arrived but the young girls don't understand it is jealousy that has made them angry.

"Father, the girls belong to us. We found them. There were no men with them," a young brave named Gray Bear explains to his angry father, Red Sun.

"You think young girls ride around with no men around, son?" Red Sun answers angrily then asks, "You do this to anger Morning Lark so she won't marry you?"

"No, father, I didn't think about Morning Lark at all. I saw these beautiful girls and we wanted them," Gray Bear answers truthfully.

"These are white girls not Indian girls. They don't know our ways. They don't live the way we do. Do you think they will adjust to our ways ever? No, they will not. They must be returned!" Red Sun states angrily.

Stepping forward Morning Lark asks, "Chief, may I ask a question?"

Chief Red Sun looks at the beautiful young maiden who loves his son (Gray Bear) very much and who he considers his daughter already so he graciously replies, "Yes, Morning Lark what is your question."

"I was wondering about the families of these girls, will they not be worried about them?" she asks smiling at Red Sun but ignoring his son.

Taking a deep breath he turns asking his son, "Would you be worried if your sisters were taken from you? And by force!"

Gray Bear (as well as the other braves) hang their heads saying, "Yes, chief, we would be worried."

Suddenly there is a shout as the guards see the riders coming in. Everyone jumps to wariness as the visitors approach.

Skinny calls out when they are within hearing distance, "Red Sun, I am your friend, Skinny Gates and my brother and friends are with me. May we enter?"

Frowning Red Sun looks at his son saying, "It seems you stole from a friend, my son," then he calls out, "Enter my friends." He walks over to where they can see him standing waiting for them to walk their horses closer to the teepees.

Hearing Skinny's voice Beth Ann and Carrie Lynn scream at the same time, "Grandpa!"

All of Skinny and Pokey's party are relieved to hear their voices and know they are here and alive.

Red Sun motions for them to dismount then the older gents and the Indian chief step to the side talking loudly so that the Indians can hear and Glory and Jay can also hear and understand.

"Grandpa just said his two granddaughters got lost and Red Sun says his son and some braves found two young white girls," Glory quietly translates for those who don't understand what is being said.

"They took'em," Jake hisses quietly.

"It's polite to say they were lost and they will be returned," Glory explains softly.

Red Sun turns to two young girls saying something to them. Willow and Morning Lark nod yes then walk over to the teepee the two girls are in, bend over and enter.

Beth Ann and Carrie Lynn fearfully look at the beautiful girls then one smiles saying something in Cherokee softly to them then taking a knife out of her pouch around her waist walks toward them.

They both let out a shriek as she softly mutters again in Cherokee saying, "Be calm, all is well," again then cuts the rawhide that tethers their ankles then reaching up cuts the rawhide strip that ties their hands together.

Both girls start rubbing their wrists as tears run down their faces at the red raw skin around their limbs.

The other young girl holds out a small jar of something saying in Cherokee, "Put this on your wrists."

Of course, neither girl understands so she takes a dab of the medicine and lightly dabs it on Carrie Lynn's wrist then holds it out for them to do the same for themselves.

They shyly take a little and apply it to their hands and ankles. They try to stand up but after sitting so long their legs are tingly with feelings. So they make a face as more tears run down their tearstained faces. In a minute or two they are able to stand and follow the girls out of the teepees.

There stands Skinny and Pokey so they rush over to them sobbing in fright.

Jake dismounts and rushes over to where both girls are as they run to him gratefully. He lets out a sigh of relief as he softly asks, "Did they hurt you?"

Carrie Lynn holds out her wrist saying, "Look at my wrist! They tied us up!"

Jake puts his finger under her chin raising it up and earnestly asks again, "Carrie did they do anything untold to ya? Did they take advantage of either of ya?"

Both girls look at each other realizing what he is asking and shake their heads no.

Closing his eyes Jake lets out a deep sigh of relief then when Skinny looks over at him questioningly he shakes his head no.

All give a sigh of relief when they see the girls are unharmed.

Glory and the men still sit upon their horses as they haven't been asked to dismount. She understands all that is said so knows it will be alright now so she just sits there waiting for the invitation to dismount.

When the girls run over to her horse she quietly tells them, "Everything is all right, don'tcha worry. Yar safe now."

Walking over Skinny explains to his group, "Red Sun sends his apologies for the braves taking the girls. It was just a harmless act on their part. He would like for us to eat with them and stay the night here."

Both girls look in horror at him as Jake asks, "Is it safe?"

"Yes, it is completely safe. Girls ya'll be with us all the time. The young braves were just having some fun. Most are about Jake and Glory's age and were just out looking for mischief," Skinny advises smiling at them.

Pokey calls over, "Glory, come over here a minute. Men ya'll can dismount and keep a sharp look out for our horses." He turns and laughs as Red Sun says, "I like that big horse the big brave is on."

Pokey has seen the tricks Jake's horse can do so answers, "That horse's name is Comfort. The brave's name is Jake and he has trained him to do some tricks. I will ask him to show them to ya'll."

Glory walks over and the Indians stare at her wide eyed then look at Beth Ann's red hair and Carrie Lynn's blonde hair. She nods pleasantly to them before walking up to the chief saying in Cherokee, "Thank ya for makin' my family welcome in yar village, chief."

Red Sun looks shocked for a minute then looking at her white blonde hair, her knowledge of their language and her buckskin clothing asks, "Are you the Glory that my brother, Good Heart, talks about?"

Smiling Glory nods yes.

"I should like to see these things that he says he has taught you to do. Will you show me so that I may not again call my brother a liar," Red Sun jokes with them.

Raising her eyebrows in question, Glory looks at her grandpas asking, "May I?"

They nod yes so she agrees, "I would be glad to, Chief."

He smiles saying, "After our meal you may show us what a white girl can learn from an Indian."

The cowboys hand over the wild game they had killed to the Indian women when Skinny tells them to then they all sit down on blankets that are brought out and drink some cool water while talking.

The girls are relaxing some now and laughing at their fears, but still not straying from their family's side.

The young maidens and braves talk to Glory and are amazed she speaks their language so well. Many know Good Heart and Yellow Moon so ask about them. Glory tells them how Good Heart had saved her papa's life as they nod yes saying, "Yes, Joe Gray." It is a pleasant time.

Jake unsaddles Comfort (his horse) then brings him to the center of attention and shows the curious Indians how well he has taught his beloved horse.

Comfort dances for them with Jake on his back going side to side then back and forth. He paws the ground when Jake asks him questions which Glory translates so the Indians can understand. Comfort rises up on his hind legs and walks following Jake's lead and lastly Jake issues a warning that Comfort will let no one ride him unless Jake says it is okay.

Many of the Indians laugh saying, "Anyone can ride a horse."

Jake shrugs his shoulders saying, "You can try. Better move back some he can be rather ornery at times." Glory translates this as a dare to try to ride Comfort. They know that Comfort will be a horse worthy of being stolen if he is unridable then they have a better chance of his not being stolen.

Many braves try to get on Comfort but he will not let any of them. A few are roughly thrown off when they try to jump upon his back but none are successful. Jake says a word to Comfort and he immediately stops and walks to Glory lowering his head he nudges her and in one leap Glory sits on his bare back smiling at the dismayed braves. Then Jake says, "Ride Glory!"

Smiling Glory nudges Comfort with her knees and he starts walking in a large circle around the fire. Glory comes up on her knees (Jake thinks again, "Those pants are too tight on her") and quickly stands up on Comfort's back. She rides around in the large circle then taking a deep breath she does a backwards flip landing on her feet behind Comfort who stops a few feet in front of her.

The Indians clap loudly for her and Comfort then the braves surround them offering money and many horses for Comfort.

Jake turns them all down saying, "He is like my son. I've had him since he was born. I cain't sell him."

Comfort allows the braves to touch him when Jake tells him to and the Indians admire the large stallion but do not try to jump onto his back again. When they are finished showing off, Jake and Comfort take a long walk and Jake feeds him a few of the oatmeal cookies he has left over which pleases Comfort to no end.

Soon they have freshly roasted meat and corn meal cakes to eat for supper. Berries are provided for dessert. Everyone is hungry so eagerly eats the tasty food given to them.

After the meal Gray Bear approaches Glory and rather mockingly asks, "You will show us what my uncle has taught you now?"

Glory nods yes then standing up wraps her long braid into a coil at the base of her neck pinning it in place with hair pins. She walks slowly into the circle of people gathered around the large fire and stands about ten feet away asking, "Gray Bear would ya like ta try ta grab me?"

Enthusiastically he nods yes so springs at her. She twists away just as he would have grabbed her and stands six feet away from him when he turns around. Again he tries to grab her and she moves too quickly for him to touch her. Laughing softly she says, "Once more and then it is my turn."

Laughing heartily he replies, "I will get you this time." When he leaps over the fire to grab her she spins around catching him behind the knees and he goes down.

She stands up saying, "Now it is my turn." She runs towards him and turning swiftly has her arm around his neck. He is taller than her five foot six inches and startled he tries to throw her off. She dances around him for a minute or two then releasing him does a backwards flip over his shoulders landing about five feet in front of him smiling devishly at him.

The Indians applaud her expertise but she keeps her eyes locked on Gray Bear. He is embarrassed that she has out maneuvered him and she is leery of him. Suddenly he rushes her so she steps aside then trips him and down he falls. She is on his back in a heartbeat softly hissing, "Ya stole my sister Gray Bear! If'n ya'd harmed her ya would be dead now!"

Realizing she could indeed have killed him and why, he understands her motives, so says, "Apologies to you, Silver Hair, I am also glad your sister was unharmed."

Glory stands up and holding out her hand offers to help him stand even though it is unnecessary.

He smiles at her impudence then nods taking it and tries to pull her to the ground but she doesn't allow that. She just laughs and pulls him to his feet.

Jake worries as he watches Glory and Gray Bear dance around. "I know Glory knows a lot about Indian ways I didn't realize just how much until now."

Skinny and Pokey are amused then astonished at how limber Glory is so thinks, "She'd be a terrific dancer. She is so light on her feet."

Glory walks over to Chief Red Sun nods informing him, "Good Heart has taught me much more but I don't wanna hurt yar braves."

He bursts out laughing and calls to the ones who had taken the girls saying, "She challenges you to take her to the ground! Are any of you man enough to do it!"

Of course all three of the other young braves leap to their feet saying, "Yes, I can do it."

Glory walks back to the circle motioning for them to come forward.

Smiling they try to grab her arms and she throws the first one into the second one then the third one she trips and he falls about five feet away. One tries to trip her as he rises from the ground but she jumps out of his reach. When one grabs her around the shoulders she goes down on one knee and tosses him over her shoulder. When a second one comes at her while she is on one knee she rolls over and over until he has to jump over her or be knocked down. Gray Bear watches and isn't quite so embarrassed and even laughs at his friends. They do manage to grab her and wrestle her to the ground but it takes all three of them to do it. She laughs slapping the dirt off of her buckskins and acknowledges them with a bow when they help her up.

She feels alive and gloriously healthy as she walks over to the chief again asking, "Chief, my future husband, Jake, is here. He is a champion wrestler. Would any of yar braves like to wrestle him?"

Red Sun smiles happily replying, "We would enjoy that."

Glory walks over to Jake saying, "Ya wanna wrestle some of these here boys, honey. Show'em what a strong handsome husband I will have."

Jake knows he needs to show he is strong enough to take care of Glory and he knows she wants them to see it and never bother them again also.

Jake rises to his six foot three inches of muscled glory stating, "I'd be right proud to and, missy, we are gonna have a little talk about your likin' to fight so much."

Glory's trill of laughter brings a thrill to Pokey and Skinny's eyes as they see the love that flows between the two young people.

Red Sun sees it also so says to Skinny, "That is one fine girl and they will have a good life. They treasure each other already."

"Yes, they do and they do some powerful arguing too," Pokey answers grinning fondly.

"Ah, but the making up is so much better after the fight. A spirited woman is to admired," Red Sun replies nodding his head then adds, "I will be forced to tell my brother that he has done well. It will be hard to eat the crow of truth but I will.

They all laugh at his true statement as they watch as Jake strips down to his pants and socks. The braves have much less on just loin cloths. The young braves eagerly wait to wrestle with the big man.

Glory looks at her beloved's chiseled chest and wide shoulders sighing thinks, "Mine....all mine."

The Indian maidens look at the bronzed glory of Jake's body letting out a sigh as they see that Glory and Jake love each other and he is already taken but what a sight.

Jake is as limber as a mountain lion and strong as a horse and he knows it. He walks to the circle and eyes the first young brave who steps up. Broken Arrow and Jake grab each other and though strong the young brave is no match for Jake so soon Jake has him pinned to the ground with very little work. Red Sun declares Jake the winner.

Standing he puts his hand out to help the young brave up then they nod and Jake turns toward the next brave. This one is older and more heavily muscled than the previous one. Rising Moon looks at Jake with eager eyes as they grab each other's shoulders and try to force each other to the ground. Round and round they go then Jake trips Rising Moon and down they fall. Unfortunately for Rising Moon Jake quickly pins him to the ground on his stomach so he is unable to get Jake off of him. Again Red Sun declares Jake the winner asking, "Are you too tired for one more Jake?"

Breathing heavily but not exhausted by any means, Jake answers, "I can do another."

"Rest a few minutes and drink some cool water then," Red Sun advises so Jake does. Soon Jake is ready for the last wrestler.

Gray Bear approaches Jake nodding he will be next. Jake knows this young man wants to show him up more than the others because Glory has bested him.

Smiling gleefully he stares at the young man baring his teeth he asks, "Ready?"

Gray Bear is around the same age as Jake and being the chief's son he has always had to be the best in every event so he is determined to beat Jake quickly. Although not as tall as Jake he is very limber and muscular so it will be a good test.

The two young men circle each other looking for an advantage when suddenly Gray Bear jumps up and tries to knock Jake to the ground with the force of his momentum. Expecting this Jake sidesteps and pushes him off to the side as he steps sideways. Smiling at each other grimly they circle again and Jake makes the next move with a powerful body slam to the ground. They roll over and over with each trying to get on top but neither allowing that to happen. So they end up with arms and legs locked around each other straining to overpower the other one. Sweat drips off of both of them as their muscles quiver and shake from the tightness of their grips. Neither will give in nor let go.

Skinny turns to Red Sun stating, "Even match."

Red Sun nods yes proud of his son as he calls out, "Enough."

Skinny calls out also, "Enough, Jake."

Each young man relaxes slowly then rising Jake holds a quivering hand out to help the other young man up. Wiping sweat out of their eyes they shake hands in the white man way then Gray Bear grabs Jake's fore arm and they clasp fore arms and shake in the Indian fashion. Gray Bear turns asking Glory, "Good man. He be good to you?"

Smiling happily Glory stands up, walks over to Jake, hugs him saying, "Yes, he is very good to me."

Looking at the lovely young woman Gray Bear knows there is no way he can have her so nods at her then Jake then walks over to his father saying, "Good Man. They will be good together." So the tension is ended.

Morning Lark watched with troubled eyes as Glory exhibited some tricks she has learned from Good Heart. She admires the buckskin pants and vest thinking, "Squaws do not wear the pants of a brave. Why does she dress so?" So she slips around the circle hesitantly asking, "Good Heart teach ya good. You have known him a long time?"

Smiling Glory walks closer answering, "Yes, Good Heart has taught me since I was a little girl. I learned with his sons."

"Good Heart and Yellow Moon come visit often. Not lately though," Morning Lark questions. She eyes the buckskin clothes as she hesitantly asks, "You make these? They look comfortable."

"Yalla Moon heped me make them last year. They are very comfortable but…I don't wear them as much as I'd like. I like the pants much better than a dress because I can move around better. Do you see my sisters over there," Glory points to the two younger girls, "They dress like I'm suppose to but I'd rather wear these."

Morning Lark looks at the two young girls with their divided skirts and bright blouses saying, "Very pretty but not easy to keep clean."

Nodding yes, Glory replies, "Yep that's the truth." She realizes the Indian girl wants to ask something and is circling around before asking (as is the Indian way) to be courteous, and then she will ask her questions.

"I wonder about Gray Bear. I love him but he ignores me. He will marry me if no one better comes along. He desires you," Morning Lark hesitantly states with pain in her eyes.

Nodding yes she understands, Glory explains, "I am different from most girls. I was raised by my Papa…my Ma wasn't around…so Papa raised me like a boy and so did Good Heart. Humm…I'm not a lady…I never plan to be one either. But I will be a good wife to Jake. That's all I want to be." Looking at Morning Lark Glory feels sorry for her so asks, "Does Gray Bear know ya love him?"

Nodding yes Morning Lark sadly replies, "He doesn't love me."

Smiling impishly Glory lays her arm around Morning Lark's shoulders and starts whispering to her. A couple of times Morning Lark looks at her in surprise but continues to listen.

"Morning Lark, ya will get his attention doing this, it might not be pleasant at times, but ya will wake him up," Glory explains as she tells about her kidnapping and the consequences of her actions.

Smiling they hug at the end of the conversation then Morning Lark walks over to Red Sun and quietly kneels down behind him. Noticing her he leans back to see what she wants as she whispers to him, troubled he nods yes.

Gray Bear watches as the two beautiful girls talk. "Morning Lark is as dark as night and Glory is as bright as the sun with completely different personalities. Silver Hair will take on the world while Morning

- 142 -

Lark will never do that." Narrowing his eyes he wonders what they are talking about. When Morning Lark talks to his father then he sees him nod yes, he wonders more. He tries to catch Morning Lark's eyes to get her to come and explain to him what is going on but she keeps her head down as she walks directly to her teepee.

When she doesn't return quickly he slips away quickly walking to her teepee. Morning Lark is sitting inside folding her clothes putting them in a buckskin bag. The flap of the teepee is open so Gray Bear realizes she is silently crying. "May I talk to you, Morning Lark?" he asks curiously.

She replies, "It is best you go, Gray Bear," then she turns her beautiful face to him explaining, "I will be leaving in the morning. I am going to ride with the white people to my uncle in Tahlequah and live there."

Going down on his knees, he asks, "But why? When will you come back?"

Silent tears stream down her lovely face as she shakes her head no flatly stating, "I won't be coming back."

Looking closely at her Gray Bear softly states, "Not coming back! Do you not want to marry me?"

Morning Lark sadly looks at him then impatiently states, "You have never asked me. You ignore me. How do I know you want to marry me especially when I see you desire the white girls? You wanted them. I saw it on your face."

Sitting back on his heels Gray Bear thinks a moment, "No, I haven't asked her to marry me...I just assumed she'd wait for me...I did want the white girls...but to marry one of them? Humm...they would not care for my comfort and I do not love them. Silver Hair would be a treasure but she won't be mine. Her heart is already given to Jake. Morning Lark has always been my choice in a mate. Humm...what do I do?" He looks up sadly asking, "Do not leave, Morning Lark."

Her hope for a declaration of love doesn't come so turning her back on him she returns to folding her belongings.

Seeing she isn't going to talk to him anymore, he stands and walks away. He walks back to the circle to sit thinking. Soon he notices Glory is watching him and when she cocks her eye brows inquiringly at him, he knows she is the one to help him or the cause of the problem. So standing he walks over and sits down next to her and Jake asking, "Morning Lark says she is leaving with you tomorrow."

Glory nods yes innocently answering, "Yes, she is ready to marry so will go to her uncle's tribe and find a mate there."

"I do not wish her to leave," he replies solemnly.

"Ya will have to ask her to stay then," Glory replies frankly.

"I did, and she said, no," Gray Bear replies then asks, "What did you two talk about earlier?"

"She asks if she could go with us to her uncles and we are going by there so I said yes," Glory answers honestly.

Quietly Jake sits and watches their intense conversation. Knowing something is going on with Gray Bear but not knowing what it is he asks Glory, "What is going on?"

Turning to him Glory explains then turning back to Gray Bear states, "Yar the only one who can change her mind. Yar father has given her permission to leave already. If 'n ya want her to stay then yar gonna havta give her a reason to stay."

Looking intently at Glory Gray Bear replies, "She is ready to marry. I'm not ready yet."

Shrugging her shoulder Glory says, "She is a lovely girl some brave will be lucky to marry her when she gets to her uncles."

Gray Bear frowns heavily at the thought of another brave taking Morning Lark to be his wife, he doesn't like this thought at all. "She has always been in my heart. I've always thought I'd marry her someday but not now. I might find someone else I want to marry more." Looking at Glory he had been very impressed by her abilities to fight and talk his language but knows she would not be his choice of a wife even if Jake were not around as she would desire things he could not and would not give her.... like a permanent home. Shaking his head in disgust at the thought of a wooden house and never being free to pack up and move on when he wants to, "I can never do that." He silently sits thinking about all the good things about Morning Lark and what their lives could be like.

Morning Lark thinks her heart is broken when Gray Bear leaves. She sadly finishes packing her belongings then lying down on her pallet she thinks of all her dreams disappearing before her. "I will no longer see Gray Bear and have a life with him. Red Sun will not be my father after all. My father is dead and my mother is dead. I have no one but my uncle in Tahlequah. I don't know if there is a place for me there. He will marry me off to some brave very quickly so he doesn't have to care for me." Tears rain down her small face as she faces a bleak future without all the ones she loves.

Gray Bear silently walks the camp thinking of changing his life, "I cannot imagine not having Morning Lark in my life, what should I do?" As he passes her teepee for the tenth time he hears the quiet sobbing and his heart goes out to her. "She doesn't want to leave us. We have been her family all her life. She won't be as happy with her uncle and he will find her a brave very quickly and she will marry and be his responsibility. I know this. Yes, he will hope to make her happy and he won't force her to marry but he will encourage it. She is so lovely. All the braves will want her... how could they not! So do I give her up or do I fight for her? Do I want to be with only her all my life? I believe she loves me. I have seen it in her face but do I love her?" He wants to go in and comfort her but knows that is against his father's rules to enter a maiden's teepee so he walks some more. Soon he finds himself at his father's teepee so softly asks, "Father, are you awake?"

Red Sun has heard his son walking the camp and knows he is thinking about Morning Lark leaving. "I know my son loves Morning Lark but he doesn't realize how much until now," Red Sun thinks. Picking up his sleeping robe he drapes it around his shoulders as he leaves his teepee joining his son outside.

"Father, I am troubled. I don't know if I want to settle down and marry Morning Lark or not. I don't wish her to leave but how can I ask her to stay if I don't know if I want to marry her?" Gray Bear asks seriously.

"Perhaps you don't love her as a woman but as a sister?" Red Sun slyly suggests.

Gray Bear thoughtfully considers then says flatly, "No, not as a sister."

"Do you desire her as a wife?" Red Sun questions cautiously.

"I desire her but I don't know that I want to marry her," Gray Bear truthfully answers.

"You would use her without marriage," Red Sun asks stunned.

"No, I would not use her that way," Gray Bear replies heatedly, "I just don't know if I'm ready to marry, Father."

"Then you don't love her enough to marry her. She is ready to marry and has been for a time now. She has waited for you to ask and turned down others. She is tired of waiting so she will leave and find another brave to marry," Red Sun states flatly then aggravated stands up and walks back into his teepee.

Gray Bear sits down right there thinking, "To never see her again, never hear her laugh, never see the sparkle in her eyes when she is happy. What do I do?" He sits the whole night thinking.

At daylight Skinny and Pokey's group are up and saddling their horses ready to head out to St. Louis. They eat a light breakfast with their Indian friends then are ready to leave.

Glory explained the situation to her grandpas about asking Morning Lark to ride with them and they (after some discussion) see no problem with it. So when she walks up with her horse they aren't surprised.

Morning Lark's spirit is as low as it can be. She sadly looks at the camp and all the people she loves thinking, "I'll never see them again. I'll never hear Red Sun's booming laughter and never see Gray Bear again. Where is he? He doesn't even want to say goodbye to me." Tears silently run down her face as she looks around then turning she jumps up on her horse and rides to Glory's side stating, "He didn't ask me to marry him."

Sadly Glory replies, "It's early yet. Give him time to miss ya."

Taking a deep breath Morning Lark sits straighter nodding yes so they trot out of the camp.

Beth Ann and Carrie Lynn are riding close to each other (as usual) talking, "I'm certainly glad to be leaving there," Beth Ann states firmly.

"Me, too. That was not an adventure I want to experience again," Carrie Lynn replies as she rubs her still sore wrist where the rawhide had been.

"Do you think Glory's plan will work?" Beth Ann asks as she looks over at the beautiful Indian maiden riding beside Glory.

"I don't know. I hope so. Morning Lark seems so unhappy," Carrie Lynn sadly replies looking at the girl.

Gray Bear is not in camp when the travelers leave as he had run to bathe in the cold mountain water that flows down the mountains a couple of miles from their camp. He strides in walking straight to Morning Lark's teepee calling out, "Morning Lark, please come out and talk to me."

No answer.

Louder he calls out again, "Morning Lark, come out and talk to me."

"She is gone, my son," Red Sun states from behind Gray Bear.

Gray Bear looks in disbelief at his father asking, "She left without saying good bye?" Disbelieving he thinks, "I never thought she would really leave."

"I believe she said goodbye last night," Red Sun replies sadly then adds, "She looked for you this morning but couldn't find you."

Shaking his wet head water cascades down his bare back as he thinks, "She did say goodbye. I just didn't think she'd leave." He answers, "I went to the waterfall and washed the dirt of yesterday off my body. I …uh…thought about my life all last night. I was going to ask Morning Lark to stay awhile and … but she is gone."

Red Sun sees the lost look in his son's eyes so knows he is coming to realize just how much Morning Lark means to him. "He has taken her for granted all his life and now that she has left he realizes what she means to him." So smiling slightly he says, "Well, my son, you will now have plenty of time to find a wife. Soon the younger girls will be ready to take to wife and you will be able to choose one. Morning Lark is sixteen years now…almost an old maid."

"Old maid! She is lovely! Old Maid," Gray Bear stares incredibly at his father and seeing his slight smile nods saying, "I see your wisdom. I had a promise of love with Morning Lark and didn't take it." Laughing for the first time he asks, "They headed north didn't they?"

Nodding yes Red Sun whispers, "Go with God, my son," when Gray Bear jumps on his horse riding off after the travelers to St. Louis.

Morning Lark listlessly rides beside Glory. She doesn't take any interest in anything around her so deep is her sorrow.

Glory keeps a good eye on her talking to her when she can get her attention.

Glory hears the galloping horse before Morning Lark does so she edges her horse over closer to Jake's forcing him to move to the left more which leaves Morning Lark riding by herself. She doesn't notice.

Gray Bear has been riding for an hour so is upset that they have gotten this far so quickly. Then he sees the riders ahead so he slows down some and immediately looks for Morning Lark's horse. Seeing her he takes a deep breath as he rides up beside her.

Hearing a horse coming she turns and watches Gray Bear riding up. Turning to Glory she gives her a big smile as Glory frowns at her slightly shaking her head no.

Immediately remembering Glory's advice she looks forward and doesn't pay Gray Bear any attention when he rides up beside her.

Gray Bear stops his stallion beside hers accusing, "You didn't say goodbye!'

Softly she answers, "I said goodbye last night." Looking straight ahead she ignores him although her heart is beating rapidly.

"I've come to take you home," Gray Bear announces aggressively.

Frowning Morning Lark looks at him replying, "I told you last night that I will be going to my uncle's teepee."

Reaching over to take her reins he is surprised when she moves her horse over so that he can't, angrily saying, "You cannot tell me what to do, Gray Bear, you have no right!"

"I will when you marry me and You WILL marry me," he replies aggressively again.

"You have not asked me to marry you. Now you demand that I marry you. You do not say you love me or even want me. Perhaps my uncle will find a brave, who will love me as well as want me," Morning Lark replies angrily.

Gray Bear successfully grabs her reins stopping their horses requesting, "Let's go over to those trees and talk."

Morning Lark looks over at Glory remembering what Glory had said about Jake's anger at her not obeying.

Glory smiles encouragingly so taking a deep breath Morning Lark nods yes that she will accompany Gray Bear to the treed area.

Glory quietly says, "We will keep riding slowly ahead. If you need us, we will be close."

Suddenly Gray Bear realizes that no one has said a word of greeting and neither has he with his obsession to see Morning Lark. He briefly nods to them still tightly holding the reins to Morning Lark's horse as they ride to the shade in a stand of trees not far away. Reaching it he jumps off his horse and gently lifts Morning Lark down from hers. Thoughtfully he watches this young woman (who holds his heart in her small hands) and he didn't even realize it until this morning. Walking over to a fallen tree he asks, "Will you sit with me?"

Morning Lark nods yes and sits down beside him. She looks inquiringly at him as she waits for him to speak.

"I always thought you'd be my wife. I'd always planned on it. I didn't realize until last night that I have been unfair to you. I gave you no promise and never told you what a treasure you are to me," Gray Bear explains looking at her intently.

"No, you never gave me a promise," she answers sadly.

"I should have! I want you to marry me, Morning Lark, and never leave me," Gray Bear answers simply.

"You want me now?" she questions raising her eye brows disbelieving.

"I always wanted you. I just never realized how much until now," Gray Bear explains rapidly.

"Just want me?" she asks sadly then standing up she walks away from him full of sadness because he won't or can't say he loves her.

Her words echoed in his mind, "Just want me...that's all?" And he knows he has to give her his heart as she already holds his in her tiny hands. So smiling now Gray Bear stands and walking over to her, he gently turns her around requesting, "Look at me."

Slowly she does with a great sadness in her lovely brown eyes.

"Yes, I want you but I love you more than the air I breathe and I don't want to live without you. I want you to be at my side every day I live and I want to take care of you and have little ones with you. You are in my soul and only you can make me happy. I love you, Morning Lark. Will you marry me?" Gray Bear gives her his heart with a shuddering sigh and waits.

Morning Lark's eyes fill with tears then she replies, "I have always loved you, Gray Bear. You have been in my heart since I was small. I would marry you but what if you decide you want another woman like the white girls you stole. Will you then put me to the side and love her?"

Laughing Gray Bear answers, "No, my love, I'll never put you aside for another woman. You are the only one I ever want or will ever want."

Laughing she happily answers, "I will marry you and give you all the joy of my heart then, my handsome brave."

Gray Bear kisses her saying, "Let's go home." He quickly lifts her onto her horse then jumps up on his own and with high spirits they ride back to the travelers.

Glory and Jake can see their happiness flowing through them as Gray Bear states, "Morning Lark will be my wife. She is going home with me. Stop on the way back if you can."

"Long life and good health," Glory blesses them then the newly engaged couple turn back South towards their camp.

"You did a nice thang there Glory. He did love her and didn't realize it," Jake states smiling at his own lovely fiancé.

"Yep, he just didn't realize how much. That is why I asked her to ride with us, hoping it would wake him up and it did." Glory replies smiling happily at him.

Raising an eye brow he jokingly asks, "Guess you think your pretty smart now don'tcha?"

"Yeah, I do!" Glory replies slapping her hat against her horse's rump and takes off at a gallop letting out a whoop of joy. Laughing everyone joins in so soon they make up for the lost time and enjoy the cool morning air as they ride along.

The rest of the ride could have been boring but doesn't turn out to be as Beth Ann talks about St. Louis and all the sights there. Her grandpas (who helped build St. Louis) are impressed by her insights of the city.

None of the other young people have ever been very far from home so listen intently to all the information she gives them.

"Did you know there is a river on the east side of St. Louis called the Mississippi?" Beth Ann asks the young people.

"Nope, don't know nothin' about St. Louie," Jake answers for them all.

"That is an odd name where'd it come from?" Glory questions as she repeats Mississippi.

Smiling Beth Ann explains, "Mississippi is a Chippewa Indian name, misi-ziibi, meaning "Great river" which it truly is. It goes from Canada all the way down to the ocean. It is the largest river in North America. It is very muddy, too, and so wide and rough only big boats can go from shore to shore. Many boats bring supplies in and take supplies out and sadly, many slaves are at the docks at all times of the day and night loading and unloading boats. Slaves are in most of the big homes in St. Louis and work in a lot of stores and shops. You will see a lot of them."

"How do you spell Mississippi?" Carrie Lynn asks puzzled.

Happily Beth Ann explains and spells it for them a couple of times.

"What about the house? What does it look like?" Carrie Lynn wonders out loud.

"Oh, it is grand. Grandmother and ..uhh... Grandfather have... uh...had a big two story house with an attic. It is bright green with white shutters. Grandmother said it was vulgar but grandfather said it stands out for all to see. It is the only home I knew until we left to see papa," Beth Ann answers.

Looking at each other Skinny and Pokey can't help smiling as they remember Lora's letter telling them that Edgar had painted the house a bright green which hurt the eyes, "It is vulgar," she had insisted.

Both had laughed as they looked around the small house they live in with very few luxuries and wondered about their girl. Memories bring up pictures in their minds of riding in and Lora opening the door and welcoming them in with hugs and kisses. Of Lora pouring them drinks from the crystal decanter into crystal goblets. "Things were so important to her. I'm glad she had them," they think as they allow the pleasant sound of Beth Ann's voice to flow over them.

"What did ya do all day?" Glory asks Beth Ann when she has the opportunity.

"Oh, I went to parties three or four times a week usually to tea parties with girls. When the weather was nice, I went on picnics with boys and girls. I had high teas with mother's friends and luncheons and dinners (in the evening) with mother's and grandmother's friends. We were running here and there all the time. When I did have extra time I read books. I attended a private school all morning. Sammy attended school, too. We were there from eight in the morning until noon Monday through Friday. Benny took us in the morning and picked us up at noon. That was part of his job," Beth Ann explains remembering so many unhappy days and hateful remarks she had made and heard.

Carrie Lynn notices the frown and sad look on Beth Ann's face, so covering her hand with hers asks, "Why are you sad?"

Smiling slightly Beth Ann ruefully looks at the others admitting, "I wasn't very nice to many of the other children and they weren't very nice to me. I wasn't asked to dance much, even though I know how, because I was so fat and hateful."

"Will you show me how to dance?" Carrie Lynn begs smiling happily at her adding, "I mean dance like I've heard they do in the big cities."

Beth Ann laughs, happy again, saying, "Certainly, I will. It isn't hard and it can be so romantic when the right boy asks you to dance to swing and sway to the music. To glide over the polished floor and feel the world is a wonderful place to be in, I love to dance. Grandmother used to say if I loved to dance so much I should do it all the time and lose some weight." She laughs and shrugging says, "She was right. But I was too lazy."

"Ya lived in a different world than I have Beth Ann. Ya could teach all of us back home so much. We would like to learn, too," Glory states with admiration shining in her eyes.

Beth Ann laughs again then shuddering dramatically adds, "Does that mean you get to teach me to shoot a deer, gut it, clean it, cut it up then cook it!"

Laughing at Beth Ann's horrified expression Glory laughs with her saying, "Yep, I could do that."

They all laugh at Beth Ann's expression of, "Oh, please not that."

REACHING ST. LOUIE
Chapter 11

"Home changes as the tides change when love no longer lingers."

Within a days ride of St. Louis Skinny states adamantly, "I am not staying at Lora's house. There are too many memories there."

"Why don't we go see Ms. Christina and stay at the Baldinger Hotel," Pokey asks his brother then turning to the young'uns he continues, "I have a part interest in the hotel and it is real nice. Christina makes sure it stays that way."

"That sounds good brother. I shoulda said something sooner but it just kinda built up inside me that I can't stay at Lora's house," Skinny confesses sadly.

"That's okay, Grandpa Skinny. We all know it's hard on ya right now," Glory states giving him a one armed hug from her horse.

They arrive in St. Louis in the late afternoon after a long tiring ride. Everyone is tired, dirty and hungry.

Riding up to the hotel they stop and dismount in front then take their saddle bags and bed rolls off the pack horses, they tiredly walk into the Baldinger Hotel on Dover Street. It is a lovely hotel with velvet covered sofas in small intimate circles scattered about six feet apart in little clusters all around the large lobby. To the right is the check-in desk and it is made of gleaming mahogany. A woman's back is turned to them, hearing them she turns around, then lets out a squeal of joy running around the desk she plants a big kiss on each of the old gent's lined faces.

"Christina it's good to see ya," Pokey says as he kisses the beautiful young woman's cheek.

Her beautiful brown eyes light up in pleasure as she hugs him again saying, "Pokey, it has been too long since you have been back. How are you doing?" Puzzled she notices a sadness about him that wasn't there before and when she glances over at Skinny she sees the same in him.

"Christina these are our grandchildren. Jake and Carrie Lynn Ewing and Beth Ann and Glory Gray," Skinny introduces then says, "Young'uns this is our good friend, Christina Baldinger."

Each say howdy do and Jake tips his hat in greeting.

Smiling slightly Skinny asks, "Can we catch up with each others news after we clean up and eat some of yar fine food, honey?"

"Certainly, you may. I'm sorry. I should have realized you'd be exhausted now. Did you just ride in from the ranch?" Christina asks as she walks back around the desk turning the registration book around for them to sign.

Nodding yes Skinny replies, "Yes, it has been a long trip."

Pokey thoughtfully asks, "Christina, if they are empty, set us up with the Patterson suite for the girls, there are three bedrooms in it. The Masters suite is my favorite and it has three bedrooms in it. Then our cowboys need a single room each so that is four more. We'll be here about a week, honey."

Leaning in Skinny asks, "Don't forget the baths, Christina. The girls will need a lot of hot water for their baths. Jake, we'll go down to the bath house for ours."

"Bathhouse? Humm…never been in one except at your ranch," Jake mumbles wondering what this experience will be like.

Skinny winks at Pokey as they hide a smile at the experience that Jake will be having soon.

Smiling Christina replies, "They are available and ready for guests. You can go right up. I'll send the maids to help the girls. We now have bathing tubs in each room in the suites so I'll send the maids up with hot water so you, girls, can have a good soak before dinner."

Glory and Beth Ann smilingly mumble, "Supper," looking at each other smile at the private joke.

The girls experience a first for them. Walking into the hotel suite they see the beautiful overstuffed furniture in the living room area and three doors opening on the sides and upon entering and looking at each room they see a bed with a beautifully embroidered bedspread and lacy curtains on the windows. Each room has a deep tub in it made of cast iron.

"Glory, you are oldest, which room would you like?" Beth Ann asks curious to see which room she will take.

Glory looks at the rooms – one on one side by itself and two side by side so smiling answers, "I'll take the one on this side so you two can be side by side. I know ya'll be in each other's rooms most of the time anyway so it will be easier for ya."

"Sounds good," Beth Ann answers after looking at Carrie Lynn for confirmation, which she receives in a quick nod.

Entering their chosen bedrooms they drop their dirty bed rolls and saddle bags on the floor and impatiently wait for the maids to bring the hot water for their baths. Glory and Carrie Lynn have never seen indoor plumbing before. The cold water comes out of a faucet into the tub but the hot water has to come from downstairs. Soon there is a knock on the hallway door as the three maids walk in each carrying two buckets of steaming water.

Smiling happily the girls open the doors to their bedrooms and the black maids pour the hot water in then start adding the cold water from the faucet asking, "Is this fine for ya, Missy?" until the water is pleasantly hot.

"I'm sure it will be fine. What is yar name please?" Glory asks curiously.

Smiling brightly the pretty young black girl replies, "Sadie, missy."

Smiling back Glory replies, "Thank ya, Sadie."

"I'ze be right back with some more for yar head washin'," Sadie exclaims to Glory as she turns to leave the room then pauses saying, "I'ze been told to take yar clothes and wash'em and iron'em for ya. Pleaze gives me yar clean dress and I'll get all those nasty wrinkles out of it while ya take yar bath. Now, Missy, I be back in a bit with more hot water for ya. So don't fret yar'self, I will be back."

Amazed at this service Glory gives the young maid the clean dress to press then standing behind the dressing screen she hands her outer clothes to the young girl.

"Missy, I'm a missin' yar drawers and petticoats. Now I knows ya don't wanna wear any dirty ones," Sadie states almost giggling then reaching up she takes them as Glory lays them over the top of the screen.

Glory peeps around the screen, when she hears the door softly shut, blushing brightly to be standing nude in a room with no clothes left in the room. Quickly brushing as much dust and dirt from her hair she looks at the steam rising from the bath tub then giggles as she walks over and slides into the warmth. Looking on a shelf beside the tub she notices a variety of oils and soaps she can use. "I could get used to this," Glory says softly to herself smiling as she ducks under the water wetting her hair then starts shampooing it. Soon the water is a muddy reddish brown and looking down into it Glory shrugs her now clean shoulders feeling much cleaner.

Carrie Lynn watches amazed as the young black maid efficiently fills up the tub with hot water then the cold water swishing it around until it is ready then says, "Missy, it be ready for ya now. If'n ya gives me yar dirty clothes, I'ze get'em washed and ironed for ya. Is this here dress on the bed the one yar gonna wear after yar bathin' time? If'n ya'll give me yar dirty clothes I'll wash'em for ya real good like."

Carrie Lynn stands uncertainly holding her hairbrush in her hand looking at the young girl not much older than herself stammering, "Yyyyeeessss."

"Then I'ze take yar clean dress and iron it right purdy for ya to wear when ya need it," she starts to leave then she turning back says, "I'ze bring ya some more hot water, too, Missy, for the washin' of yar hair. It is right purdy if'n ya don't mind me sayin' so."

Pick up Carrie's dirty clothes as she starts to leave the room Carrie Lynn calls out, "Wait! Thank you and what is your name please?"

Surprised the young black girl curtsies answering, "Bessie, Missy."

"Thank you very much, Bessie. I appreciate it," Carrie Lynn answers sincerely.

"Just doin' my job, missy, and thank ye right back," Bessie replies smiling at the nice young girl.

Beth Ann is sitting at the dressing table in her petticoat brushing as much dust and dirt out of her hair as possible when she hears first Glory then Carrie Lynn talking to their maids. She realizes, "I ignored the maid and just pointed to the tub for the hot water instead of thanking her for carrying it up the flight of steps. Then I said, "I'll need two more. Please get them now." "Why didn't I think of saying thank you and asking her name and being pleasant instead of just acting like I'm a queen or an important person?" Beth Ann is humbled by the knowledge that she still doesn't appreciate all that is given to her. So she sits wistfully watching the hot steamy water cool until the young maid huffs in with the other two required buckets and sets them beside the tub.

Beth Ann smiles pleasantly at her saying, "I'm sorry I rushed you for these buckets of hot water. It was rude of me and I apologize."

The maid's eyes widen at being apologized to so smiles saying, "No problem, Missy, just doin' my job." She curtsies to Beth Ann then continues hopefully, "I'd be right pleased to take yar dirty clothes and wash 'em for ya and if 'n ya gives me yar clean dress I'ze get the wrinkles outta it for ya."

"I would appreciate it very much. I'm sorry ...what is your name please?" Beth Ann asks smiling again.

Startled the young girl cautiously answers with another curtsy, "Etta May, missy."

"Thank you, Etta May, for your kindness and I would greatly appreciate your help," Beth Ann replies as graciously as her mother ever could have.

Etta May backs out of the room stunned at being spoken to so kindly. "Normally people just ignore me and order me around...well, she did at first but she treated me right nice this time," Etta May smiles all the way down the back staircase to the kitchen.

Bessie and Sadie are already there ironing the wrinkles out of the other girl's dresses when Etta May walks in saying, "I cain't believe how nice that young lady is in the Patterson rooms up thar. She talked real nice to me and even asked my name saying, "Thank ya, Etta May."

Bessie and Sadie have been talking about how nice their young ladies are so they explain the same thing happened to them. They finish ironing the girl's dresses then all hum a song as they wash out the girl's dirty clothes and hang them on the clothes line behind the kitchen. It takes some work to get the red dirt out of the clothes so they scrub hard on them.

"Let's take'em some more hot water. They would appreciate it bein' so nice like," Bessie advises and the other two agree so they all pick up another bucket and fill it with hot water before walking back up the stairs to the young ladies' rooms. It is quiet inside so when they walk to the closed door of each girl's rooms they knock on the door.

Glory is half asleep in the tub so blinking she calls out, "Yes?"

Sadie opens the door a little saying, "I'ze brung ya some more hot water, Missy, can I come in?"

Glory looks down into the dirty water blushing but doesn't know what to say, "Huhh...I guess."

Sadie walks right in unmindful of Glory's nudity then looking at the dirty water states, "Let me hep ya with that dirty water." Reaching down into the tub she lifts the plug and the water starts draining. She looks up at Glory's horrified face and puts the stopper right back in. Humbly she says, "I'ze right sorry to upset ya, Missy. I thought ya'd like some clean water to finish the rinsing of yar hair. I'ze sorry," she stands with her head down waiting to be yelled at.

Reaching out Glory lays her hand over Sadie's tight fist softly explaining, "Sadie, I'm sorry. I'm not used to anyone waiting on me. I'm not sure what I'm supposed to do." Then giggling she says, "This is the first time I've ever been in a fancy hotel and I've never had a bath in a tub like this with running water so it's all new to me."

Sadie beams with pleasure saying, "Missy, don'tcha worry about nuthin' I'ze take good care of ya. Do ya want the rest of that ole dirty water out and I'll hep ya wash that purdy hair of yars, if'n ya let me."

"I'd be grateful for any help ya give me, thank ya," Glory answers still blushing slightly at her nakedness.

So quickly Sadie mixes the hot water with the cold water then dips it out and pours it over Glory's hair until the soap and dirt are all gone. Glory thanks her then picking up a towel she quickly wraps it around her body saying, "Ya've been wonderful, Sadie, I do appreciate yar help." She thinks the young maid will leave but she just stands there so Glory states, "Uhhh...I can do the rest."

Glancing down at her feet Sadie asks, "Would ya let me comb that hair of yars? It's so purdy, I'd really like to."

Knowing how tangled her hair is and that it will take a long time to get it tangle free Glory ruefully replies, "It's a real mess. We've been on the trail for weeks so it is pretty bad. I always have a lot of tangles in my hair. It ain't any fun gettin'em out."

Smiling Sadie replies, "I'ze might know somethin' that will hep ya. I'ze be right back."

Carrie Lynn and Beth Ann have similar reactions to the young maid's williness to help. Soon all three girls are clean and sitting at their dressing tables having their long hair combed. The maids are amazed at the colors and textures of the young ladies hair and repeatedly say so.

With freshly ironed dresses and smelling of French soap the girls are ready to face the city, that is, after they eat as they are very hungry. They walk down to the front desk to see if they can find out where their grandpas and Jake are.

THE BATH HOUSE
Chapter 12

"An alluring experience leaves you with welcome memories."

Skinny and Pokey know the routine of a bath house well as they have been here many times. They helped finance this one and the owner, Lee Adams, knows them very well. So when they walk into the Adams Bath House they are warmly welcomed by him.

Lee is a bruiser in size. Large, well muscled and kind, which is one of the reasons Skinny, financed him buying the bath house ten years ago. Lee was one of their cowboys who were injured in a stampede so walks with a limp now. Unable to ride well anymore Lee decided to settle down and run a business. He has done very well.

"Wa'll bust my buttons, it's the bosses: Skinny and Pokey and hello, young fella, hope yar here for a while. He practically breaks the older gent's ribs hugging them hard, before continuing, "It's been way too long since ya'll last entered these doors."

"Just got here and needin' a bath before we can go anywhere. Know ya got the biggest tubs anywhere and young Jake here needs a horse size one, he's so big," Skinny states laughing and slapping Jake on the shoulder.

"Ain't never been in a tub big enough for me," Jake replies smiling impishly at Skinny then adds, "Don't know if'n I'd believe thar is one unless I put my own eyes on it."

Lee likes him at once so answers, "Well, son, here we do have one big enough for a giant. Boss, we now have running water in the bathing rooms, ya ain't gonna believe it. A few months ago a salesman came by saying he could fix it so each bathtub had its own water supply – even hot water – so I said, "You prove that and I'll buy six of 'em. By dingy he did it. So now I have six tubs with hot water in'em. I'll show them to ya. Ya need private rooms?" he wiggles his eye brows at them suggestively.

Jake doesn't understand what this means so when Skinny and Pokey look at him questioningly he replies, "Don't matter to me. What is the cost of these here baths?"

Skinny and Pokey exchanges glances then bite their tongues to keep from smiling before turning to Jake explaining, "Ya can have company with yar bathin' if'n ya want it and this bath is on us."

Jake looks at them with a…what are you talking about look when Skinny wiggles his eye brows at him and Jake understands they mean a woman. He blushes saying, "No, sir, I'm not wantin' that kind of thang atoll. Glory would kill me if'n she knew and it wouldn't be right."

Pokey waves his hands up in the air as if warding him off replying, "Just askin'," so turning to Lee answers, "Just hot baths this time."

Lee leads them to a big room with four bath tubs in it. One big enough for two or even three people and large enough for Jake to take his first totally submerged hot bath in. Jake looks at it then at Lee saying, "I'da never believed there was one big enough for me to get in and outta. This is somethin', much obliged."

Lee grins wolfishly before replying, "It usually holds three."

"Three? Oh," Jake questions then blushes again. "Drat I've got to stop blushing like a girl," he fumes to himself, "Just ain't used to seein' these thangs nor even ahearin' about'em."

Skinny and Pokey can't stop laughing at Jake's incredulous look as he looks at the large tub.

Jake takes it good naturedly saying, "I'll get ya back ya dirty ole men."

"Yep, right now we are both "dirty old men," Pokey snickers and they all laugh at his jest.

They lay their saddle bags with their clean clothes to the side while Lee starts the water running – one tub at a time. He draws half the water for Skinny then Skinny climbs in then Lee pours in more hot water as needed.

"Give me yar clean shirts and I'll have Ginny iron the wrinkles outta them for ya," Lee asks so Pokey hands him his and Skinny's then Jake hands him his.

Jake motions for Lee to do Pokey's tub next while he takes his shirt and boots off just leaving his pants on. Soon Pokey lets out a sigh of pleasure as he also enjoys the warmth of the hot water on his ole body.

Jake watches and is amazed at this new experience as Lee walks over and starts working the faucets on his tub. He asks Lee, "How hard is it to put these pipes in? We are gonna be building a new house real soon and this here be a great new thang to have."

"I can show ya. It takes time but it ain't hard," Lee replies smiling at the handsome young man, then asks, "What'cha doing with these old coots?"

Smiling brightly Jake answers, "I'm marryin' their granddaughter."

"You're marryin' Miss Beth Ann?" Lee asks in astonishment.

Shaking his head no in amazement, Jake laughingly replies, "Naw, her big sister, Glory."

Looking very surprised again Lee turns to Skinny asking, "Ya never said ya had two granddaughters?"

Skinny waves his hand saying, "Later Lee, I'm too tuckered to talk right now." Feeling embarrassment flow through him Skinny realizes they had just given Glory up because they had believed Elizabeth's lies for all those years and poor little thing she'd grown up without any grandpas as he mutters, "I'll fix that mistake." Looking over at Pokey he softly says, "We need to fix that mistake, brother."

Pokey is feeling guilty, too, so answers, "Yep, we do. We did'em a big unkind thang." Then smiling he continues, "They forgave us," he snaps his fingers then continues, "Just like that."

"Yep, they are good people. Didn't hold it against us neither, coulda and I wouldna blamed'em if'n they had," Skinny answers sorrowfully.

Pokey splashes water on Skinny saying, "The past is done but the future looks real good so let's just enjoy it and make it up as good as we can."

"Yep, let's do that. What'cha say about gettin' one of these big tubs for Jake and Glory? It's big enough for two," Skinny suggests with a wink and a grin.

"Yeah, I bet Lee would give us one of these here ones if'n we bought him a new one then Jake could have one to put in their new home real quick. Bet Kevin and Josh could take it down in a wagon and hep them with the buildin', too. They are both real handy," Pokey thoughtfully says, "Yep it could work."

"Think so," Skinny replies leaning back smiling at the pleasure of the hot bath.

"Maybe get Joe and Lizbeth one too. It would be a real nice present to Joe," Pokey slowly suggests as he looks over at Skinny.

A bright smile lights up Skinny's face as he nods yes.

Suddenly the door opens to the bathing room and in walks a beautiful woman very scantily clad. She has very little on...very short skirt...lacy bloomers...and a low necked white blouse falling off the shoulders and she is barefoot. She slowly saunters over to Skinny and Pokey and in a low southern drawl asks, "Ya didn't ask for me? I'm hurtin' beyond redemption, sirahhs."

Smiling the older gents look at her long naked legs then Pokey answers, "Hello, sweet Gay. How are ya, gal?"

"Doin' fine, Pokey, but I'm crushed ya didn't ask for me," Gay answers with a velvety voice as she bends forward and they look down her gapping top to her firm naked breast and behind her Jake gulps at seeing the beautiful fanny through the lacy bloomers.

"Gay, honey, yar's as beautiful as always," Skinny states winking at her wolfishly.

"We brung our grandson with us, Gay, so we are showin' him the ropes," Pokey answers truthfully with his eyes staring at the lovely brunette in front of them.

Gay turns her luminous eyes upon Jake then saunters over to him.

Jake immediately puts his hands over his privates in embarrassment as he looks at the beautiful woman. He gulps then gives her a goofy smile saying, "Afternoon, madam."

Gay sits on the edge of the tub touching Jake's black curly locks with her fingertips as she sulkily asks, "Shorely ya want some company in that water, don'tcha handsome?"

Jake's mouth drops open as he looks over at the two old gents who are smilingly waiting to see what he will do. Warmth fills his eyes as he looks at Gay answering, "Madam, nothing would pleasure me more but I'm a marryin' their granddaughter and she'd skin me if'n I did but I'm much obliged for the offer."

Resigned Gay sadly smiles saying, "Lucky girl," then rising she winks at the old gents then slowly and sexily strolls out of the room.

Jake looks over at the grandpas saying, "Wow, what a woman! I thought my bath water was hot until she walked in."

Both roar with laughter at his statement because they feel the same way. "Maybe a cold bath is what we all need now!" Pokey answers laughing.

Supper that evening in the Baldinger Hotel is something three of the young people wouldn't have believed could ever happen. The men meet the young ladies (who are sitting in the lobby talking with Christina) asking, "Are you hungry?"

All three girls nod yes as Glory replies, "Starvin'!"

"Follow us," Pokey advises as he and Skinny walk over to a door on the left side of the lobby where it opens to a restaurant. They immediately hear glasses clinking and people talking. Standing on her tip toes Glory looks over her grandpa's shoulders peeping in. She sees elegantly dressed women and men in suits. Looking down at her clean but plain dress she realizes they look out of place. She tugs Skinny's arm saying, "We ain't dressed as nice as they are."

Looking at her beautiful young face Skinny smiles answering, "Yar beauty is all you need to look grand, Glory. Don'tcha worry about it, you look fine."

He looks over at Beth Ann and is pleased to see she isn't embarrassed at not having on a silk dress and slippers.

She smiles at him saying, "It smells good, Grandpa."

He hugs her before replying, "You look lovely, Beth Ann."

Blushing slightly she answers, "Thank you, Grandpa. I feel pretty," and she does. She chose one of her nicest dresses that her papa had Miss Ella make for her and she feels pretty even though it isn't a fancy dress.

Glancing over at Carrie Lynn she smilingly says, "This is really nice."

Carrie is awestruck never having eaten in such a fancy place and a little scared so she takes Beth Ann's hand whispering, "I'm afraid I will drop my fork or spill something."

Beth Ann smiles kindly explaining, "If you drop your fork they will bring you another one and if you spill something the waiter will clean it up. That is their job and people do it all the time."

Taking a deep breath she sighs, "Okay."

Glory grabs Jake's hand after she looks inside the restaurant shakily saying, "Jake?"

Pulling her close Jake states, "Head high, yar your mother's daughter, and one who can out fight Indians and outlaws plus you are a beautiful woman. They will be looking at your lovely face most of all."

Squeezing his hand she smiles naturally for the first time.

A man in a black suit seems to sail across the floor to them. He smiles and formally says, "Welcome back, sirs, it is very nice to see you again. Have you brought your family with you? Hello, Miss Beth Ann, it has been a while since we've had the pleasure of your company."

Beth Ann blushes a little then smiling answers, "Thank you very much, Mr. Stephen, it is very nice to be back." Remembering the last time she had been here when the beef steak had been too rare and she had thrown a fit (mainly just to get Mother's attention) and she had given Stephen a hard time. "I was rude and obnoxious to him. I know his job is to be pleasant to everyone no matter how badly they act…I'll have to think of a way to …uh…redeem myself," Beth Ann thinks as Stephen escorts them to a table against the wall.

Stephen has known Skinny and Pokey for years as they helped him start the restaurant and he also knows Pokey never sits in front of a window where some bushwhacker can take a shot at him. Better to be safe than sorry is Pokey's attitude. Stephen glances over at the table next to the one he escorts them to and nods to Skinny's four cowboys sitting there.

Greetings and small talk are made then they turn to their table to sit down.

Beth Ann moves to sit in between Glory and Carrie Lynn. They look at her as she just stands behind her chair. Beth Ann whispers, "Mr. Stephen will seat us."

"Seat us? What's that mean?" Glory whispers back.

"He will pull your chair out and you sit down in it," Beth Ann whispers back.

Carrie Lynn and Glory raise their eye brows at this fancy notion.

Stephen walks to Glory first saying, "May I?" and he pulls her chair out so she gracefully sits down in it then he does the same for the other girls who all graciously say, "Thank you."

Then he hands a menu to each of them. Half of them almost gasp aloud at the prices. Greatly concerned Jake looks at Glory and Carrie Lynn.

Glory whispers urgently, "Grandpa Skinny, these are high prices."

He whispers back, "It won't cost us anything. We own the restaurant." It isn't exactly a lie but not really the truth either as he intends to pay the bill but he does have a part interest in it. Three of the young adults sigh in relief because the prices to them are very high.

"What are ya hungry for? After all the good food you girls cooked for us on the trail it might be kinda hard to pick out somethin' different, might'en it," Pokey asks and teases the young people.

Concerned Carrie Lynn looks over at him saying, "I don't know what a lot of these are. I've never heard of them."

"Beth Ann knows, don'tcha honey, explain to the others," Pokey advises nodding at her.

"I intended to," Beth Ann answers smiling and she begins explaining what the fancy names mean on the food items.

"Why cain't they just say steak instead of those fancy words," Jake mumbles as he listens to Beth Ann explain.

"Ya certainly know a lot about thangs," Glory states with admiration when Beth Ann finishes.

Beth Ann giggles saying, "Remember showing me how to milk a cow, gather eggs and clean out the chicken coop. That was something I knew nothing about. We learn what we are taught and this is what I have learned growing up here."

Chuckling Glory states, "Well…that makes me feel better."

They enjoy steak, mashed potatoes and gravy, green beans with peach pie for dessert. Brought out on platters of silver and plates so delicate it seems they will break to eat off of them. The crystal goblets they drink from are heavy and delicate at the same time. The tea is fragrant with mint and the napkins set at each place are linen.

When they rise to leave Jake asks Glory, "Let's ask the grandpas to eat somewhere else next time. I was too nervous I'd break somethang to enjoy the food."

Breathing a sigh of relief Glory replies, "Me, too."

Pokey and Skinny did notice the panicked looks on the young people's faces as they watched Beth Ann like a hawk and did exactly what she did. So Skinny pulls Pokey to the side saying, "Let's take'em somewhere else next time. They were scared stiff they'd do something wrong and embarrass us. No need for that."

Pokey nods yes agreeing, "They got good manners, didn't embarrass me none."

Smiling Skinny nods yes the same for him.

It is dark outside when they walk back into the lobby of the hotel and they are all tired. Pokey looks at Skinny saying, "We'd better go see Marshal Wheeler and tell him about the deaths."

"Yep, let's do it now," Skinny agrees, "Then we will sleep better."

Pokey tells his cowboys they'll be at the Marshal's office for a while so they follow them over there then Bradford stays outside smoking while the old gents go inside to talk to the Marshal.

Marshal Garth Wheeler is a quiet man. He doesn't say much so when he does you listen, rather like Pokey. Garth rises from his desk and walks across the floor shaking hands with each of them then pounds Pokey on the back saying, "Ready to come back to work, old fella."

"Nope, gave it up a long time ago but thanks for the askin'," Pokey replies smiling at the good looking man.

Garth is all muscle and a fast draw with a gun. He is an even tempered man even though he is known to yell on occasion. Almost six feet tall with sandy brown hair and blue eyes he has made many a maid's heart flutter. Nearly forty years old he has been happily married for many years.

"Good to see ya. How have ya'll been?" Marshal Garth asks pleasantly.

Troubled Pokey answers, "Not good, son. Lora was killed down south by the ranch along with Edgar and Franklin Potter."

Reaching out he lays his callused hand over Pokey's saying, "Sorry, man. I'm so sorry," he looks over at Skinny asking, "How are you two holdin' up?"

"Pretty good. Pretty good," Skinny replies smiling sadly.

"What happened?" Garth inquires.

Pokey looks at him through his watery blue eyes as he asks, "Ya want the truth or what we want people to hear?"

Leaning back Garth replies, "Oh, it's that way, huh?"

"Yep, ain't good," Skinny answers sadly.

"Well give me the truth, then tell me what ya want people to know," Garth advises compassionately.

Skinny starts with, "I'll start the tale. First off we found out that Elizabeth was stolen from a woman named Nona James when she was about two years old. Edgar stole her from a wagon train that was a passin' by St. Louie."

"There are a lot of wagon trains go through here," Garth states surprised.

"We weren't on talkin' terms with 'em for about five years cause we weren't happy with the way Edgar was doin' and treatin' Lora," Pokey adds sadly, "So when Lora wrote saying she'd had a baby we were thrilled and it seemed to break the hard feelin's some and we came right up. It seemed like Edgar was doin' better so we had high hopes of 'em bein' happy. He was buyin' the store and Lora loved that big ole house so there was debt but it was to us. We didn't know he was a borrowin' a lot from Franklin Potter until recently."

"Truth be told, it seems that Franklin Potter was set up to marry Elizabeth when she turned sixteen. Edgar was allow'in it to pay him back all the money he owed him. Then Elizabeth met Joe and fell in love with him so that ruined their plans. Then she upped and married Joe and they moved down South. Joe has a big ranch down there called the Rocking J. Lora and Edgar never gave up on gettin' Elizabeth back so when she complained that she was tired of cookin' and cleanin' they sent her the money to come back here, which the spoiled girl did. Joe had too much pride to come get her and make her go back home so they just let it ride," Skinny explains then looks at Pokey to continue.

"Then Potter decides he wants Elizabeth to marry him like he'd always planned but she can't marry him without a divorce or Joe's death. So Elizabeth wrote and asked Joe for a divorce and he said come down here and git it here. So she went down South except Joe had no thought to really divorce her since he still loves her. She realized she loves him, too, so they got back together," Pokey explains in detail.

Frowning Garth states, "I'da whopped her fanny good for leavin'."

Laughing Pokey replies, "Oh, Joe did that. Poor girl couldn't sit down for a long time."

Nodding yes Garth replies, "Rightly so."

"Elizabeth wrote her parents saying she wasn't comin' back so they decided they'd go get her and bring her and the children back. If Joe wouldn't give her the divorce, quiet like, then they'd fix it so he had an accident and be dead," Skinny explains with a sigh.

"I see," shaking his head he understands Garth states looking sadly at the old gents.

"They tried to kidnap Elizabeth but kidnapped Glory instead," Pokey continues explaining.

"Wait, who is Glory?" Garth inquires confused.

"Glory is Elizabeth's oldest girl that she left with Joe when she ran away," Skinny explains.

"She left a little girl and didn't go back and get her?" Garth asks astounded.

"Yep, she did," Pokey answers sadly.

"I hope he whooped her real hard," Garth states frowning heavily.

"Oh, he did. The men grabbed her at the house and took her about ten miles away where they were camped and waited for Joe to ride in and rescue her then they'd kill him. But we were too smart for that so we snuck up on'em," Pokey exclaims proudly.

"Ole Potter and Edgar got drunk as skunks. Never had the nerve to do anything without liquor and decided that Glory would be a good one to take advantage of," Skinny frowns in anger remembering seeing it happen all over again in his memory.

"They tried to...uh...take advantage of your granddaughter Glory?" Garth asks amazed.

"Yep, they were gonna and Lora tried to stop'em and they killed her for it. Edgar hit her a few times then kicked her in the head and that is what killed her. I hope she didn't realize how far they would go. She told Glory she didn't know they could be so crazy. Anyway when they tried to take Glory, she fought back, and first chance we had we took'em out.

We killed Franklin Potter and Edgar Hawkins," Skinny states sadly but still angrily.

"The girl is all right?" Garth asks concerned.

"Yep, they didn't harm her. We buried the varmints down there and took Lora to Elizabeth's and Joe's home and buried her thar," Pokey explains sadly.

"I'm real sorry to hear this sad tale. I know it was hard on you tellin' it. Cain't say I'm upset at losing Hawkins or Potter. I'm sorry, but they weren't worth the effort to even spit on'em," Garth replies truthfully then continues, "I'm real sorry about Mrs. Lora. She was a nice lady. She was always polite to me. Elizabeth, well truthfully, I hope she learned her lesson. How are Beth Ann and little Samuel doing?"

"Radiant with love from their father, never seen a turnaround in young'uns in my life. Sammy is a happy little boy now and Beth Ann, well, you won't believe it when you see her. Joe showin' her love has taken the meanness and hatefulness right outta her. She is as sweet a child as I've ever seen. She insisted on comin' back and helpin' us take care of unfinished business," Skinny explains smiling again.

"We'd like for ya just to say that they were killed on the way home and not tell our business to everyone around," Pokey states frankly.

"Done, it ain't nobodys business but yours," Garth answers nodding his head yes sadly smiling at the two older gents he respects.

"We got some papers to go over with ya tomorra. If'n ya don't mind, we are pretty well tired out tonight so we'd like to git to bed," Skinny states rising.

"Sounds good to me," Garth answers then walking to the door opens it and looking out he sees Bradford sitting there so asks, "Hey Brad, life treatin' ya good?"

"Nothin' to complain about Marshal," Brad answers smiling then standing up looks around some more before saying, "It's clear as I can see."

Skinny and Pokey walk sadly back to the hotel but are glad to have that piece of foul business done with. "I don't wanna talk about this anymore, brother, it's too hard," Skinny admits to his brother.

"Yep, it has taken a lot outta me lately," Pokey answers truthfully then turning to Brad says, "Thanks for stayin' Brad. Go ahead enjoy the evening. We're gonna go to bed."

When they reach their rooms there is a note from Beth Ann asking them to come down to the Patterson suite so they walk to the suite next to theirs.

Beth Ann opens the door at the first knock asking, "I hate to ask but grandpas we only brought two changes of clothes. When we go to the store tomorrow may we get an extra set so we don't have to wash our clothes every day?"

"Hummm…she didn't ask for fancier clothes and just one set not three or four… interesting," Skinny realizes then putting his arm around her shoulders answers, "Beth Ann, do you realize that everything in the store and your grandparent's house belongs to your family now."

"Oh, no, I didn't realize that," Beth Ann replies frowning, "But it was yours…"

"It was ours at one time but as I told yar ma and pa, Edgar paid us back all the money he owed us so it all belongs to ya'll now," Skinny replies kindly.

"But I…uh…don't know how to feel now," Beth Ann looks beseechingly at her grandpas before continuing, "I mean before I took it for granted that I was entitled to it but now….are we?"

"Yes, honey, ya are. Edgar and Lora loved ya very much and ya were their grandchild as much as any young'un could be. They would want ya to have it," Pokey answers as he kisses her forehead.

Looking down as a tear slips down her cheek Beth Ann replies, "I do miss them. Especially Grandmother…she did love me…I know she did. She spoiled me a lot, too. Grandfather…he always treated me nice. He yelled at us all a lot. He … never did anything to make me think otherwise."

"That's good child," Skinny replies as he also hugs this precious little girl thinking "So young and innocent of any of the deceptions that have been played on her."

"What will I tell people when they ask about Mother and how will I explain about Papa being alive when Mother said she was a widow?" Beth Ann asks bewildered then explains, "Papa made me promise not to lie anymore. What do I say when they ask me?"

"Come in here and let's discuss this with everyone," Pokey requests.

Jake, Glory and Carrie are in the sitting room of the Patterson suite so when the other three walk in Pokey says, "Beth Ann's reminded us we need to know what to tell people here about everything that happened back home."

Skinny walks over and sits down in a chair then leaning forward taps his fingers together asking, "Beth Ann says Elizabeth told everyone she was a widow. Now we all know this ain't true so what will we tell people?"

Pokey thinks a minute before saying, "She ain't a widow, never was one. Don't know how to explain this."

"Uhhhh...Mother didn't tell many people about Glory either," Beth Ann admits sadly looking at her lovely sister.

"So we come in telling everyone that Elizabeth is not a widow and has a daughter older than the daughter they know...Beth Ann," Skinny thoughtfully admits.

"So people will want to know where she is, how come she's still married and how come she didn't talk about me," Glory repeats thoughtfully.

"I'm sorry, I should have asked Mother about this before we left, but I just didn't think about it until now," Beth Ann admits.

"It is not on your shoulders, Beth Ann, it's on your mother's," Skinny states frowning then smiling says, "Truthfully I don't think Elizabeth will care what we tell people here. She doesn't plan on coming back. We are closing the store and the house when we leave. So we could give the gossips a lot more to gossip about than Edgar and Lora's deaths."

Jake looks at Beth Ann sad face before replying, "But Beth Ann might want to come back some day when she is grown and is a lady. We don't wanna do anything to make that difficult for her."

Looking up at Jake, Beth Ann smiles (at her soon-to-be brother) answering, "Thank you for thinking about me, Jake. I might come back some day. I don't know what the future will be. I've always liked St. Louis; of course, it was the only home I knew until recently."

"So we just tell the truth and say Elizabeth and Joe decided to live separate lives for eight years but are back together again. Glory stayed with her pa and Beth Ann and Sammy stayed with their ma. That is the truth and all they need to know. We can say Elizabeth was upset about it so just told a little lie about Joe being dead, laugh it off as a vanity of hers," Carrie Lynn answers the question nodding as she considers it.

Smiling Beth Ann states, "That is the truth and we won't be lying. I can do that. People will believe it, too."

Skinny answers, "We can truthfully say that Lora and Edgar died while on the way back to St. Louie. Then just say we can't talk about it. It ain't like it is anyone's business anyway."

"But if they say how did they die? What do we say?" Jake questions.

"Let's just say an accident while they were camping out. It not exactly the truth but I don't think Grandfather would have killed Grandmother if he hadn't been drunk," Beth Ann states sighing softly.

Looking at each other they agree they will tell this story. Now mentally exhausted they all stand up ready to go to bed for tomorrow is going to be a busy day.

THE HAWKIN'S MERCANTILE
Chapter 13

"An excess can be shared for the good of all."

Early the next morning, they eat breakfast at a café not far from the hotel then walk a block to the Hawkin's Mercantile.

Smiling as they walk in Beth Ann remembers all the times she had run into the store and her grandfather had given her whatever she asked for. Her grandmother and mother had brought her here weekly for material, thread, candy and the latest patterns.

She smiles when they walk in as she sees the young man who runs the store for her grandfather when he is out of town. She calls out, "Hello, Randy." Then seeing the shelf stocker in the back she calls out to him, "Hello Chris."

Walking over to greet her, Randy Ford smiles saying, "It is good to see you, Miss Beth Ann. Did your grandfather and grandmother make the trip back okay?"

Walking up from the back of the store Chris joins them saying, "Welcome back home, Miss Beth Ann."

Beth Ann introduces Chris Ball and Randy Ford to everyone before turning back sadly explaining, "No, they were killed on the way back, Randy."

"What about your mother?" Randy asks looking around for her.

"She decided to stay down South and Samuel stayed with her," Beth Ann explains then continues, "Do you remember my grandfathers? They have brought us back to close the store and house."

Both young men look at each other in dismay then Randy repeats, "Close the store? We made good money? Everything I've sold are at Mr. Hawkin's prices. I haven't lost any money while Mr. Hawkins was away. I've done the best I can."

Stepping up Skinny replies, "I'm sure ya have Mr. Ford, it's just that no one will be living here now. Elizabeth and the young'uns will be staying down South so there ain't any need to keep the store open."

"Oh," Randy softly says looking down at his feet thinking, "What will I do now?"

"Mr. Ford...," Skinny starts when Randy smiles saying, "All my friends call me Randy...hey, Beth Ann?"

Nodding yes Beth Ann replies, "Yes, grandpa, Randy is one who was always kind to me even when I wasn't so kind to him. He has been my friend for a long time."

Randy's beautiful blue eyes light up happily as he smiles at Beth Ann saying, "You are an angel compared to my little sister. Now she is a tyrant!"

"Catherine is a peach. I've always liked her. She is beautiful and she has a good heart," Beth Ann states chuckling happily.

"No, you have a good heart but so far Catherine is heartless but hopefully she will grow up one of these days," Randy replies frowning as he looks at Chris standing to the side of them.

Smiling Chris answers, "I'll wait for her to grow up, Randy. She is only sixteen so she still has time."

Jake cockily walks over to Chris saying, "Maybe you and me otta have a little talk about women."

Smiling Chris nods yes so they walk towards the back of the store talking and chuckling then Chris states, "No! You didn't do that! What'd she do?"

Glory inelegantly snorts saying, "Telling tales on me, I bet!"

They all smile at her as she stomps away. Looking around Pokey states, "Too many memories here, Randy. We don't plan on comin' back too often anymore. Pokey and I are gettin' old and tired. If'n ya want to buy the store then we might be able to work out a deal but we don't want the handlin' of it anymore."

"No, sir, I'm not really interested in running the store. I've been talking to Mrs. Christina about working for her. She has a really nice hotel and she has told me she needs help at the front desk. I'm getting married soon and I need to have a job I can count on. I appreciate the offer but, no sir; this is not the job I want to do the rest of my life. I'm sorry to say, Mr. Hawkins wasn't a fair man. He did a lot of things that I have had a hard time stomaching and I was going to tell him when he returned that I was leaving," Randy explains.

"We understand that, Randy. We will pay you the wages yar owed and would appreciate if you would help us clean out the store," Skinny replies shaking his hand.

"I'd be happy to," Randy answers smiling at them, then he stops and sadly states, "Uh…oh, dear, there are a lot of people who owe money to the store. The credit line Mr. Hawkins had is a bit steep but there are a lot of poor people out there that can only get by on credit."

"We'd appreciate all the help you can give us, son," Pokey states understanding it will be bad.

"Beth Ann come to the back and help us with the books please," Skinny asks so she follows them into the back office where Randy picks up the ledgers laying them on the desk in the small cramped room.

Randy explains, "I don't normally do the ledgers, just when Mr. Hawkins is gone, so I only know the last couple of months worth of entries. He…uh…well… it is all listed here for you." He looks sadly at Beth Ann.

"He is definitely uncomfortable," Beth Ann thinks as she listens to him talk and seeing his hesitation.

Skinny takes the ledgers, opens one and starts reading it with Pokey looking over his shoulder. Pokey frowns as Skinny flips back page after page glancing down at each thoughtfully then looks over at Randy, who stands with uncertainty on his young face. When Skinny pages back to where the writing is different – stiff and scratchy and not nearly as neat he looks closely at the entries. Leaning back he looks at Randy stating, "Looks like Edgar was gouging some of his customer especially the ones who didn't come in often."

"Yes, sir. He did. They were usually the poorer ones who couldn't afford much in the first place. He'd tell them one price then write down a higher price after they left. I've worried about it," Randy admits.

Looking at Beth Ann Skinny asks, "Beth Ann, do you want a job? This list needs to be gone over and any grossly over charging noted on it. See what you think and let me know." Disapproval is written all over his face as he stand up then turning to Randy he asks, "Will you help her?"

"Oh, yes sir, I'd be delighted," Randy answers smiling over at Beth Ann.

Skinny slaps him on the shoulder saying, "I believe you know the candy Beth Ann is most fond of. Why don'tcha get you two a bowl of it to snack on.

Smiling he answers, "Thanks," and walks back into the store to get the candy.

"That was nice of you, Grandpa," Beth Ann answers smiling at him.

Skinny walks over to her seriously saying, "I did it for a reason. Beth Ann, Edgar has been cheating a lot of people. This ledger proves it. The money is your families but I don't think yar Pa or Ma for that matter would want money taken this way. It is up to you but any amounts you think are overcharged mark them out. Work from yar heart, honey." He and Pokey leave the room shaking their heads at Edgar's greed.

Walking around to the back of the desk Beth Ann sits and starts reading the pages. She notices immediately that some of the figures are added incorrectly and always in the store's favor. Frowning she picks up a pencil and starts correcting the mistakes. She pulls some paper out of a drawer and starts writing names and figures down. When Randy returns she looks at him in despair asking, "Oh, Randy, how could he?"

Solemnly Randy looks down shaking his head no before answering, "Because he could. He wasn't a fair man."

"Please help me make it right," Beth Ann begs as a tear rolls down her red face.

"That I can do, let's start here where they paid the last time," Randy replies then adds, "You look like a hundred dollars, girl, what did you do to lose so much weight?"

Smiling brightly Beth Ann looks up saying, "I worked! My papa made me do chores and watch my eating. Oh, Randy, I do wish you could meet my papa. He is the most wonderful man in the world."

"I can see he is good to you and I'm very happy for you. You deserve it," Randy replies sincerely.

"Thanks, Randy," Beth Ann answers humbly.

They work an hour on the books so soon Beth Ann and Randy have a list of charges much less than the ones Edgar had entered.

Randy explains to her about the people she doesn't know and how poor some of them are and that helps a lot.

Beth Ann sadly hands the list to Skinny when they are finished saying, "I believe this is correct now, Grandpa."

Skinny looks at Randy asking, "Son, I need you to see what you can collect from these people. If'n they don't have it don't press them, we don't wanna cause anyone any difficulties. Tell'em they have thirty days to pay it all up. Don't threaten'em and don't scare'em just tell'em the facts. Can you do this?"

"Yes, sir, I can," Randy states positively.

"Go to it then," Skinny replies nodding sadly as Randy leaves the store with the list.

While Beth Ann and Randy worked on the books, the rest of the young'uns have been looking through the store seeing what is here. The country kids are amazed and mystified at some of the items but admit it is a thrilling experience.

Carrie Lynn can't keep from staring at the silver brush, comb and mirror sets all boxed up with a red bow on them. She smiles as she strokes the silver handle wonderingly. Pokey notices she walks around looking at everything but always comes back to admire these sets.

Jake's interest is in the hats and boots picking up one then another and trying them on. Glory looks at everything amazed and impressed with all this stores holds. They all look at the large candy jars full of all kinds of candy wondering what some of them taste like thinking "That looks good…ohhh that one looks good, too."

Walking out of the office Beth Ann's shoulders are slumped as she thinks, "How could grandfather have cheated people like that? He cheated the poorest ones the most. The ones who needed help the most he cheated the most. Why would he do it? Where was his heart?" Sadness overwhelms her as she realizes it wasn't too long ago she wouldn't have cared about any of this – her only consideration was where it concerned her own welfare. How can we make it right? *"Dear Lord, what can we do to make it right?"* she prays as tears run down her sad face.

Glancing up Glory sees her troubled face so walking over asks, "Bethy, what's wrong?"

With tears running down her face she explains, "Grandfather cheated many people, Glory. The ones who needed help the most he cheated the most. I feel so bad about it."

"Then we will find a way to fix it. That is what Papa would do. So what can we do to make up to those people who need it?" Glory asks decidedly.

Looking at her sister in awe Beth Ann sputters, "I'm not sure but.." then smiling happily again she states, "We will figure it out. The two of us can figure it out, can't we?"

"Certainly, we are Nona's granddaughters, after all," Glory replies hugging her caring younger sister.

"Yes, we are," Beth Ann smiles still amazed at this fact.

"Let's pray about it and let God tell us what to do. *Dear Lord, we want to make up for the bad things grandfather did. But we don't know how, please hep us to hep those people. Amen,*" Glory prays then hugs Beth Ann again as they join the others.

Beth Ann and Glory approach Pokey as Glory says, "Grandpa we are feelin' real bad about Grandfather Edgar cheatin' people, we prayed and asked God to hep us find a way to hep'em. Is this okay with ya'll?"

"Shorely is. I'm proud of ya for havin' such a good hearts," Pokey replies kissing each girl's forehead, "Now we gotta get busy. How about we move some stuff around and set up a place for each of you to put thangs to take home with ya'll."

Frowning Jake asks, "Each of us?"

"Yep, yar family, too, so bring those trunks stacked in the corner over here and set up one for Joe, Zak, Minnie and Benny, Good Heart, Nona and Glory and Jake's house. Ya'll decide what ya want to put in'em and wrap it up good so it don't get broke." He crosses his arms across his skinny chest then looking at them Pokey continues, "Wa'll let's get busy."

"But sir…we cain't," Jake starts to say when Skinny lays his hand on Jake's shoulder saying, "Let it be, Jake, this is the way it's gonna be."

"I..uh…I don't know what to say," Jake replies helplessly.

"Say thanks and get to work," Skinny states smiling at him as he slaps him on the back and pushes him towards the trunks.

"Thanks," Jake readily repeats frowning as he looks intently at them. He nods then turning around starts picking up the trunks as he was asked to do. They scoot merchandise around until a space is cleared then Pokey requests, "Beth Ann, put a name on each trunk so we don't get'em mixed up, honey." Happily she does so.

"First thing first! I want some candy! How about ya'll? Girls, why don'tcha divide it between your homes and git me some lickerish and Pokey some of those peppermints sticks. I see thar are some tins on the shelf over that – use'em to put it all in. You can just set it on the counter and eat what you want while we work," Skinny advises then chuckles watching all their eyes light up happily.

All the young'uns say, "Thanks a bunch."

"I have been advised that ya'll are needin' more clothes to wear while in St. Louis. So, girls, go get the clothes you want to wear and put'em together in a stack and we'll send one of my boys down to the hotel with'em," Skinny advises firmly.

"Grandpas, I have a lot of clothes at the house," Beth Ann states smiling slightly.

"Are they all fancy clothes or everyday clothes?" Pokey asks knowing the answer.

"Oh, mostly fancy clothes," Beth Ann answers blushing.

Wiggling his eyebrows Pokey says, "Get you some every day clothes then, girl. Yar gonna need'em. Git!"

"Yes, Sir!" Beth Ann replies laughing as she runs to the rack of store bought dresses.

"That girl sure is one to be fair, now ain't she?" Skinny states smiling and liking the way Beth Ann has grown up in the last couple of months.

"Yep, right proud of her," Pokey replies slapping his brother on the back.

"Jake, come with me. We's gonna look at some other thangs and hav'em ready to pack next," Pokey states then with his bow legged and stiff walk marches over to the mens area of the store, "I figure you know more about hats, boots, belts and stuff than the girls do. First thang is pick out three sets of clothes for yarself so ya got some extra clothes to wear while we are here then get some for Joe, yar pa, grandpa and brother, Benny and Arty and what you think Good Heart and sons would wear. I know ya'll be fair so this is your job. Now man afore ya start arguin' with me about anythang anymore – don't… just do as I ask you. Yar tirin' me out!" He stomps off (as if mad) but winks at Skinny when he passes him.

Jake shuts his open mouth as he watches Pokey leave then turning he looks at all the clothes then smiles and gives a full belly laugh calling back to Pokey, "Yes, sir!" Jake picks up a stack at a time and separates them as best he can. He starts with the pants then shirts then boots and lastly hats. When he has his stacks full there are still a number of clothes that won't fit any of them back home so smiling again he pulls them out making two more stacks that will fit Skinny and Pokey. "Old codgers don't know what I can do when I sets my mind to it," Jake mutters with a chuckle. Walking back to the trunks again he picks up another one and carries it up front then writes OLD CODGERS on it before setting the clothes beside it. When it is not even half full of clothes for them Jake still has a lot of pants and shirts left over so he begins filling another trunk with clothing and hats for Skinny and Pokey's cowboy sons.

All the girls easily find three dresses each with new underwear to wear under them. Then they sort the readymade clothes to take home. They pick out a pink dress for Stephie, a blue one for young Payton, a lovely aqua blue for Elizabeth and a soft violet for Grandma Nona.

"There's not any for pregnant ladies ready made. Why don't we just choose some material for Minnie and Yellow Moon?" Glory advises and the other two girls agree.

The girls wrap up their clothes to wear in St. Louis and young Kevin (one of the younger cowboy guards) gladly carries them back to the Baldinger Hotel.

"Uh, Mrs. Christina, would ya mind keepin' an eye on these packages of clothes for the young ladies and Jake. Pokey asks if'n ya wouldn't mind could ya hav'em ironed for the young ladies. Their names are written on the paper here which ones are theirs," Kevin asks blushing to be talking to the lovely lady.

"Certainly, thank you so much for bringing them to me. I appreciate it," Christina replies sincerely. She calls the young maids and they take the packages and immediately start ironing the young ladies new dresses.

With the last job completed Skinny and Pokey look at the young people as Skinny advises, "Next get busy filling up these trunks with breakables. Girls go to the material and divide it up between yar houses and pack the breakables in it. That is the next thang to do."

Thrilled the girls quickly walk to the bolts of material. First they look at the bolts of material and fairly divide them then they pick out matching thread for each bolt and chose the buttons they guess will work best.

Carrie Lynn blinks rapidly in amazement as their stash grows larger and larger. The material they choose for Minnie's family are all bright colors but they do add some dark colors for pants. A bolt of soft cotton material is added for diapers for the babies as well as a good supply for Elizabeth's and Glory's, when she has some.

"I know I'll be needin' some in the future, just hope it ain't for a while," Glory states giggling to her sisters of the heart.

The girls pick up a stack at a time and carry it to the trunks then set it beside the carefully labeled trunks. Carrie Lynn gasps when she sees three beautiful silver hair brush sets with red ribbons on them setting by her trunk. Each set has different designs on them. She looks up at Pokey, (who is standing close by) stuttering, "I can have one of these?" tears start running down her cheeks because she really does want the lovely comb, brush and mirror set.

"You betcha. Every girl needs a pretty hair brush and mirror," Pokey replies firmly.

Jumping up Carrie Lynn runs over to him grabbing him and kissing his cheek three or four times.

Laughing Skinny says, "Don't forget me."

So she runs over to him and kisses him also. They both hug her and she can't help going back and kneeling down to sit looking at the beautiful silver hair brush, mirror and comb, which is in each set. "I'll save this to open until we get home, I don't want to take a chance on breaking it," Carrie Lynn explains happily to the grandpas.

Thoughtfully Glory stands in front of some expensive items looking at them when Skinny walks over and looks at them with her. Hesitantly she says, "I'd really like to have one of them mantle clocks. It would look really nice in our new home. We have one at home that was my grandma Grays and it is fine lookin'."

"Well tell Jake which one ya want then wrap it up good and put it in yar trunk," Skinny states positively.

Smiling Glory calls over to Beth Ann, "Bethy, come here a minute, please."

Happily Beth Ann walks over as Glory points out the mantle clocks on the shelf saying, "I'd like to have one for me and Jake for our new house is that okay with ya?"

"Sure," Beth Ann answers sincerely then walking closer she looks at the other clocks on the shelf and turning thoughtfully says, "Wouldn't this one look nice on Minnie and Benny's mantle." She fingers an oak clock with gold filigree trimming on it.

"Oh, Beth Ann, that would be wonderful. There are four clocks let's put one in Minnie and Benny's trunk, one in mine, one in ma and pa's for you to have later and one for our grandpa's. They don't have no clocks in their house. We'll surprise'em," Glory whispers to her.

Beth Ann's eyes light up happily as she nods yes. So they quickly reach up and pick up each clock then wrapping them very carefully set them inside the trunks.

Walking over to Glory and Beth Ann, Carrie Lynn asks, "There are two sets of silverware over here. A set for twelve and one for eight, which trunk do you want them in?"

Thoughtfully Glory and Beth Ann look at each other than smiling Glory asks, "One for Beth Ann and one for me?"

Shaking her head no Beth Ann replies, "Grandmother has three really nice silver sets at the house. Let's send Minnie and Benny the set for twelve and one for eight can go to your house, Carrie Lynn. So you will have a nice set for your hope chest."

"Oh, thank you!" Carrie Lynn says and quickly does as she is asked.

They look at the sets of dishes next and there are some very pretty ones. Glory asks Beth Ann again, "What should we do?"

Beth Ann replies, "Mother wants the nicest set, which is at the house. There are two other sets of twelve at the house that are really pretty. Why don't we give Carrie the pretty set of eight and send Minnie and Benny the other set, it has little blue flowers all over it and Minnie would love that."

"Sounds good. Carrie Lynn is working hard at helping us. She deserves to have some nice thangs. That set of tin ones would do good for our grandpa's house. They prefer them to the breakable ones," Glory states giggling.

In the store room where Jake is working, he finds some crates that have him very curious. Walking to the doorway he calls out, "Girls come back here a minute."

Quickly all three girls walk back there and see a large crate. Jake is in the process of opening it then they see it is full of dishes and silverware for a restaurant.

"I wonder who these belong to?" Jake asks the girls.

"I'll put a note on this crate that says dishes. Randy should know who they belong to," Beth Ann advises and does so.

When Jake opens another crate he lets out a cry of joy for inside are the prettiest lamps he has ever seen. The shade on the lamp has ten little crystals handing down from it. Gently he picks it up and setting it aside starts digging deeper and finds another one just like it. Digging deeper he finds three more just like the others except all five have different irridescent colors with the sparkling crystals hanging from the globes.

"Oh, my, oh my, these are beautiful," Beth Ann exclaims watching the crystals reflect off of the light that is coming in the back door.

Looking at each other they say, "Ma and Stephie," at the same time.

Looking at the beautiful lamps Glory says, "Well these have to come home with us. What color would Stephie like best...ya'll know I gotta keep in good with my future mama?"

"The pink one!" Jake and Carrie Lynn reply at the same time.

"One for Mother. What color Beth Ann?" Glory asks and Beth Ann cocks her head to the side replying, "You chose. Let it be your surprise."

Glory looks at the blue, green, orange and yellow lamps left saying, "Green like Papa's eyes."

"What color for your house, Glory and Jake?" Beth Ann asks hiding a smile.

"Ya mean it?" Glory asks happily looking at the beautiful lamps then turning to Jake asks, "Which one, honey?"

"I like the blue one," Jake replies with sparkling eyes.

Glory hugs him saying, "Blue is my choice, too. See how well we agree!"

Skinny and Pokey are talking to Randy in the front of the store and warding off customers who are coming in and asking questions about all that is going on in the store. Everyone is curious about what has happened so they give them all the same story. The young people don't realize this is one of the reasons they have been shooed to the store room is that so many people are nosily asking questions (which are none of their business). So Pokey and Skinny had requested Jake go back to the store room knowing he will find things and ask the girls to come back there to help him.

Hearing Randy's voice Glory walks out of the store room asking him, "Randy are the lamps with the crystals on them for anyone special?" Hoping desperately they aren't.

Shaking his head no Randy explains, "No, Miss Gloria. We just received them in yesterday. I ordered those and hoped to sell them before Mr. Hawkins returned. I know they will sell fast as they are so pretty."

Glory jumps up and down clapping her hands replying, "Oh, I'm so glad! They are so pretty. Oh, Randy there is a big crate of dishes back thar. Are they for a restaurant here?"

"They were ordered for a restaurant then it burnt down and the people left town without paying for them so we have been trying to resell them. They have a pretty design on them," Randy explains ruefully.

Looking at her grandpas Glory states, "Well, we know just where they are going!" Giggling happily she walks back to tell the others that Grandma Nona has new dishes for her café.

Everyone smiles happily at the surprise Nona will be getting with the dishes when they open another crate full of large cast iron pots and pans. They label them for Grandma Nona also.

"Sir, Mr. Hawkins planned to surprise Miss Beth Ann on her birthday with the little piano in the store room. It is one of those small ones that can be put into a bedroom. Miss Beth Ann plays beautifully," Randy explains in a low voice.

"Then we will be sure it is taken with us. Thank you, Randy. We really appreciate all yar doin' to help us," Skinny says slapping his back heartily.

After Randy walks away, Pokey exclaims, "Cain't forget Glory, brother. What can she get? She will be sixteen soon."

"Joe asked me to get all the new jewelry here and bring it back to him so that on special occasions he can give the girls somethangs so that can be Glory's special gift," Skinny advises thoughtfully.

"That be nice but ...we need somethin' else...somethin' special like," Pokey replies thinking hard about it.

"How about that stallion back at the ranch? It already loves Jake," Skinny states suddenly.

"Then we can give it to him for a weddin' present. Glory's got her own horse already. She won't want another horse unless it was to breed with the stallions," Pokey's eyes light up as he continues, "What about that pretty filly that was in the same herd as the stallion. That white faced one with the heart shaped spot on her chest...that is a beautiful little filly?"

"Yeah, she is a pretty one. She'll be just right. When we go back home let's have two of the boys follow us with 'em. Make a good weddin' present too," Skinny replies smiling then nodding at his brother says, "Good thought, brother, real good idea!"

Excited, but getting tired of all the hard work, at dinner time Glory asks, "Grandpas we're gettin' hungry. Where do ya wanta eat at?"

Pokey looks at Skinny before saying, "I know just the place. It is a little bit of a walk but I bet ya'll won't mind that. Skinny and I will ride as we're old. Ha ha It's about six blocks from here called Johanna's Café. She is one good cook. She makes pies almost as good as yar Grandma Nona. What do ya think?"

"Oh, sounds good to me. Beth Ann, have ya ever gone thar?" Glory asks turning to her sister.

"Yes, Mother and I have a few times. They have the best chicken pot pie. No one makes it as good as Miss Johanna and Miss Johanna is... well you will just have to wait and see her," Beth Ann replies with a smug smile.

Puzzled but content to wait and see they all start to walk out the door when shots ring out. Jake pushes all three girls to the floor before drawing his pistol as Skinny and Pokey grab for them and all hit the floor pretty hard.

Women scream, grabbing their young'uns hands, and run for the shops and dart inside. Men jump behind posts or whatever is close by. Everyone is looking around to see where the shooting is coming from.

Pokey and Skinny have their pistols out looking all around. They slowly stand up still leaning against the wall on each side of the door looking outside when Bradford calls out, "You low down skunk get outta here or we are gonna drill ya with holes, Cully." He fires a couple of shots to the side of the building across the street and they see a man run away.

"Cully again?" Skinny states angrily.

"Yep, boss. Sorry, I didn't see him atoll until he fired," Bradford sadly reports then firmly continues, "I'll be on the lookout for him now. There won't be another time."

Pokey looks at the fear on the young girl's faces saying, "Sorry girls this happens occasionally. Some outlaws didn't like gettin' sent to jail so sometimes one of 'em shows up and tries to get even. My boys are good at lookin' out for me though. Good job, Bradford. Ya did good."

"I'll be on the lookout more, too," Jake states in a firm voice.

"So will I," Glory mumbles feeling the pistol in the pocket of her skirt.

Marshal Wheeler jogs up asking, "Who was it this time, Pokey?"

"Steve Cully. That man don't know when to stop," Pokey fumes.

"Wa'll I'll keep an eye out for'em," Garth Wheeler replies then leaning back against the door asks, "Wondered if'n you two would go down to Potter's Bank and help me sort through some of his belongings after dinner?"

Skinny and Pokey nod yes they will do this then the Marshal leaves to patrol the city.

Josh rides up with the horses for Skinny and Pokey while Bradford and Jay ride in front and behind the two old gents keeping an eagle eye out for trouble.

Kevin runs up at the same time so Pokey looks down at him commanding, "Keep an eye out for Steve Cully. He is in town. Keep my young'uns safe. Young'uns we will ride ahead and get us a table. Josh go with Kevin and watches out for yourselves and our young'uns."

Both say, "Yes, sir!" So Kevin walks with Jake out front and Josh follows right behind the girls.

Glory steps up closer to Jake in the front line, he gently but firmly says, "Git back Glory."

"I'm a better shot than ya are, Jake, and ya know it," Glory states quietly.

"But I'm bigger and meaner and I've already proven that to ya, haven't I. Don't make me have to take my eyes off the street, Glory. I'm watchin' out for all of us," Jake softly explains.

Stepping back Glory mutinously says, "Yes, SIR! But I'll be watchin', too."

She scans the area around them because she knows all too well what can happen when you don't pay attention when danger is around.

Smiling Jake replies, "That's my girl! Thanks Glory."

His answer is a hand in the middle of his back giving him a hard shove, which causes him to chuckle.

They arrive safe and sound at the café to see Skinny and Pokey are already inside and Bradford and Jay are sitting at a table for four close to the front door while a bigger table for six is in the back of the room and away from any windows.

Jake, Glory and Carrie Lynn stop in their tracks when they see Miss Johanna for the first time. She is a rare beauty.

Jake's mouth drops open as he mutters, "My goodness, she is beautiful, a goddess."

Black hair, flashing brown eyes with the pure white complexion of the southern gals, Miss Johanna Light has long eye lashes and a perfectly formed cupid's bow for lips, a ripe figure and an eye for a handsome man.

She gravitates to Jake (as a fly to honey) and huskily states (licking her luscious lips), "Well this is my lucky day. Who are you handsome?"

Stepping closer to Jake, Glory coldly states, "My future husband!"

In mock distress Johanna asks Jake, "This can't be true that would be too cruel!"

Jake gulps but doesn't utter a word until Glory elbows him in the ribs sharply then he smiles sheepishly saying, "Yes, madam. Glory and I will be wed this summer."

"What a shame," Johanna replies then turning she sweeps the floor with the side to side swishing of her skirt as she leads them to the table where Pokey and Skinny are sitting.

Jake is jabbed sharply in the ribs again when Glory notices what his eyes are following. He smiles and winks at her then taking her hand leads her to the table.

Jake holds out the chairs for the girls (as he remembers Stephen did at the fancy restaurant) then sits with his back to the wall so he can keep an eye on the door also. Johanna's Café has one small window in front so it is easy to watch it and the back door at the same time.

Johanna waves away Bill Collier (the usual waiter) when he walks over to take their order and writes it down herself. She stands VERY close to each of the men when they order and they can't help but smell her expensive French perfume.

Glory keeps her eyes on Jake and glares at him when he looks at the lovely Johanna.

Johanna finds it delightful to be so scrutinized by the beautiful young girl but would have been horrified if she'd been able to read Glory's mind and see how Glory would love to scalp her of her beautiful hair.

Glory is shocked to realize she can be so jealous. "I've never been before and I don't like this feeling," then she remembers hearing the men whispering about a Miss Gay from the bathhouse and how beautiful she is then Mrs. Christina is a beautiful woman but she is married, thank God. Now THIS woman who fawns over the men like they are sugar and she is ready to lap it up. Frowning she can't even think what to order.

Beth Ann notices how angry Glory is so leaning over explains, "Miss Johanna is always this way. She likes men to admire her and Glory, she is beautiful, but that is all there is to it."

"All men? Even Grandfather Edgar and Mr. Potter?" Glory asks amazed.

Shaking her head no, Beth Ann chuckles replying, "No, she has good taste in men. Jake is one good looking man," then she smiles and winks at Glory so like their father that Glory laughs. The meal is brought and they enjoy delicious chicken soup then have applesauce cake and cherry pie for dessert.

Soon it is time to go back to work. Cautiously they leave and quickly walk back to the store.

Soon as they enter Skinny starts laying out the jobs to be done. "We've got to go over to the bank that Potter owned and hep the Marshal out for a while this afternoon. Jay and Josh will stay here with ya'll and Randy I'd like you to stay out here in front and let the young people keep on doin' the work and packin'," Skinny directs as Randy nods yes.

Skinny motions for the young people to come closer then he quietly advises, "There is bound to be a stash of money here in the store that Edgar has hidden. When you find it, pocket it, until we get back. Then we'll get it safely put away. Jake, keep the girls in your sight as we will be gone for a time. Not sure how long. Girls stay in the store. If'n ya need to go to the outhouse take one of the men with ya. No use takin' chances."

"We will," Glory replies firmly looking at the younger girls.

Both remember her kidnapping so nod yes. Smiling they all return to working as Jake replies, "We'll wait right here until ya return, don'tcha worry about us."

Bradford and Kevin walk with them to the bank while Jay and Josh stay at the store watching over the young people and helping out as needed.

A pretty young girl enters the mercantile door, looks around then calls out, "Beth Ann, you are back!"

Beth Ann swings around seeing her friend Kathy so smiling she quickly walks up front saying, "Yes, Kathy, I'm back."

Kathy does a double take when she sees Beth Ann close up. No pimples on her face, her skin is glowing, she has lost a lot of weight and she is smiling. Seldom does Beth Ann smile and not so happily either.

Good naturedly Beth Ann asks, "I look different, don't I?"

"Yes, you are beautiful. Your skin is so pretty it makes me want to feel its softness," Kathy replies laughing as she hugs her friend then turning around requests, "Wait a minute." Walking over to the door she calls out, "Come on in, Beth Ann is back." She giggles as she walks back in whispering, "Get ready." Three more girls and three boys walk in. Rather one of the girls seems to float in she is so light footed and the three boys are pushing and shoving each other playfully.

Beth Ann blushes prettily when all six stop abruptly to stare at her. She smiles saying, "Good afternoon Gina, Denisa, Lea, Rodney, Dennis, and Marcus."

Their mouths are wide open in astonishment so raising her eyebrows at them questioningly Beth Ann asks, "I look different, don't I?"

"You look like an angel," Dennis states with awe.

"You talk different, too," Gina answers thoughtfully (not taking her eyes away from Beth Ann's lovely skin and smile).

"I knew you'd look like your Mother, Beth Ann, and you certainly do," Marcus replies smiling happily at her.

"I can't believe it is you," Rodney replies awestruck at the changes in her.

"I had to look twice to make sure it is you," Denisa states softly.

"You still have style in dressing even if it's not fancy clothes you are wearing," Lea states smiling happily at Beth Ann.

"I always like to be "In Style", Beth Ann replies hugging sweet Lea.

"You always have been," Lea states hugging her back.

"Would you like some candy?" Beth Ann asks as she reaches behind her picking up her tin of candy. It is an assortment of different candies she likes.

"You never offered us candy before," Dennis states shocked.

"My grandfather wouldn't let me but honestly I didn't know how to share then. I've learned better manners now," Beth Ann replies smiling as she passes the candy around then sets it on the table so they can have some more.

"You look wonderful, Beth Ann!" Gina states belatedly hugging her, "I was so shocked that I couldn't move for a minute or two."

"How about going to the dance with me on Thursday at Rippetoe's? It's going be the dance of the month. Old Rip's got a newfangled music machine, can't remember the name of it right now," Rodney asks smugly looking at Dennis and Marcus.

"I'm sorry but we won't be here but a couple of days so I won't be able to but thank you very much for asking me," Beth Ann refuses graciously.

"What do you mean? Won't your grandmother make you go to the dance as usual?" Kathy asks very surprised.

Looking sadly at her feet Beth Ann replies, "She would tell me to go if she were here but she can't anymore. My...uh...grandparents died on the way back and we are here to clean out the house and store. We will be leaving permanently at the end of the week."

All the girls hug Beth Ann again saying they are sorry to hear this sad news.

The boys awkwardly pat her back saying they are sorry to hear of her loss.

"We will miss you a whole lot," Lea states hugging her friend again.

"Yeah, it ain't fair," Marcus states as he takes another piece of candy from the tin.

"That's right you just got back and now you say you are leaving and not coming back....when will we see you again," Rodney asks looking at her sadly.

Shaking her head no sadly, Beth Ann answers, "I don't know, Rodney."

Looking at how lovely Beth Ann is now Dennis replies, "That is not fair! You just got back and you are leaving and won't be coming back."

Beth Ann smiles at her good friend, Dennis, replying, "That is so sweet of you, Dennis. I will miss my friends here when we leave."

"What about your Mother, is she here?" Kathy asks looking around the room for her.

"No she stayed down south with my father. She won't be coming back to St. Louis either," Beth Ann replies smiling at the thought of the new baby now that she has adjusted to the idea.

"Little Samuel? Where is he?" Rodney asks looking around for him.

"He stayed down there, too. He wasn't interested in coming back. I wanted to help with moving our things back so I came to help," Beth Ann explains as she looks around the store.

Beth Ann is very surprised at their wanting to be around her as they never seemed to want to in the past. "I wasn't popular with any of the boys in the past, maybe because I was so hateful to them," she ponders this thought.

Carrie Lynn walks over saying, "Hello, I'm Carrie Ewing."

Beth Ann introduces her and the boys are in awe again. Here is another beautiful girl maybe she can go to the dance with them so they ask.

"Will you go to the dance with me next Thursday?" Marcus quickly asks after being introduced.

"I think she'd rather go with me," Dennis pipes in then continues, "I am the oldest one of us."

"Like that makes a difference," Rodney exclaims shaking his head no.

Regretfully Carrie Lynn replies, "I'm sorry but I'll be leaving with Beth Ann after we finish packing. I won't be able to go. But thank you very much, Marcus, for asking me." Carrie has never been asked to attend a dance before and it doesn't make any difference that she doesn't know how to dance yet, it is the thought that she has been asked that counts.

Jake and Glory have been keeping an eye on the young people as they choose food for the trip back. When it looks like they are talked out and the boys are looking wistfully at the two girls Jake chuckles then calls out, "Git back to work, girls, we gotta get this done."

The boys glance into the back of the store and see the big man so ask, "Who is that?"

Smiling Carrie Lynn replies, "My older brother. I'd better get back to work. It was nice meeting you." Then she returns to her job.

Beth Ann smiles graciously at her old friends saying, "I'd better get back to work, too. We are cleaning out the store today."

Looking around the St. Louis children realizes there aren't any black people doing the work just the young white people so Rodney asks, "Where are your slaves? Why aren't they here doing the work for you?"

"We don't own any slaves anymore. My father freed them," Beth Ann answers still smiling but now ready to return to work.

"Freed them! Whatever for," Kathy asks shocked then continues, "Who does the work around your house now?"

"We all do. We share the work and it gets done very quickly," Beth Ann explains knowing this will be a novel idea to any of them as it would have been for her a few months ago.

"You work! What do you do?" asks Gina wonderingly.

"Whatever my Papa tells me to do," Beth Ann replies honestly.

"Like what?" Lea gasps more than astonished.

Hiding a smile Beth Ann answers truthfully, "Cleaning out the chicken coop, milking cows, washing clothes, washing dishes, cooking and setting the table…." She stops at their shocked expressions before continuing, "I'm no better than anyone else and I want to be a good wife to my husband when I marry someday."

"Boy, you sure changed down there," Kathy replies with conviction, "You wouldn't even pick your clothes up off the floor the last time I was at your house."

"That's true but my life has completely changed now. I really have to get back to work. It was very nice seeing you. Take care and hopefully I'll talk to you again before we leave," Beth Ann graciously says turning around. She notices they have made a considerable dint in her candy supply and finds she can laugh about it.

The St. Louis children walk out in a daze and keep repeating words as they walk down the street together…"She gave me candy…. She is beautiful!…Did you see how pretty she is?…. Her grandparents are dead….They are closing the house and the store…Samuel didn't come back. …Mrs. Gray stayed down there and is not coming back…Mr. Gray is alive!" when suddenly they look at each other and as one say, "I'm going to tell my Mother and Father. They won't believe this."

Beth Ann walks back to the others wonderingly saying, "I can't believe they were so interested in talking to me. They seldom said much to me at all except Kathy she was always nice. She is my only best friend here."

"You have a friend for life, Beth Ann, I'll never let you leave me," Carrie Lynn sincerely replies.

Back at the ranch Joe and Elizabeth are enjoying a second honeymoon. Joe's cowboys are working harder making up for the time that Joe and Elizabeth are spending together inside the house and down at the hot springs.

"Cooking for two is so much easier than the nine I've been cooking for," Elizabeth states one morning then adds, "Although I do rather miss making all those biscuits every day."

Joe laughs replying, "Don't worry, honey, ya'll be making lots of biskuts the rest of yar life. They are wonderful and our grandpas and Uncle Max do love'em."

Stirring her coffee Elizabeth wonders out loud, "I wonder how Beth Ann is doing in St. Louis. I am sure the other children are shocked at her appearance now. She has lost probably thirty pounds and her skin has cleared up. She is so happy and contented now. I didn't realize how unhappy she and Sammy were in St. Louis, mainly because I was so unhappy." Frowning she keeps stirring her coffee thinking about St. Louis and all that they will be doing packing up everything. Then she adds, "I should have gone back and taken care of all those details. It was just so much easier to stay here with you. I don't want to be separated from you ever again. But it was selfish of me to leave it all to the children to take care of."

"It will be fine. Jake and Glory need to see the big city, it will give'em a new insight on life after livin' on a ranch all their lives. Beth Ann needs closure and maybe to adjust to her new life here. Beth Ann is so smart that I've wondered how she can keep on larnin'. I wonder if'n we telegraphed the grandpas we could get'em to bring some educatin' books back while they are up there so that she can keep larnin'," Joe replies as he looks at his lovely wife.

"Oh, Joe, that is a wonderful idea. Why don't we write it and send one of the men in today with it?" Elizabeth answers smiling at the pleasure it will give Beth Ann.

"So be it," Joe states smiling then walking over to a cabinet he picks up a box with paper in it and they compose the telegram. A little later Joe walks over to the bunk house calling out, "Pete?"

"Yep, boss," Ole Pete replies walking out of the store room.

"I need ya to go into Roy and send a telegram for me. Do ya need any supplies from the store while yar there?" Joe asks smiling at his old friend.

"Betcha want me to check on that purdy mother of yars too, don'tcha?" Pete asks smiling and wiggling his bushy eyebrows at Joe then continues, "Never did tell ya that when I went in and got her when Glory was taken that she near broke my bones on the way back and me aholdin' a kettle of chicken soup for the sick young'uns. Neva had such a wild ride in my life and well, maybe, I respect her for it."

"She is some woman. Ya might even be able to eat dinner thar and have some of her pie with yar meal. Tell her Lizbeth and I are having our second honeymoon with all the young'uns gone and we will see her in about a week," Joe advises knowing that Nona will respect their privacy.

"Shorely will," Pete answers smiling his almost toothless smile then adds, "Ya'll was talkin' about building on the house. Did ya talk to Hank and Ralph about it yet?"

Nothing is a secret on a ranch (as Joe knows firsthand) so even though he hasn't directly talked to Pete about adding rooms onto their house he isn't surprised that Pete knows about it so explains, "No, I haven't done that yet. Why don'tcha get ready and I'll write another note to Hank and ya can give it to him while yar thar. Maybe I'd better wire Ray Johns over in Ernest about the lumber I'll need, so I will only have to make one trip over thar."

"If'n ya are gonna build a bunch of rooms it'll take ya a couple of trips to get it all," Pete replies thoughtfully.

"Yeah, it will, but maybe I can get a couple of wagons going at the same time. Might count on ya to go over there for me and get some of that wood as ya know lumber so well, Pete," Joe states thoughtfully.

"Be obliged to hep ya all I can, Joe. Ya's always been good to me and I knows a little carpentry myself so could help out with the buildin' some too," Ole Pete answers smiling and Joe notices he is down to three front teeth now.

"Sounds good to me, Pete. Get the buck board and meet me at the house in a few minutes," Joe asks returning to Elizabeth (who is just finishing the breakfast dishes) explaining, "Pete just reminded me I'd better order up that lumber for the rooms. He is gonna take a note to Hank ta git his help, too. We can get those rooms built on pretty fast with Hank, Ralph and my men helpin'."

"I can hardly wait to get it done and paint it. We are going to be in the back more with a nursery right beside our room aren't we?" Elizabeth asks hopefully.

"Yep and we'll put Sammy and the grandpas at the far end of the house so they won't be disturbed when the baby cries. Maybe put ma on the other side of the nursery then Beth Ann," Joe thoughtfully points out.

"Yes, ma will want to help out all she can and we will let her," Elizabeth replies smiling knowing that this baby will be extra special to her mother because she will help raise it.

"Need anything from the mercantile while Pete is thar?" Joe asks as he sits writing the note to Hank.

Elizabeth thinks a minute before thinking, "Maybe some more coffee we have enough for us but we will need more before everyone gets back."

"Will do," Joe picks up another piece of paper writing coffee on it then scribbles a note to Frank as he smiles, folds it, and writes Frank's name on the front of it. Hearing the buckboard at the door he stands and taking the notes walks out to meet Ole Pete. Laughing when he returns he takes Elizabeth's hand and they walk back to their bedroom to continue the honeymooning.

Sammy is having the time of his life at Minnie and Benny's farm. He has shown them he can milk a cow, gather the eggs and ride very well without a saddle.

"Sammy boy, I'm so proud of ya. Yar growin' into a man so fast I cain't keep up," Minnie exclaims as she kisses this precious little boy of hers.

"I'm gonna be big and strong, Minnie. No one will ever pick on me, not ever again!" Sammy states positively.

Wrinkling her forehead thoughtfully Minnie asks, "Sammy come over here a minute." She sits down and even though she has virtually no lap she finds room for Sammy to sit on her knee then worriedly says, "Sammy, I don't like hearin' ya say thangs like that. I knowd better than anyone how ya was treated but, honey, ya got to forgive'em. I thought ya had."

"Oh, Minnie, don'tcha worry I've forgivin' them for all the hittin' but I ain't gonna allow no one to do that to me again," Sammy replies firmly.

"Does this mean yar gonna be a mean man who hits on others just cause yar big and strong," Minnie asks puzzled.

"No, Minnie, I wouldn't do that. You know I wouldn't do that," Sammy replies horrified.

"Then Sammy boy, I don't rightly understand what'cha was sayin' then," Minnie asks puzzled.

"I'm gonna protect others, Minnie. I ain't gonna allow no one to hurt others just cause they can. I didn't like it when it was done to me so I'm gonna stop others from doing it," Sammy states firmly.

Thoughtfully Minnie ponders this a moment then sadly says, "There's a lot of mean people in the world, honey, ya cain't stop'em all and it means that yar plan on spendin' yar life fightin' and hittin' others. That cain't be a good life for ya."

"But doing good is what I wanna do Minnie. I don't want others to pick on someone just cause they want to. It ain't right," Sammy replies firmly.

Looking at this child of her heart Minnie knows he is referring to how hatefully she and Benny were treated by his grandparents and even by his own family so knows she has to make him understand. "Sammy, listen to me, honey, and let me explain a few thangs to ya. One thang is that there will always be people who will be mean to others. That is just a fact. Seconded there will always be good people like yar Pa who will stand up and fight those who are mean and ya do well to be like yar pa. Third sometimes people have to larn to take up for themselves. Now this here is me and Benny. It's taken us some time and with a lot of nice people hepin' us'ns we are larnin' and sometimes it just takes larnin' to make things right. Sometimes it ain't easy, like with yar ma and Beth Ann, but, honey child, don'tcha see a big difference in them now. They were unhappy and so they took that unhappiness out on ya and…us'n. But they larned differently and were real sorry like. Remember. So think about the larnin' people need to do afore ya start knockin' people around. Will ya promise me that, Sammy? I don't want'cha to be a hittin' on people, I really don't," Minnie begs from the heart.

Putting both hands on her velvety brown cheeks Sammy looks her in the eyes and solemnly promises, "I will think about it. I promise ya, Minnie. I never want to make YOU unhappy."

Hugging him Minnie sighs happily saying, "That makes me feel much better. Thank ya."

Impishly Sammy explains proudly, "I already told Beth Ann someday I'm gonna give her a spanking she won't forget for all the mean things she did to me. She said real sassy like, "Maybe you will and maybe you won't." But I'm gonna keep that promise to myself."

"Well, honey, it ain't like she don't deserve it for what she did afore but now she treats ya right nice and that is somethin' to think about, too," Minnie advises thinking of the stinker Beth Ann was and how her whole attitude changed when they moved down here and she found out her pa really does love her.

"I have a long memory, Minnie," Sammy states raising his eyebrows knowingly at this second mother of his.

"Then use that good brain of yars and make some good memories to remember the rest of yar life," Minnie replies wisely.

POTTER'S BANK
Chapter 14

"Sadly, some enjoy the evil they surround themselves with."

Skinny and Pokey follow Marshal Wheeler into Franklin Potter's Bank and meet the smiling face of Charles Sloan.

"Good Morning, Gentlemen. What can I do for you?" inquires Charles as he looks at the three older men.

"Charles, could we talk in the office for a few minutes?" Marshal Garth requests politely.

"Certainly, come over to my desk," Charles requests leading them behind the teller's cages to a lone desk in the corner.

"I think we'd better go into Mr. Potter's office, Charles," Marshal Wheeler states smiling slightly.

"I don't have a key to it, sir. I'm sorry but Mr. Potter took it with him and said no one was to go in there until he gets back," Charles explains truthfully.

Putting his long bony arm around Charles's shoulder Skinny replies, "He won't be coming back, Mr. Sloan, he died."

"Died? Uncle Franklin died?" Charles asks shocked. The two tellers hear his statement so turn around looking over at the men questioningly.

"That's true, son. They died on the way back to St. Louis," Pokey answers stiffly.

"They? Mr. & Mrs. Hawkins died, too?" Charles asks shocked again.

Skinny nods yes.

"What about Mrs. Elizabeth and the children? They weren't hurt were they?" Charles immediately asks.

"No, they are fine. Beth Ann came back to help us close the store and their home," Skinny answers pleased that this young man cares enough to ask.

Dropping into a chair Charles mumbles, "Well, that is all to the good."

Marshal Wheeler pulls a key out of his pocket saying, "I imagine this fits the lock on the door," then walking over tries it and, yes, it fits perfectly and the door swings open.

Hesitantly Charles follows them as they walk into Franklin Potter's office saying, "Please have a seat and tell me what I can do for you."

The office is stuffy so Charles opens a high small window propping it open then sits on the front of the desk while the older men take the only available chairs. Glancing at the chair behind the desk Charles doesn't feel he should sit there.

Appraising the young man standing before them, Pokey thinks: "About thirty years old, brown curly hair, brown eyes with long lashes, quick smile and a direct look. This is a man I trust." So he says, "Mr. Sloan, you said Uncle Franklin, is that true?"

Blushing Charles replies, "Yes, sir. It is. My uncle didn't want anyone to know I was related to him thinking they could go through me to get loans or money from him. But that wasn't possible; he was very tight fisted with his money." Then Charles straightens his shoulders continuing, "I should say right off that I didn't care much for my uncle. My mother loved him dearly and, I believe, he cared for her but he has no love for me or my sister. He pays me enough to survive, but that is all. I'm sorry to say that I have very little respect for him because he isn't…uh… wasn't a very nice person."

Marshal Garth smiles sadly replying, "There ain't many who would or could say somethin' good about him. He cheated a lot of people but I couldn't prove it or do anything about it."

"It broke my heart to see it happen over and over again. He caused a lot of farmers and ranchers to go bankrupt. But what could I do? I tried a couple of times but never was able to help many," Charles explains sadly.

"Is your Mother still alive? Do you have any other family other than yar sister?" Skinny asks.

"No, none. Mother died a year ago and Uncle Franklin was her only sibling," Charles answers puzzled.

"Then that means if there ain't a will saying otherwise that everything Potter has will belong to you and yar sister," Marshal Wheeler states matter of factly.

Charles looks up sharply saying, "I hadn't thought of that. He probably does have a will but I've never seen it."

"Then we will go through his desk and see if we can find one. Does he have a deposit box in the bank's safe?" Marshal Wheeler asks.

"He has three! Never figured out why he needed three but there are two small ones and one large one," Charles explains thoughtfully.

"Let's see if we can find a key to them and see what is inside of 'em," Marshal Garth replies. Walking around to the back of the desk he tries to pull open one of the drawers and it won't budge. Looking at the second key on the string he tries it and the drawer opens. The drawer is neat as a pin and as he leans closer he notices little pencil dots that show where everything is lined up. Looking up smiling faintly he states, "Didn't trust anyone, did he. There are little pencil marks around every object here so he could tell if anything has been moved. He musta thought he had some reasons to be so careful like or cautious like."

"None that I know of, he just didn't trust anyone," Charles sadly answers.

The other three men watch as Garth Wheeler takes every item out of the drawer laying it on top of the desk. Six sharpened pencils, an expensive eraser, small pen knife to sharpen the pencils, small used notebook with pencil smudges on it, black ink and pen, a small key and some small change.

Picking up the key Marshal Garth asks Charles, "Will this unlock a bank box?"

Charles takes the key, looks at it closely answering, "No, sir. I'm not sure what this goes to," then hands it back.

They look at each item then put it all back into the desk, except the notebook and the key, which Garth leaves laying on top of the desk.

Opening each drawer he takes out everything in it and they look at each item...nothing of interest except they find two more keys that will fit two bank boxes. After Charles leaves with Pokey to find the two bank boxes Garth and Skinny look in the last drawer blinking look at their find. A small leather whip, a bottle of liquor and pictures of naked ladies are all hidden underneath a beautiful silk scarf which has a rainbow of colors in it.

Stumbling back Skinny states, "That scarf belongs to Elizabeth. We bought it for her when we went to Fort Worth two years ago." Looking back inside the drawer his face pales as he continues, "I don't think Elizabeth would have enjoyed what Potter had in mind to do to her."

With a snarl Marshal Wheeler answers, "Don't think anyone would enjoy bein' whipped with this," nodding towards the small whip.

"Guess there's some but none that I knowd of," Skinny states shaking his head sadly.

"Oh, there are saloons and houses of ill repute that have women who will do anything for money. Reckon he visited them some," Marshal Garth explains sadly shaking his head.

Charles walks in with one large box with Pokey carrying the second one, a smaller one and both wooden boxes are full. The small one is full of twenty dollar coins. It is so heavy Pokey has a hard time carrying it.

The large box is full of papers which just about pop out of the box when it is opened. Many deeds, wills and other papers are in it.

"Charles looks like you have some work ahead of ya with these," Marshal Garth states looking at the large pile of deeds. Then he looks over at Skinny and Pokey saying, "Judge Burnfin is in town. You both know him. Maybe we should take Charles over there and get a paper statin' he and his sister are the only living relatives of Potter so Charles can start takin' care of this mess and can see what we have to deal with here. What do ya think?"

Charles nods yes when they all look at him and Skinny and Pokey agree then Charles requests, "The bank closes in an hour. Could we do this then? I don't like leaving the bank while we are open."

"Sure thing," Marshal Garth replies then looking at the papers asks, "Want some help with these?"

"I believe I will know most of the farmers and ranchers on these deeds. I'd like to check out their payments and especially the percentages of interest that my uncle charged and see what I can do about helping these people. That will take some time. What about the key to the other box? We don't know what is in it?" Charles explains then asks.

"It must be at his home. After we visit the judge then we'll go over there and see what we can find," Marshal Wheeler explains thoughtfully.

Charles' eyes widen then he says, "Oh, I'd forgotten about his house. It is huge and now…it will be ours! It's a fine house."

"You will make it a fine house, Mr. Sloan. That is the important thing," Pokey states nodding at young Charles.

"Yes, sir! I'm going to make a lot of changes at the bank and the house. I have never been inside the house. I was never allowed over there. When he visited my mother he always came to our home," Charles replies with a decided twinkle in his eyes.

Later that evening at supper Skinny, Jake and Pokey stand when Johanna approaches their table and the young people are ready to sit down.

She smiles in appreciation explaining, "My specialty is Chicken Pot Pie tonight but we have steak or wild game also. All the meat is fresh."

"Give us a minute please, Johanna, and we'll get right back to ya," Skinny requests smiling at the lovely woman. She walks away in the same sweeping motion which causes many a male eye to follow.

Leaning forward Pokey explains, "The chicken pie is real fine. It is tender and comes in a small pie pan but I can tell ya from experience that it is a lot of food. She also has the best fruit pies around here so you might want to save some room for dessert."

Looking at Jake Glory whispers, "What'cha wanta eat?"

"I'm right fond of steak or the fried chicken. I cain't think what a chicken pie would be like," he replies frowning slightly puzzled.

Leaning over Beth Ann explains, "It is really good. The chicken is in a creamy sauce with carrots, onions and green peas in it. The portions are good sized, too." She looks worriedly at Carrie Lynn then whispers, "I wonder if I can eat a whole pie now? My stomach is a lot smaller. Do you want to share one and then we could each have a piece of pie? Or should we just have chicken pie and no dessert?"

Laughing softly, Carrie Lynn answers, "What a dilemma! Chicken pie and no dessert, or half a pie and dessert? How about half a pie and dessert? I'd hate to miss a good piece of pie."

Beth Ann bursts out laughing saying, "Yes, I agree. Grandpas Carrie Lynn and I will share a chicken pot pie and then have dessert."

Growing up where you don't waste food at all Glory looks over at Jake asking, "Could ya eat half my pie if'n I cain't?"

Smiling Jake winks at her saying, "Never passed up good food in my life, Glory. Cain't wait til you start cookin' for me. I love your biscuits."

Joy lights Glory's eyes as she replies, "I'm a real good cook and if'n we like the pie it will be another recipe that I'll have."

Everyone orders what they want and soon the wonderfully browned chicken pot pies are delivered to the table and they are large.

Laughing to herself, Carrie Lynn thinks: "It wasn't so long ago that I'd have gulped this down as fast as I could and not even tasted it. I so enjoy the flavors of food now. Back then I never knew when I was full but now by eating slower I fill up faster and my stomach is smaller. I'll be full with eating just half the chicken pot pie but I'll never be too full for a piece of peach pie."

Beth Ann's thoughts are similar and looking around the familiar café she remembers all the changes she has experienced in the past few months. "My looks have changed drastically. I don't have those horrid spots all over my face. I've lost a lot of weight and I have a waist now. Grandmother would be proud of me for that. She ate all she wanted and never gained any weight. I've always wondered why some people can do that and others can't. Glory seems to eat whatever she wants and she is thin…well, not thin…she has curves. Glancing down she realizes for the first time that she has some curves now too. Smiling she thinks, "I'll have to tell Carrie Lynn about this discovery. We both have some curves now."

Skinny and Pokey watch all the young people smiling at their joy in life. Both notice how thoughtful Carrie Lynn and Beth Ann are and that they both seem to smile all the time now. Both gents remember a time just last year around Christmas when Beth Ann was a sullen little girl who frowned all the time and spoke sharply to anyone and everyone. Skinny grins again seeing her happy and smiling now and mainly due to her father's love, "Father's love…well… we gave our girl all the love we had to give and for some reason it was never enough for her. I wonder why? Maybe you have to choose to be happy and not expect others to make you happy. That is something to ponder on."

"Jake, I've eaten all I can," Glory whispers as she pushes her more than half full plate of chicken pie over to Jake.

Smiling Jake winks at her as he takes it and set it on top of his now empty plate. He has eaten a large steak with green beans. Picking up a spoon he takes a small bite of the pie and is pleasantly surprised to find he likes the chicken pot pie. He nods to Glory saying, "We'll have to tell Nona about this. It is very good."

Nodding yes Glory replies, "Grandma will love it." She turns to Beth Ann asking, "Do ya know what's in the gravy in the chicken pot pie?"

Beth Ann thinks a moment before replying, "Yes, I believe I do but not the exact recipe. Johanna might give us the recipe." Then she looks at her grandpas before continuing, "If the right person ASKS she might give us the recipe."

Both Skinny and Pokey raise their eyebrows and hands at the same time asking, "ME?"

Beth Ann and Glory nod yes then folding their hands under their breasts keep looking intently at the two older gents with raised eyebrows. Suddenly both girls burst out laughing begging, "Please."

Winking at them Pokey says, "Let me see what I can do." He stands up and walks with his bow legged walk to a table where Johanna is sitting drinking tea by herself.

Chuckling as he leans forward Skinny explains, "If'n he loses, I'll give it a try but I don't reckon I'll have to. Some women go for the bow legged scrawny type instead of the tall good lookin' type."

Everyone laughs with him as they watch Pokey charm the lovely Johanna into giving them her recipe for the delicious chicken pot pie.

Johanna smiles as Pokey walks up to her table asking, "Care if'n I sit with ya, Miss Johanna?"

"Certainly I want you to. Sit down Pokey and tell me what has been happening in your life," she answers grinning at him.

Pokey sits then taking a deep breath looks Johanna in the eyes sadly answering, "Our daughter, Lora Hawkins, died so we came to St. Louie to close down the store and clean out the house. It ain't been easy but everyone has bad times and we ain't no better than anyone else."

Immediately Johanna lays her lily white hand over Pokey's with understanding in her eyes says, "I know all about loss. You and Skinny helped me out a lot when my mother died three years ago. I'd have fallen prey to Mr. Potter if you hadn't helped me keep the café. I'm very sorry to hear about Mrs. Hawkins. She was always kind to me." Looking down she remembers the bad days of not knowing what to do and where to turn to. Remembering her parents were good friends of these two fine men and they had eaten many meals here at the café over the years, she had asked them for help and gotten it. "Father died so many years ago that I don't really remember him," Johanna sighs with regret, "I remember his laughing eyes and wonderful sense of humor most of all. He was always a blessing to be around." Looking up she asks, "Is there anything I can do to help you?"

Pokey smiles at this beautiful young woman who he has known most of her life so with tongue in cheek asks, "Well there is one little thang. The girls love yar chicken pot pie and would like yar recipe."

Johanna is completely caught off guard and her trill of laughter lights up her beautiful brown eyes as she leans forward teasing back, "Well, sir, that is a big secret. Most the women in this city would kill for my mama's recipe but for you...well...I'll make an exception, with the stipulation that they don't give it to anyone in St. Louis."

Pokey leans over looking at his girls at the back table nods yes with great enthusiasm then leaning towards Johanna states, "That is a promise! Thank you, sweet girl, for making my granddaughters happy." He kisses her cheek and they continue talking for a few minutes.

Skinny sighs dramatically saying, "Darn it, looks like he won again. I don't know exactly how he does it but he just kinda slips up on women and they do whatever he asks."

Pokey escorts Johanna back to their table, pulls up a chair for her to sit on then says, "Listen carefully, girls, Johanna is gonna give ya the recipe for this fine chicken pie we just ate."

Johanna sits down and after smoothing out her skirt looks each girl in the eye saying, "I've never given my recipe away. I've never sold it even though many have offered me a great deal of money for it but as a favor to my adopted fathers here I'm going to tell you in detail ONCE how to make it. Only once so listen carefully. First I want your promise not to give it or sell it to anyone other than yourselves."

"Can we give it to our family? That is who we'd like to make it for," Beth Ann asks hopefully.

Smiling Johanna nods yes agreeing, "Of course," then she explains every step of making the wonderful chicken pot pies saying, "You will have to stir the sauce all the time it is cooking to keep it from getting lumps of flour in it. It should always be made fresh and if you have left overs you can make up a little more sauce and it will be almost as good."

After she finishes, Skinny looks over at her asking, "Johanna where is that good looking young man of yours? Ya'll were talkin' about gettin' married the last time we were here."

Johanna looks down then frowning explains, "He said he had to do something before he could settle down and get married. He left a month ago saying he'd return when he finished it. He was very closed mouth about it." She looks worried for a minute then shaking her head asks, "Pokey said you are going to sell the Hawkin's house. How much are you asking? I might be interested or know someone who is?"

"Johanna, if'n ya are interested, then it is yars and we'll come up with a price for you," Skinny states shaking his head yes.

"Let me think about it. If Jim was back....I could ask him...it would be so much easier but I'm not sure what to do right now," Johanna replies as she looks out towards the street as if her Jim will walk in the door any minute.

"There's no rush, honey. We will be here a few more days and we'll be back to eat so just think about it," Pokey advises patting her clenched hands.

Smiling Johanna lifts her troubled eyes saying, "Thank you, I will seriously think about it."

Watching for Steve Cully they return to the store to work on it some more. Opening the door they are shocked to see a man sitting in a chair by the stove eating some candy.

Frowning (with his pistol in his hand) Pokey demands, "Who are ya and what do ya think yar doin' breakin' into this store."

Raising his eyebrows haughtily the man scowls at him hatefully answering, "I'm Race Jacks and I can come and go here anytime I want! My father owns this store! Who are you to be questioning me?"

Pokey and Skinny look over the man who appears to be in his late thirties and do see a resemblance to Edgar Hawkins. Small eyes, low forehead, thinning brown hair, weak colored blue eyes and thin to the extreme in build. "Who did you say yar pa is?" Skinny asks looking Race straight in the eye.

"Edgar Hawkins," Race answers belligerently.

"How come yar name is Jacks and not Hawkins?" Pokey asks with a steely look in his eyes.

Leaning back Race explodes loudly with a snarl, "Cause he wouldn't marry my ma when he shoulda!"

"Sounds like he didn't want you," Jake states aggressively from behind the counter.

Race jumps and looks over at the big man behind him then keeps looking up until he sees a rigid jaw with eyes like ice staring back at him. Gulping he states, "No one gets away with sayin' that!"

Jake lifts his eyebrows stating, "I wouldn't say anything like that. I have better manners, but by what you just said it is true."

Race's mouth drops open then taking a deep breath he plans to get even with this smart mouthed man as he thinks, "Very idea sayin' it to my face! I killed the last one that did that." He clenches his teeth in anger and hatred for the man who is his father for giving him this humiliation.

"What are you doin' here and what do you want?" Skinny demands frowning at Race.

"I came to see my father, if'n it's any of your business. He's usually here at this time of day," Race answers as he looks around the room for Edgar.

Feeling sorry for the man, Skinny explains, "Sorry to tell you but Edgar Hawkins died recently and was buried down South."

"Died! He cain't be dead! He promised me...," Race sputters as he wildly looks around the store.

Compassion fills Jake's eyes as he calmly states, "He is dead. Sorry for yar loss. We have come to close down the store and the house."

"Close down the store and house?" Race repeats looking stunned.

"Yes, sir, that is what we are doin'. Do ya have any proof that yar Edgar's son?" Pokey asks quietly as he watches the distraught man.

"Proof! I'm livin' proof! I look just like him," Race yells belligerently.

"Don't mean ya are, now does it?" Pokey replies watchin' Race closely. He has seen many odd things happen when a fella is told bad news.

"Don't think you will cheat me outta my inheritance, man," Race states looking wildly around the room seeing all the empty spaces, which were full the last time he was here.

"Then show us proof that yar his son," Pokey repeats adamantly.

"Ain't got none," Race answers coldly.

"Where is your ma? Her word would count," Skinny asks him.

"Left with a no account man years ago. Don't know where she is. Said she was fed up with me and Edgar wouldn't help none with my raisin' so she left and I ain't seen her since I turned sixteen," Race answers angrily.

Gently clasping his hand on Race's elbow Skinny leads him to the door saying, "Well we will check into this and get back with you. Don't know what to tell you right now but come back tomorrow and we will see." He literally pushes him out the door then turning back to Pokey says, "We need to talk to Garth about this, maybe he knows if it is true."

Nodding yes, Pokey agrees, "Yep, he may and when Randy gets back we can ask him."

Randy walks in the door at that moment saying, "Collected quite a bit of the past due money, sirs, but there are some that just don't have it."

Nodding yes Skinny answers, "Fine, good job there Randy. We had a visitor a few minutes ago. A Race Jacks, he says he is Edgar's son. Do you know anything about this?"

Nodding yes reluctantly Randy explains, "He says he is. He tells everyone he is. Mr. Hawkins never admitted it but he did give him money a few times. Yelled at him every time for being a "no account weasel" but that is all I know."

"Didn't seem fond of him?" Jake asks interested.

"No, sir! Acted like he was a pest and wasn't nice to him at all," Randy answers thoughtfully then adds, "I heard him tell Mr. Jacks to quit trying to sponge off of him. Asking did he think Mr. Hawkins was made of money."

"Randy will you stay in the store and talk to people as they come in. Pokey and I need to visit with the Marshal and, Jake, keep the girls in the store and watch out for'em," Skinny advises then nodding to Pokey they walk out of the store.

Randy and Jake agree then they all go right back to work.

Back at the bank Charles Sloan finds some interesting information on his Uncle Franklin Potter in the form of a notebook. Reading it he is astounded at the information inside:

In the section on <u>Deeds</u>: names changed over and over on them where Franklin had sold and resold the same property and making money each time.

Charles can't help praying: *"Oh Lord, how could my uncle have cheated people over and over and so many of them he caused to lose everything they had worked so hard for. Lord, please allow me to help these people. I don't know how but somehow please help me to do this. In your precious Son's name I pray."*

Tears trickle down his young face as he looks at the lists and startled he reads the heading of the second section:

<u>Outlaws</u>: Gulping he blinks at the names and descriptions of what his uncle had paid men to do. Laying the book down Charles realizes he will have to tell Marshal Wheeler about this but how can he protect the innocent ones who seem to have gotten caught up in his uncle's schemes. The ones who have been abused and the ones killed. Taking another deep breath he turns to the next section expecting the worse and sees it.

<u>People Who I have had disappear</u>: Charles looks in horror at the names and dates and even the places where the bodies have been buried. Eyes almost bulging with shock Charles closes the book praying again: *"Oh, my dear Lord, what can I do to make amends? How could he have done such unspeakable things and how can I make it right? Please help me, Lord, to do what I can to help these people. Amen."*

Hesitantly he turns to the next section and pales as he reads the word: <u>Women</u>: looking down at the many pages dating back over 20 years Charles reads the names of women Franklin had forced to have sex with him and in the way he wanted it done. Charles' eyes widened at the sadistic way Franklin had treated women and is shocked to learn he knows many of the married ladies on the list. He looks down the many lines of their gambling debts – very small ones to large ones that Franklin had been collecting on. He notes the saloons that sold their IOU's to his uncle for the money and saw how Franklin had collected them.

The last section says: Edgar Hawkins: page after page of money loaned, deeds done to pay back money, ways both had enjoyed hurting women, burning out settlers, evicting people off their farms etc.

Turning with disgust Charles takes a deep breath and closes the book. He prays a long time then lays the book back into the drawer and locks it. He walks out into the twilight and looking up into the sky begs, *"Lord, you tell us with your help we can do anything. Please help me."* A very sad young man returns to the small house he has grown up in along with his younger sister, Donna. She is surprised at the bear hug she receives when he walks in the door so just smiles and hugs him back. "Donna, I thought I knew Uncle Franklin pretty well. I knew he cheated people but I couldn't do anything about it. Well, now, I can do something about it and, oh, my God, Donna I have found out some horrible things he has done and I'm not sure how to fix them but I have to try," Charles admits sadly then continues, "It will take a lot of Uncle Franklin's money to make it right."

Donna takes Charles face in her small hands saying, "Make it right, Charles, in every way. We don't want anyone's blood money on our hands. We knew he wasn't a good man so we will do whatever we need to do to make it right for those he made suffer. It is his money anyway not ours. So pay back what is owed to others and we will be free to live as we choose."

Smiling Charles takes a deep breath of relief saying, "Now you can marry James Albert and not old man, Manuels that Uncle was forcing on you."

Shuddering Donna states positively, "No matter what Uncle Franklin plotted for me. I'd never have married that old man. He is horrible. James Albert and I had already planned to elope next week."

"Good I'm glad to hear that. I would have helped you do it, too. James Albert Michaels is a good man. You will be happy with him," Charles answers kissing his sweet sister's lovely face.

"Yes, he is and now you can marry Francis like you have wanted to do for so long," Donna replies smiling happily at her big brother.

"Lovely Francis, she is my dream. She has waited this past three years for me to have the money to wed her. I'm going to see her tonight and set the date. In the next week or so, would be my choice," Charles answers dreamily then remembering says, "Oh, what are we going to do with Uncle Franklin's house? Tomorrow let's go over there and see what's inside."

Clapping her hands happily Donna nods yes saying, "Finally my curiosity will be full filled."

Charles nods yes then remembering the book and all that was written in it he wonders, "What will we find tomorrow at Uncle Franklin's home?"

The next morning the young people continue working on the store going through every shelf and every drawer finding all kinds of treasures. Glory and Jake take one section of shelves pulling down each item and looking at them when Jake finds a metal box so chuckling says, "Well, lookee here, what I've found, honey." He hands down the box and Glory grunts as she takes it.

"This is heavy," she groans as she gives it a little shake and clearly hears the sound of coins in the box. Raising her eyebrows she chuckles saying, "Looks like we found Grandfather's money box, let's see if we can open it."

Putting his hand on top of hers Jake frowns saying, "Maybe I'd better look inside first before the girls see what is in it. He might have somethangs you shouldn't see."

Puzzled Glory starts to question him when he just nods no and taking the box he turns his back to her and slowly opens the box. It is full of coins and paper money, full to overflowing to be exact. He runs his hand over the bills looking for anything that shouldn't be seen by the young impressionable girls and finds only a small sketch of a woman. It is crudely done but a remarkable resemblance of Nona. Jake turns the sketch over and sees Nona written on the back of the worn piece of paper. Raising his head Jake wonders, "Did you love her, Edgar, or were you just fascinated by her? I'm glad she escaped you. You woulda made her miserable."

"What did ya find?" Glory asks stretching on tip toe to look over his shoulder.

Looking at the sketch once more Jake replies, "A lot of money and a sketch of a woman," turning around he sets the metal box down on the counter showing her its contents.

Glory gasps at seeing so much money and tentatively she reaches out and picks up a twenty dollar gold piece as she quietly explains, "I've seen some Papa has but I've never seen so many of 'em at the same time."

"Neither have I. What should we do with it?" Jake whispers as he looks around.

"Grandpa said to keep it hid til they git back, why don't we wrap it up like a present and put it under the counter here and then we can take it to our rooms later," Glory wisely advises still staring at the money.

Jake eyes search the room looking for a place to hide it then softly agrees, "That sounds good to me, too, let's just make sure one of us is close to it all the time."

"Okay," Glory agrees as they quickly wrap the box in brown paper then tie it tightly with string and set it under the counter close to where they are working.

Beth Ann and Carrie Lynn are sitting in chairs going through drawers of gadgets. Beth Ann explains what some items are to Carrie Lynn then Carrie Lynn explains what some items are to Beth Ann. Both have a greater respect for each other after finding out each knows a lot about some things and the other knows a lot about some other things.

Beth Ann notices some dusty boxes under the counter so getting down on her hands and knees she pulls them out one by one. Opening them she finds school items – rulers, books, chalk, erasers along with miscellaneous other items. She picks up one of the books and caressing it says, "I read this book a long time ago. It is a good one." She looks at two more books saying, "Oh, I haven't read this one nor this one." She looks up at Carrie asking, "Do you think there will be room to take these books home?"

Smiling Carrie Lynn replies, "I bet we can find room if we look hard enough. Why don't you set what you want by your family's trunk like the grandpas requested we do then wait and see?"

Smiling happily Beth Ann nods saying, "Yes, I will do that." She picks up each small box and after looking through them carries them over to their trunk hoping there will be room for them.

She passes Glory and Jake as Jake starts handing down some items from the top shelf of the open cabinets they are cleaning out and stares intently saying, "That looks familiar."

Glory hands the odd shaped container over to Beth Ann and taking it she looks intently at it saying, "Grandfather used to keep...uh...

something important in this box…what was it? It was at the house for a long time then it disappeared. I always liked the box and after he saw me reaching for it one day he took it away. I've wonder what is inside of it?"

She starts to open it when Jake quickly takes it out of her hands saying, "I'll open it for you." Turning his back and setting it down on the counter Jake opens it while hiding its contents. Closing his eyes he lets out a sigh of relief that it isn't something bad then looking again he knows the contents hold a lot of sorrow. He slides the lid back on then turning around sadly says, "I believe it is some jewelry Mr. Hawkin's took as payment instead of money." He opens the lid wider and inside it is filled with jewelry…rings with stones in them, wedding rings, earrings, many watches, stick pins, and a thick piece of paper with writing on it.

Picking up the paper and looking at it Beth Ann sadly replies, "Yes, you are correct. Grandfather took these items and made notes on who they belonged to and where they came from. He has notes on pieces that he sold or gave away to women." Slowly she lowers the paper then looking down at the jewelry says, "I don't believe people should have to give up a wedding ring to pay a bill," then turning she walks back to Carrie Lynn with her head bowed. She silently prays, *"Lord, I know I don't know much about life. But Lord, how can there be so much cruelty and loss in people. Why…oh, my dear Lord, why would Grandfather do the things he has done and Lord, how can we make it right?"* A single tear runs down her face as she thinks of the women whose wedding rings lay in that pretty box. No, it is not a pretty box anymore. I certainly don't want it," she thinks suddenly. Silently she goes back to work all the joy of finding new things fails for a time.

Glory and Jake look in the box of jewelry then at Beth Ann, Glory whispers, "Jake, I don't think we should show Beth Ann anythan' else like this. She is hurtin' too much now."

Nodding yes Jake replies, "She is just a little girl. She don't need to see no more bad thangs from someone she loved." They wrap the odd shaped box in brown paper, tie it with string, and place it beside the other box before returning to work.

Skinny and Pokey leave Marshal Wheeler's office without any additional information on Race Jacks. "Garth said Race has been around for a long time and that he don't seem to work none and is always short of money then, seems me like, he has money and spends it freely," Pokey explains thoughtfully as they walk back to the mercantile watching out for outlaws (as usual) as they walk.

"Randy said Edgar gave him money. I wonder if'n he made him earn it?" Skinny wonders out loud but softly.

Stopping suddenly Pokey looks at Skinny asking, "We ain't found no illegal stuff have we? No jewelry or notes of owed money yet have we?"

"Nope, not that I know of," Skinny replies before adding, "Maybe the young'uns have while we were gone."

Returning to the store and seeing Randy they ask, "Randy, where did Edgar keep the jewelry...wedding rings and thangs like that?"

"Oh, I forgot all about them. They are in the back. Shall I get the box for you? I'll bring the key, too," Randy replies then he disappears into the back returning he hands a large box to Skinny saying, "Here is the jewelry. Mr. Hawkins kept it under lock and key. Here is the key."

"Does he have any other items or boxes back there where the jewelry was?" Pokey asks wonderingly.

"Yes, come back and I'll show you where he hid them. I should have thought about these before but haven't been back in the office since we worked on the books," Randy explains as he and the two older gents walk back to the office.

As they walk past Jake and Glory, Jake reaches out and taps Skinny on the shoulder. When Skinny sees his face he knows he has something important to tell them. He calls out, "Pokey, come back here a minute, I need to ask you something."

Turning around Pokey (frowning in concentration) sees Jake nodding yes to come back so he says, "Randy, be with ya in a minute, son. I gotta ask Jake somethang."

Jake quietly confides, "We found Edgar's stash and a box of jewelry that looks like it was taken for payment from people."

Pokey and Skinny smile at this good news then sadden when Jake continues, "Beth Ann saw the jewelry and knew why Edgar had it and is upset about it. Glory and I decided not to show her anything else like this so it won't upset her. We tend to forget she is just a little girl and shouldna know some of these thangs."

Both look sorrowfully over at Beth Ann who is sitting quietly going through a shelf of toys. Sorrow is written all over her face. "Yar right.

We didn't realize how right you are til now. Thanks Jake," Skinny replies and glancing sadly at Pokey they slowly walk back to the office.

"Wondered when we'd find that jewelry, knowd he weren't above takin' thangs people treasured," Pokey states looking at the floor and shaking his gray head.

"Yep, me, too," Skinny sadly admits, "You know I don't think Lora was very happy with him the last few years. Maybe he weren't happy with her either and that is why he was so mean to her in the end."

"No reason to beat on her! No reason a toll," Pokey angrily states.

"Never a good reason for that," Skinny agrees shaking his head in wonder at the cruelty of others.

Randy walks over to a cabinet and reaching behind it pulls a lever and it opens a door. Taking the key he unlocks it and inside are shelves filled with boxes. Smiling ruefully Randy says, "The only reason Mr. Hawkins showed me his secret hiding place was so I could make him money while he was gone. He never wanted to miss selling anything and making money off of it. Look here…see these marks on the shelves…he showed them to me saying he'd beat the living tar outta me if I touched any item on these shelves that they are personal items of his. I believed him and never did but I have to admit I'm curious about what is in them."

"We'll let you know, son. Ask Jake to come back here and will you stay up front with the girls for a time. Ask Jake to bring me those boxes too," Skinny requests.

"Certainly, sir," Randy nods yes then walks out of the room.

"Think Edgar has some secrets hidden in here?" Pokey asks as they look at the large boxes on the top and bottom and the smaller ones on the middle shelves.

"We'll see," Skinny replies sighing then reaching in he picks up the first of the little boxes. He opens it and it is full of wedding bands. Leaving it open he reaches in and pulls out the second flat box and opening it they see it contains watches. Picking up a third box he opens it and it has lovely rings with colored stones in them.

Jake walks in carrying the two boxes he and Glory had found and seeing the jewelry sets them down before looking at the beautiful rings. Looking at Pokey and Skinny he asks, "Can I buy one of these rings for Glory's weddin' ring?"

"Shorely can," Pokey answers shaking his head yes.

"They shore are pretty. Wonder if'n she'd like to pick it out herself or should I pick it out?" Jake thoughtfully asks.

"Ask her later, Jake, right now we need your help," Pokey replies then pointing to the cabinet explains, "We need to see what are in these boxes and Jake prepare yarself, it may not be good."

Squaring his shoulders Jake walks over to the cabinet saying, "I've already seen some bad some more ain't gonna bother me none."

Skinny closes the jewelry boxes setting them to the side of the desk as Jake lifts a large box down and sets it on the desk. Opening it they pick up a long black (duster) coat, black mask that will cover a man's face, black shirt and pants and wrapped in an oil cloth two six shooters along with a box of bullets stuck in one corner of the large box.

"Guess he used these quite often to keep them here," Jake states shaking his head sadly, "Wonder how many times he raided people."

"Probably kept them here so Lora wouldn't find out, she was always curious," Skinny answers looking at the offending items.

"He probably used them a lot, too. Let's sit this box aside for Marshal Wheeler," Pokey also answers shaking his head sorrowfully.

Jake lifts each item out and they carefully look them over then he sets the box by the door after Skinny marks a W on it for Wheeler.

The next box is very heavy and when Jake opens it he jumps back in surprise for inside contains a variety of whips, ladies boots...red, black and green ones along with some things Jake doesn't know what they are. Looking up he asks, "What do you wanta do with these?"

Shaking his head Skinny replies, "This will take some thinkin' about. Just set it in the corner for now, please."

Jake carries the box to a corner then returning he picks up another box and set it on the desk then tentatively opens it. Opening it he finds ladies clothing, surprised he picks up one piece after another blushing as he looks at garments he didn't even know existed. When he lifts up a pair of red silk stockings and garters with red bows on them he raises his eyebrows saying, "Wooeee! What'cha gonna do with these?"

"Now that is a thought, Jake. I would guess that Edgar's lady friends wore them or he planned for them to wear them. They look new to me. I wonder if Glory and Elizabeth might like to hav'em. They are made to entice a man and if'n that man is thar husbands that is all to the good, don't'cha think?" Skinny states with a wolfish grin on his face.

Blushing even more, Jake looks at the sheer lacey material and chuckling says, "I imagine Glory would wear this for me especially after I showed her how to put'em on. Maybe some of them boots over thar go with these. I'll talk to her about it."

"Maybe we'll talk to her about it and let it be a surprise for you," Pokey states raising his eyebrows and looking at Jake menacingly, "Or maybe we will let her mother explain how to wear them."

"Course that would be best," Jake answers picking up the box and setting it in the corner on top of the other one.

Jake lifts the two large boxes from the bottom of the closet/cabinet and opening them finds they are full of colored glass plates and cups. Rainbow colors sparkle on the different colored sets. "These are real purdy. Wonder what they are for?" Jake asks as he holds up one of the lovely plates to the light.

"These are party sets. When ladies have high teas they have little plates and matching cups and they put cookies and little sandwiches on'em," Skinny advises then looking closely he sees a piece of paper so reaching in he picks it up then reads it. It says, *Edgar, order Elizabeth a set of eight tea party sets in eight different patterns so we will have enough for her wedding to Franklin. Don't be stingy either. Get her the nice ones. Lora*

"So Lora wanted these for Elizabeth, they are purdy. We'll tak'em to her," Pokey firmly states as he wipes a tear from his ole eyes and taking the note from Skinny he touches the words their girl had written.

"Jake will you carry these up front and ask the girls to wrap'em really well. Maybe get another trunk to put them in, we don't want'em to get broken," Skinny requests as he rubs a hand over Pokey's back since he is still staring at the handwritten note.

"Yes, sir. I'll do it myself right now," Jake replies leaving the room to return a few minutes later with another trunk and a couple bolts of material with cotton batting to wrap the boxes in. He personally layers the trunk with quilt batting and material to cushion the lovely dishes then sets each box in wrapping them individually. "I think when we put this trunk in we otta put it right behind the driver as that is the best and safest place for it."

The trunk is only half full so Skinny asks, "Son, why don't we put a layer of those clothes you like so well on top of these boxes then we can put some other breakable things in thar, too."

Smirking Jake replies, "I'd be delighted." So he goes back to the two boxes he'd set in the corner and taking the clothing he fits them all around the boxes then looking inside the other box he pulls out the boots and a few other items of interest then looking at Pokey asks, "Is there anything else in this box worth keepin'?"

The older gents haven't been paying much attention so they look in the half full box explaining what some of the items are used for.

Jake's face reddens again at finding out this kind of information. He replies, "Just put in what you think Elizabeth would like. I don't think Glory would like any of those kinds of thangs."

Chuckling Skinny replies, "I don't think the paddles would be a good idea. Elizabeth wouldn't like them a toll."

Shaking his head no Jake states, "Got no use for'em either! I wouldn't use'em, if'n I had'em."

"Thank God for that. Let's burn this stuff, brother. Wouldn't want anyone to suffer for it," Pokey replies positively.

"Sounds good to me," Skinny answers while closing the box.

Jake leaves the room and walking up to the girls asks, "I got a trunk going to your ma that has some breakables in it. I need some thangs to put in the top of the box. What'cha think we could put in thar?"

"What breakables? Let us see'em," Glory asks curiously.

"Think grandpas want it to be a surprise. Just wanna fill it up some more then we can close it." Jake answers truthfully.

"How about some of the clothing we picked out for Mother and Grandma?" Beth Ann asks then continues, "We could put some other small breakables inside the clothing too. Remember those music boxes over there. Mother loves music boxes. That could be a couple of things. Humm…what else?"

"Those lovely lamps with the crystals could be wrapped in the clothes and we could make a special tag for this trunk saying breakables in it," Carrie Lynn replies thoughtfully.

"That is a good idea but we should set them in each family's trunk so we don't have to open the trunks and separate them later," Jake advises as he thinks then hugs his little sister for her good idea.

Glory brings the clothing over and helps Jake wrap each lamp protectively in the material. Soon the lovely lamps are in each family's trunks carefully wrapped to keep them from getting broken.

Curiously looking at the trunk Glory wonders, "What's the big secret and why is Jake putting everything in himself and why won't he let me hep him." She frowns when she sees what she thinks is the heel of a red boot sticking out, as Jake quickly covers it up.

Since the trunk is rounded on top as most of the trunks Edgar has are, they find they can stack some of the hats on top of each other and close the trunk lid without crushing them. Smiling happily he closes the trunk and turning the key Jake locks it and pockets the key thinking, "This is gonna be a big surprise." He finds a small piece of red ribbon so ties it to both handles to remind them this is the trunk to be very careful with.

Marshal Garth along with Pokey, Skinny and Charles Sloan arrive at Judge Burnfin's home late that afternoon. Mrs. Leslie answers the door with her bright smile saying, "Come in gentlemen. What can we do for you?"

"Evening Mrs. Leslie we came to see the judge. It won't take but a few minutes if he has time to see us," Marshal Wheeler requests with his hat in his hands.

"He is still in his office so it shouldn't be any trouble at all. Come with me," Mrs. Leslie Burnfin advises. Walking across the room she knocks on the open door inquiring, "Judge, you have company."

"Come in…come in. I'm just finishing some paperwork so I can help you in a few minutes," booms the voice of Judge Dean Burnfin.

"Thank ya very much Mrs. Leslie. It is right nice to see ya again," Pokey states as he smiles at the judge's lovely wife.

"Oh Pokey, it is nice to see you, too. Hope you haven't gotten young Charles here in trouble and trying to fix it now," Leslie teases smiling at her old friend.

"Nope just trying to help out, Charles, here. Remember my brother, Skinny Gates, he and I are here to close up Edgar Hawkin's store and Lora's house…they died down south and won't be coming back," Pokey sadly explains to the lovely Leslie.

"Lora died! I am so sorry to hear that. She was a pillar of the community in all of our committees. Is Elizabeth okay?" Leslie asks sadly patting Pokey's hand in sympathy.

"Thank ya. Elizabeth is okay. She stayed down south with her husband, Joe, and is very happy with him again," Pokey answers for the seemingly thousandth time.

"I never did think she was a widow and she certainly never seemed to entertain any gentlemen callers so I always wondered about Joe," Leslie states smiling at them.

"She is a hard headed woman but she is finally growing up. Joe is seeing to that," Skinny adds chuckling.

"I imagine she is very happy then," Leslie states nodding yes.

"Yep, she certainly is," Pokey agrees.

"Don't just stand in the doorway, men…come on in," Dean Burnfin hollers out then asks, "What can I do for ya'll?"

They all shake hands and sit when Judge Burnfin points to the chairs around his desk.

Marshal Garth starts out, "Franklin Potter died down south and young Charles here is his only male relative that we know of. We're looking for Potter's will but ain't found one yet so need to give Charles permission to carry on the banking business and taking care of Potter's bills, house and all that."

Turning to look at the men Dean Burnfin asks, "How do you know Potter is dead?"

"He and Lora and Edgar Hawkins died down south while visiting Elizabeth and her husband, Joe," Pokey explains sadly.

Standing up Dean walks around his desk and pats Pokey and then Skinny on the back saying, "Sorry to hear that men. Knew Mrs. Lora a long time and she was a good woman. Truth be told no one will miss Edgar or Franklin but everyone will miss Mrs. Lora…she had a kind heart and was always helping people. I'm so sorry for your loss."

Both brothers thank him before Skinny explains, "We saw their bodies and helped bury them so know they are all dead. Now Charles here doesn't know of any other relatives that Potter had so that leaves him with having to handle the bank business where, you know, he works then there is Potter's house and slaves. Someone needs to take charge and see things are done right so we came to ask you to give him permission to do this."

"Is this what you want Mr. Sloan?" Judge Burnfin asks giving him his judge's stare that seems to look right down into your soul.

Straightened up Charles answers, "Yes, sir and I will do my best to fix all the problems my uncle caused and help the ones that I can."

"Since I was a lawyer before a judge and did most of the wills around here and I don't have any knowledge of Potter having a will then I don't see any reason not to give Charles Sloan here permission to take over Potter's affairs," Judge Burnfin announces after he thinks a minute.

"Thank you, sir. I appreciate your help," Charles states nodding his head yes.

"Well then let's get this done," Judge Burnfin states and sitting back down starts writing on a fresh piece of paper stating all of Potter's belongings now belong to his nephew and niece, Charles and Donna Sloan. After finishing writing it up the paper is witnessed by Marshal Garth Wheeler, John (Skinny) Gates and Ernest (Pokey) White.

A few minutes later and a few dollars changing hands for the paperwork the men depart going their separate ways.

Charles stares at the piece of paper in his hands and taking a deep breath realizes the problems have just started.

THE POTTER HOUSE
Chapter 15

"A house is not a home when terror fills it."

After receiving permission from Judge Dean Burnfin to take possession of all Franklin Potter's property, Charles and Donna knock on the door and enter their Uncle Franklin's home. Marshal Wheeler accompanies them on this fine day.

The butler opens the door saying, "Good Day."

"Good Afternoon. I'm Marshal Garth Wheeler," Garth answers smiling at the black man.

"Yas, sir! I knowd who ya is?" replies the tall muscular man named Lucien.

"Would you gather the other members of the household I need to talk to ya'll," Garth requests rather sternly.

"Certainly, sir. Just a minute," Lucien answers then rushes to the back of the house then to the staircase calling for everyone to come down to the parlor.

When six black servants rush into the room they nervously look at the Marshal and the young couple in front of them.

Nodding thanks Garth advises, "I have some news for ya'll. Mr. Potter will not be coming back to St. Louis. He died on the trip down South and was buried down there."

"Dead? He really is dead?" Lucien asks stunned.

"Yes, he is dead and won't be coming back. This young couple are his nephew, Charles Sloan, and his niece, Donna Sloan. They have inherited the house and the bank. They are sole owners and I don't want to hear that you have run off or been stealin'. I won't take that lightly. This here young couple are gonna need your help and I'm hoping ya'll will give it," Marshal Wheeler states with a stern look.

"Yas, sir! We do whatever Mista and Missy Sloan asks of us," Lucien answers immediately with a bow.

The three women curtsy and keep their heads bowed, eyes down.

Charles and Donna walk closer then Donna says "It is so nice to meet you. The house looks sparkling clean."

"Masta Potter, he whup us if'n it ain't," looking up one of the women coldly states.

"She can't be forty years old yet. She is lovely with golden brown skin and luminous brown eyes," Charles thinks as he looks at her surprised by the statement.

Startled Donna blinks not knowing what to say so Charles smiles faintly at them replying, "Uncle Franklin was a difficult man. I hope you will soon see that we are not cut from his cloth. We do not beat or whip anyone. We will try very hard to always be fair to each of you and please if there are any problems come and tell us and we'll figure out a way to fix them."

The women look up at him in astonishment then when he looks at the men they also have an astonished look on their faces as if this is a new concept to think about.

"We'd like to wander around the house and see it. Uncle Franklin never invited us to visit so we are interested in what it is here," Donna states smiling at the not so nervous servants now.

Nodding the servants all leave the room and gather in the kitchen. Lucien stands inside the door saying, "Wa'll this is a right nice surprise."

Looking at him Dottie replies, "Think he be as bad as Masta Potter? He says he don't beat slaves but white people do."

"Just don't give him any reason to, Dottie. Ya know yar place and keep to it," the tall pretty black woman states sharply as she thinks about this new development.

"But Ila Kay what if'n he is as bad as the old one?" questions Dottie again.

Smiling grimly Ila Kay answers, "No one could be that bad, ain't we got the scars to show it. Let's give'em a chance and do whatever they say just like we did Masta Potta and maybe we be much better off."

"Right, Ila Kay, we best do what we be told. Chester git yarself back to the stable and clean it up good afore the young masta gets out there. I knowd ya ain't got it as clean as Masta Potta told ya to keep it," Lucien advises with a frown at the younger man.

Slowly nodding yes Chester answers, "Yep, I'd better do that Lucien," and he quietly slips out the back door.

Molly, the youngest of the group, happily explains, "I dusted everthang yesterday. They should be happy with it."

Looking at her Ila Kay asks, "Did ya sweep off the back steps like I told ya to do, Molly? If'n not, go do it now."

"Yes, mama, I'ze do it right now," Molly answers grabbing the broom as she runs out of the room.

"It's a good thing Masta Potta ain't the one comin' in today or Molly would be gettin' a whippin' for not doin' that," Lucien states sadly looking out towards the back door.

"Wa'll we don't know anythang yet either good or bad about these white folks so let's just keep on our toes and do our best," Ila Kay states adamantly as she returns to scrubbing the kitchen counter.

"Yep, best to do that," Lucien admits as he walks back into the parlor looking for the young couple to see what they are doing.

Donna and Charles stand in the doorway looking at the lovely oak furniture in the formal parlor then they wander from room to room looking at the glossy finish of the beautiful wood.

"Oh, I knew this would be beautiful. I've heard about the parties he has had," Donna gushes as she looks at the stained glass window in the dining room then looks at the crystal in the china cabinet. She runs her finger down the table that can hold twenty people easily thinking about the wonderful parties that must have taken place here.

Charles looks at everything also but with an eye for unusual things. He notices that in every room there is a switch or a piece of a belt lying ready to be used and wonders again at the cruelty of his uncle. He remembers how lovely all three of the female servants are and sees again the youngest who looks to be about twelve years old then shudders at what his uncle could have already done to her.

Walking up the staircase he asks, "Donna will you look in the guest bedrooms and let me look into Uncle Franklin's room by myself?"

Puzzled she smilingly replies, "Certainly, if that is what you want."

Walking into the room Charles shudders at the feeling of despair that fills the room. Looking at the bed he sees places rubbed white on each of the four posts and knows what that means…someone has been tied to the bed posts many times before. Looking up he notices something hanging down from the end of the bed's canopied top and touching it realizes it is a chain. Looking closely at the posts he realizes each end of the bed at ankle height more chains are attached behind the curtains. Taking a deep breath he knows what Uncle Franklin enjoyed most was hurting people. *"Dear Lord, how he must have hurt these servants and how they must hate him and probably me and Donna, too. Give me the wisdom to stop this hurting right now. Please Lord, show me the way. Amen."*

Charles finishes concealing the chains just as Donna knocks on the door before walking in asking, "May I come in now?"

Smiling Charles answers, "Certainly. He has some nice furniture in here."

"All the furniture is beautiful and so beautifully polished. The servants do a very good job of cleaning the house," Donna states as she looks at the bookcase on the inside wall of the bedroom before continuing, "Look at all these books. It will take a life time to read them all."

Charles can't stand the room any longer so taking her arm says, "You have a lifetime to read them…every one of them…if that is what you want to do, sis."

"Yes, please. I do so love to read," Donna replies happily.

"Have you talked to James Albert about all this yet?" Charles asks knowing she wouldn't be able to keep it from her beloved fiancé.

"Of course, I was wondering if we could have the reception here at the house after our wedding," Donna asks looking around at the lovely house.

Charles considers this a bare second before saying, "Mother wanted you to have it at our home. I think that would be best in honor of Mother. Besides now we can fix up our home much better and even buy some new furniture or move some of this furniture over there. Whatever you like we can do."

Looking around Donna asks, "We haven't talked about where we will live when we marry. Where do you want to live, Charles?"

"I've been thinking about buying or building a home. This will always be Uncle Franklin's house and I want something that is mine. I thought we could fix up our home for you and James Albert if that is what you want. What do you think?" Charles asks wonderingly as he hadn't really thought about it until he had walked in and felt the unhappiness that envelopes this house.

Donna's face falls a little as she hesitantly replies, "Oh, well, that would be okay. This is so lovely. Why don't you want it?"

"It feels sad and lonely to me. Francis and I don't plan on entertaining in a big way and all this would be wasted. Do you and James Albert plan on entertaining in a big way?" Charles inquires.

"No, not really, just small ones like we have always done," Donna replies thoughtfully as she looks around the elegant house.

"This would be a big house to clean, too. Do you think you could do it or have servants to clean it for you?" Charles asks seriously.

"We've never had but two servants Charles....I don't know if James Albert and I will be able to afford more than two after we are married," Donna thoughtfully answers.

"I don't plan on having such a big home and more than two servants so this wouldn't work for me either," Charles explains seriously.

Taking Donna's hands Charles faces her asking, "Let's think this through. My idea right now is to move the furniture that we want into the homes we want and then sell this big house and split the money. It is big and we could live a long time on the money from its sale. This house doesn't seem like a home to me...it is just a house... and I want a loving home for my family."

"Yes, I want a loving home for my family, too, and if you think it would be best to do this your way then we will," Donna answers kissing his cheek.

"Let's get some paper and you can write down the furniture that you like best and we will talk about it," Charles suggests as he kisses her rosy cheek.

So they each take some paper and a pencil and start making their lists as Charles makes a mental note to go over every piece of furniture in this house and especially in Uncle Franklin's bedroom to see what he will find.

Back at the Hawkins's Mercantile Skinny and Pokey sit counting the money from Edgar's stash of coins and bills that Glory and Jake had found. The young people continue to go through the shelves checking each for items they might want to take home. What they don't think they will need they are leaving on the shelves to find a use for them. Setting them on the lower shelves for easier access is Jake's idea.

Hearing a baby cry Beth Ann looks toward the front window and notices a wagon stopping in front of the store. As in a trance she watches the wagon and all the occupants in it.

Carrie Lynn hears the baby crying also but hasn't moved yet so is startled when she sees Beth Ann staring out the window so she stands up and looks also. They see a wagon bed full of young children. The young couple are talking softly and going through a small pouch counting money. The baby continues to cry loudly.

Randy notices their interest so walking closer explains, "That's the Peabody family...Cindy is the ma and Howard is the pa. They have five little ones. Two sets of twins just a year or so apart then the baby girl. She has been sick a lot. I haven't ridden out to their farm to collect the money owed from them yet. They live about five miles south of town on a little farm. They never have much money and the farm doesn't produce much."

Still looking at the family Beth Ann softly asks, "How much do they owe?"

Pulling out his list from his pocket, Randy answers, "Eight dollars and six cents."

"I remember a lot of canned milk on that account," Beth Ann realizes as she sees the column in her mind's eye and sadly remembers Edgar had overcharged almost three dollars on it. Without blinking an eye she says, "Mark it off the list and don't try to collect it." Turning to

Glory she states, "Let's get some stuff together for them. They need it much more than we do."

Glory's eyebrows rise as she looks at her younger sister's no nonsense manner then smiling ruefully she asks, "What'cha wanta giv'em?"

"Food …flour…sugar….canned milk…whatever we can," Beth Ann states firmly while turning and wiping a tear from her eye.

Hugging her caring little sister Glory whispers, "We can do that and more." She turns to Jake asking, "Jake will ya git us a box or two and hep us fill it up with food for that young family out thar."

Jake stops what he is doing and looks out the front window then smiles nodding yes. He picks up two boxes and sets them on the counter saying, "Those young'uns could use some clothes, too. There's some extra ones back here."

Beth Ann stands rooted to the same spot feeling her soft young heart breaking at seeing the young children and parents in threadbare clothes while she has an over abundance.

Young Howard quickly walks in the door then seeing the shelves being emptied slows down asking Randy, "Are ya closin'?"

"Yes, sir. Mr. Hawkin's died and his family is here to close the store," Randy explains respectfully.

"I'd shorely appreciate a can or two of milk. My Cindy…well… she ain't got enough," Howard Peabody requests handing him the coins for the two cans.

Randy looks over at Glory, as she walks up saying, "We have a special today, Mr. Peabody…six cans for the price of two." Smiling she nods to Randy as he hands the surprised young man six cans of milk taking the coins that would normally have purchased just two.

Howard smiles gratefully asking, "Thank ya, Miss. Like to have deals like this all the time…uh…Randy…. when will our bill be due? If'n we can, we'll pay it in a couple of weeks. Know Mr. Hawkins will want it soon."

Smiling at the young man Glory explains, "I'm sorry. I didn't introduce myself, I'm Gloria Gray and Mr. & Mrs. Hawkins were my grandparents. They both died on the trail down south so won't be returning to St. Louis. Mr. Peabody we found an error when re-adding yar bill and found ya don't owe us anything. So don't worry about it anymore."

Shocked Howard Peabody replies, "But Mr. Hawkins said we owed it and had to pay it....don't want to cheat yar family, miss!"

Glory pats his arm saying, "Ya ain't. Ya don't owe us anythang. God Bless ya'll." She turns and walks back to Jake leaving Mr. Peabody staring after her.

Howard turns back to Randy questioningly so he answers also, "You don't owe anything Mr. Peabody. We have appreciated your business."

Howard looks down at the cans of milk then back at Randy then softly asks, "Randy, what about Cindy's wedding ring? I owe a dollar on it before I can git it back."

Glory hears and shudders at the thought of her grandfather taking a woman's most prized possession away because of a debt so lifting her chin she walks back over smiling saying, "That was taken into consideration, Mr. Peabody. What does the ring look like and I'll git it?"

"Just a gold band with a bird on it, it was my ma's and she gave it to me to give Cindy when we married four years ago," Howard answers smiling at the pretty young lady.

"I'll get it," Glory repeats then walking back to the office says, "I found a home for one of the rings." Pokey hands her the box and she looks through the twenty or so rings until she finds the worn gold band with a bird sketched on it. Taking it and smiling happily she walks back and hands the ring to the young man saying, "Here it is."

Puzzled the man looks at Glory asking, "Yar sure everythangs paid up?"

Smiling Glory nods yes saying, "Yes, everthang is paid up." She walks him to the door and as she passes Beth Ann she is handed a bag of candy which she hands to Howard Peabody saying, "We know how young'uns love candy. Heres a few pieces for ya'll to enjoy on yar ride home."

He stares in amazement first at Glory then at Beth Ann, who are standing smiling at him, then he states heartfelt, "God Bless ya'll." Turning he quickly walks back to the wagon handing his wife the milk then taking her hand slides her wedding ring back on it. He kisses her ring finger as they hear him say, "Never again will I do this. This is more than a token of my love for ya, honey, it is a promise for the future and I'll never lose it again."

Hugging him Cindy cries tears of joy as she looks at the returned wedding ring but mainly by his promise to never lose it again. She looks at the six cans of milk asking, "How did you get so many? We didn't have enough money for six?"

Kissing her hand again Howard explains as he climbs back into the wagon and they start for home. As he starts explaining about their wonderful good luck, Cindy turns around waving to Glory and Beth Ann as they stand in the window watching them drive away.

"Well we heped one family who needed it, Beth Ann," Glory states wiping a tear from her cheek.

"I think we can help them some more, don't you?" Beth Ann asks pleadingly.

Jake has been watching and listening so he walks up closer saying, "We have some toys here that those little ones could use and clothes, too. Did ya see how threadbare theirs are? We could play Santa Claus and leave it on their door step tonight."

Smiling Glory agrees saying, "Randy can show us the way tonight and we'll drop off some boxes of goods for them. There is plenty here that we can't use and they need it very badly."

Beth Ann's eyes light up with joy as she replies, "Let's fill those boxes up, Jake!"

All four young people jump in and soon have four boxes full of food, canned milk, clothing and toys for the Peabody family. Randy helps by looking in the ledger and finding out what they normally purchase and the sizes (which all good shopkeepers keep for further reference). Clothes are a joy to pick out as each young person chooses a child or adult and picks out new clothes and shoes for them. This fills one full box. All of the young people are tired but happy when this little job of joy is completed.

Looking at the boxes Randy asks, "I can get Chris to go with me and deliver these boxes late this afternoon, if you want us to. I know you don't have much time to spend doing your good deeds and we'd be happy to do it for you."

Jake slaps him on the back (nearly knocking him down) saying, "Sorry, Randy. That is right nice of ya. If'n yar sure you want to then we'd greatly appreciate it." Reaching in his pocket Jake pulls out some coins and drops them into Randy's hand saying, "Much obliged."

Randy opens his mouth to say he doesn't want the money but Jake raises his hand up halting him saying, "Thank you again, Randy."

Chuckling Randy replies, "Thank you, Jake." He pockets the coins then walking into the back room asks Chris about doing this errand with him.

Hugging Jake for his thoughtfulness Glory says, "That was real nice of ya, honey. Ya know they ain't got much money. We are gonna give'em a bonus before we leave. I bet grandfather didn't pay him much for all the hard work he has done."

"He is a good man, Glory. I think that would be right nice of ya'll," Jake exclaims smiling at his lovely young fiancé.

Walking out of the office Pokey and Skinny notice how happy the young people are so ask what is going on and they explain as they walk down to Johanna's Café for dinner.

"How long do ya think it will take to finish cleanin' out the store?" Pokey asks the group as they sit eating chicken noodle soup with homemade crackers.

"Over half of it is gone through now. I'd say one more day and we should be about done. Is thar an attic? I went through the store room and Randy has contacted some people who have ordered things and just not picked them up yet. He is a right nice young man and a hard worker," Jake explains.

"Yes, he is. Edgar was lucky to have found him," Skinny agrees then asks, "Let's see if we can finish the store by tomorra and then we'll go to the house and start cleaning it out. Pokey how many wagons are we gonna need to tote this home?"

"I talked with Jessie at my wagon company and he has a couple of big wagons and about six buck boards that we can get. I figure we can fill the big wagons with furniture and take the extra trunks in buckboards," Pokey replies thoughtfully rubbing his chin.

"Well, we can git a bunch of furniture in those big wagons and wrap'em up real good and that will work out just fine," Skinny answers as he thinks about it then adds, "When we get to our ranch we can put extra men on the big wagons and we can go faster with only the buck boards. I'm sure by then these young'uns are gonna be ready to git home."

Leaning over and lowering his hand Pokey put up two fingers for only his brother's eyes Skinny knows that means that there are actually eight buck boards available and that two of them will be taking tubs and piping down to Joe and Jake's homes. This is gonna be one big surprise for both of'em," Skinny smiles nodding yes.

"That sure sounds like a lot, grandpa?" Beth Ann asks worriedly, "Do you think we should ...."

Patting her hand Skinny interrupts answers, "You are to take whatever you want and we will see that it gets home for ya'll. This is yar legacy and Lora would want you to have it. So don't worry about anything but choosin' your thangs for your homes cause we know ya will care for it and remember our girl when you have it."

Sternly looking them in the eyes Glory states, "We will pay all the men their wages and the rental for the wagons and all the expenses, Grandpas, we will NOT debate about this."

Chuckling both older gents raise their eyebrows then answer, "Sure thang Glory. We know how proud Joe's girls are."

Beth Ann and Glory look at each other knowing they are being hoodwinked by their grandpas so Beth Ann pursing her mouth inquires, "Guess we could keep track of it for you then we'd know for sure."

Squinting at her Pokey replies, "Young lady, ya ain't too old to get yar fanny whacked by me. Don't try my patience too much. Skinny and I will take care of this and give yar Pa the details. You girls don't need to worry about it none!"

Raising her eyebrows inquiringly Beth Ann gives them a look so much like Elizabeth's that both older gents can't keep from chuckling at her.

Leaning closer Glory earnestly replies, "Grandpas we do not want to take advantage of ya'll. We want to be fair about everythang. Papa will want us to be. Ya know that, don'tcha."

Both smile at her then Pokey answers, "We know and we will take it up with yar ma and pa when we get back."

A tired, but happy, group eats supper at Johanna's that evening and talks over all they have accomplished at the store today. They enjoyed seeing Randy and Chris set off an hour before so they could sneak up and leave the boxes for the Peabody family and get home before it is totally dark.

Walking over Johanna reaches them just as they are finishing with a slice of her wonderful pie each then asks, "Do you know we have a new theater in St. Louis now?"

Leaning back Skinny thinks a moment then shaking his head answers, "No, honey, don't reckon I knew that. What play are they doin'?"

"Romeo and Juliet and tonight's the last night. I thought maybe the young people would enjoy seeing it," Johanna asks looking at the three young girls then continues, "I'm going so I thought if you are interested we could meet there. The theater is just down the street from the Baldinger Hotel so it is not far."

Looking at their grandpas Glory answers, "I've never seen a play. I'd like to go."

Carrie Lynn nods yes saying, "Me, neither."

Shrugging his muscular shoulders Jake replies, "It might be fun. I ain't never been to one either."

Hiding a smile Beth Ann explains, "It is a love story. I have read the book but I have not seen the play."

Looking at each other (as if in pain) Skinny and Pokey reply, "If'n ya want to go we'll go with ya'll."

"You don't have to grandpas cause Jake will be there and we will all stay together," Glory states smiling sympathatically.

"What do you say, Jake? Can you watch all our girls for us?" Pokey inquires and jokes smiling at him.

"Shouldn't be too hard," Jake smiles back nodding yes.

Smiling happily Johanna says, "I will see you there." She smiles again as she walks away thinking, "You will have a surprise coming when you get there."

Skinny calls after her, "Thank you for asking Johanna."

She waves her small hand as she stops to talk to some people at another table.

Watching carefully for bushwhackers they leave the café hurrying back to the hotel and quickly change into clean clothes to go to the theater. All three girls are excited and enjoy helping each other dress in their new dresses (even though none are really fancy).

Beth Ann thoughtfully looks at their dresses realizing they will be under dressed for the theater as she has attended the theater many times then realizes with a new found confidence that she doesn't care if they are.

Mrs. Christina sends the three young maids up to help the girls dress when Pokey tells her they are going to the theater for the first time.

They help by brushing the girl's long hair and arranging it in a becoming fashion. All are very excited to be going out even though they are all tired from working all day.

Marshal Wheeler walks over to Pokey and Skinny's suite after Bradford delivers the box of black clothing they had found in the mercantile to him. Shaking his head Garth sadly says, "Don't surprise me none that Edgar was in on some of those raids. It happened ever so often but I never could prove who did it. Actually I never once saw Hawkins or Potter ride a horse anywhere. They always went in a buggy so I'd kinda ruled them out and they always had an alibi. Now it makes me really wonder. I ain't talked to young Charles Sloan yet. He sent me a note that he'd be down tomorra to talk to me that he'd found some information he thought I'd like to know. Bet'cha it is about some of thar doin's. I'll find out more and let'cha know."

Frowning sadly Pokey replies, "Never figured he was as bad as it looks like he was. He weren't a strong man, but I never figured him a murderer."

"People will do most anythang for money and we now know he was in need of money," Skinny admits sadly.

Pokey looks at Garth stating with disgust, "He was into power and control. We found whips, chains and all kinds of thangs like that."

"I have a feeling that is something he and Potter were into. I think I'll mosey over to the saloons tonight and ask around. I'll let'cha know what I find out," Marshal Garth explains with a frown.

Holding up one hand Pokey sadly answers, "Garth, I don't want any details. If'n he was mistreatin' any women and they need help that is all I need to know."

Skinny nods yes saying, "I don't want that on my conscience so if'n you find out we can hep just let us know.

Nodding wisely Garth answers, "As you wish," and returns to his office.

"How about a drink before we go to bed, brother. We can wash this filth from our mouths and prayer will wash it out of our hearts," Pokey sadly advises walking over to the table and pouring each of them a small drink.

Taking their drinks with them they walk into their bedrooms and wearily sit on their beds. Skinny prays: *"Dear Father in Heaven, how could*

I not have seen what was goin' on and stopped it. We came up here a couple times a year. We just couldn't take Edgar more than that. To know he did such bad things to people and enjoyed it makes me sick to my stomach. Please show us a way to hep the ones he hurt. In Jesus' name I pray. Amen."

Pokey kneels down on the hard wooden floor as tears run down his lined face as he prays: *"Lord, I feel like we let'cha down. I don't know why we didn't see or know what was goin' on so we coulda stopped it. It pains me to know he musta hurt a lot of people especially women. I don't see how he coulda done what I think he has done and maybe he has done even worse. Lord, we need yar hep to make any of this right. In yar Son's beloved name, I pray. Amen."*

Wearily they lie down in their beds and quickly fall into an emotionally exhausted sleep.

The young people pay the entrance fee before entering the theater. They are startled as the noise level is very high. Beth Ann and Carrie Lynn are pleasantly surprised when Rodney, Marcus and Dennis show up at their sides asking to sit with them. Both eagerly look at Jake for permission so he nods yes then he and Glory sit behind the girls.

The announcer walks onto the stage saying, "Ladies and Gentlemen you will have a special treat tonight as we have an unexpected talent for you to see and hear...Miss Johanna Light! She will bring you the brilliant shining light of entertainment tonight folks as Juliet. She is replacing Miss Patty Carter, who was injured during last night's production. Welcome and enjoy the evening!"

All of the young people are spell bound with Johanna's marvelous performance. When she walks out as Juliet everyone is entranced at seeing her as a young girl with her long black hair decorated with ribbons. She plays the role to perfection and Romeo (being a handsome young man and an excellent actor named Josh Matthews) acts his part exceptionally well.

Beth Ann (is very impressed with the performance of the actors) whispers to Carrie Lynn, "They are really good. I have been to a few plays and this is the best one I've ever seen."

In the last scene when Juliet kills herself over Romeo all four have tears running down their faces. Jake isn't even ashamed of it and Glory is impressed again by his humble heart thinking, "He sees so much and grieves over the wrongs in the world." *"Oh Lord, I am so blessed. Thank ya so much. Amen."*

The audience rises as one clapping in appreciation for the wonderful entertainment of the evening. Johanna walks out four times bowing to the mountainous applause. Men yell and stomp the floor in approval of her performance. Afterwards Johanna sends a young boy out with a note inviting the young people, "Come back stage and see me if you want."

Eagerly they follow the young boy as he leads them to a small dressing room then after rapping three times on the door Johanna opens the door and ushers them in asking, "Did you like my surprise?"

Laughing the girls all hug her as Beth Ann replies, "Best performance I've ever seen."

"That is a real compliment Beth Ann as I know you have been to the theater quite often," Johanna answers smiling happily.

"It is a powerful story. I'm not ashamed to say I had a few tears when Juliet took her life," Jake declares sincerely.

"It is sad that they felt there was no other way to be together," Carrie Lynn admits sadly.

Looking at Jake Glory adds, "But to know a love that deep is a blessing from God."

Johanna's joy and smile seems to seep right out of her. Turning she sits at the dressing table staring at her reflection replying, "Yes, it is a blessing and a torment as well." Slowly she starts removing the heavy makeup from her lovely face.

Leaning down Glory (gazes into the mirror meeting Johanna's unhappy eyes) smiles slightly saying, "All will be well. There is a reason Jim has been gone so long and he will return to ya. Yar love is so strong, it will bring him back."

Smiling slightly Johanna whispers, "I hope so."

Glory nods yes saying, "I know so."

They talk a few minutes before Jake states, "It's gettin' late ladies. Why don't we let Miss Johanna change clothes then we'll walk her home before goin' back to the hotel." His three girls walk out with Jake turning at the door saying, "I'll be waitin' right outside and Miss Johanna it will all work out for the best for you and your man. We will pray for ya'll."

Within a few minutes Johanna walks out dressed in her street clothes again and they slowly walk her to her small apartment above the café and watch as she pulls a curtain open and waves to them that she is safely inside.

Jake and Glory are ever alert on the way back to the hotel but Beth Ann and Carrie Lynn seem to float as they relive the wonderful play.

The next morning when the bank opens at eight a.m. Marshal Wheeler is standing at the door waiting to talk to Charles Sloan. Opening the door and seeing the Marshal Charles takes a deep breath saying, "Come back to the office, Marshal, I have something to show you."

Garth states with sympathy, "Ain't good is it?"

"No, sir, it is not," Charles replies sadly as he closes the door. Charles sits in the chair behind the desk explaining, "I prayed about this a long time last night, Marshal, on what to tell you and what not to tell you." He looks sadly down at the book in his hands before continuing, "I knew Uncle Franklin was not a nice man but not a cruel man until I read his journal and visited his house, it can't be called a home." Sighing he lifts his eyes to Garth as he hands him a bunch of pages of paper saying, "I've copied all the information that you need to know from his journal."

Looking at Charles inquiringly Garth notices Charles unhappily staring at the book in his hands before he continues, "Uncle Franklin did a lot of cruel things to women and I don't want that information to become public knowledge so I'm not giving you that information. If you want to read the journal, that is all right, but it is not something that should be talked about to embarrass these ladies. I'm going to try to fix what I can of the hurt he has caused and in the papers here I told you in detail where the gambling is taking place and who is doing it as well as the blackmailing Uncle Franklin did but I didn't give you the ladies names. It just isn't right to do so."

Charles raises his chin stubbornly and Garth respects him for his choice so answers, "That is a good idea. After I read the journal it will be just between you and me and I'll help you, however, I can, son."

Charles smile is tight and pain fills his eyes as he reluctantly hands the journal to the Marshal and walks out of the room.

Marshal Garth Wheeler thought he'd heard of everything that could be done to a human being but finds his face blush then pale as he reads of the cruelties Franklin and Edgar had come up with. When he finishes reading the book, he walks to the door calling out to Charles then he returns to his chair in the office. Garth looks at Charles saying, "Yar right. No one needs to know these thangs. Burn it if'n ya want to."

Charles sorrowfully looks at Garth before replying, "I'm making a list of the people that he caused injury to and after that I am burning the thing! Thank you, Marshal, for understanding."

They shake hands and a troubled Marshal walks back to his office with much on his mind and a thick packet of papers in his coat pocket.

Reaching his office he sits down at his desk and putting his head in his hands prays, *"Lord, I don't wanna remember these thangs. Cain't understand human beings hurtin' the weaker ones and especially enjoyin' it. Please let me help Charles to fix what can be fixed. Thank you, Lord. Amen."*

He sits reading the many pages that Charles has written so clearly for him thinking, "Pokey and Skinny don't need to know this. They are troubled enough as it is. I'll just keep this to myself." Garth makes a mental note of which saloons he will be visiting and which men he will manhandle on these charges. Smiling slightly he realizes, "I can stop some of this and I believe I'll ask the preacher to talk about gamblin' and its consequences at the Sunday service. Maybe we can get the message out about this and stop it. I'll be praying about this some more."

Seeing a shadow pass his open doorway, Garth glances up seeing Steve Cully. Quickly standing up, he folds the papers sticking them back into his vest pocket, he quickly runs out the door. Looking in both directions, he can't see Cully so mutters, "You won't outwit me for long Cully, you ain't that smart," he starts walking down the boardwalk looking into the stores and alleys looking for him. When he reaches Johanna's Café he looks in the doorway and sees Pokey sitting with his family in the back so Marshal Garth walks to the side of the open doorway. He stands waiting to see if Cully will come for Pokey again. Thinking back he remembers why Cully keeps trying to kill Pokey: "Janette was a lovely young lady that Cully wanted to marry. She was as sweet as pie," Garth thinks as his eyes keep scanning the street looking for Cully. "Janette was as prim and proper as her mother, Ernesteen, had taught her to be. Ernesteen was a lovely woman with blue black hair and a ramrod straight back." Garth shakes his head saying to himself, "Get back to the start of it, Garth. Cully wanted to marry Janette somethin' fierce especially when he found out what a talented horsewoman she was. Yeah, Cully raises horses. Pokey found out that Cully was still married even though he'd told everyone he was a widower. His wife, always sickly, was still alive and living in a hospital. Now it wasn't right of Cully to lie like that and Pokey being a Federal Marshal at that time had not hesitated to tell Miss Janette these facts. So course she quit seein' Cully and ended up she and her ma moved to Mustang to git away from him when he kept pesterin' them." Shaking his head he remembers, "Heard how Cully's wife died not long after that but it was too late for him to win back Janette as she had already married a bookkeeper named Gary by then. Cully never re-married and keeps trying to shoot Pokey in his frustration over Janette. I've jailed him a couple of days a few times but this time I'm gonna make a believer outta him. I'm gonna wing him and teach him a lesson," Garth promises himself.

Seeing the Marshal standing at the door, Bradford walks over to him asking, "Cully hangin' around again?"

"Yep, just saw him a little while ago so figured I'd better keep a close look out for Pokey this morning. I hate to have to shoot Cully but I will if'n I have to," Garth replies as his eyes continually scan the street.

Bradford's eyes also look carefully all around them then he sees the tip of a rifle barrel coming out of a window in the building across the road. He pushes Garth down as he yells into the cafe, "Hit the floor, Boss!"

Skinny and Jake leap over knocking the girls and Pokey out of their chairs onto the floor of the café so everyone is on the floor as a couple of shots ring out hitting the wall behind Pokey's chair. The front window shatters and glass covers the floor and the customers close to it with its sharpness. Shots ring out as Marshal Garth and Bradford shoot at the window across the street where the rifle is.

A figure stands up, wavers then falls through the window across the street as Cully falls through it, hitting the roof of the porch before rolling down it and with a thud lands in the red dirt below.

Garth yells in asking, "Everyone okay?" then jumping up runs across the street checking on Steve Cully. Cully is indeed dead with two bullet holes in him, one in his chest and the second one in his throat.

"I was aimin' at his arm and he moved. I didn't intend to kill'em," Marshal Garth admits to himself.

Bradford rushes into the café towards Pokey as soon as he sees the Marshal go towards Cully and helps both older gents stand up saying, "We got'em, Boss. Don't think he will be shootin' at ya again."

Sadly Pokey replies, "He's dead, Brad?"

"Believe so, Boss," Bradford answers then explains, "I just happen to see the Marshal outside so stepped out to join him then saw the tip of a rifle come outta the winda across the street and knew he was a lookin' through the winda out front so yelled for ya'll to hit the floor."

"You saved my life, Bradford," Pokey replies unashamedly hugging the young man.

Skinny slaps him on the back saying, "Much obliged, Bradford. Much obliged. We owe you big, son."

Bradford shakes his head no replying, "No, sir. You don't owe me nothin'. You two have been like fathers to me since I was just a kid of fourteen and you picked me up off of the street in Abilene after those cowboys like to have kicked me to death for stealing from'em. I deserved it and I knowd it but I hadn't eaten in a coupla days and was real hungry. Wasn't right and I paid a price for it but ya'll heped me get well then took me home with you and made me your family. I ain't never gonna forget that. No, sirs, you don't owe me nuthin'." He sits down heavily in a chair facing the wall as he works at controlling his emotions. All three girls surround him shielding him from prying eyes then hug him and kiss his cheek as tears run down their faces from the scare and emotions they have just endured.

Both Skinny and Pokey put their hands on his shoulders and squeeze hard as their emotions are overflowing, too.

After seeing all are okay, Jake runs out the door to check on the fallen man. He walks back in quietly saying, "The man is dead. You won't have to worry about him anymore Grandpas."

Sadly shaking his head Pokey answers, "It ain't like I'll ever be able to forget him. His death will hang on me like a shroud til I die... poor man."

Walking closer to him and looking into his sad face Glory declares softly, "He done wrong Grandpa and he has paid for it. It ain't on yar soul that he took a dislike for ya after ya did what was right. Ole Satan got in him and kept him riled up at ya. But Grandpa it ain't yar fault so don't let the ole Devil get in yar mind and tell ya it is, cause it ain't!"

Skinny lays his hand on Pokey's shoulder replying, "She's right, brother. You only did what was right and he took it wrong. You saved young Janette from disgrace and that was yar job. Never be sorry for it."

Shaking his head yes Pokey answers, "Your right, both of you. Thank you. I'll be a prayin' about this for a time."

Pokey hands Johanna money for the broken window as they walk towards the door to leave then they walk back to the mercantile to work some more on cleaning it out.

Seeing Race Jacks standing by the closed door of the mercantile doesn't help anyone's mood. Sighing Skinny invites him inside (after the young people walk to the back of the store) saying, "Mr. Jacks we can't find any proof that you are who you say you are. You do look like Edgar and even act like him (a slur that goes right over Race's head.) So we decided to give you an inheritance from him. Not that he said to but cause we feel it is the right thang to do." Reaching in his pocket he pulls out a fat bag saying, "This is payment in full there won't be anything more ever. Here's five hundred dollars."

Race's eyes eagerly look at the money bag then looking up he squints saying, "Hey, five hundred dollars ain't much. This store and his house are worth ten times that amount! I deserve more."

Pokey snatches the money bag back then fiercely replies, "This is all yar gonna git, if'n ya want it. Take it and go, if'n not then just go!"

Looking at him angrily Race replies, "Oh, I'll take it but I should get half of everything. It is my right!"

Shaking his head no Skinny angrily states, "Man, ya ain't got no rights! Edgar never claimed you and we don't gotta give you nothin'. But we wanna be fair and give you five hundred. Don't come around here again! Now git out!"

Sulkily Race walks slowly to the door then turning around he sees that Skinny, Pokey and Jake are all watching him closely with their hands on the butt of their pistols warily. He smirks then tipping his hat walks out of the building.

"That ain't the last we'll see of that critter," Jake states as he watches the man slink out the door.

Taking a steadying breath, Pokey replies, "Probably not. I'm tired of all this trouble. I long for some peace and quiet. Let's finish up here and git over to the house and get that done and go home. I'm ready for some peace and my comfortable rocking chair."

Hugging his younger brother Skinny answers, "Just a couple more days and we'll be on the way."

Looking at Jake Skinny advises, "Let's make this the last day in here. I'm gonna take the jewelry over to Marshal Wheeler and see if he and the pastor can find out who owned it and let'em see about gettin' it back to the rightful owners, that will ease my mind some. Pokey, I want'cha to go in the back and hep the girls with the packin' then pick out a few boy things for Arty and Sammy. You can choose something they will really like, okay."

Pokey's mood lightens some so nodding he replies, "I can do that," and he slowly ambles away towards the toy section.

Glory glances up towards him so Jake motions for her to keep an eye on Pokey for them. Smiling happily she nods yes.

"Grandpa, where's the box of jewelry. Let me take it to the Marshal and you hep the girls, too. It won't take me very long. Just tell me what you want me to tell the Marshal. You look tired to death," Jake requests with a friendly one arm hug.

Taking a deep breath Skinny hands the box to Jake saying, "That would be nice. I think I'll take your advice and go back and help Pokey. Tell Marshal Wheeler we just wanta return the rings we don't want no payment on'em if'n they ain't got it. Just to git'em back to their owners. Mayhaps the Pastor at the church will recognize some of'em, if there ain't a name for it. Oh, give him this gold piece to bury Cully with. Thanks, Jake." Slowly (as if with a great burden on his shoulders) Skinny walks back joining Pokey who is sitting with slumped shoulders in the back while the girls make an attempt to cheer him up by showing him different toys on the shelf.

Sitting in a chair across the street from the mercantile Race watches every movement made inside the store. Seeing Jake walk over to the Marshal's office carrying a box, Race mutters, "Givin' more of my property away," mumbling he continues, "It all belongs to me. He was my pa even if'n he didn't claim me. If'n he'd lived he would have, yeah, he would have." Frowning he doubts his own words but wants to believe them badly. Looking at Jake and seeing his youthful muscular build Race thinks, "If I confront him it'll be in the dark, wouldna be smart to any other way."

Jake notices Race but completely ignores his presence as he walks over to the Marshal's office doing as he was instructed. He hands over the gold piece to Marshal Wheeler requesting, "Grandpa Skinny said to pay to have Steve Cully buried with this."

Looking at the money Marshal Wheeler nods yes then asks, "Don't surprise me none that they would do this. They are the fairest men I've ever known. Did ya ever hear how they came to get all the land around about here and down South?"

Shaking his head no Jake sits down in a chair across from the Marshal to hear the story.

Leaning back Garth closes his eyes remembering then starts, "They were just young'uns when they helped an important family. Seems me like, they were just in their twenties when traveling up North and "seein' the world" they happened to save the life of a young couple fleeing from outlaws. The young lady had just had a baby a week or so before and was real weak. Her husband was over powered and was bein' beaten at the time they rode in. They got rid of the scum and helped the couple get to her parent's home. Her parents were very rich important people and the husband and her father visited the President of the United States requesting a grant of land to repay them for their help. St. Louis was growin' from a small evil town to a big city at that time so the President requested both to become Marshals and help clean up St. Louis. Skinny told 'em he had a ranch to run and parents to take care of and he couldn't for very long so the President enlarged the land grant his and Pokey's pa's had and gave him a whole lot more land. Pokey took the Marshal's job and with Skinny as his Deputy, for a time, they cleaned up St. Louie then thar cousin came by. You know Reverend Max Roy?"

"Yep, know him real well," Jake admits as he listens with an open mouth.

"Wa'll he'd just got hitched to a right purdy little lady named Bonnie Jean and Skinny and Pokey got him to go back up North and find some decent families to come back to St. Louie with and some for down South. He did a right fine job of it too. Miss Johanna's parents moved here for one and she was born here. They were good people, both have died now and she is alone. I hear there are some really nice folks down South that you probably know."

"Yep, my ma and pa are two of 'em that Rev Roy found in Iowa and Joe Gray is another one," Jake replies smiling happily then asks, 'Who was the important family? Do you know?"

"I only know it was someone related to the President of our United States. They were that important," Garth admits while shaking his head no.

"Wow," rising Jake shakes hands with Garth saying, "Gotta git back to the mercantile. Thanks for the story." Thoughtfully he walks back to the store wondering who that important couple had been.

Late that afternoon they finish packing the trunks to take with them and leave Randy with boxes of items to deliver and some to sell. They are all exhausted and dirty. Jake walks down to Johanna's Café and pays her to send steaks up to the hotel to them as they are too tired to visit the café that evening.

Graciously she answers, "No problem at all, sugar. I'm sorry they are so upset. Cully was trouble just waiting to happen for a long time."

Soon everyone has a bath and is sitting in the Patterson Suite eating steak, potatoes and green peas with apple pie for dessert as they relax.

Looking at her grandpas Beth Ann explains, "I am so excited about taking the surprises back home. It is going to be such a wonderful surprise for everyone. Grandpas I am so happy to be here with you and I want you to know I appreciate you allowing me to help close the store and I know going to the house tomorrow will be hard because there are so many memories there but it will be good to get it finished. Don'tcha think?"

Smiling warmly at them she is rewarded when both old gents smile fondly at her as Skinny chuckles answering, "Never knew any girl who likes surprises as well as you do, little girl. You make everythin' more interestin' cause you find the fun in it. I never used to look for enjoyment in the little things of life but I'm enjoyin' seein'em through yar eyes. You have given me a new outlook on so many thangs that I didn't have afore. Thank ya, honey. I'm enjoyin' the time spent with you, too."

Nodding yes Pokey answers, "I couldna said it better."

Blushing Beth Ann blinks a few times as she absorbs this information then looking down at her feet softly says, "No one ever really wanted to be around me before we went down to Papa's ranch. I wasn't a very nice person then Papa said, "If you want people to like you...you gotta be likeable," so I decided I want people to like me so I try to be likeable. What you see when you look around is new to me so I find enjoyment in the everyday now," smiling she looks around the room further explaining, "I see a great difference in St. Louis now because I see it through different eyes. I see the excitement of the city as I always did but now I see the people and I am enjoying them."

Smiling at her younger sister Glory replies, "Yar loved now and ya know it. It makes a world of difference in how ya look at the world. When Jake and I were at odds, nuthin' made me happy. I felt there was no joy in the world left for me. Then we made up and the sun was brighter. The days seem happier when I wake up and when I go to bed. It is love that makes a difference in our lives and how we choose to live it."

Beth Ann looks stunned for a minute then thoughtfully says, "Yes, I see you are right."

Carrie Lynn smiles looking at both of the sisters realizing that even though everything is just the opposite: looks, thoughts and desires for the future they have a bond of love that will be with them forever.

BUILDING ON
Chapter 16

"Happiness, love and joy make a house a home."

Back at Joe's ranch Hank and his family ride up with a wagon full of tools as Hank greets Joe with a yell, "Hey, lazybones, git outta bed!"

Joe walks out of the barn with a pitchfork in his hands saying, "Well git down from yar wagon and come into the house. We got some hot coffee and pie ready for ya'll."

Looking behind Hank Joe spies the scarecrow form of Aunt Ella as she stands talking to one of her son so Joe stealthily walks up behind her then laughs loudly when he taps her on the back and she jumps like she has been shot.

Ella smacks his muscular arm saying, "Joseph Gray don'tcha scare me like that again. You could give me a heart attack!"

Grabbing her he tosses her slight body up in the air causing her to squeal and grab him around the neck as he laughingly answers, "Yar gonna hug me, Aunt Ella, if'n I have to make ya."

Ella smiles lovingly at the handsome young man who so easily holds her in his strong arms so stroking his tanned cheek replies, "Ya just rushed me, boy. Ya didn't give me time afore ya grabbed me."

Kissing her cheek and setting her down on her own feet Joe answers, "Sorry, Aunt Ella, but next time ya'd better give me a big hug first thing." He laughs again as she hugs him, swats him, then walks into the house.

Elizabeth has the table set with plates and cups waiting for her family to come in the door. Walking over she hugs her Aunt Ella kissing her cheek asking, "Didn't Ma come with you?"

"She will be out next week like Joe asked. Rosie is heping her out today and when I go back I'll do the cookin' at the café for a while so she can hep you out here. My boys and Hank eat a whole lot of food," Ella answers as she can't help stroking Elizabeth's soft cheek as she looks at her lovely face.

"We have plenty of food for everyone. Good Heart brought over a deer last night so we will have some fresh venison steaks today and stew tomorrow," Elizabeth advises happily.

"That is one fine man, Good Heart is, and he is real good with animals. Hank sent him another horse yesterday. Poor thang just cain't take the noise of town and was so skittish that Hank felt it would kill itself with anxiety," Ella explains sadly.

"That must be the reason he brought the deer over. That was nice of Uncle Hank to do that," Elizabeth replies as she smiles at her only known aunt.

"Hank loves his animals more than he does people," Ella states with a rueful smile.

Looking out the door Elizabeth enjoys seeing Hank kid around with Joe so answers quietly, "He loves people a lot. He must really love his animals."

"Yep, I married a very carin' man. I'ze been blessed for a long time. God is good," Ella answers as she watches Hank lumbering after his sons and Joe as they tease him then adds, "Joe's been like a son to us since he was just a young fella. When he said he had no one in the whole world who loved him after his ma died, well, we just took him as one of ours, ain't never been sorry for it neither!"

Turning back around Elizabeth hugs her aunt gratefully saying, "God Bless You all for taking such good care of him and Glory, while I was gone."

"It was our pleasure," Ella answers as she lovingly looks at Elizabeth.

The men walk in and eat pie and drink large cups of hot coffee then start building on the addition to the house. With help from Joe and his cowboys they add on the bedrooms that are needed so in just four days most of the rooms are roughly completed.

"Uncle Hank, ya do the work of two men," Joe states as he wipes sweat from his face as he looks over at Uncle Hank carrying more lumber over to the side of the house where it is needed.

"God made me the size of two men, maybe three, so I do's the work I can," he smiles then teases, "Wanna hold these boards for me for a minute. I gotta scratch my nose."

Laughing Joe answers, "Ralph's the only one who could hold even half of what yar a carryin'. No thanks, but I'll hep ya lay'em down."

Hank smiles his toothless smile replying, "No need. I was just a jossin' ya."

With seemingly no effort he sets the huge load of boards down then makes a joke of rubbing his nose. Within a week all the rooms are finished and mostly empty of furniture.

"Ma is gonna be so surprised when she sees her room. I can hardly wait for her to come tomorra and see it," Joe says happily as he and Elizabeth stand in the doorway of Nona's new bedroom.

"She will be shocked at the size of it. You have more than doubled the size of the house, Joe," Elizabeth exclaims as she looks around at the changes in the house. It had been a one bedroom house with a parlor, kitchen and a small loft made into two very small rooms. Now it has a total of eight bedrooms (counting the nursery), a parlor and a kitchen plus a larger loft with only one big room for storage. Smiling she looks at the kitchen (which used to be the biggest room in the house) realizing their bedroom with the nursery beside it is just as large. She twirls around saying, "There is plenty of room for any and all the furniture they bring," as she giggles happily.

Joe smiles sadly replying, "I know thangs are important to ya, Lizbeth, but guess I didn't realize how much till now."

Startled Elizabeth stops twirling around before replying, "It isn't things, Joe, not the furniture, the dishes or whatever, it is the feeling of home and a place for everyone. See this room (she points to the one they have chosen for Beth Ann) see the windows. Can you feel the joy she will feel when she looks out the window and sees the flowers growing? She can hear you working in the barn or riding in for a meal or coming home for the evening. Joe, she will always look for you to come home. Sammy will, too. We have put him beside the grandpas and they will teach him so much. Then the grandpas each have a room and Uncle Max has a room for when he is close by. They are all three getting old and it pleases me greatly to know they KNOW they have a home with us and that we will be here for them whenever they need us. I love this feeling of family close by. I've never had these feelings before." Elizabeth's eyes sparkle with her happiness and the joy she feels rolls over her like the joy of Heaven smiling down on them.

Chuckling at her happiness Joe admits, "I'm sorry, Lizbeth. I judged ya wrongly. I thought for a time it was the possessions ya were cherishing not the people."

Twirling around again and laughing she replies, "Joe, believe what you see. I love you and with every breath I take I love you more. I love our children. I love our whole family. I love our home and I love cooking and doing all the things I used to think were just work. Now they are a labor of love, I will NEVER take life or family for granted again. Please believe me."

Humbled Joe nods yes saying, "I'm sorry, honey. I guess I'm still a little insecure. I'll try really hard not to be."

Kissing him then hugging him Elizabeth answers, "I'm happy, Joe. So very happy that I feel like I can fly, please fly with me."

"That I can do," Joe answers tenderly kissing her again.

CLOSING THE HAWKIN'S HOUSE
Chapter 17

"The needs of the heart vary as the birds of the air."

Taking a deep breath Skinny knocks on the door to Lora's home. It is immediately opened by Jasper, their butler. Jasper's solemn expression turns into a smile of welcome as he opens the door wider then stepping back says, "Welcome, sirs! Welcome!"

Skinny and Pokey lead the group inside and when Beth Ann eyes meet Jasper's she smiles sincerely saying, "It is good to see you, Jasper. I hope Bootsy and Mertie are doing well."

Jasper's eyebrows rise almost to his hair line in shock at Beth Ann's softly voiced inquiry (as she has never spoken to him unless it was to order him to do something for her) so he stumbles over the words, "Fine, Missy, jest fine."

Beth Ann is a little bit subdued as she realizes, "He doesn't know what to think about my friendly question," so she says, "Jasper, this is my sister, Glory, and her fiancé, Jake and his sister, Carrie Lynn Ewing."

Almost shocked beyond words at Beth Ann introducing young white people to him Jasper nods his head looking at Beth Ann almost in terror just waiting for her to do something more outrageous then is even more shocked when Glory holds her hand out to shake hands with him then Jake and Carrie Lynn do also. His eyebrows rise even higher in confusion when Beth Ann smiling happily at him leans closer saying, "It is so nice to be home for a time."

Gulping Jasper replies politely, "It's nice to have ya home, Missy."

Beth Ann walks slowly into the parlor and stands there remembering all the parties and visits that have been held here. She looks at the straight back chair that her grandmother had always sat on. "Never slouch, Beth Ann! A woman's spine should always be as straight as a board!" Lora's words echo in her ears and a trickle of a tear rolls down her face as she thinks, "She'll never be back here again." Blinking rapidly she wipes the tear away. Turning she hears her Grandpa Skinny request, "Jasper would ya ask all the staff to come out here. We need to talk to ya'll."

Jasper's eyes fill with fear for a moment then he looks over at Beth Ann who nods yes with a small smile. He walks quickly to the staircase and calls for the maids to come down to the hallway then walks into the kitchen asking them to come out.

Fearfully they all line up in the hallway and taking a deep breath Skinny explains, "My daughter, Lora, and Edgar Hawkins are dead! They won't be comin' back to St. Louie or this house. We are closin' the house in the next few days. All of ya'll will be freed. You can leave as soon as we git everythang done here. We'd really appreciate yar help in gettin' the house cleaned out. Beth Ann came back to help us do this. Elizabeth and Sammy stayed down South with Joe."

"Cowboy Joe? He be alive?" Bootsy asks surprised then looking at Beth Ann asks, "Yar Pa is alive?"

Beth Ann nods yes knowing her mother told everyone that Joe was dead then turning to the servants she introduces, "This is my big sister, Glory. This is Jake and Carrie Lynn Ewing, our good friends, who have come to help us move the furniture and belongs down South."

The six servants are surprised almost beyond words then Bootsy asks, "What about us'ns? What will we do? Where will we go?"

Stepping forward Glory answers, "Where ever ya want, ya can go. We will be sure and pay all the wages owed ya and give ya a month's pay to help ya with a new start." She glances around the house before continuing, "Ya'll have done a nice job of keepin' the house clean. It looks real fine."

Bobbing a curtsy the four women smile delighted at the praise then Bootsy anxiously asks, "Whars Minnie and Benny? An Arty? Whar they be?"

Beth Ann quickly replies, "Oh, they are fine. My papa freed them and paid them their back wages and they have bought a farm not far from us. Minnie is going to have twins real soon so they couldn't come back."

"Arty is growing up good and gettin' bigger ever day," Glory adds smiling at the black servants.

"Benny gots his own farm?" Jasper asks very impressed.

"Yep and he is doin' real good. His crops are comin' up now and he couldn't leave'em to come back. They said they didn't think they had left anythang they needed back here," Jake answers nodding politely to them all.

"Nope, guess they ain't got nothin' here....cain't think of anythang," Jasper replies as he looks over at Bootsy.

"Minnie is gonna have twins. Betcha she is dancing in the air over that," Old Marta states smiling happily.

"Oh, she is and is taking very good care of herself so they will be healthy," Beth Ann answers smiling happily as she explains.

Pokey steps forward asking, "Jasper would you get a couple of men to bring down all the trunks outta the attic. We will need two in each bedroom. We have a wagon comin' with some more trunks anytime so would ya set them in these rooms down here."

Nodding yes Jasper answers politely, "Yas, Sir!"

Smiling at the maids Beth Ann explains, "We will need all the sheets, towels and blankets for the trunks. Please get them out and set some by each trunk. I've made some signs for each trunk too. I'll show them to you so you will know which trunk things will go into."

"Want'cha need some sheets for the beds? Where ya be sleepin'?" Old Marta questions as she looks at Skinny.

"We are stayin' at the Baldinger Hotel so we can quickly clean out the house," he sadly explains very softly.

Old Marta (looks a hundred but is actually only in her fifties) looks at Glory stating, "Ya have the look of yar Pa and Masta Samuel, Missy. He was one good lookin' fella."

Glory smiles (giving a trill of laughter) saying, "Thank ya very much. I'm right proud of that fact."

Skinny and Pokey are having a hard time being in the house as they can almost see Lora in every room they look in. Memories cloud their minds to the extent they can hardly stand it. Seeing their anguish Beth Ann walks closer and taking an arm of each of them leads them to the back of the house to a room that is seldom used. Passing Jasper she requests, "Please bring some strong coffee and cookies to the sun room."

Nodding yes Jasper immediately walks Bootsy back to the kitchen advising her of their needs.

She sadly nods yes seeing their grief and immediately starts making refreshments.

The other young people follow Beth Ann as she quickly leads their grandpas to a part of the house they didn't visit often so it won't have memories of seeing Lora in it.

Docilely they allow her to lead them away from the parlor and past the dining room to a large airy room in the back of the house looking out over the garden.

Beth Ann smilingly says, "I love this room. I have read many books back here. The sunlight is good and the chairs are comfortable. Grandmother seldom came in here as it was too close to the outside and she didn't like it. It became my room." She twirls around then looking over gives a giggle as she sees the color coming back into her grandpa's faces at her actions. Grinning again she thoughtfully states, "I feel hungry just walking into this room. I wonder how many boxes of candy I ate while reading."

Skinny and Pokey can't help smiling back at Beth Ann's delight in this lovely room. Looking around they realize they have never been in here before on their visits so it doesn't bring any memories back and that is a blessing. Wandering around looking out the large windows they sit in two rocking chairs with big over stuffed cushions on them.

"Mighty comfortable chairs, Bethy." Pokey states with a small smile.

Beth Ann smiles happily saying, "Just wait until you get a taste of Bootsy's ginger cookies. I'm going to ask her to make some for us." She almost runs from the room but she doesn't fool Glory nor the other young people.

Glory stands up explaining, "I want to talk to Bootsy, too." She follows her younger sister and soon finds her back in the parlor with tears running down her young face as she sits on the floor by their grandmother's favorite chair.

"Ya did a nice thang, Bethy, ya took care of our grandpas. Now let me take care of ya, okay?" Glory sits down on the floor beside her and turning Beth Ann towards her she cradles her young sister as she cries.

Glory feels tears run down her face also as she realizes she will never know the good side of this grandma like Beth Ann did. Then suddenly she smiles saying, "Beth Ann, we lost Lora and Edgar but we gained Nona. She's gonna be a wonderful grandma to us and our young'uns. Remember Ma said, "Lora and Edgar held our past but Nona holds our future." We can be glad of that, cain't we?"

Beth Ann's sadness lifts some as she says, "Yes, it does help."

"Why don'tcha call Carrie Lynn and have her go upstairs with ya and show her yar room. Jake and I will help the grandpas for a time," Glory advises as they stand up.

"Good idea," Beth Ann agrees sniffing. They walk out of the room just as Jasper is coming out of the back room so he walks over to them asking, "Do ya want some tea upstairs, Missy?"

Sniffing a little Beth Ann replies with a smile, "I would greatly appreciate it. My friend and I will be in my room. Thank you."

Jasper smiles at Beth Ann (the first time she can ever remember) then he pats her shoulder saying, "We'd be happy to, Missy." Turning back he returns to the kitchen.

Beth Ann's mouth drops open as she whispers, "I've never seen him smile at me before!"

"Times change and people change, honey. Ya've changed a lot and he is seein' it," Glory explains smiling down at Beth Ann again.

"Thanks, Glory, for all...uh...everything," Beth Ann replies softly.

"What are big sisters for anyway, but to boss ya around," Glory gives a low chuckle then orders, "Git Carrie Lynn and git to it!"

Beth Ann's smile reaches her eyes this time as she runs to the doorway asking then explaining, "Carrie Lynn want to go up to my room now? Grandpa's I'll be up there for a while. Glory is going to help down here."

Carrie Lynn immediately joins her at the door and holding hands they race up the staircase to Beth Ann's room on the second floor.

Carrie Lynn runs her hand along the glossy finish of the wood on the staircase admiring the shine and beauty of it. Looking at the walls covered in silk wall paper she thinks, "I've never seen anything like this before."

Entering Beth Ann's bedroom she lets out a gasp of delight. Beth Ann has a canopied four poster bed finished in a light honey color. Carrie Lynn just stands in the doorway looking at the matching dresser, chest of drawers, two night stands with drawers, clothes closet, desk and a lovely dressing table. "Beth Ann this is lovely! I'm so impressed. This is the nicest bedroom I've ever seen."

Looking around at the bedroom set Beth Ann remembers Carrie Lynn's room which has two twin beds and a small dresser with a mirror on it and pegs for hanging her clothes on and she shares all this with Payton.

Beth Ann thoughtfully says, "I never appreciated it, Carrie Lynn. It was just always here. It is nice, isn't it?"

Shaking her head emphatically yes Carrie Lynn answers, "Wow, nice. Really really nice, Beth Ann."

Slowly turning in a circle Beth Ann sees her room in a new light. Her furniture glows from frequent waxing and not a scratch is allowed to show. Grandmother wouldn't stand for it. Smiling she remembers when she'd gotten a water stain on the night stand and her grandmother had yelled at her and made her go to bed without supper that night, which was a terrible punishment for Beth Ann. Turning she looks at Carrie saying, "Furniture is just things, Carrie Lynn, but all this meant the world to Grandmother and Grandfather Hawkins. Showing the world they had them was very important to them. But this wasn't a happy house. I never felt loved here but at Papa's home I feel loved and it is just a small home. The room I share with Glory would fit into a storage closet in this house.

But I wouldn't trade it for anything because of the love there. This is just a house but Papa's is a home."

Smiling Carrie Lynn nods yes, she understands, saying, "I understand, Beth Ann, but it is very nice."

Walking over to the clothes closet Beth Ann throws open the doors as she watches Carrie Lynn's face.

Carrie Lynn blinks a couple of times at the silk dresses she sees hanging in the closet and the colors all run together like a rainbow. Slowly she walks towards them holding out her hand as she touches the lovely dresses. She notices most have lace at the neck and wrists and the vibrant colors just jump out in beauty. "My, oh, my, they are beautiful," Carrie Lynn finally states as she glances over at Beth Ann then giggles saying "You were spoiled rotten! I'm never going to let you forget it either!"

Giggling with her Beth Ann answers, "The best thing is that they are all too big for me now which means when we cut them down it won't show on the silk and there are enough dresses for both of us."

"Both of us?" Carrie Lynn whispers afraid she has heard wrong.

Nodding yes, Beth Ann explains, "Yes, both of us. I just counted and there are fourteen silk dresses and seven dressy ones that aren't silk. Some of the colors never looked good on me anyway so we will just divide them up. Help me take them down and lay them on the bed, please."

A knock comes from the open doorway and there is Jasper with a large trunk nodding at Beth Ann saying, "Here be the first trunk for ya, Missy."

Smiling warmly Beth Ann replies, "Would you set it over here please and thank you very much for bringing it to me."

Jasper smiles again answering, "My pleasure, missy." He sets it down where she asks then opens it for her then walks out of the room smiling and wondering, "What happened to that mean little girl to turn her so nice?"

Both girls look at the large trunk then Beth Ann thoughtfully ponders, "Let's see what needs to go in first? My books!" Walking over to a bookcase she starts going through the many books in it then frowning says, "I don't know which ones to give away. These books were my best friends until I met you."

Looking at the books Carrie advises, "Choose your favorites and let's see how many we can line the bottom of the trunk with, then you can take the ones you aren't as crazy about."

Smiling Beth Ann nods saying, "Good idea, Carrie Lynn, you are very smart."

Smiling happily at this compliment Carrie Lynn replies, "Life smart not book smart like you."

"Life smart is better than book smart. I will be life smart someday," Beth Ann replies as she promises herself she will be.

"It will hold forty books on the bottom, Beth Ann," Carrie Lynn answers as she is half bent over the trunk filling it up with the books that Beth Ann hands her.

"That's quite a lot, maybe I'd better stop and see what else I need to take home with me," Beth Ann states thoughtfully looking around her old bedroom. Picking up items that mean something to her she set them in the trunk. Soon she has cleaned out her desk, dresser and chest of drawers by wrapping her breakables in the clothes she wants to take home with her. She lays a pile of clothes that are well worn or she doesn't want in another pile to be gotten rid of. She slowly and thoughtfully goes through every drawer in the room.

Carrie Lynn watches as she methodically saves or discards items as she goes. Finally she can't stand it anymore so asks, "What is it that tells you to keep it or discard it? Something's are really nice that you are getting rid of and some things are old that you are keeping. My curiosity is killing me."

Looking down into the trunk Beth Ann explains, "These old things are mostly things my grandpas gave me, some are things my mother, my Hawkin's grandparents and a few friends have given me. I don't want to leave my school things. I plan on studying a whole lot more and becoming a school teacher when I turn sixteen. I want to teach children to love books and learn about places they will never have the opportunity to see. It is very important to me."

Smiling Carrie Lynn answers, "It makes sense now. Let's take a break and see how the grandpas are doing."

Looking at the small clock Beth Ann answers, "It has been three hours since we started. We deserve a break. I wonder if Glory asked Bootsy to fix lunch...uh...dinner for us." They giggle at Beth Ann immediately getting back in the habit of saying lunch here instead of her papa's version that it is dinner not lunch.

Walking downstairs they see a lot of activity. Glory is giving orders to everyone around her to do this and that. Amazed Beth Ann stops and watches as Glory requests this be done then something else be done and the servants jumping to do it and smiling not frowning or grumbling about the extra work. Sniffing the girls smell something wonderful to eat so running down the last few steps they glance over as Glory smilingly says, "Dinner is almost ready. I asked for a cake and puddin' as a reward for all our hard work and it will be ready in just a few minutes. By the time we wash up it should be ready." Turning back to the servants working so hard for her she requests, "Why don't we all take a breather and come back in an hour and try to finish up this room. Thank ya so much for helpin' me out. I really appreciate yar help."

Walking over Beth Ann quietly says, "I never knew you would be able to order people around like that and so nicely. They didn't seem to mind working for you at all."

Glory looks thoughtful for a minute before explaining, "People don't mind bein' asked to do somethin' but most people shorely don't like bein' ordered around. I just asked."

Beth Ann becomes thoughtful as her mind works out this simple explanation, "Ask not order and people are willing to help not grumble. I like being asked not ordered around. I can do this also."

"Come on lazybones, let's eat," Glory calls out as she swiftly walks towards the kitchen to wash her hands.

Tilting her head to the side thinking Beth Ann thoughtfully realizes, "Glory isn't waiting to ask someone to bring her water to wash her hands in, she is going to the water and washing her hands. Humm… well, I'm still learning," she murmurs as she hurries after her long legged sister.

Applesauce cake with apple cream pudding is served after dinner at the Hawkins' house and everyone praises the cooking highly. Glory glows in the pride that she had requested the meal and it has turned out wonderfully.

Leaning over Jake kisses Glory's cheek saying, "Ya did good Glory. First time you ever requested a meal, ain't it."

"Yep, and Bootsy is a good cook," Glory replies smiling at him.

"Glory good job on the meal, Pokey and I are gonna go through the desk in the library next. Beth Ann, we want'cha to come down and pick out all the books from the library you care to keep. Then we are gonna donate the rest so take all you want. We asked Jasper to bring in a trunk just for these books for ya'll," Skinny advises then turning to Jake he asks, "Jake, would you help Beth Ann with the books… hand'em down and all. Then get the rest of the books ready to go."

A look passes between the two men that means go through the books to see what might be in them and look for the hiding place they know Edgar has somewhere in the house. Jake nods yes replying, "Be glad to."

Walking into the library Jake glances at the rows of books thinking, "Most all look new. Better look in every one to see what's inside of it." Glancing at the books he estimates there are about a hundred books that need to be looked at. Taking a deep breath he pulls the ladder over then climbing level to the top shelf starts taking the books down.

Carrie Lynn and Beth Ann hurry back to Beth Ann's room to finish packing the trunks. Beth Ann looks at the four candy boxes all half full sitting around her room so says, "No reason to let this candy go to waste. Why don't we pick out the box we want to keep then take the other ones downstairs and share them with everyone?" Smiling gleefully she continues, "We can eat as much as we want with all this exercise."

Carrie Lynn's eyes light up as she replies, "Yep! What a nice thought but let's limit ourselves to a few …uh…six an hour?" They laugh and laugh at this then Beth Ann rushes back downstairs while Carrie Lynn finishes wrapping a towel around the small clock in the bedroom to take with them.

Looking around the room Carrie Lynn smiles at all the work they have accomplished in just half a day. The room is almost bare. The two trunks are fully loaded and everything is just about packed up. Glancing at the pile of things Beth Ann didn't want she sighs, "I've never have many nice things and to just give them away. But we have to limit how much we can take with us." Sadly she looks away.

After picking up the three candy boxes Beth Ann runs down the stairs then stops at the bottom thinking, "If Grandmother was here she would be yelling at me for running up and down the stairs like this. Ladies do not run ever." Smiling she holds her head up and continues walking down the last few steps then giggling quickly walks over to the room Glory is in and hands her a box of the candy saying, "Here is some candy to share."

Glory's eyes light up as she looks at the half full box of candy then she answers, "Thank ya! Beth Ann, that is right nice of ya." Looking intently at the candy she picks up a piece, eats half of it then asks, "What kind is this?"

Beth Ann is startled for a minute as she looks at the half eaten candy before replying, "Cashew with caramel."

"Cashew with caramel? I've never tasted a cashew afore. Thanks," Glory thoughtfully says laying the box down on a table she turns to the servants in the room saying, "Hep yarself to some of this here candy when ya want it." She immediately starts working again wrapping breakables to put in the trunk so doesn't see the shocked expression on the servant's faces as they look at her then the box of candy then back at Beth Ann. They all know she NEVER shared her candy with them.

Blushing a little Beth Ann picks up the box and smiling at them offers them each a piece of candy saying, "Have some candy, it is really good."

Smiling they each take a piece replying, "Thank ya, missy."

Beth Ann returns to the library and hands the grandpas a box of candy which they eagerly take. She hands one to Jake (who surprises her by leaning down and kissing her cheek) saying, "Thank ya, honey."

This time she isn't surprised when Jake offers Mertie (the young serving girl) a piece of the delicious candy.

Mertie looks at Beth Ann (who smiles nodding yes) before she takes a piece.

Beth Ann earnestly explains, "I'm almost finished with my room. I can tell Carrie Lynn what to start packing for Samuel then come back down here and help you, Jake."

"Sounds good to me," Jake replies as he chews another piece of chocolate candy.

Slowly walking towards the stairs Beth Ann realizes, "I never thought about offering candy to the servants but Glory and Jake both did. Humm...I still have a lot to learn."

Suddenly she stops and turning towards the kitchen she walks in then seeing no one calls out, "Bootsy? Marta?"

Both are in the cold room so quickly walk out carrying some meat for supper.

Taking a deep breath Beth Ann blushes slightly then runs her tongue over her bottom lip before saying, "Thank you for the lovely meal you prepared for us. The cake and pudding were especially good." Looking down and taking another deep breath and biting her lip Beth

Ann explains, "I never said thank you for all the wonderful meals, desserts and cookies you cooked while I was growing up." Sadly looking up she half smiles adding, "I really appreciate all the kindnesses you have shown us and I'm sorry I didn't say thank you when I should have. I...uh....wish I'd been more pleasant to all of you."

Bootsy and Marta look at each other then Bootsy replies, "It is mighty nice of ya to say thank ye to us, Missy. We'uns can tell yar a happy girl now and we are right happy about that. Looks like yar Pa took ya in hand and showed ya what yar ma and grandparents didn't."

Blushing Beth Ann nods yes then smiling answers, "Yes, he definitely took me in hand immediately and when he said he loved me and always wanted me...well...it means everything to me."

"Sounds like ya got a good pa there, missy," Marta states smiling then she smiles saying to Bootsy, "I recollect that Missy here loves that peanut brittle ya make so well, why don't we make up a couple of batches of it for'em to take with'em when they leave?"

Nodding yes Bootsy replies, "We'uns could do that. Sound good to ya, Missy?"

"Yes, madam! That would be wonderful. Thank you!" Beth Ann answers smiling happily then saying goodbye leaves the room.

"That is one changed girl. Wonder what her pa did to change her into such a good girl?" Marta asks as she looks over at Bootsy.

"Reckon a good spankin' started her change of mind then him a tellin' her he loved her made the biggest change. All young'uns need to know they is loved," Bootsy states positively.

"Yep, yar right," Marta answers, nodding her head yes, agreeing.

Returning to her room Beth Ann and Carrie Lynn walk across the hallway to Sammy's room and again Carrie Lynn can't believe how nice the bedroom set is. Dark wood this time with almost as many pieces as Beth Ann has.

Walking over to his closet Beth Ann opens the door saying, "No short pants are to go home with us but pretty much everything else. Would you get all his good clothes out and lay them on the bed then put his books in the bottom of the trunk, toys next and then breakables like we did in my room, please. Anything worn out or torn please put in another pile. Here is his list of what he especially wants."

"Got it. I'll ask if I have a question on anything," Carrie Lynn answers with a nod.

Beth Ann returns downstairs and walks into the library explaining, "Carrie Lynn is working on Sammy's room. My room is almost finished. I can start going through the books now."

"Good, start with this stack first," Jake advises as he points to a large stack. Jake quickly flips through every book as he takes it down from the bookcase. So far he has pocketed a number of sheets of paper but hasn't had a chance to really look at them yet. As soon as he finishes looking through a book he hands it to the young maid, Mertie, and she dusts it then sets it in whichever stack he requests her to put it in.

Beth Ann lets out a little scream of joy when chuckling Jake hands her a set of books. She giggles saying, "I wonder why Grandfather would have these. She wonderingly looks at the set of encyclopedias about animals and their care. Wild animals, farm animals and many she has never seen before.

Seeing a piece of paper stuck in the first book Jake pulls it out then laughing hands it to Beth Ann to read. She reads: "Edgar, be sure book covers match the wall paper. Lora." Beth Ann giggles then sobering replies, "How sad that she didn't care for the reading of the book just its cover."

Nodding wisely Pokey replies, "Caring people in the world open up and read the books on people by gettin' to know'em and helpin' when they can. I'm sorry to say that Lora wasn't that kind of person…the carin' kind."

"I saw Grandmother help people a few times," Beth Ann states then explains, "I know a girl at school, she didn't have nice clothes like the rest of us, so Grandmother told her mother she would pay her to help with a party she was giving. She didn't need any help because Mother always helped her. Mrs. Marks was very happy and Jaci came to the party in a new dress. Grandmother paid her then gave her some of my clothes that I didn't need or couldn't wear anymore. I bet Mrs. Marks was able to get two dresses out of one of mine." Beth Ann giggles at the memory but at the time it had been embarrassing. She remembers seeing tiny beautiful Jaci with two dresses fashioned out of one of hers. Cocking her head to the side she thinks about it for a moment realizing it doesn't hurt anymore to think about it. "Humm…I wonder if that is because I'm growing up or because I'm thinner now."

Skinny and Pokey smile (at her attempt to make them feel better) and appreciate her kindness.

Beth Ann takes the handwritten note from Jake and carefully tucks it inside one of the books.

Continuing to hand the books down, Jake touches a book that isn't leather but wooden. Running his hand over the set of books beside it he notices two others are wooden as well. Pulling the first book out he is shocked by its weight. Looking around to see what Beth Ann and Mertie are doing, he slowly opens it and sees it is filled with money. "Grandpas could ya hep me a minute?" Jake asks looking meaningfully at them.

Both realize Jake has found something so turning to Mertie Skinny asks, "Mertie, why don't you go help Carrie Lynn upstairs in Sammy's room for an hour or so."

Mertie bobs a curtsy then smilingly answers, "Yas, sar," and leaves the room.

Looking up Beth Ann asks, "What have you found?"

"Fake books, don't know what's in'em all," he replies as he hands all three down.

Pokey takes one book and opening it they see it is full of money, envelopes full of coins.

"Wow, wonder how much that is?" Jake asks shocked as he looks down.

Looking at the envelope, Beth Ann advises, "Look in the corner of the envelope. It should say the amount. Grandfather didn't like to recount money. So he'd write it down then scratch it out and put the new amount under it." Sure enough in a corner amounts are written on each envelope. Looking inside the last book, which says Bookkeeping on it, they find some letters. Opening it the brothers find they are love letters written by Lora many years ago.

Glancing at one of them Pokey states, "Well, this is somethin'. She did love him when they married and he kept the letters all these years, this says somethin' to me."

Skinny also glances down to read a line or two of the letter nodding yes unable to speak.

The third book is full of envelopes, some old and well-read and some new ones. They set this one aside to read later.

After Jake helps carry the fake books over to the desk he and Beth Ann return to the bookcase to finish sorting through the books. When the trunk is full they close the lid but don't lock it as Jake advises, "We can fit lots of little thangs down the sides of it and in-between the books."

"I will go see if Carrie Lynn needs any help and I will be back in a few minutes," Beth Ann advises and leaves the room.

Looking at Jake puzzled Skinny advises, "There's over five hundred dollars stashed in this one book. If'n he needed so much money and was always a borrowin' from Franklin why didn't he just pay him back with this money?"

"If'n ya'll forgive me for a sayin' it, cause I didn't even know the man, but it seems me like he enjoyed gettin' money from his friend. He liked doin' the payback, I think. Ya know the thangs we found at the store, I believe he enjoyed doin' those kind of thangs."

Nodding sadly Pokey answers, "I wouldn't doubt that for a minute. I don't think he had a conscience left."

"Sad, but true," Skinny states sadly shaking his head he looks at the floor.

Walking in Glory smiles sadly at them then sets a hat box on the desk dully saying, "Look what I found." She opens the box and they raise their eyebrows at the amount of money and jewelry inside. Glory explains, "This jewelry is nothing compared to what is upstairs in Grandmother's room." Looking at them she explains, "She has Beth Ann's name written on some of the pieces upstairs." She doesn't have to add that none have her name on them, they can tell it by her expression.

Laying his muscular arm around Glory's shoulder Jake gives her a little squeeze as he softly explains, "You had Nona, honey, she gave ya lots of pearls of wisdom, gems of truth and the brightest diamond of love that anyone could have."

Nodding yes Glory looks over at him then turning to her grandpas says, "Never wonder why I love this big ox. He soothes my soul whenever I need it."

Standing on tiptoe she kisses Jake's cheek saying, "I've got work to do." In her usual way she quickly walks toward the door.

Jake's eyes follow her lithe figure then he loudly questions, "OX???"

Looking over her shoulder Glory gives him a sly look asking, "Should I have said mule or stud?"

Giving her a haughty glare Jake replies, "If'n ya don't know the difference, I'll just have to show you after we're married." Then jumping down he quickly grabs her before she can leave the room and starts tickling her. Her giggling fills the air and everyone hearing it grins.

Back at the ranch the bedroom floors are being sanded down to a smooth finish. Resting a moment Elizabeth sits back on her heels as she glances over at her dirt covered husband exclaiming, "Joe, I'm enjoying this. Can you imagine that? It feels good to be doing hard work for this wonderful surprise."

"They will surely be surprised, my love. It is certainly labor and done in love for our loved ones. It amazes me sometimes when unexpectedly I feel the joy and the blessing in what I'm doing. Hey, Lizbeth, I just had a thought. Ya might not like it, but think about it, and see what ya think. During calving time we just don't have enough hands to watch out for all the cows having calves. Next calving time why don'tcha come out with us and see the miracle of birth? Usually we just watch but sometimes we haveta help with the first time mothers."

Turning her head to the side laughing Elizabeth answers, "I'll go and learn. We, mothers, need to stick together."

"That's my girl!" Joe replies smiling at her again then returns to sanding the floor thinking, "I'da never have imagined she'd say she'd like to hep with the addition much less jump right in and even sit on the floor sandin' it. She has really changed since comin' back home."

Sammy and Arty are white washing the house over at Benny's farm and half covered in it. Arty asks, "Sammy, why do ya think women bawl all the time when they's havin' a baby?"

"Don't know" Sammy replies as he moves his whole body practicing his side to side stroke as Benny had told them to do.

"Mama, she is a bawlin' all the time. I'ze be right glad when these babies be born," Arty advises as he also does the side to side stroke of the whitewashing.

Thoughtfully Sammy explains, "Papa said that mamas go through some changes when they are gonna have a baby, ya know, in their bodies. They are makin' food for the baby so sometimes it makes them act different. Now Minnie she got two babies in her tummy so she has twice the bawlin' and other stuff that mamas get."

"Aw...I see. Well, I hope those babies come real soon afore me and pa go crazy," Arty adds with a chuckle.

"Guess I will have to go home soon. They must be missin' me somethin' terrible," Sammy states regretfully.

Frowning Arty answers, "I shorely like ya bein' here Sammy. It's a lot more fun doin' the chores when I got'cha to hep me. Will ya stay just awhile longer?"

"I'd better ask Benny and see what he says," Sammy thoughtfully replies, "Maybe he will let me stay longer."

Laughing Arty gives him a little shove saying, "Ya know ya could live here all the time and we'd love it."

Sammy hugs Arty unashamed to feel a tear come to his eyes as he says, "I'll always love ya'll. Do ya think the babies will like me? I mean I'm not like ya'll."

"What do ya mean ya aint like us'ns?" Arty inquires confused.

Putting his hands on his hips and getting more paint on his pants Sammy explains, "Cause I'm white and not colored like ya'll are. The babies might not like me." He sadly sticks his bottom lip out as he seriously looks at Arty.

Arty starts laughing so hard he can hardly catch his breath.

Frowning and gritting his teeth Sammy mutters, "I don't like being laughed at!"

"Wa'll yar so funny! Lookee here, Sammy, do ya like me less cause I'm colored. Would ya like me more if'n I was white?" Arty asks still smiling.

"Nope. Yar being colored don't make me no difference. I like ya because of yarself!" Sammy replies adamantly.

"It won't make the babies no difference neither! Ya treat'em nice and they'll like ya, jest like any other person," Arty explains to his adopted younger brother.

Hanging his head Sammy replies, "Guess I shoulda known that."

"That's why ya got me, Sammy boy. Big brothers explain stuff like this, ya know," Arty boasts happily.

Smiling Sammy replies, "Yeah and yar a great big brother!"

Minnie and Benny are inside the house listening to the boys talking then wiping a tear from his eyes Benny softly says, "We got some good boys don't we, honey bun?"

Wiping tears from her eyes as well Minnie replies, "We'uns are very lucky, Benny. God has blessed us so much. Can ya believe it's true… ya know….I still find it hard to believe that we'uns has our own farm. We own it and no one can take it away from us'uns. We'uns own land and cows and horses and chicken…lots of'em too. I can fix us whatever we'uns want to eat and we can eat <u>anytime</u> we'uns want to and where we want to. I don't wash nobody's clothes but us'uns and yous take care of yar own horses not someone elses. Ain't God great in sendin' Big Joe to us'ns! I wake up happy ever day cause I'm free, yous free and specially cause Arty, he be free and now these babies be born free."

"I thank God every day for all these blessin's, too. I ain't gonna ever let Arty take it for granted and these babies ain't gonna know what it means to be a slave but we'uns are gonna let'em know what it was like and we'uns are gonna teach'em to be responsible for themselves and thar actions. Freedom ain't never to be taken for granted," Benny states firmly.

"Lucky Penny, yous is so smart. I'ze so proud of all yous done since we got this farm. Yous works days and nights to make it a home and it will always be extra special, cause yous made it," Minnie exclaims kissing her beloved husband.

"I ain't worked no harder than yous has, my love. We'uns make a good family cause we keeps God in our hearts every day," Benny answers sincerely.

The Freed family celebrates the four months they have had their own home with cake and pudding that evening. Minnie even cuts the yellow cake to look like their home and they all enjoy it greatly.

Back in St. Louis Skinny and Pokey stare at all the jewelry and money in Lora's hat box then smiling Skinny states, "Guess Lora was makin' sure Edgar didn't leave her penniless."

"Guess she had reason to worry about it the way he killed her," Pokey admits sadly then asks, "Gonna give all this to Elizabeth?"

Looking closely into the box Skinny states, "Glory coulda taken anything she wanted outta this box afore she brought it down…"

"She ain't like that! She don't steal from nobody!" Jake states angrily.

Sadly Skinny pats Jake's tense arm continuing, "Ya didn't let me finish, Jake. I was a sayin' she coulda but she wouldna taken nothin' not given to her. She was disappointed that Lora didn't have her name on some of the jewelry. I'm wonderin' why? The only thang that comes to mind is that she was gonna let Glory pick out whatever she liked when they came back. What'cha think Pokey?"

"Ya musta been reading' my mind cause that is what I think she intended also. Jake would ya ask Glory to come back down here, no wait, let's go up there and let her pick out the same number that Beth Ann has," Pokey replies shaking his head yes.

"Hey, Grandpas I'm sorry I jumped on you like that. I know ya'll don't know Glory like I do and I jumped when I shoulda. Sorry," Jake says with a half-smile.

"No problem, son. We love Glory, too, and we wouldn't have talked about her behind her back anyway," Skinny explains grinning at him.

"And especially not IN FRONT of you, son," Pokey adds slapping him on the back.

"Sorry," Jake repeats humbly.

"Let's go upstairs now," Skinny advises so they put all the money in a drawer then locking it they walk out of the room. When they met Beth Ann in the hallway Pokey pulls her to the side explaining about the jewelry and that Glory is upset.

Shaking her head yes she understands she follows them upstairs.

"My feelings are hurt," Glory realizes, "And I don't like feeling left out." She reasons, "It don't make any difference cause she didn't know me but it hurts just the same." When her grandpas, Jake, and Beth Ann walk into the bedroom she turns away wiping a tear away before facing them.

Beth Ann walks right over to the drawer the jewelry is in and taking it out explains, "Grandmother let me look at my jewelry, which I can wear now on special occasions, but I can't have until I turn sixteen." She picks up the pieces that have her name on them then looking around asks, "Glory, where are the boxes with your name on them?"

"I didn't find any boxes with my name on'em," Glory states flatly.

"Well they are usually right here," Beth Ann replies as she searches through the drawer then asks, "Did you find any other jewelry?"

"Ye…sss," Glory answers puzzled.

"Did you see a set of emeralds and a necklace with a diamond pendant and a pearl necklace?" Beth Ann inquires.

Looking bewildered Glory answers, "I don't know…what's an emerald and a diamond? I know what a pearl is."

Shocked Beth Ann smiles stating, "Oh, goody! I get to show off again." Laughing happily she takes the hat box from her Grandpa Skinny then starts opening the boxes of jewelry explaining, "This is the emerald necklace and earrings that Grandmother was going to give you on your sixteenth birthday. She thought they would match your eyes. This is the pearl necklace she bought to give you on your wedding day and the diamond necklace is for your eighteenth birthday or when your first baby is born."

Narrowing her eyes suspiciously Glory frowns accusing, "Are ya jokin' with me?"

"No, not at all. See this ruby ring it is for Mother's birthday, which is real soon. This box," she holds it up, "Is cuff links for Sammy's coming out party when he turns thirteen. Grandmother didn't want any of us to be left out," Beth Ann explains in detail.

"How do ya know all of this?" Jake asks surprised.

Blushing a little Beth Ann explains, "Grandmother and I talked all the time. Mother was gone so much that we spent a lot of time together. She told me about how life should be lived as a lady and how hard it was for her at first. Did you know Johanna's mother taught her how to be a lady? She was younger than grandmother but coming from the East she was very sophisticated."

"Constance taught Lora about bein' a lady?" Pokey asks surprised.

Beth Ann shakes her head yes.

Pokey and Skinny look at each other thoughtfully then Pokey explains, "Constance and Jonathan had to leave New York real quick after Jonathan got shot. Ya see Constance was a rare beauty. Johanna looks like her quite a bit but she looks like her pa, too. Constance had the purest white skin and rosy cheeks. She sang like an angel, too. Well this varmint calling himself a man was gonna kidnap her and take her down South to be his wife. She loved her husband and two young'uns and weren't gonna leave'em. So this varmint shot Jonathan in the back and thought he was dead. We just happen to come by and took him to a doctor. He told us what was goin' on so we hid his family for him. We hid him out until he was well enough to travel. I stayed with him while he recovered and Skinny stayed with Constance and the boys and we got'em safely away."

"Wow! What happen to the varmint?" Glory asks angrily.

"He went back South when he couldn't find'em. Course it took a month for him to give up then they sold everythang they couldn't bring with'em and we brung'em down here and they started the café. Jonathan was a chef at a big restaurant up thar," Skinny explains then adds, "Makes sense why Constance woulda helped our girl out."

Looking at the jewelry then eye-to-eye with Beth Ann, Glory softly asks, "Really and truly she left these for me?"

Smiling happily Beth Ann replies, "Really and truly she did."

Beth Ann and Glory hug then Beth Ann explains, "Grandpas I was working in Mother's room and I remembered that she had a couple of dresses ordered from Mrs. Mary. Mrs. Mary makes her living sewing so I know she will need the money even though Mother will not need the dresses. There is also a dress for Glory…Grandmother said it is special and uh…I don't know if there are anything else. Grandmother was keeping it as a surprise."

"No problem, honey. We'll go over thar tomorra morning and see what she has," Skinny advises patting her head.

"Thank ya, honey, for remembering," Pokey states as he hugs his thoughtful granddaughter.

Everyone returns to their jobs so very quickly most of the rooms have been gone through and trunks are packed in every room.

When they talk about the furniture to take back Glory tells a tale about needing each bedroom of furniture. (In this way there will be plenty for the new bedrooms back home. Both Jake and Glory are in on the secret of the grandpa's bedrooms.) Pokey and Skinny shake their heads in amazement but do as she requests and arranges for enough wagons to carry it back home. Soon everything is packed except they haven't looked in the attic.

"I don't like to go in there. There could be spiders," Beth Ann exclaims when asked about the attic by Pokey.

"Well we need to clean it out," Jake replies then opening the door he walks in then stands absolutely still as he gasps out loud. The room is as clean as it can be and has two sets of baby furniture in it. "Everything Elizabeth will need and a second set is here," he states in amazement.

"Grandfather didn't believe in wasting money on new furniture so everything was stored up here. This is my baby furniture and this is Sammy's," Beth Ann explains, "I forgot it was up here."

Running her hand down the side of the beautiful high chair Glory advises, "Jake can make beautiful furniture like this. He has a gift with wood."

Smiling lovingly at her Jake replies, "I enjoy makin' thangs, especially chairs. Should we take both sets home with us?"

Looking at the expensive sets Skinny answers, "We are gonna need'em so we'd better take'em."

Glory jumps up and down giggling with joy. Opening a drawer she sees that each drawer is full of clothes, blankets and diapers. Her eyes glowing she exclaims, "Another trunk, Jake! Oh, this is soooooo nice! We can share some with Minnie, too."

Smiling Jake explains, "No need for cradles for Minnie's babies. Pa is gonna take two of'em over to Minnie while we're gone."

"Ya made two cradles for the babies?" Glory asks as she rubs his cheek lovingly.

"Yep, finished'em right afore we left. Pa said he'd paint'em then take'em over to Minnie. Bet she cries when she sees'em. I carved some pretty words on'em, too," Jake explains proudly.

"That was right nice of ya, Jake," Pokey states slapping him on the back.

Embarrassed Jake replies, "Well the cradles will match the chest of drawers that Pa and Shorty are makin', we wanta do what we can to hep'em out. Well... cause they need it."

Nodding Skinny advised, "Never be embarrassed for doin' nice thangs for others cause that is what God wants us all to do."

"Ma's been making little cradle mattresses for the beds. She said her fingers were hurtin' from sewing the heavy material together so guess with the little sheets Granny Jo made the cradles will be real nice for the twins," Jake explains thoughtfully.

A very tired but well-pleased family returns to the Baldinger Hotel, eats an appetizing supper, then retires to bed for an early night.

While all the hard work in cleaning out the house is being done unknown to them Race is watching and waiting for his chance to get inside the house. Waiting, and not pleasantly either, Race watches every movement from the windows he can see in. He has hidden himself in Sammy's small tree house in the back yard. When curtains are taken down he grins softly saying, "So they are cleanin' up the house ready to live in it. Wonder where the high and mighty Elizabeth is? Never would give me the time of day. Real purdy but a snob! I'll sneak in tonight and find pa's hidey hole where he stashed his loot. I hope they ain't found it yet. If'n pa had'na hired those men to watch over the house I'da gotten in a long time ago. Tomorra I'll just mosey on over and walk right in. Bet those guards are gone now. Then I'll just search the house till I find that money. Those coloreds will be sleepin' and never know." A very disgruntled Race slips up to the Hawkins's house and tries the side door. "Locked, darn it! I'll get in somehow," he mutters as he tries every window on the ground floor (without any success). Muttering revenge he finally gives up and sliding from shadow to shadow arriving at his room around two a.m. tired and hungry.

A sad and disheartened Charles Sloan walks into the hotel lobby early the next morning carrying a wrapped package. He sits in the lobby waiting until Skinny and Pokey walk down then he meets them saying, "I've been through all my uncle's papers and these pertain to your family. The young people should not see these. They are very disturbing. I don't know if Mrs. Elizabeth should ever see them but you should know what Uncle Franklin and Mr. Hawkins had planned for the family. I'm sorry but you should read them or have Mr. Gray read them real soon. It pertains to the children's future."

Taking the package Skinny replies, "We found some notes that Edgar signed that shows that he owed your uncle about $800. That is just recent ones. We don't know how much money he actually owed him."

Shaking his head sadly Charles answers, "Not much more than that. I believe both liked owing each other and they enjoyed doing the rotten things they did. I gave Marshal Wheeler a detailed report of what uncle said they did. I was wondering if you'd like to give the money owed to Uncle to Marshal Wheeler to help those that can be helped. I'm going to have him contact me with whatever money is needed. I'm not sure how to do this but I'm going to make it right for as many as I can."

"We gave him a list of what we found out, too. We are havin' a hard time realizin' the things they did," Skinny admits sadly shaking his head.

"They were depraved, sirs! It has made me physically ill reading about all they did to poor innocent people due to greed. I'll never tell my sister about it and I'm going to do my best to forget it after I help the ones that I can," Charles exclaims shaking his head sadly he looks them in the eyes continuing sadly, "There are so many of them."

"Garth is a busy man and outta town some. You let us know… wait. Pokey let's deposit some money in the bank for Charles to use as he sees fit. We'll take the money that Edgar hid and then just tell Marshal Garth to ask Charles here for some when he finds the needs," Skinny advises steadily.

Pokey smiles one his rare smiles agreeing, "Good idea. Yep, let's do that."

"I promise I will not misuse it, sirs, it will all go to the families that were injured. I promise you that," Charles returns urgently.

"We trust ya," Pokey replies firmly.

All three men shake hands then Charles leaves for the bank.

Skinny takes the packet of papers and walking over to the desk asks Mrs. Christina, "Honey, would you mind putting this in the safe until we git back. I'd appreciate it."

"Certainly, anything else I can do for you all?" Christina asks with her pleasant smile.

"Yep, we gotta go by a Mrs. Mary's house about some clothes. Would ya care to accompany two old men?" Pokey asks with a wink and a smile.

"I'd be delighted. Let me get someone to take my place and I'll be right with you," Christina answers happily. Taking the package she disappears into the office behind the desk then walking back out she rings a bell three times and a young man comes down the stairs.

"Yes, madam?" Brian inquires.

"Watch the desk for me until I return. I won't be gone long," Christina advises. Then taking each of the older gent's arms she walks out with them.

Seeing Bradford and Jay stand up to follow, she blushes then smiling at them walks on with the old gents. Bradford and Jay continue walking behind the three on the alert for bushwhackers again.

"We thought it would be a good idea to have a lady go with us when we go see Mrs. Mary about the clothes that Lora and Elizabeth ordered. Don't want her to feel scared or anything," Skinny explains.

"Mrs. Mary! Afraid of anyone, not her! You must not know her. She is a wonderful lady and full of spunk. Just wait and see," Christina advises with a smirk.

They talk all the way to Mrs. Mary's home where they take their hats off before knocking on her door.

A small dark headed lady opens the door upon seeing Christina and smiling teases, "How did you get so lucky to find four good looking men and why are you bringing them to my house. Mayhaps you are bringing one for me?"

Christina laughingly replies, "Mary these men are Lora Hawkins's father and uncle. These other two men are their cowboys. I'm sorry to tell you but Lora and Edgar Hawkins died down south and her kin have come to close the Hawkins's store and the house. Beth Ann said she thought you were working on some dresses for Elizabeth and Lora so they have come to pick them up and pay you for them."

"Oh, you poor dears, I'm sorry to hear about Lora an…well, I'm sorry to hear about Lora. Is Elizabeth alright?" Mary asks looking from face to face.

"She is fine, madam. She stayed down south with her husband. Sammy stayed with them, too," Skinny explains nodding yes.

"Joe? The one Elizabeth mooned over all the time," Mary states nodding yes then turning requests, "Follow me please." She leads them down a small hallway into a large bedroom with clothes hanging all around it. She picks up a lovely deep blue dress and a sunny yellow dress and shows them to the men.

"What a beautiful color! I can see these would look nice on Elizabeth," Skinny admits as he fingers the material.

"Yep," Pokey agrees nodding his grey head.

"Lora picked up the last dress I made for her already but I do have one other dress that Lora requested for her granddaughter Gloria. She said she is getting married and ordered a wedding dress for her. I've spend considerable time on it. Would you like to see it?" Mary can't keep the excitement out of her eyes as she asks.

Politely Skinny agrees saying, "We'd love to."

Regally Mary walks over to another door, opens it, and disappears inside. When she walks back out they all gasp at the white wedding dress she carries. It is in the princess style with a full skirt with small puffed sleeves and a low bodice. The skirt is layers of net with white seed pearls sewn on over a white satin underskirt. Then on top of the layers of net is a silver skirt which is parted in the middle then pulled up and gathered on each side.

Whistling in approval Skinny states, "Lordy, Lordy, that's the purdiest dress I've ever seen!"

Pokey's eyes smile gleefully as he adds, "Won't that look wonderful on Glory. Lora did a fine job of pickin' out this one. Lordy, Lordy is it purdy!"

"Mary, it is dazzling. Absolutely wonderful, where did you find the pattern?" Christina asks as she also stares at the lovely dress.

"Lora found a picture of a princess named Cinderella and she requested I make a dress just like that one for her granddaughter. It's taken me almost six months to finish it," Mary answers proudly.

"Well, whatever the price is, it will be worth it. Please figure up what we owe ya and would ya pack these up real special like for a trip down south," Skinny requests with stars in his eyes.

Biting her bottom lip Mary hesitantly asks, "Would that include the money owed to me by Lora and Elizabeth on old orders?"

"Yes, madam. We'd like to pay the whole bill they owed ya," Pokey states firmly nodding yes.

"I'm afraid it is rather large," Mary replies hesitantly.

Grinning Skinny answers, "If'n I ain't got enough on me then Pokey will pay it and if'n he ain't got enough, well, I'll go get it from the bank."

When she hesitantly hands Skinny the bill he looked at it then back to her asking, "Is this all? I believe you cheated yarself on the wedding dress," so he pays the bill giving her extra money saying, "You done us a big favor and we thank you. We'd also like to give Mrs. Christina and Miss Johanna a present for all the help they have given us. Please put this (he hands her another coin) towards a dress for each of 'em."

Christina opens her mouth to object when Pokey sternly states, "We's already decided and we's seen this lady has a talent with the needle and we want to give ya a present so don't say no. Don't know when we will get back here to see you again."

Closing her open mouth Christina replies, "I'll never forget you two. You saved my life five years ago. You have been like fathers to me since I met you. I would be proud to have a beautiful dress as a gift from you." She kisses each of their cheeks then wipes a tear away.

"We got to git back to work. We'll see ya later. Christina, will ya ask Johanna to come over here and choose her dress?" Pokey states then requests.

"Yes, Pokey. I will be delighted to be the bearer of your gift," Christina answers smiling happily at them.

Mary beams happily at the men as they leave her house then turning to Christina requests, "Someday you must tell me how you met them."

Wiping another tear away as the old gents walk away, Christina says, "Yes, I will do that." Then she and Mary talk about her new dress.

"Christina will enjoy havin' a new dress. I'm glad we thought about askin' her to come with us so we could surprise her," Pokey quietly states remembering her happy face.

"She deserves all the happiness she can get. Ever little bit of joy we can give her will make up some for what she has been through," Skinny agrees nodding his head yes.

"Yep, there is too much meanness in the world, Skinny. The older I get the harder it is to forget all the bad thangs I've seen. I'm a thinkin' about maybe stayin' with Lizbeth and Joe for a spell would be right nice," Pokey explains shaking his head no to bad memories.

"Yep, we deserve some restin' time. I'm gonna think on it serious like. I knowd this would be a hard time…just bein' here…much less all the bad thangs we have found out. Glad to be headin' home soon," Skinny answers with a long sigh.

"Me, too," Pokey agrees as he looks down at the boardwalk as they walk back to the hotel to get their horses.

Quietly Bradford and Jay walk behind them (about six feet), enough to give them privacy but not enough that they can't get to them quickly if they need to.

Jay softly says, "They are gettin' mighty tired of all this heart breakin' theys been gettin'."

"Yep, they's aged a lot in the past few months," Brad replies sadly.

"Ain't ever day you see yar daughter kilt right in front of ya," Jay stares at Skinny's back before continuing, "A smaller man woulda killed all of 'em. Shoulda! I woulda if'n he'da let me."

"Yep, me, too. Mrs. Lora, she weren't the nicest woman I've ever met but she didn't deserve what she got," Bradford states flatly with anger in his eyes.

"Nope, she didn't," Jay softly confirms.

They all work hard again and finish packing all that they want to take back to Joe's ranch and all the other places. It is an exhausted but jubilant group that meets at Johanna's Café that evening for supper.

Johanna meets them at the door. Crossing her arms under her breast and tapping her foot she says to Pokey and Skinny, "You two have been busy, haven't you?"

Both smile at her then Pokey answers, "Yes, we have. Found out about our little surprise for ya?"

"Yes, I have and I'm wondering why. What do you want to me do for you? Scout out some outlaws for you, Pokey, or maybe butcher a cow for you, Skinny? You know I like chickens best!" She raises her eyebrows at them while smiling inquiringly.

"Well, honey, it's like this. You was so generous to give us yar recipe for yar wonderful chicken pot pie and our girls here are gonna fix it for us a lot. Ain't ya girls?" Pokey explains encouragingly.

"Yep," Glory answers as the other two younger girls nod yes.

"Sooooo, we decided we want to give you a nice present as a thank you," Skinny continues explaining then leaning closer whispers, "Mrs. Mary needs the work, too, honey. She made a beautiful weddin' dress for our Glory but that is a surprise and we wanted to give her some more business."

Smiling ruefully at them she answers, "Sounds just like you two softies. Thank you very much for the present and I will continue to do business with Mrs. Mary, if she is as good as you say. Our theatrical group always needs more costumes."

"She is," Pokey replies nodding yes then says, "Young'uns go ahead and eat while we talk some business with Johanna."

"What'cha been thinkin' about the house, Johanna?" Skinny inquires.

"I would love to have it and I think I can afford it but I'm not sure about some things that I'd like to do with it and you might not like my ideas," Johanna admits sadly.

"If'n you want it then ya'll be able to afford it. What's troublin' ya?" Pokey asks very interested in her answer.

"Well it's like this. There are a lot of people who lose their homes and their way of life - whites and coloreds. I'd like to give them a helping hand in starting a new life. I'm just not sure how to do it?" Johanna explains earnestly.

"What'cha want to teach'em?" Pokey asks very interested.

"Women ...cooking, sewing, honest jobs so they aren't forced into being saloon girls, so they have a choice. And men ...that is harder...I'm not sure exactly…maybe find them someone who can teach them a trade like horse shoeing, farming, saddle making…you know something they can make a living at," Johanna explains with a light in her lovely brown eyes that speaks of her conviction.

"That is a right nice plan, honey, and we can help ya with it," Pokey states shaking his head yes.

"Yes, definitely that would be a wonderful thang to do. Johanna, you could move yar café over to the house. It has a large kitchen and dinin' room and you could make the parlor and sittin' rooms into eating rooms real easy like. Also the coloreds that live there might want to stay and work for you. They are really good cooks and they keep the house real clean. It has six bedrooms and an attic that could be made into one maybe two bedrooms. The coloreds need better places than those shanties they live in. I'd change that real quick like. We plan on givin'em enough to start over and they could do it with you right there where they's worked for so long. It won't hurt a askin' them tomorra," Skinny explains with a happy light in his eyes.

"You have talked me into it. I'll be praying really hard tonight that God will show me the way to help these homeless and hurting people," Johanna answers happily.

"God Bless yar givin' heart!" Pokey states smiling at the lovely young lady.

Early the next morning the details are ironed out as Johanna walks to the bank and deposits the money for the house in an account for Elizabeth and Joe and takes possession of the former Hawkins's home.

Delighted she accompanies Skinny, Pokey and Marshal Wheeler to the house to talk with the servants.

Skinny asks they all assemble in the parlor explaining, "Miss Johanna has bought the house today. She is gonna change it into a happy place. Even the color outside is gonna change to yalla cause her famous Chicken Pot Pie is gonna make this house famous. One of the reasons Pokey and I are here is to give ya'll your freedom papers. Marshal Wheeler is here to answer any questions you have on that, too."

Pokey explains, "We know you have worked here for a long time and will be needin' money to start out on. So each of ya'll be given some money to do this," Pokey hands out the envelopes of money as

Skinny hands out the papers stating they are free people now and can go anywhere they like at any time.

Wiping a tear away Jasper shakes hands with Pokey and Skinny when they offer him their handshakes saying, "Neva thought I'd be a free man. Thought I'd always hafta do others biddin'. This is a wonderful feelin' knowin' I'ze can go anywhere and dos anything I want. But, sirs, I don't know what to do or where's to go?"

Johanna smiles her lovely smile answering, "You can stay here at the house and help me if you wish to. I'm going to make this a happy home. I'll be moving my café over here and there are some changes that I will be making. I'm going to need some help. One of the main reasons I'm buying the house is to help people who don't have homes learn a trade so they can earn their own living. There's not a reason in the world that you can't be the first ones. We can talk about what you'd like to do the rest of your life and I'll see what I can do to help you do it. Of course, with my café I'm going to need people to help me with it. Right now my café is fairly small just one room but here I can enlarge it and I'll need more workers for it. If you choose to do this then I'll be paying you a wage to work for me. Also we are going to tear down those shanties in the back and build some nice little homes for the workers I hire. Today is your freedom day so think about what you'd like to do and talk to me about it tomorrow."

"Where will we go tonight?" Mertie asks looking at Johanna in terror.

"But how we live?" Bootsy asks fearfully, "We ain't got nobody to go to."

"You may stay where you are for a week whether you decide to work for me or not. This should give you time to think about what you'd like to do," Johanna kindly offers.

"I knew when the house be empty that we would hafta find a new home, cause they be nothing to do here. But I'ze never expected this to happen," Jasper states smiling then continues, "I'ze say right now that I'ze likes to stay and work for ya. Bootsy be my wife and Mertie is my little girl so after we'uns talk we tell ya, okay, Missy?"

"That is okay by me and please call me Miss Johanna not Missy. I'll call you Mr. Jasper, if that is acceptable. You are going to work for me. I don't own slaves and I don't have servants. I have paid workers," Johanna advises them all.

"Miss Johanna will we be able to…uh…learn to read and write now?" Mertie asks with excitement in her eyes then continues, "I seen Missy Beth Ann a readin' all the time and she loved it. I'ze think I'ze love it too."

Chuckling Johanna rubs Mertie's stiff little pig tails saying, "Yes, Miss Mertie, I can arrange that."

"Honest and truthful you will teach us to read and write?" Bootsy asks in amazement.

"It will be my honor to do it," Johanna answers smiling at her then turning to Skinny and Pokey says, "Why didn't I think about this before. Everyone needs to learn to read and write. I can make a school room available for any and all who want to learn. I'll just have to find a willing teacher. But I can do that."

"Yes, you see God is working to help you already," Skinny answers smiling at her.

"We were gonna donate some books from the store to a school or the library instead we will send them over here. We'll stop by the store and tell Randy to send'em to you when you are ready," Pokey states with a grin.

"Thank you so much. You are making my dream come true," Johanna exclaims hugging each of them.

"We gotta get goin' we are leavin' in a while to head home. You take care and Marshal Wheeler will be keepin' an eye on you for us," Pokey advises as they hug her again.

Marshal Wheeler walks out the door meeting Bradford and Jay waiting for them as he promises, "Yes, I'll keep an eye on her and her new enterprise. She may have some trouble over it. Some whites don't like the idea of educating the coloreds but I believe it just makes us all better people. I'll be around when she needs me and I'll check in with her every day until things shape up for her."

"We really appreciate it, Garth. Remember the money at the bank for the families or anyone who needs help from whatever Franklin and Edgar did to'em," Skinny reminds him.

"I'll take care of it and send ya a letter occasionally and let ya know what is happenin'," Garth promises.

"Thank ya, son. We are leavin' a lot of our problems on yar back, sorry for that but know ya to be a real fair man and that is what we need,"

Pokey states sincerely then hands him a fat envelope saying, "Don't think about returning it, son."

Garth stares down at the heavy envelope and starts to open his mouth to say something when Brad pats his shoulder softly saying, "Ease their hearts as well as thar minds and take it, Garth."

Taking a deep breath Garth nods yes calling out to Skinny and Pokey as they walk away, "Thank ya and God Bless ya on yar way home." Looking down he smiles and shaking his head thinks, "Well Sue now yar gonna get those improvements to the house you've been awantin'. He smiles at the happiness it will bring his lovely wife to have some new furniture and a rug or two for their home. Smiling and thinking out loud he says, "I believe my three young'uns would like to have a few new toys and store bought candy. Think I'll mosey over to the mercantile and see what they have for'em."

Late that evening Race breaks a window at the old Hawkins's house and climbs into the library. He quickly moves into a corner then squinting in the moonlight realizes the room is empty. As quietly as he can he moves from room to room seeing they are all empty. Taking off his boots and carrying them he runs upstairs in his holey socks and stares in astonishment at the empty rooms. All the way up to the attic he runs looking for something...anything...left for him to steal and finds nothing. Disappointment runs through him like a plague then he grits his teeth promising, "I watched the back of the house all day. They musta loaded the furniture out the front door. Don't they know ya never load out the front door... just the side or back door! Don't they got any edicut to know that! Guess this means I'm gonna haveta get some men and follow'em south and get what belongs to me." Slipping out as quietly as possible he leaves the Hawkins's house for the last time. He moves from saloon to saloon getting and paying off men to go with him to collect HIS belongings from Skinny, Pokey and their family.

HEADING SOUTH
Chapter 18

"The way maybe long but the fellowship is grand."

Soon the wagon train leaves St. Louis with a group of riders riding their horses beside the wagons. Three large Conestoga wagons follow the buck boards all loaded with belongings going home with the families. Each piece of furniture has been lovingly wrapped in protective covers to keep them looking new. Dishes are carefully wrapped and stored in barrels and breakables wrapped and rewrapped to insure their safe arrival.

Happiness and a little tiredness surrounds the travelers as they start the long ride back to Skinny and Pokey's ranch then onto Joe's home with a few deliveries to be made around there.

"What a life! To be in the open air, ridin' my horse beside my favorite men, and with the best sisters in the whole wide world, this is so wonderful! I can hardly wait to git back home and show'em everythan' we brought'em. They are gonna be so surprised," Glory exclaims with a trill of laughter.

Smiling at his radiant young wife-to-be Jake answers, "It has been so much fun. I'll never forget this trip Grandpas. Thanks for lettin' me come with ya'll."

"Thank you, Jake! We couldna done it without you. You lightened our load considerably. Proud to have you with us and in the family," Skinny answers smiling at the young giant of a man.

Bowing Jake replies, "Thank you back and ya'll are most welcome. I will remember always the nice hotel...and" he slides his eyes over to Glory and softly says, "The bathhouse....Yar shower house was somethang I've neva seen before. The food was really good. I ate in a fancy hotel, too. I've stored up a bunch of memories to last me a long time. I enjoyed it, sirs."

Leaning over closer to him Glory loudly says, "I heard the part about the bathhouse. Yar gonna tell me about that....I ain't gonna forget it."

"Someday, my love, someday," Jake replies smiling smugly at her.

Leaning forward Carrie Lynn explains, "Grandpas, it was a dream trip for me, too. I've never stayed in a hotel like that before or even seen an indoor bathing tub. It was wonderful. I'd never had anyone to wait on me like those nice girls did either. We left them some money as a thank you gift. They were really good to us. I can't wait to tell Ma and Pa all about the fancy restaurant and fix them chicken pot pies. They will love them, too."

"Well ya'll earned yar stay that is for sure. We worked ya like horses and not once did I hear any of ya complain," Pokey compliments the young people.

"It was hard work but we did it for ourselves. Remember ya said ya'd be givin' Pa an accountin' of the expenses. We don't want to take advantage of yar good natures," Glory replies giving them the "Joe look" squinting her eyes and raising up her left eyebrow.

Both of the old gents chuckle at her menacing look as Skinny answers, "We will explain it all to your Ma and Pa."

"We are going to have so much fun with all the surprises we have planned. I can hardly wait to see Minnie and Benny's faces when they see what we have brought them," Beth Ann exclaims laughing gleefully.

"How about Ma's face when she sees the lamp with the crystals on it?" Carrie Lynn giggles answering.

"We'd better give it to her last or she won't see anything else," Jake suggests laughing at the delight their mother will experience with the lovely pink lamp they are bringing her.

"True enough. She does love sparkles," Glory giggles with him.

"I wanna see Joe and Pa's faces when they see the Stetsons we brung'em. Their mouths will drop open and they will stutter...me???? Ya brought ME a new hat? Then when they see the nice furniture we have for our new home, wa'll they ain't gonna be any containin' their happiness for us," Jake's laughter mingles with the other young peoples as they envision all the joy they will be bringing to their families.

Pokey nudges Skinny saying, "It was worth it all to see the young'uns so happy. It was hard but we did what had to be done. Now we can just sit back and enjoy the blessin's of doin' it."

Smiling back at his brother Skinny says, "Yep! The hard times are about over."

"The young'uns think they know all the surprises but they don't," Pokey chuckles as he winks at his brother.

"Always nice to keep a few surprises going for the ones who like to giv'em so much," Skinny agrees.

"I cain't wait til Jake sees the bathing tub we are carrying for him and Glory. Think we can just leave it in the wagon at the ranch until their home is built?" Pokey asks as he thinks about this wonderful surprise.

"That sounds like a good idea...maybe deliver it when the house is bein' built cause the floors gonna hafta be strong to hold that big tub on it," Skinny states as he thinks about it.

"Yep, yar right. That will be some fun, won't it?" Pokey chuckles delightedly.

The first day is full of joy. Everyone remembers things that they haven't told someone about so it is spent in remembrances and even a few tears but happy ones.

Sitting around the campfire the first evening, Pokey asks, "I've been thinkin' about the Indian braves a takin' the girls on the way up here and I think we otta teach ya to shoot a gun. Carrie Lynn, do ya know how?"

"No, Pa said he'd teach me someday but hasn't yet," Carrie answers honestly.

"Beth Ann, do ya know how?" Pokey asks her as she stares shocked at him.

"No, I'm not fond of guns, Grandpa," Beth Ann grimaces as she thinks about it. They can just hear her thinking, "Ladies don't shoot guns."

"It's a fact that everyone should know how to use one, it could save your life someday," Skinny explains to the reluctant girls.

"That's a good idea, grandpa. Both the girls need to know how. Maybe we could practice with'em some during the day and in the evenings," Jake answers thoughtfully.

"I'll teach'em all I know and girls it ain't hard to do. You just put yar eyes on what ya want to shoot and point the gun in that direction. I'm sure we got some guns that won't be too heavy," Pokey advises as he thinks it through.

Beth Ann and Carrie Lynn glance hesitantly at each other then Carrie Lynn shrugs and giggling replies, "Okay, I will make a bet with you that I will shoot better than you will, Beth Ann. I know because "I" was born in the south and have been around guns all MY life and YOU have probably never even seen a gun." She giggles and giggles after offering this dare to get Beth Ann interested.

"Have you ever touched a gun, my dear?" Beth Ann asks in her Elizabeth voice.

"Why, yes, my dear. I picked up my Pa's gun and handed it to him once," Carrie Lynn states in a high toned nasal voice then giggles some more.

"She doesn't say she dropped it twice cause she picked it up with two fingers as if it were a rat," Jake explains laughing as he tells on his sister.

"Well, my dear, I did touch it. Have you ever touched one, deary?" Carrie Lynn inquires in her nasal tone again trying not to giggle.

"No, madam. I have not but TODAY I will. So who wants to explain how we do this new acquisition to our education," Beth Ann states in her new teacher style.

So everyone starts explaining the way they shoot and the way to hold the gun so this discussion takes them through noon the next day when the girls have their first lesson.

Pokey shows them first and after getting used to the weight of the large guns they lift them and aim at a tree and fire. Both completely miss the tree. This aggravates the girls because due to the challenge both are striving hard to beat the other one. The second shot is closer but still misses the tree by five feet. Glory strolls over and talks to them a few minutes helping each one aim their gun and this time both girls hit the tree. Both jump up and down in joy at their accomplishment.

Glory ducks and grabs their guns as the girls dance around wildly pointing their guns in all directions.

Chuckling Jake leans over to Bradford and Jay saying, "We'd better stay far away when they are shootin' in any direction we are in."

"Betcha a dollar Beth Ann does better," Bradford replies with a smile.

"I'll take that bet. Gotta protect my sister's pride here and bet on her," Jake answers so they shake hands.

Watching all the girls Jay says, "I shorely wouldn't wanna tangle with Glory. She looks like she could be a mite mean, if'n she had to be."

"Yep, she can be. She whispered something to Gray Bear when she had him down on the ground and by his startled look I don't think it was a nice thang. She wouldn't tell me what she said but I can just imagine," Jake explains looking proudly over at his little love as she instructs the younger girls in shooting.

Race and his outlaw buddies are not far behind and hearing the shooting decide to stay farther back from the wagon train.

Thoughtfully Race advises, "Tonight we'll sneak up and see if'n we can get a good look at'em. With all those wagons they are havin' to go real slow so it shouldn't be hard to trap'em somewhere. Albert, you and Patch ride around'em and git in front of'em and see where they are going so we can trap'em."

Both men nod yes while chewing on jerky then lay down on their blankets and are quickly asleep.

Some of the outlaws grumble at not having a hot meal or at least hot coffee with their cold biscuits and dried jerky. They mumble until Race states, "Okay tomorra night we'll have a hot meal and fresh game, but we cain't do any shootin' so Golden Eagle will hafta get us some meat with his bow and arra's."

The brave nods yes so soon everyone is snoring.

At daybreak the girls fix hot coffee, hot biscuits with bacon for breakfast with plenty for everyone to eat all they want. They all start out well fed and happy while the group following them has two day old biscuits and more dried jerky along with stale water from their canteens.

Albert and Patch (Race's men) ride to the west of the group they are following and by noon have made a half circle and ride a mile or so to the southwest of them.

Once or twice Jay stops and looks in their direction but can't see anything but is still very watchful. His senses tell him something isn't right and he always goes by his Indian senses.

Brad notices he keeps looking towards the west so asks, "What wrong, man?"

"Nothing I can see but it feels bad," Jay answers as he searches the landscape finding nothing menacing in his view.

"Wa'll I know if'n ya say so to keep an eye out so I will, too," Bradford replies watching the horizon for any sign of danger.

"Pokey, me and Jay gonna take a little walk around the campsite tonight so don'tcha shoot us when we come back in," Bradford advises his bosses.

"Some one followin' us?" Skinny inquires surprised.

"Don't know, boss, just feel somethang ain't right," Jay answers thoughtfully.

"Do what you need to do and thank you," Skinny replies smiling at his men.

After a good meal that evening Jay and Bradford slip out and run a mile to the west then circle north looking for any sign of followers but come back with nothing to report.

"Still don't feel right, Brad. Somethings out there, I feel it," Jay whispers quietly to his pal.

"We'll keep our eyes open, partner," Brad whispers back then exhausted both sleep but very lightly.

Beth Ann's sleep is interrupted by a nightmare. She dreams she is running through a valley when suddenly an Indian man with blood red stripes across his face and a vivid scar across his chest along with a crazed expression on his face is in front of her. She moans in her sleep turning one way then another trying to out run the man chasing her. She raises her arms to protect her face when in her dream the man says something and lunges at her. She gives a loud piercing scream and wakes up fighting.

Jake tries to hold her saying, "It's okay, honey. It's okay. Jake is here. I'll not let anyone hurt'cha. I promise. No one will hurt'cha."

Sobbing loudly she hugs him tightly as he comforts her.

"What'cha dream about honey?" Pokey inquires feeling helpless.

"A big mean Indian brave was chasing me! He said he'd been sent to kill me. He grabbed me and I fought with him screaming," Beth Ann stutters as she shakes violently.

"Was it one of the braves who kidnapped you?" Glory asks as she rubs her sister's arm feeling the goose bumps on them. Frowning she looks at Jake saying, "It was real to her."

Nodding yes, Jake says, "Honey, it's all right no one will hurt'cha. None of us will let'em."

Looking around them Beth Ann quietly explains, "I've had bad dreams before about something happening and it does. I don't talk about it because it scares people, but it usually happens. I know this man will come to kill me."

Kneeling down beside her Jay sincerely asks, "Miss Beth Ann, the Indian man wasn't me was it? Don'tcha know, I wouldn't hurt'cha for anythang in the whole world."

Astonished Beth Ann looks up at him then laying her trembling hand on his arm she wanly smiles explaining, "It wasn't you, Jay. I know you wouldn't hurt me. This man was older and he had red stripes across his cheeks, there was a long ugly scar across his chest and he wore a red loin cloth. He had a big knife and he was going to kill me." She looks around blushing as her face turns from white to red in a moment of time as she becomes embarrassed. Everyone is watching her then looking at Jay she explains, "Jay, he said: Boss, said to kill ya," and he was going to.

Jay sits down on the ground beside her Indian style then taking her hand he asks, "Let us pray to our Father in Heaven and ask for guidance on your dream. He knows all and will give us an answer. Then he prays, *"Father, we are most upset by Miss Beth Ann's dream. She is afraid now and we know you know all and see all. Please let us know what we should do. Blessings on the young lady, Lord. She is precious. Amen."*

They had all gather around Beth Ann to comfort her when Jay asks to pray so they all kneel around her, touch her and pray their own prayers.

Skinny requests, "I always feel God more closely when I recite Psalms 121 will ya say it with me?"

Everyone nods yes and joins in, if they know it. Glory, Jake and the girls are surprised when most all the cowboys know this bible verse.

Skinny and Pokey start it together, *"I will lift up mine eyes unto the hills, from whence cometh my help. My help cometh from the Lord, which made heaven and earth. He will not suffer thy foot to be moved: He that keepeth thee will not slumber. Behold, He that keepeth Israel shall neither slumber nor sleep. The Lord is thy keeper; the Lord is thy shade upon thy right hand. The sun shall not smite thee by day, nor the moon by night. The Lord shall preserve thee from all evil: He shall preserve thy soul. The Lord shall preserve thy going out and thy coming in from this time forth, and even for evermore."*

Everyone takes a deep cleansing breath as stress is relieved for God is always in control of our lives, if we give ours to him.

Lifting his head Jay states firmly, "Danger follows us. We must not be slow in reachin' the ranch, boss."

Looking at Jay intently Brad asks, "What do ya know?"

"Danger to us all. We must not tarry to the ranch," Jay repeats then rising he walks to the side of the camp and kneels down to pray some more.

Both younger girls look wild eyed at their grandpas then smiling Glory questions, "Little sisters do ya doubt we are able to keep ya safe?"

Both look at her then shake their heads no as Beth Ann answers, "No, I know you will."

"Then don'tcha worry we are all on the lookout now. Tomorra ya'll stay close to the grandpas and Jay and I will scout around some," Glory advises then turning to Jake she raises her hand in a stop motion before continuing, "Nothing will stop me from lookin' and Jay is much quieter than ya are. I'm not going to argue over it." Walking to her horse she takes her buckskins out of her saddle bags and lays them down ready to put on. She picks up her blanket and moves it over between the two younger girls spreading it between them with her arm across Beth Ann's stomach in reassurance. Beth Ann and Carrie Lynn both cuddle as close as possible and she smiles faintly before she falls asleep.

"She won't be stopped and she is right. Jay moves quieter than I do," Jake states with a sigh. Turning to Jay he sees he has lain down and is breathing deeply. "I'll talk to them in the morning and see which direction they plan to look in," is Jake's last thought before he also falls asleep.

A few hours later Glory and Jay slip out of camp without waking anyone. They nod to the guard (Josh) as they pass him, startling him as he hadn't heard them at all. They run a couple of miles west but see nothing so head north. Kneeling down to take a breather Jay states, "I smell horses but I don't see them."

"I do, too, but not wild horses," Glory whispers back as she scans the landscape again, "We are being followed but they are very good. I cain't see them anywhere around us. Could they be farther behind us? If so, why and what do they want?"

"We're traveling with a lot of wagons full of goods, they might be after them. But why would Beth Ann have a night dream about someone trying to kill her? It must mean someone means us harm," Jay rationalizes.

"No one is gonna hurt my sister!" Glory's eyes glow with a green fire as she says it.

"And no one will harm Pokey and Skinny unless they kill me first," Jay promises himself and Glory, "Let's git back to camp now. Let's not scare the young girls but we will inform the men to be on alert. Okay?"

Smiling grimly, Glory nods yes saying, "Yes, we had better make light of it for the girls but all the men will be alerted to danger." She looks at Jay and smiling faintly says, "I'm glad you are with us. I trust you."

Chuckling softly he replies, "I'm glad YOU are on our side. I'd not like to tangle with you!"

Smiling smugly Glory answers, "No one better try to tangle with me. I won't take it lightly."

"Nor will I," Jay promises her. They run swiftly back to camp and find Jake with hot coffee waiting for them.

He is pacing around watching and waiting for them. The moon is barely visible but the sun hasn't started to rise yet when he hands them a cup of hot coffee. Glory notices that it has been boiling awhile.

"Waitin' up for me, handsome?" she whispers to Jake.

Scowling at her he quietly replies, "Yep! Did ya see anyone?"

"No, we didn't see anyone but we know they are out thar," Glory explains frowning then continues, "They are good. There is more than one. We could smell horses but they ain't real close to us."

"Then we will be more careful," Pokey states from his pallet. He raises his hat from his forehead saying, "Let the girls sleep awhile and Glory and Jay take a nap now. It's gonna be a long day." He settles his hat back over his face and they hear him snoring very quickly.

Jake pulls Glory over to his side to make her lay down and quickly she falls asleep tired from the exercise. He sits looking at his young beautiful girl thinking, "I ain't gonna let anything happen to you either, Glory. Whether you like it or not, I'm gonna be on you to be careful like."

"Clench those teeth any harder and you'll break 'em. Let it be, Jake, and sleep while you can," Skinny advises as he softly walks around on guard duty.

Jake nods yes then leaning over lays his arm across Glory's slender body as she curls into him. He smiles sleepily letting his guard down falling into a deep sleep.

Skinny stands with rifle in hand looking at his loved ones promises himself, "No one will hurt'cha, none of ya'll." He looks at Bradford and Jay thinking, "My boys. Not of my seed but of my heart." He glances over at the younger men, Kevin and Josh, as they patrol the other side of camp and smiling faintly thinks, "My younger sons. They have all had hard lives but love and compassion changed their lives. *Yes, Lord, they are my sons in all ways. Hep me watch over'em.*"

Race has Albert watching the other campsite this night so when Albert reports, "There was activity during the night but I didn't think they are alert to our presence." Race shrugs it off saying, "We are too smart for'em and we've been careful. Ain't nothin' to worry about right now."

Meanwhile back at Minnie and Benny's home a wagon pulls up about supper time and Zak and Shorty climb down.

After looking out the window Minnie opens the door saying, "Come on in. How is everythang goin' at yar home?"

"Everthang is goin' well, hope ya'll are too?" Zak answers smiling at the blooming figure of Minnie as he thinks, "She looks as wide as she is tall now."

"Pa, Jake and I have a surprise for you," Shorty announces as he walks around to the back of the wagon pulling a tarp off the furniture.

"What??? Oh my, those are lovely," Minnie states as she sees two cradles and a 3 drawer chest.

"My boys and I do love makin' furniture. Jake made the cradles afore he left and Shorty and I made the chest with drawers for the twins. Jake is still gone to St. Louie so Shorty and I decided to bring'em on over so you'd have them when the little ones come," Zak explains slightly blushing.

Looking at the beautiful furniture with carvings on the cradles saying "God's Love and Blessings on you and Jesus Loves You" Minnie's tears start again and Benny's mouth is wide open in surprise. "I'ze don't know what to say. This is so nice of ya'll to make these for us'uns. I tries real hard to make purdy thangs but ain't had much time to make'em nor would they look this purdy," Benny states wiping a tear away as he kneels down beside the cradles looking at them.

"Glad you like them. Me and my boys find it relaxin' workin' with wood. It's soothin' to the soul," Zak explains happily looking at this nice family.

"Jake's got the real talent of workin' with wood. He just sees in his mind how it should look then makes it that way. Pa and I have to work out a pattern," Shorty explains smiling at their happiness.

"I'ze think all of ya'll has a lot of talent and great hearts to make these for us'uns," Minnie declares then hugs each man (as much as she can as she is so heavily pregnant).

Standing Benny holds his hand out to shake then hugs each friend also saying, "Thank ya so much for the beautiful furniture. We shorely do appreciate yar kindness."

"Lookee at the purdy mattresses Ma. See how nice they are and ma look here," Arty states then hands Minnie a material wrapped package sitting in one of the cradles.

Minnie's eyes just sparkle at the present then opening it she laughs happily at seeing four little sheets to fit the mattresses and two quilted blanket just the right size for the cradles. "Oh, they are so nice and so purdy. See the embroidery on them and how purdy the flowers are. Thank you so much. Please tell Stephie and JoyAnn thank you so much for the lovely pretties," Minnie states as she hugs both men again.

"They wanted to come with us but ma wasn't feeling real good so Stephie stayed with her. They said they'd see ya this week sometime so ya'll can talk," Zak explains happy to see how much their presents are liked.

"Oh, I'ze just loves'em. Ya'll are just too good to us," Minnie states smiling broadly.

"Cain't never be too good to yar friends," Shorty states happily.

The men carry the furniture into the house and set them up inside Minnie and Benny's bedroom so they will be able to use them easily.

On the trip home the girls practice their shooting for thirty minutes with Jake this time and they can see improvements. Nerves are high so when they are ready to leave Glory asks, "Ya'll can we gather for a minute and say a prayer?'

Smiling everyone makes a circle then Glory prays first: *"Lord, we are upset about this business goin' on here. Please hep us to enjoy bein' together and make this a wonderful trip full of good memories. Watch over us and hep us when we need it. In Jesus' name I pray. Amen."*

Each one who wants to whispers a few words of prayer before saddling up or climbing onto the seats of the wagons as they head to the ranch.

During the day (when nerves seem to be high again) Jake announces, "I'm gonna entertain ya'll with my beautiful voice." He starts singing and it is very loud and sometimes a little off key but good. He winks at the girls when they look questioningly over at him so soon the girls join in. Glory has a lovely voice so soon it is a Heavenly choir singing as they ride towards the ranch.

Pokey, Skinny and all the cowboys (that know the songs) join in if they want to and it does seem to relax their nerves. When it is time to walk the horses Jake comes up with new words for a song about walking on the Lord's highway and after the first verse the others join in laughing and start making up new verses for it.

At times during the day Jay and Bradford ride off and watch for anyone following and at intervals so does Jake and Glory. Beth Ann and Carrie Lynn ride beside the grandpas and feel safe.

This sets the pace for the days to follow. Someone comes up with some type of entertainment and they all fall into doing it. It becomes an educational one when Beth Ann suggests they find something starting with a certain letter and name it as they see it. The cowboys riding beside the wagons and driving the wagons play along as well.

Race and his men realize the second day that they are being watched so have to drop farther behind to stay concealed. They hear the shooting going on twice a day and wonder about it but don't ride any closer to check it out. Race angrily states, "What are they doin', if'n they know we are followin' them, why are they wastin' bullets like that? It don't make no sense." Then turning to Golden Eagle, he accuses, "Why ain'tcha found a good place to trap'em in? Ya've been lookin' for a long time."

"Boss it is flat country. Cain't find no where's that we can sneak up on'em," the Indian man replies angrily.

Race glares at him saying, "I'm a payin' ya to kill'em and take those wagons! I want results!"

Pokey does limit the number of bullets each girl uses to a minimum and they are greatly impressed with how quickly the girls become accurate in their shooting. Pokey tells his young girls, "When we get home I'm gonna find ya each a smaller gun and holster kinda like Glory's got. These guns are too heavy for your hands."

Skinny pulls him over later saying, "With all the leather we are bringing home, we can make the girls a holster and decorate it like we done for Brad and the boys."

Pokey's faded blue eyes glow as he replies, "That would be fine with me. It's relaxin' workin' on leather. Oh, Skinny, we can make'em much nicer than boughten ones. Great idea, brother."

So after traveling as fast as possible they arrive on their land. Cowboys herding cattle meet them and they all breathe a sigh of relief with the extra men around. Nerves relax and Beth Ann decides that her nightmare isn't going to come true so she becomes her bubbly self again.

Race jumps up and down cussin' when he sees the cattle and the abundance of cowboys with them saying, "Cain't sneak up on'em here. Start scoutin' around and find a way in or somewhere we can watch'em. Don't imagine they are gonna stay here long."

Two days later the tired group arrives at the ranch house. It is quite a little wagon train that pulls into the yard next to the small house. Curious everyone walks over to the ranch house to see their bosses and find out what is going on.

"Did ya buy out St. Louie?" Big John bellows from his kitchen window.

"Nope and I didn't bring you anythang neither!" Skinny bellows back then laughs at the joke because he has brought him back some new dishes and cooking pans along with numerous other things.

Jake, Carrie Lynn, Beth Ann and Glory look at each other and smile at the secret they have in store for their grandpas. Gleefully Jake remembers he has tied a piece of yellow ribbon on the trunks and boxes for their Grandpas ranch and made sure that they are all loaded together on the same buck board. He'd decided in St. Louis it would be easiest to tell which trunk will go to each family by tying a different colored ribbon on them. So the large wagons and buckboards each have trunks and furniture with the same colored ribbons on them as much as possible.

That evening Big John fixes a meal fit for royalty with big steaks, baked sweet potatoes, green beans, pecan pies with a mountain of biscuits, jelly and butter. Everyone eats until they can't eat anymore then takes turns using the shower house.

Lying in bed that night Beth Ann smilingly says, "I must have been mistaken because no one tried to harm us on the way down."

Yawning Carrie Lynn replies, "Well they couldn't have gotten close enough to you to be able to get you ....you were protected all the time."

Nodding yes in the dark Beth Ann realizes Glory and Carrie Lynn can't see her head move so replies, "Yes, I felt safe."

Yawning also Glory adds, "Yar safe. I ain't gonna let anythang happen to ya."

After the girls go to bed Pokey, Skinny and Jake sit at the table drinking coffee when Skinny remembers, "I've got all those papers in my saddle bag that Charles Sloan gave me. We'd better look 'em over."

Yawning Pokey replies, "I've got all the papers from Edgar's desk in my saddle bag. Guess we otta look 'em over, too. We got a little time now…so let's do it."

Standing up Jake walks over to the table by the door and picks up the saddle bags and carries them to the table laying them down for the old gents. Both open their bags bringing out a piece of oilskin then open it pulling out a handful of papers.

They start opening papers and glancing at them when Skinny exclaims, "Mother of God this cain't be true!" He shuffles through the papers and finds other letters with the same handwriting on them and setting the lamp closer to him starts reading. His face turns white as he reads the following:

Dear Franklin Potter,

I have received your letters to the fact that in the near future you will have available to us the following for marriage:

Miss Gloria, being sixteen years of age, and pure in heart and body, to marry my son, Armond, in the fall of 1850.

Miss Beth Ann, being sixteen in the year of 1854, to marry my nephew, Wilford the Third. Bring her with Miss Gloria and her education will be seen to.

As per our agreement, the sum of ten thousand dollars will be paid upon our satisfactory completion of each marriage. The young ladies must be pure in body, Mr. Potter. Nothing else is acceptable. Upon the last of our transactions, the beautiful Elizabeth will be welcomed with open arms into my home as my mistress when you deem the time is right. If she is as beautiful as you say, AND if her WILL is not completely broken by you. You must remember that I will not take this woman if she is scarred in any manner. You see, dear Franklin, I remember your rather perverse ways with women.

Your Servant, Count Albany Etinne, Paris, France

Skinny reads and rereads the letters and finally he holds them out to Pokey to read while he just shakes his head in shock.

Pokey doesn't even notice as he also is suffering from shock at reading the letters that Edgar had hidden:

Dear Mr. Hawkins,

It is with great excitement that I accept your sale of land in the wildlands South of St. Louis. I understand that I may not purchase the whole tract of land but a partial section. I am interested in the mountainous part as it will remind me of home. As soon as you have acquired this land then I will be glad to come and inspect it before the sale begins.

Humbly, Pierre Du'mont, Duc of Hogshead Castle, France

Pokey glances up just as Jake takes some papers from Skinny's shaking hands and sees that Skinny's eyes are dilated and he seems to be in shock. "What is it, Skinny? What did ya read?" Pokey asks worriedly.

"Franklin was gonna sell the girls to royalty in France!" Skinny states quickly looking towards the rooms where the girls are sleeping.

"Sell them!" Pokey stutters in shock.

"Yep, he has lined up husbands for Glory and Beth Ann and he planned to make Elizabeth the mistress of this Count Etinne," Jake explains with blazing anger in his eyes then continues, "That low down son of a skunk was gonna send 'em to Europe so we'd never find 'em and keep the inheritance from ya'll."

Pokey shakes his head then holding out his papers explains, "Edgar's letters say he planned on selling our ranches to some Duc in France. They weren't gonna let our girls live to tell about it or put up a fuss about it to my way of thinkin'!"

"He was gonna sell our ranches? To whom?" Skinny questions leaning back in his chair totally stunned by this information.

"Someone named Pierre Du'mont of Hogshead Castle in France. He has it all set up to take it away from Elizabeth and the young'uns and make a lot of money off'n our hard work, brother," Pokey explains sourly.

Raising his head up suddenly, Jake inquires, "What does it say about little Sam?"

"Nope, ain't read nothin' about him a tall, yet?" Pokey answers as he quickly scans the letter he just read.

"No, I didn't read anything about him either," Skinny replies then looking at Jake sadly states, "I'd imagine they would have killed him so there wouldn't be anyone to make a claim on the inheritance." Standing up Skinny walks outside to the corral and stands there trying to take all this in then bowing his head he prays, *"Lord, I thought I'd found out all the evil things that could happen to a fella in my life but this seems more than I can bear. What can we do about this? How can we handle this?"* He slides bonelessly onto his knees and prays for quite a while.

Pokey and Jake keep a careful eye out for him as they continue to go through the letters.

A long while later Skinny walks back in saying, "I've been a prayin' about all this and I believe we otta give Joe the letters about the girls. He will handle it for us and we will tell him about what Edgar had planned for our land, too. Pokey, we gotta make out another will real quick and state exactly what we want done with our property. Right now our will says it's to go to Lora and Elizabeth. I think we need to change it up some and not forget our boys. They will need a home when we are gone and we got plenty to share. Before we head out to Joe's let's talk to them about what section they'd like to have. Jake will you put all those letters together for me, please. I don't think I can touch 'em again."

"Yep, we will do that. You go on to bed, Jake and I will get these papers together, brother," Pokey states as he notices that Skinny walks like a tired old man to his bedroom.

"I'll keep an eye on him tonight and make sure he is okay," Pokey advises Jake as he quickly starts picking up the papers from his bag.

Jake folds the papers and rewraps them in the oilskin, then puts them back into Skinny's saddlebag. Then he does the same with Pokey's set of papers then quietly asks, "Pokey, how can anyone be so low to do what they had planned. They planned to send all three of our girls to a foreigner and to another country. Maybe Beth Ann woulda been happy there bein' she is a lady now but Glory would neva been happy. Lizbeth, a mistress to a Count, someone who knew Potter so well that he knew he liked to mistreat women. They would have ended up killing her physically and especially mentally. How could they do that?"

Taking a deep breath, Pokey replies, "I don't know, son. It is beyond me to understand the workin's of their evil minds. Greed…most of all. Greed! Let's git to bed we got a day to relax tomorra and think about all this before we head on over to Joe's. Lord, I can use peace of mind again."

The girls wake up early and after fixing coffee giggle as they think of all the surprises they have in mind to do today.

Jake wakes up quickly at the sound of their joyful voices. He shakes the bad memories of last night out of his mind as he quietly says, "Good Morning Ladies! How did you sleep?"

All smile as Glory answers, "Like a sack of tators! I was dead tired." She notices something is troubling Jake but when he smiles it is gone.

Beth Ann and Carrie Lynn are almost jumping up and down with excitement at the surprises they have in store for their grandpas.

Carrie Lynn whispers loudly, "Come on Jake let's get the trunks out!"

Smiling he complies and quickly finds the right trunks and carries them into the house as quietly as he can.

Glory opens up one and Carrie Lynn and Beth Ann open the second one as they quickly start decorating the house. Jake walks out to one of the large Conestoga wagons then quietly picks up two bundled chairs carrying them inside. Glory and the girls quickly take the coverings from around them then set the two rocking chairs in the sunlight by the windows. The two old rickety rockers Jake picks up and sets in the barn for the time being. They can't stop giggling at the surprise they will see on their grandpa's faces when they see their home has become a home with the help of the four young people.

Skinny sits up in bed and after taking a deep breath sighs wearily muttering, "Didn't sleep a wink last night. All these problems just gettin' me down! Cain't believe Edgar and Franklin could be so bad and downright evil to do what they planned on doin'. *Thank you, Lord, for savin' our girls. I cain't imagine the horror they would suffer at those people's hands.*" Hearing the girls giggling in the next room he smiles mumbling, "Better git out there and see what they are up to."

Pokey hears the girls giggling quietly and it brings a smile to his old face also as he thinks, "I could get used to this happiness in my house. Just hearin' em makes me feel good about life and I can put the bad behind me. It was like that when Lora was a child. She brought such sunshine into our lives. Ma and Pa loved Lora just like their own child. I'll never forget the happiness she brought me, maybe, that's why God let us have her. *Thank ye, Lord, for the blessin's ya've give me ever day. It makes me happy to be around these young people, to see the joy they find in everthang. Like on the way down here the songs and thinkin' up words that Beth Ann came up with. Thank ya so much. Amen."*

The old gents walk out of their bedrooms at the same time then stop in amazement seeing the changes in the kitchen area.

Smiling and chuckling Skinny asks, "A table cloth and new dishes. Now where did these come from?"

Giggling delightfully Beth Ann answers, "From the store, grandpa. We want to share with you and bring some pretty things to your home."

Pokey walks over to the open fireplace in the small living area and looks at the clock sitting on the mantle. "This here looks pretty familiar to me." He smiles as he humbly says, "Thank ya for thinkin' about us."

Smiling hugely Jake replies, "Oh, keep lookin' you ain't seen it all yet."

They both look back towards the kitchen seeing two new pots and a brand new coffee pot on the stove along with a set of silverware sticking out of a pretty pottery jar sitting on the table. It is yellow as is the table cloth.

"You certainly brightened up the old room. I like the color Yalla makes me feel right good seein' it," Pokey states happily seeing their hard work.

"Look behind you, grandpas," Jake asks them beaming.

They turn as one and notice their old rockers are gone and in their place are two nice rocking chairs from Lora's sitting room with padded seats. Walking over Skinny sits down in one smiling brightly says, "Mighty comfortable."

Pokey sits down in the other one then looking at the table that holds their Bibles says, "Well lookee here Skinny. This is a fancy table and it has little drawers on it to keep stuff in. Well, ain't this nice. You young'uns shorely surprised us with these nice thangs."

"That's not all either," Jake advises then nods to the girls as they pick up the clothes Jake had picked out for them from St. Louis. Each has three completely new sets of clothes.

Both of their eyes widened then they squint at Jake saying, "This is your doin'. You was suppose to git them for your families back home."

"I did and these were too skinny for any of us!" Jake replies laughing at his own joke. Everyone chuckles at the smiles that grow over the grandpa's faces as they enjoy the receiving for a change.

Glory nods to the girls as they start setting supplies on the table for their home as she explains; "Now ya'll have plenty of coffee, salt and jelly. We even found a bucket of molasses for ya'll. We know ya like yar sweet thangs."

Skinny and Pokey laugh and all the bleakness of the past evening is temporarily forgotten in the joy of this moment.

Big John bellows from outside the door, "Breakfast is here."

Jake quickly opens the door for him and his helper, Danny, as the girls clear the table off.

Big John doesn't miss much so after walking in he pauses saying, "I do declare this is right purdy. I always liked Yalla. You did a good job ladies and gent." He nods to the girls and Jake then looking at his old friends says, "Those chairs look mighty comfortable boss."

Both keep rocking as Skinny replies, "Yep, they are. See that clock over thar. They picked it out for us, too. See over there we got some new cooking pots. It'll take a while but we'll get that coffee pot to tastin' like our coffee soon."

Big John nods smiling brightly then quietly whispers to the girls, "You did real good, ladies. Real good. Thank ya. Well lookee here ya got some fancy sorghum. We don't git it hardly atoll. Are ya gonna share it boss?"

"Maybe and maybe not," Pokey states (raising his eyebrows up) then continues, "Depends on how good yar biscuits are this morning." Then chuckling he adds, "Pull up a chair, John, and join us."

"Be glad to," John states smiling broadly as he sits down. Glory hands him a new tin plate and he looks at it saying, "Now yar gettin' fancy on me, new plates and new pots and pans. We ain't gonna know how to do without you young ladies takin' care of us."

All three girls giggle and smile happily at the men as they fill their plates and everyone enjoys a wonderful breakfast. While they are eating Glory asks, "I'd like to invite ya'll here for breakfast tomorra morning before we leave. I'm gonna fix flap jacks for everyone like Papa makes. Ya'll will lov'em, Big John."

Laughing Beth Ann leans forward to Big John explaining, "That is if you will give us the fixings for the flap jacks, syrup, butter and bacon or sausage."

"Be glad to. I'll be here, too. I love my food," John replies happy to be included.

They rearrange the trunks after taking the furniture out of the big wagon and are able to leave with one less buck board on the way to Joe's home.

After breakfast Jake and Big John help unload two large trunks for Skinny and Pokey carrying them into the cooking shed for distribution later.

Skinny and Pokey carry a crate into Big John's domain (the smaller bunk house where the cooking shed is attached to) saying to him, "Big John we brought ya some new thangs we thought you might need," Pokey states with a smile at their longtime friend.

"So you did bring me something…what'cha got?" Big John's blue eyes sparkle at the surprise he is getting.

"Open this crate and see," Skinny states smiling at their suprises for Big John.

"Gladly," Big John answers and with Jake's help pries the boards off the top of the crate and John sees a new set of cast iron pots and pans….large ones that will feed a bunch of cowboys. "Woweee, these are nice. Thank ya boss we can really use these," John states happily pulling them out.

"Gosh boss these are really fine. John and I will have a lot of good times cookin' in them," Danny states looking happily at the cookware.

Digging farther down, John pulls out metal stirring and serving spoons as well as four large forks that he can use to lift the heavy roasts from the oven to the table with. "Now this is somethang I've needed for a long time, thank you for remembering and getting them for us," John states laughing heartily at the surprise.

"Danny look in the corners of the crate," Skinny advises as Danny and John sit back admiring the cookware.

Danny's eyes light up so leaning over he pushes the straw around until his hand hits a bucket which he pulls out laughing happily saying, "Sorghum! We got us some sorghum! It has been a long time since we had any. Thank ya boss! Thank ya."

"Keep looking there are more surprises," Pokey urges smiling at their happiness.

Eyes lighting up happily both men lean over and run their hands around the crate pulling up boxes and bags stuffed in, around and inside the pots and pans.

"We bought ya a bunch of new spices to cook with and ….," Skinny stops when Danny (who has a big sweet tooth) laughs loudly pulling out two large cans of maple syrup.

"Yar the best bosses ever! John we got maple syrup…real maple syrup!" Danny laughs delighted with the surgary surprise.

John laughs with him asking, "So you don't like my homemade syrup Danny?"

"Oh, I like it fine but I love maple syrup so do the boys. Can we have flapjacks tomorrow John? That would be wonderful….maybe even tonight we could have them?" Danny asks hopefully.

Patting him on the shoulder John says, "We will see. Soon we will have them."

Looking at Skinny and Pokey (who are smiling happily at the happiness they have brought to John and Danny) John says, "Thank ya boss. This has been a wonderful surprise. Guess the trunks are more surprises. Do ya need help with delivering them?"

"Yeah we do, John. Got to separate the surprises and could use yar and Danny's help to do it. Would now be a good time?" Pokey asks.

"Surely would. Just tell us what you want us to do," John states happily.

So opening the trunks they separate the clothing, tobacco, candy and even some toys for the cowboys who will be coming in this evening for supper. The men even get inventive and wrap the cowboy's blankets around their presents when they leave them on each man's bunk.

Later that evening as the cowboys come in from the pasture and their jobs completed for the day they stop off at their bunks (as usual) and see the blanket wrapped package.

"Can we open it now?" Branden asked happily looking at the large bundle on his bunk.

"Is this like Christmas when we all take turns opening our presents?" Matt asks Big John who is standing in the doorway watching them.

"One of you better ask the boss…no, here they come," John answers watching Skinny and Pokey walking towards them.

More and more of the cowboys walk into the bunkhouse and since they have talked to both Skinny and Pokey during the long day are happy to see them again. They all crowd around talking and laughing with them before Mike calls out, "Did ya look at your bunk yet?"

All the men quickly look towards their bunks and with eyes sparkling look back at their bosses.

Holding up his hands for silence Skinny states, "How about we eat first then ya'll can open yar presents? Give us an hour and we will be back so we can enjoy seeing you open them. Okay?"

Smiling the cowboys look at each other and together yell, "Yes, Sir!" laughing as they do it.

Leaning in Pokey laughs saying, "After ya eat if'n ya help Big John with the dishes, it will make time go faster!"

Since it is a rule that each cowboy washes his own plate, cup and silverware and sets them on the long counter to dry, to help with the pots and pans is not a big deal to the men. Most all of the cowboys have grown up on Skinny and Pokey's ranches. They have all had a time period where they were on clean up duty. They know the rules and follow them without comment (usually). So call out, "Yes, boss!" laughing and carrying on as young men will do.

Soon everyone has eaten and helped clean up the cooking shed and is patiently waiting to see what their presents are. Skinny and Pokey walk in from having their supper with their grandkids saying, "We brung our grand kids with us cause they chose some of the presents for you boys."

Jake and the girls excitedly walk in happily waiting and watching the cowboys eagerly waiting to open their presents.

"This ain't Christmas so dig in boys. If'n yars don't fit see if'n you can switch around with one of the other boys…we did the best we could to fit you all," Pokey advises then laughs as the men quickly start opening their presents.

Looking at their happy faces Skinny thinks, "Why don't we do this more often, we can afford to do it." Laughing he watches as the men stand up and not thinking about the young girls strip off their dirty shirts and pull on the new ones they have just received. They aren't thinking of anything except seeing their presents.

Beth Ann is shocked at first seeing the good looking young men strip off their shirts as this is the first time she has experienced this then notices how happy they are to receive presents so just laughs happily with them.

Each cowboy receives two new shirts, two pair of pants, long johns, socks, candy and some receive tobacco or chewing tobacco whichever one they use. Some of the younger men receive toys to play with or a small musical instrument. The laughing and happiness is contagious so everyone is smiling happily watching their fun. Soon the young men are shaking hands and hugging Skinny and Pokey saying thank you over and over and enjoying these unexpected presents. Skinny and Pokey have known all their cowboys for a long time so know what each one likes and dislikes. As they leave the hear their cowboy sons exchanging pieces of candy with others and looking at each others clothing admiring what everyone has received.

Back at the ranch Elizabeth and Joe are sitting at the table talking about their children and wondering how everything is going with them. "I can hardly wait to see their faces when they see the room additions we've made. They will be so thrilled," Elizabeth gushes happily.

"I'm a hopin' Glory won't mind sharin' a room for a month or so til we git her house built. I know she is ready to git married but that is kinda hard for me to accept. My little girl gettin' married," Joe replies looking down into his coffee.

"She will make a beautiful bride, Joe. She has your looks in most every way. She is absolutely beautiful. I will miss being around her though," Elizabeth agrees sadly then continues, "It will take more time for her to get to know me." She looks up at Joe asking, "I will always wonder what she thought about me when I left her like that?"

"She cried for ya for a long time. Every day she cried … near broke my heart. I couldn't go anywhere without her bein' with me. Then Good Heart and Yalla Moon came into our lives and they were real good to her. She took to Yalla Moon right off and they accepted her as their daughter. Good Heart has much more patience than I do with young'uns. They heped make it right for ya, honey. Now see my dilemma is about Beth Ann and Sammy, I know I deserted'em like ya deserted Glory. I hope they will forgive me for that, too," Joe explains then sadly adds.

"They blame me, Joe, not you. I shouldn't have left and even after I did I should have come right back but I was too proud and young to realize it at the time. It is easy to look back on my mistakes and see what I should have done but it is hard at the time to know what is right to do," Elizabeth explains sadly.

Taking her hands in his large ones he says, "Then we will just do the best we can every day and pray it is enough."

Smiling she leans over kissing him answering, "Yes, we will do our best to make it up to our young'uns."

Joe chuckles at her Southern talk promising, "We will do the best we can."

Running in the door Sammy slams it behind him. He winces at the sound saying, "Sorry, Ma and Papa. I got good news though." His little face lights up happily as he continues, "Good Heart said I am gettin' real good with my sling shot and that soon I'll be able to get some small game for the table."

Raising her eyebrows Elizabeth swallows asking, "Please ask Good Heart to teach you how to clean the wild game you kill. I don't know how."

Opening his eyes wide Sammy asks astonished, "YOU will cook it for me, Mama?"

Smiling down at her happy son Elizabeth replies, "Certainly I will cook it for you. It wouldn't hurt to ask Yellow Moon HOW I should cook it but yes, you catch it and you can eat it."

Sammy does a little dance around the kitchen table then leaning over kisses Elizabeth's cheek (which is one of the few times this has happened). She blushes with pleasure as Joe winks at her in approval.

"I'm gonna tell Good Heart the good news. Be back in a while," Sammy explains then runs back out the door shutting it quietly this time.

Lowering her head to the table Elizabeth woefully asks, "Oh, Joe, what have I just agreed to do?"

Smiling he chuckles replying, "Ya just agreed to make our son happy, that is what ya wanted to do and ya did. Most wild game is roasted or fried so ya will be able to do either. One thang you gotta always remember is to soak it in salt water to get some of the gamey taste outta it."

Lifting her head she smiles ruefully saying, "I guess, I did so I will."

Before daybreak Skinny and Pokey have everyone up and ready to leave for Joe's ranch, so sleepy eyed but full from the large breakfast they just ate they head out just as the sun is rising.

Golden Eagle's knuckles are raw and dripping blood from the beating he has just given Davey Raymond, one of Skinny's young cowboys. The young cowboy was captured as he was making his rounds checking the cattle. After much persuasion as well as blood spilt Davey mumbles through the blood dripping out of his swollen mouth, "They are heading towards the City of Roy but I don't know when."

Golden Eagle smugly wipes the blood off his knuckles onto Davey's tattered and torn shirt then laughing harshly he does the same with his large bowie knife. Since Davey's blue shirt is red with blood already and half torn off of him it makes little difference to the shirt or the knife.

"Ya want me to kill ya now or let some animal eat ya?" Golden Eagle harshly asks the weakened cowboy, then continues, "Yar gonna bleed to death real soon anyway so it makes no difference to me."

Davey struggles to raise his head after his hours of torture and cockily replies, "Let the animals do your dirty work. At least that I can respect."

Golden Eagle shows his yellow teeth as he roars with laughter as he tightens the ropes holding Davey to the tree. He pulls the ropes holding him upright tighter then looking him in the eyes states, "Ya just killed yar bosses, man. We are gonna kill ever one of'em!" He continues to laugh all the way to his horse which is tethered close by.

Davey struggles until his shoulders and wrists are raw and bleeding trying to get free but to no avail. Blood drips from his nose and mouth and from cuts all over his face. Davey spits blood out and gritting his teeth states to himself, "Well if'n I can't get free then I'll have to think of somethin' else. Pray man, pray. Psalms 27:1 glad the bosses taught it to me: *The Lord is my light and my salvation; whom shall I fear? The Lord is the strength of my life; of whom shall I be afraid.*" He whistles for his horse so Spirit runs right up to him. "Come on, honey, I need your help. Bite through these ropes and git me free," Davey begs the beautiful mustang.

After much encouragement she starts biting on the rope across Davey's chest and soon bites through enough that Davey is able to strain forward and break it. He falls forward tangled in the rope and lays there for a minute catching his breath.

Spirit leans down and grabs the back of his leather vest with her strong teeth lifting him to his feet.

Davey laughs softly saying, "Yeah, nag nag nag. I gotta stand up and git to the ranch and warn our bosses." Painfully he stumbles to the side of the horse and after four tries is finally able to lift his sore and aching body onto his saddle. His hands (which have been numb) are painfully tingling and tears come to his eyes as the pain in his body seems unbearable. *"Please, Lord, help me git to the ranch. I gotta warn'em of those gunning for them. The Lord is the strength of my life. The Lord is the strength of my life. Help me, please Lord, help me!"* He makes himself sit up in the saddle (while blood runs down his hands) he grabs the reins turning Spirit towards the ranch and help. He almost falls off so after a couple of minutes he pulls his lariat out wrapping it around his body tying himself to the saddle then taking a deep breath he orders, "Spirit, GO HOME!" He swats her with his hat then drops it as she takes off towards home at a dead run. Davey lets the reins fall down and leaning forward wraps his arms around her strong neck just holding on as well as he can. Every time she slows down he nudges her with his boots to go again. Soon she is covered in sweat as well as blood and it covers Davey making it harder to hold on but Davey keeps urging her on muttering over and over: *"The Lord is my light and my salvation. The Lord is my light and my salvation."* Finally he sees the ranch come into view and gives her one more kick to get her the last quarter of a mile. Spirit runs straight to the bunk house and stops her sides heaving.

Looking out the window Big John sees Davey and Spirit and all the blood. Running out he yells for help, "Need some help out here! Davey's hurt!"

Almost unconscious Davey focuses on Big John explaining, "Ambush...they are gonna ambush the bosses...gotta send help. God, I'm sorry. I told'em where they are goin', I couldn't take anymore! I'm sorry, so sorry!"

Patting his shoulder Big John answers, "We'll take care of'em, Davey." Then he starts giving orders and within a few minutes a dozen cowboys are riding to the rescue. Big John and Tom Snell (older cowboy of Skinny and Pokey) carry Davey into the bunkhouse grimacing as they get a good look at his injuries then get to work fixing him up. Big

John's blue eyes blaze in anger after ripping Davey's shirt completely off of him, he sees the damage that had been inflicted on the handsome young cowboy. "Don'tcha worry none about your good looks, Davey, I'm gonna do a good job on sewing up these cuts on you. Who did this to you and with what?" John asks worriedly as he sees the many cuts on Davey's chest and face.

"An Indian with an ugly scar across his chest and a big knife," Davey replies breathing painfully.

"Wish Doc Ron was here, he be better at this than me," Tom Snell exclaims as he tries to help Big John stop the flow of blood running out of Davey.

"Here drink this and take a little nap while I take care of all your hurts," Big John forces some liquid down Davey's swollen lips so soon he falls into a deep sleep while Big John starts washing all the cuts then starts sewing up all the nasty cuts on his face and chest. Later Big John sits back wiping sweat off of his face, he counts the places he has stitched up and grimly says, "No one otta hurt a fella like this. Looks me like, he cut him with a knife about twenty times or more. Poor Davey's gonna be in pain for a while cause he's got two broke ribs, too."

"Otta hang that Indian for hurtin' the boy like that," Tom Snell states firmly.

"Yeah, wish I was on the wild ride the boys are on to catch up with the bosses and those nice young'uns," John states more than a little worried.

"We can just send our prayers with'em and God will take care of our boys and bosses," Tom states firmly.

"Yeah, we can always trust God to take our troubles away. He brought Davey home and I will be thankin' him for that for a long time," John agrees whole heartedly as he looks down at one of "his" boys. John steps over to the window and looking up into the sky prays, *"Lord, we got a passel of trouble following the bosses and the young'uns plus our boys. Please send some angels to help'em out and keep'em safe from harm. We know you can do anythang and you see everythang...please watch over our friends. In your blessed name I pray. Amen."*

Everyone is in high spirits as they ride for home. Skinny and Pokey are riding side by side talking. Pokey says, "Skinny let's plan to stay awhile at Joe's and relax thar. We've done all the thangs we had to do and now it is time to rest up some. The bunkhouse is right nice and it's got good beds, what'cha think?"

"Sounds real good to me. We gotta teach little Sammy how to shoot that sling shot better, too. We don't wanna git him in trouble with his ma and pa over it. Remember it was YAR idea in buying it for him," Skinny teases his younger brother.

"Yep! That's a good reason," Pokey chuckles at the fun it is playing with little Sammy.

Jay looks over at Brad saying, "Something bad is gonna happen. I feel it, seems like I've got a hundred eyes starin' at me but I cain't see no one yet."

Looking around Bradford answers, "About five miles ahead is that valley we gotta cross. It's the only place close by where anythang bad could come at us. Let's get the girls in a wagon and warn everyone to be on the alert. No use takin' chances."

"Wish we could get the bosses to hide in a wagon, but know they won't. They are gettin' too old for shoot outs," Jay states sadly looking at Pokey and Skinny riding at the front of the group then narrowing his eyes he smiles saying, "Glory will get'em back to the wagon or Beth Ann can. Watch out for'em while I fix this up."

Turning his horse around he moves over towards Glory speaking softly, "Trouble is a comin' we feel it strong. Gotta git the girls in the wagon and Glory we need to git the bosses in with them, too, for their own protection. Can you do this?"

Glory looks at him thoughtfully then motions for Jake to get closer and explains to him then says, "Yes, we can. Where do ya think it will happen?"

"There is a valley not far from here. It'll be thar," Jay explains looking intently at her.

Smiling grimly she states, "I'll take care of it. I'll get Beth Ann and Carrie Lynn into a wagon. I'll have them act like they are sick and need the grandpas then we will hav'em safe."

Nodding yes, Jake replies, "I'll go up with the grandpas and be ready." He slowly walks his horse up to theirs saying, "It a beautiful day today. Can ya believe what wonderful weather we've had?"

Glory maneuvers her horse between the two younger girls then explains, "We need to get the grandpas into a wagon for safety. There is a valley comin' up and it is the only place around we can be ambushed."

She looks intently at Beth Ann before continuing, "Ya'll be protected at all times."

Beth Ann stutters, "A valley? I was in a valley when he tried to kill me!"

Narrowing her eyes into slits Glory looks Beth Ann in the eyes replying, "We won't let anyone hurt ya. Ya can take my word for it. Now I need ya to act sick like…stomach ache real bad and carry one somethin' fierce so our grandpas will get in the wagon and stay with ya when the shootin' starts. Can ya do it? Their lives depend upon it."

Gulping Beth Ann faintly agrees, "Yes, I can do it."

"So can I," Carrie Lynn answers as sweat breaks out on her face in terror.

"Okay, start now. Moan and groan loud," Glory orders sitting back and trying to act normal.

After a few minutes Glory calls out, "Grandpa's! I think the girls are sick. Both are carryin' on something awful back here!"

Skinny and Pokey jerk their heads around and sure enough both young girls are lying across their saddles groaning loudly. The grandpas turn their horses rushing back to them with Jake following close behind.

"Let's git'em in a wagon, quick like so they can lay down," Glory urges so Skinny and Pokey help the girls back to one of the Conestoga wagons and quickly move furniture around for the girls to lay down on a feather mattress. Glory and Jake help and in the helping move mattresses to cover both sides of the wagon, leaving the front and back open for shooting hoping it won't come to that.

Pokey starts to get back out when Glory pitifully says, "Grandpas will ya both stay with'em for a while. Ya seem to be the only ones to calm'em down." When he turns and looks down at the girls Glory looks down at the girls arching her eyebrows at them urging them to confirm this.

Both understand and beg the grandpas to stay with them for just a little while.

Worried Pokey and Skinny agree after seeing the girls are sweating heavily and their breathing is quick and jerky. They don't realize it is fear that is the cause. So they instantly agree to stay and sit down beside the girls talking softly to them as the girls continue to moan and groan.

Jake, Jay and Bradford are leading the wagon train when suddenly Brad drawls, "Ya know what? They are gonna try to take us out first. We are the biggest and meanest looking fellows here."

Jake and Jay look at each other a little stunned then nodding yes agree with him. Jay looks over at Brad who is his brother in all ways except blood thinking, *"God please take care of Brad and my other brothers behind us and Lord please take care of my bosses...they are just like pa's to me. God please give me strength to do what I need to do. Amen."*

Jake is praying also, *"Lord I know you watch over us every day and I appreciate it will ya watch over Glory, Carrie Lynn and Beth Ann...Lord, especially Beth Ann, please, don't let that injun get her. Help us all to protect her and keep her safe from all harm. In Jesus name I pray. Amen."*

Brad is quietly looking all around when he realizes, "I could lose everyone I love right here. I ain't told many of them how much they mean to me. I will do that when we survive this...no, if but when. *Yes, Lord I know you are warning us and I appreciate it. Please protect us all especially the bosses and the young girls...I believe they need it more. In Jesus name I pray. Amen."*

Jake's eyes light up as he says, "Remember all that leather we are carrying. It's in big pieces. Let's wrap a piece around our chests and see if'n that'll help. I know where it is so I'll go git it and when I ride back up ya'll can slide it around yarselves. I'll give the other cowboys some, too, when I tell them to get prepared for an ambush."

They agree so quickly he rides back to the correct wagon, climbs in and taking his knife cuts the covering off the big leather stash and starts cutting it up into pieces that will fit completely around them. Then he unbuttons his shirt and fits one around his chest and back. He estimates the size of Glory's middle then cuts one for her then taking the pieces he has cut he rolls them up and goes from wagon to wagon handing them out. He motions for the others to do as he has done then riding up beside Glory (who is riding behind the wagon the girls and grandpas are in). He loudly states, "Glory, come over here and give me some sweet talk. I'm gettin' bored."

Startled she looks over at him as he motions for her to come to the far side of the wagon so she quickly does. He whispers urgently, "Slip this around yar middle and back so if'n a bullet hits ya it won't go in. I ain't takin' no chances with you."

Nodding yes, she asks, "Hep me." She quickly undoes the buttons down the front of her long sleeved shirt and Jake sees the silk camisole underneath. Taking a deep breath he watches as she fits the leather around and over her firm young breast sliding it completely around her. Smiling she whispers, "Ya done good. It fits all around me. Stop lookin' at me like that. We gotta be on the alert!" She quickly rebuttons her shirt then gives him a little shove as she pulls her horse back over so that she continues walking him at the back of the wagon again acting like nothing is going on.

Quickly Jake rides up to Brad and Jay (who are still in the lead) when Jay quietly states, "There are two men watchin' from the North."

Jake rides over to that side of them as if he is having trouble with Comfort and quickly hands them the leather saying, "I'll git'em to watch me for a coupla minutes while ya'll put that leather in place." Leaning down he whispers to Comfort (his beloved horse) then pulling the reins to the side Comfort starts bucking up and down all over the place stirring up the red dirt. Jake stays in the saddle keeping Comfort going in a circle to stir up as much red dirt up as he can, for about five minutes, then he softly calls out, "Enough. Good boy. Enough." Comfort immediately stops and nodding his head regally starts walking beside the other horses again.

Both Jay and Bradford have their leather coverings in place under their shirts so state admiringly, "That is some trick. Comfort is a great horse."

"I raised him and he will do lots of tricks," Jake explains as he scans the area behind the other riders before continuing, "There are two more men in the rocks ahead."

"Yeah, we saw'em," Jay agrees saying, "Brad, ya need to tell the others we are gettin' close and it will soon."

"Oh, no, ya don't! I ain't leavin' ya out here by yarself!" Brad mutters angrily.

Jay gives him a sharp look explaining, "I need ya back by the bosses, Brad. I can handle it up here if'n I know yar watchin' out for them. Do it for me, okay?"

Brad gives him a helpless look but reluctantly nods yes and sorrowfully replies, "What should I do save my fathers or my brother?" He turns his horse riding back to the wagon the young girls and grandpas are in.

A tear glints in Jay's beautiful long lashed brown eyes and a small smile lights his face as he continually scans the area.

Back at the ranch Zak and family ride up as Zak asks, "Joe, shouldn't the young'uns be back today? I thought they would be here yesterday at the latest. Think somethin' coulda happened to'em?"

Joe thoughtfully rubs his chin before replying, "It's later than I thought it would be. Wonder if'n they had some bad weather or somethin'. Wanna ride out thar and meet'em? We shouldn't be gone long."

Shifting uneasily in his saddle Zak immediately nods yes.

"I'm gonna go with you, Pa," Shorty states firmly.

"We will visit with Elizabeth for a while then head on home," Stephie advises as she and Payton dismount and walk into the house.

Joe walks into the kitchen saying, "Lizbeth, we are gonna ride out and meet the wagons. They otta be close by but we might be gone a day or so. Glad ya made some extra biscuits this morning."

Elizabeth picks up a couple of napkins then quickly makes sausage biscuit sandwiches then picks up some fried pies she has just taken out of the oven and wraps them up for them to take.

Joe reaches up on top of a cabinet where they keep dried jerky and pulls out some for each man then grabs some apples from the cabinet and is ready to go.

Quickly walking over to the bunk house he informs Randy and Earl where he is going and when he expects to be back.

Shorty fills up the canteens and Zak grabs some feed for Joe's horse.

Smiling the wives kiss them then the three men ride out.

Skinny's cowboys are riding at a furious pace trying to get to their bosses and friends as quickly as possible. No one talks much as they are too worried about not reaching the wagon train in time.

Frowning Branden Barns narrows his eyes concentrating on the terrain thinking, "Where could an ambush take place?" Sitting straight up he yells over to Mike and Matthew saying, "They will ambush them in the valley! It's the only place I can think of. What do ya think?"

Matthew frowns as he also thinks about the way to Joe's home then nodding agrees, "Yep that is the only possible place they can trap'em in."

Mike grits his teeth advising, "We will be there in time! But it won't hurt to pray about it anyway."

"Oh God I know you love our bosses, Skinny and Pokey, like we do. Please take care of them and our friends and don't forget the young people with'em. They have been real good to our bosses," Branden silently prays as he wipes a sudden tear from his eyes.

Matthew and Mike prayers are very similar as they hasten to help their friends so with their eyes following the wagon's tracks they quickly ride towards the wagon train to help them out.

Greg Wiley (another young cowboy of Skinny and Pokey's) rides up beside Branden calling out, "Branden think Davey will live? He looked hurt pretty bad."

"God willing he will. Big John will take real good care of him. He always has taken real good care of all of us. Wish Doc Ron was back though…he be a better doc but he and JC ain't back yet," Branden answers frowning and says another prayer this time for Davey.

"They are both good," Greg answers and says his own prayers both for help and for healing.

Joe and Shorty sense Zak's anxiety so following his lead they ride hard down the trail to meet the wagon train.

Shorty frowns thinking, *"Lord I don't know why Pa's so anxious to reach Carrie Lynn but he seems to be about to jump outta his skin. If'n you've told him to rush then we will shorely rush. Please watch over all our friends, Lord, they are precious to us. Amen."*

"Lord, I think something is wrong. Cain't imagine what just like Zak but feel trouble is abrewin' for my girls. Please watch over'em and take good care of'em. They are precious to me. In Jesus Name I pray. Amen," Joe prays as he rides hard and fast with the other two men.

Gleefully Race rubs his hands together saying to Golden Eagle, "Soon! Soon it will all be mine!" He turns and looks at Golden Eagle demanding, "No one survives ….no one! Kill'em all!"

"Why kill the girls they can be sold as slaves?" Golden Eagle questions thinking of the beautiful white haired girl.

"Cause they have inherited everything that shoulda been mine. I deserve it all! They gotta die! Ya just want more money, don'tcha! Ya do what I say," Race states firmly.

Smiling cruelly Golden Eagle runs his hand down his knife before replying, "Don't worry, boss, I'll do it."

Looking down into the valley they see the wagon train finally approaching so Race waves to his men to be alert.

Foolishly he is wearing a red shirt and it shines like a beacon to the men in the wagon train but they continue on impatiently awaiting the attack.

"Kill that big white man in front first," Race demands of Golden Eagle (as he remembers the remarks Jake made to his face about his father never marrying his mother).

So Golden Eagle aims his bow and arrow at the two men leading the wagon train.

Suddenly an arrow flies through the air hitting Jake in the middle of his chest knocking him off his horse. Comfort immediately moves directly in front of him shielding him from anything coming in that direction again as he conceals Jake's body from the front of the valley. Comfort's eyes are wide as he looks around him with nostrils flaring.

A second arrow flies fast at Jay but he quickly leans forward so it flies over his head knocking his hat off as Jay yells out, "Ambush! Take cover."

The cowboys (driving the wagons) quickly roll into the back of them and grab their guns ready for the shootout.

Glancing around the back of the large wagon Glory sees Jake lying in the road motionless so jumps down to run to him when an arrow hits the wagon the girls and grandpas are in so gritting her teeth she yells, "Git down we are under attack!"

Looking at Jake she sees he isn't moving then glares at the arrow muttering, "That Indian won't live the day out!" Seeing movement she aims her gun and shoots one man. Smiling grimly she lowers her hat farther over her eyes to keep the sun's glare out of her eyes as she watches for the next outlaw to appear in her sights. Feeling someone behind her she whips around shooting the man coming down the hill behind her. Rolling under the wagon she calls out, "Stay in the wagon they are on both sides of us. Grandpas watch the front and back!"

Skinny and Pokey are shocked when they look at the girls and see them clinging to each other in terror but no longer moaning and crying. They realize they have been tricked into the wagons out of danger.

Angrily Pokey states, "I otta paddle yar bottoms for trickin' us like this! We otta be out thar with the men."

Terrified Beth Ann looks at him wailing, "They mean to kill us, grandpa. You promised to watch over us!"

Skinny and Pokey look at Beth Ann remembering her nightmare. Skinny softly replies, "We won't leave ya, honey, he won't git to ya."

Nodding grimly Pokey states, "That's a promise, honey!"

"Give us a gun! We can shoot now," Carrie Lynn begs them.

Reaching into a nearby crate Pokey pulls out the extra guns and ammunition saying, "Load'em and keep ours loaded."

Both girls know how to load a gun so quickly they reload as Pokey and Skinny aim and shoot at the bandits. As soon as one falls another outlaw seems to appear.

Opening his eyes and blinking at the bright light hitting his eyeballs, Jake frowns wondering about the sharp pain in his chest and the throbbing in his head then looking down he sees the arrow sticking out of his shirt. Moving slightly he realizes it hurts a little but not much. Slowly he reaches up grabbing the arrow shaft he pulls it straight out giving a gasp at the sharp pain that follows. Looking at the arrow he notices that only the very tip has blood on it and there isn't any blood on the shaft at all. Smiling he realizes the leather around his chest has saved his life. Taking a breath he says, *"Thank you, Lord!"* Slowly looking around again he sees Comfort is practically lying on top of him so patting Comfort's back he says, "Good boy. You saved my life!" Looking back towards the wagons he sees Glory under the grandpa's wagon shooting and everyone else shooting from their wagons. She glances over at him and he sees tears are running down her cheeks so he calls out, "Don't give up on me yet, Glory! I ain't dead!"

Glory can't stop the tears from running down her cheeks as she thinks about Jake lying dead. When she hears his beloved voice she raises her tearful eyes to him and smiling brilliantly at him calls out, "Ya just scared ME outta ten years, Jake! I'm gonna git ya for that." Wiping the tears from her cheeks she grimly yells, "Git'em Jake! We ain't givin'em nothing!"

Jay smiles when he hears Jake's voice and is relieved he isn't dead as he'd first thought, "The leather saved our lives!" Happily he yells over,

"Glad yar still with us, Jake! I'm gonna steal that horse of yours. I ain't neva ever seen a horse like him afore."

"Nay, cain't let that happen," Jake answers smacking Comfort on the neck lovingly saying, "Hide!" Jake rolls over half a dozen times into the cover of a large rock as Comfort immediately gallops away to safety.

Brad rolls under the wagon (that the bosses are in) asking, "We are all okay boss! Ya'll okay?"

"Yep, doin' fine. Shootin' these varmints as quick as we can," Pokey answers grimly.

Smiling Jay and Bradford sigh in relief watching to see which direction the bullets will be coming from next. Both say their own prayers of thanksgiving and prayers of help from this ambush.

Race mumbles angrily, "Why haven't we already taken the wagon train," then demands, "How did they know! It shoulda been a surprise attack and they were ready for us. I thought we killed that big giant and he just rolled over to those rocks. Ain't he human?" Looking over at the men he has hired, he notices three are down already. "We gotta take them out fast and git the job done. Move in men and kill'em," Race yells as he slides down a boulder and moves closer to the wagon train.

Skinny's cowboys coming to the rescue hear the shooting and even though their mounts are tired from the hurried ride they urge them on. Soon they are close to the wagon train and can hear the shooting much better.

Branden raises his hand in the air and all the men stop. With their horses heads down breathing heavily he orders, "We need to ride in quietly. Let's git a little closer then hide the horses and creep up on'em and git'em."

"Want me and Mike to go on the North side and you and Greg go to the South side. The rest of ya can evenly follow either side ya want," Matthew asks looking at the rest of the cowboys.

"Yep, sounds good! Now, quietly men, let's git'em!" Branden orders firmly.

Jesse and Norman (Skinny and Pokey's older cowboys) smile at the take charge attitude of their young cowboys (almost sons) so follow their orders and split up following the younger men.

Norman smiles then spits as his mouth fills with red dirt as he says, "They are younger and move quicker than we do but we are tougher and meaner than they are."

"Yep and we ain't gonna let'em forget it either," Jesse states smiling then adds, "Young pups are growing into good men. I'm right proud of'em."

"Yep, me, too," Norman agrees as he runs.

Zak and Shorty hear the shooting at the same time as Joe calls out, "Seems like ya was onto somethang Zak! There's trouble ahead."

Drawing their guns they ride quickly towards the valley. When they see the shooting coming from the rocks ahead of them Shorty holds his hand up and lowing his voice states, "Let's git in behind them! I'm goin' for the North side ya'll go on the South side." Then jumping off this horse he is off like a shot.

Watching his son move quickly Zak quietly replies, "He didn't give us a chance to say nay, did he?"

Lowering his hat over his blazing eyes Joe answers, "Nope, let's go!"

Quickly and quietly they move up behind the outlaws.

Watching the shooting coming from the wagon train Race calls Golden Eagle over ordering, "Shoot an arra into that wagon that purdy girl is under. Betcha her sister is in that wagon and will run out then we can shoot'em both. As soon as ya shoot it git down there and make sure they are both dead!"

Nodding yes and smiling widely in anticipation Golden Eagle replies, "Yes, boss!" He stands straight, lights the arrow on fire, aims it then shoots it into the canvas of the wagon that Skinny, Pokey, Beth Ann and Carrie Lynn are huddled in waiting to see which direction the next attack will come from.

Carrie Lynn screams shrilly when the fiery arrow hits the canvas and it starts to burn.

Both Zak and Shorty jerk when they hear her scream because they recognize her voice and know she is in danger.

Shorty mumbles angrily, "They better not harm her or they will deal with me!"

Brad quickly runs to the back of the wagon to get the ammunition out then sets it on the ground under the wagon and grabs a mattress off the side of the wagon. He pulls it out and lays it under the wagon as he orders, "Girls git under the mattress for protection! We won't let the fire git to you!"

Skinny and Pokey jump down as Bradford (grabbing one of their arms) literally runs them to the buck board behind their wagon throwing them down on the ground. Two cowboys stay with Brad as they carefully look around for more outlaws.

Pokey and Skinny try to crawl out and go back to Carrie Lynn and Beth Ann but are stopped when shots ring out all around them. Pokey mutters, "They harm my girls and I'll kill'em bare handed."

"I'll hep ya, brother!" Skinny answers as he watches the large wagon in front of them.

Grabbing the girls Glory pulls them under the wagon then taking her knife she climbs back into the wagon hacking off the burning canvas throwing it out the back of the wagon.

Jake crawls over to the girls and comforts them saying, "I'm here and nothin' is gonna happen to you! Don't worry. Do you still have your guns? Good, keep'em ready!"

"Yyyyes, we bbbrought them with us," Carrie Lynn stutters as she holds tightly to Beth Ann's arm.

Beth Ann's hands are sweating so much she can hardly hold the heavy gun but she has a death grip on it and extra bullets, too.

Suddenly two men run out from behind some rocks right behind Jake and Glory. Beth Ann sees them first so screams loudly, "Behind you!"

Both swing around in time to dodge the knives that are thrown at them so they thud harmlessly into the side of the wagon.

Screaming wildly Beth Ann scoots down farther under the heavy cotton mattress.

Joe knows the screams are coming from Beth Ann and sweat pops out on his forehead as he moves faster towards the outlaws thinking, "I've gotta git there and save my baby. *Please Lord, watch over our young'uns!*"

Zak keeps pace with Joe as they quickly climb over rocks to get to the men shooting at their families.

Shorty is making good time climbing from the other side as he is younger and quicker. He comes upon the first man and they wrestled for a few minutes until Shorty's knife ends the outlaw's life. Looking at the long jagged cut down his arm Shorty just shrugs and is quickly on his way to the next man.

Branden's men are climbing quickly and quietly from the other end of the valley when they come upon the outlaws shooting at the wagon train from back there so they start making their counter attack.

Hearing shooting from behind them as well as in front of them Pokey and Skinny look at each other asking, "Who is behind us? Are they with us or against us?"

"Must be with us or they wouldn't be shootin' against them," Pokey reasons wonderingly.

Gasping they see the two men rush Jake and Glory then see them miss being stabbed.

Race charges Glory pulling out another knife. They gasp again as Glory kicks it out of his hand then come up with her other foot kicking him right on the side of the head and he drops like a stone.

Without pausing she leaps up and brings her whole body weight down while putting her hands together and comes down sharply on Patch's (a very large man with a patch over one eye) wrist. His second knife falls from his hand as they hear a sharp crack as she breaks his wrist. Patch lets out a yelp of pain and glares at her angrily.

Jake's whole attention is on Patch (Race's muscle man) so he jumps on him and they roll around on the ground punching each other unmercifully in life and death hand to hand combat. They roll all across the rocky ground but neither can best the other.

Race groggily starts to stand up when Kevin (Skinny's cowboy) grabs him and drags him over to a nearby tree where Josh (another young cowboy of Skinny and Pokey) is waiting.

Suddenly the large Indian (Golden Eagle) drops out of the tree and with a powerful slap back hands first Josh then Kevin and they fly backwards. Holding his large wicked looking bowie knife the Indian smiles evilly at Glory saying, "Come on little Indian girl! Come and git me! I know yar tricks! I larned 'em myself!" He passes the large knife from hand to hand as he approaches her.

Glaring at him Glory cockily answers, "Ain't had to kill an Indian yet so ya'll be my first!" She notices the long jagged scar on his chest seeing Beth Ann's nightmare has come to life.

Standing back up Race bellows, "Kill them" and races towards Skinny and Pokey when Jay and Bradford shoot him dead center in his chest.

Outlaws rush out of the rocks attacking the cowboys guarding the wagons. Suddenly it seems everyone is busy fighting hand to hand even Skinny and Pokey. Jay and Bradford are close to them and anxiously watching out for them as they fight.

Jake's outlaw (Patch) is nearly as big and mean as he is so their fight is a grim one with neither giving way as they slug it out. Patch turns his good hand over and grabs the knife Glory knocked out of his hand and with a powerful grip brings it down towards Jake's unprotected throat.

Glory dances around Golden Eagle as he slashes out with his wicked bowie knife. Carrie Lynn and Beth Ann scream shrilly time and again as he comes close to slashing Glory. Moving quickly he backhands her and knocks her rolling across the hard red dirt then turning he starts advancing towards the two young terrified girls cowering under the wagon when Glory yells, "Take another step and I'll shoot ya in the back!"

Golden Eagle believes her so slowly half turning around he drops his hand positioning his knife to throw it.

"PUT IT DOWN NOW!" Glory demands then advises, "I won't hesitate to kill ya!"

In a swift move he starts to throw the knife but hits the ground hard as a shot rings out hitting him in the back. Stunned at the pain he lays there alive and thinking furiously.

Both terrified girls slide out from under the wagon and start running. Carrie Lynn runs to the wagon behind them where the grandpas are but Beth Ann is beyond terror so she runs to the horses' heads squatting down there panting heavily as she clutches their reins. Gasping for each breath she takes she peeps through the impatiently moving legs of the horses watching Golden Eagle. He is lying on the ground with his head turned towards her. A red stain is seeping from his bare back and running down his side. Glory's smoking gun is lying on the ground where she had been standing. But she isn't standing there now. Wildly Beth Ann looks around for her buckskin clad legs. Gasping for breath she almost smiles when she looks back towards Golden Eagle and sees his eyes are open and he is smiling evilly at her with hatred in his eyes.

"Where are you, Glory!" Beth Ann screams shrilly, "He's alive!" She can't keep from screaming shrilly again and again in terror.

Shorty is wrestling with a much larger outlaw and they are rolling all over the hard packed red dirt when he hears Beth Ann's shrill screams. Clamping his jaw down he urges his body to move faster as he rolls the outlaw (Albert) towards a large rock and cracks his head against it. Albert doesn't move again as Shorty jumps up and runs toward the covered wagon and Beth Ann.

Zak reaches the wagon that Carrie Lynn and the grandpas are under so is shooting it out with the outlaw cowboys behind them. Carrie Lynn is covered by her father and the grandpas now.

After Glory shoots Golden Eagle she runs to Jake and hits the outlaw called Patch as hard as she can across his throat then turns back to look at Beth Ann just as she screams shrilly.

Gulping Beth Ann can't take her eyes off of the scarred red man.

With lightning speed he rolls under the wagon and stands up looking at her smiling his evil smile.

Startled and hypnotized she watches him advance towards her (with the big bloody bowie knife) just as she dreamed. Screaming she turns and runs around the horses' heads terror completely filling her.

Joe is closing fast so when he sees the large Indian roll under the wagon towards Beth Ann he runs as fast as he can towards her.

As she rounds the horses heads he grabs her and swings her behind him with his left arm as he shoots the Indian three times dead center in the chest.

At the same time as the bullets hit the man Glory leaps out of the side of the wagon (through the torn and burnt canvas). She launches herself at the brave knocking him to the ground, but Golden Eagle is already dead.

Shorty tackles Golden Eagle at the same time that Glory flies through the wagon so all three roll around the red dirt with Golden Eagle really dead this time.

Joe grabs Beth Ann pulling her back under the wagon as Glory rolls under from the other side with her knife still in her hand. She grabs Beth Ann hugging her hard saying, "I thought I'd already killed him. I'm so sorry, Beth Ann."

Shorty rushes back to his father and Carrie Lynn after he sees Beth Ann is safe. He wipes dirty sweat out of his eyes as he watches for more outlaws to appear.

"Papa's here! You saved me!" Beth Ann exclaims through her tears as she clings to her beloved father. Looking up at him she cries out, "I needed you and you came ...just as I needed you...you were here!"

Rocking her back and forth Joe says over and over tearfully, "My baby....my baby, I'll always be here for ya...always and forever."

As Shorty slides back under the wagon that Carrie Lynn is under she grabs a hold of both of them sobbing wildly.

"Baby, it's alright I'm right here. Pa's here," Zak croons to his distraught daughter as Shorty rubs her back and pats her shoulders as she cries in fear.

A short time later when she is calmer Shorty nods at Zak stating, "We'd better see how many are alive." He rolls out looking around then sees Jake lying on the ground not far away with a dead man lying beside him and there is blood all over Jake's chest so he rushes over asking, "Jake! Jake, are ya all right?"

Breathing heavily Jake replies, "Yeah, I'm alright. This outlaw nearly did me in. If'n Glory hadn't helped I might not be alive now."

"Are you bleedin' here?" Shorty asks as he runs his hands over Jake's bloodied shirt.

"A little, I got an arra wound in my chest but don't think its bad," Jake replies weakly.

Seeing all the blood on him, Shorty is worried it is more than a little cut.

Branden, Matt, Greg and Michael (Skinny's young cowboys) walk up first to report to their bosses, "Ain't none alive back thar. We searched the hills for the rest of 'em."

Jesse and Norman (Skinny's older cowboys) smile and nod yes as they stand behind their boys as Pokey looks over at them for confirmation.

Jay and Bradford return from jogging around the area checking for the outlaws so Brad reports then asks, "Don't think thar are any alive here either. Boss, ya want us to bury'em here?"

"Nope, I want ya to take'em to the Sheriff in the City of John and let him see about identifyin'em," Pokey states as he angrily looks at Brad and Jay.

Walking close to them and coming almost eye to eye with them he promises, "Ya ever pull a trick like ya just did, boys, and you and me are gonna visit the wood shed again!"

Both grown young men look at skinny little Pokey but dutifully reply, "Yes, sir!"

Looking at the men he considers his sons Skinny angrily states, "That goes double for me! I can take care of myself and ya'll ain't never gonna protect me like that again. You understand!"

Jay starts to explain but Bradford elbows him so they both answers, "Yes, sir!"

Skinny points to six of his men saying, "Load up the bodies on their horses and take them to the Sheriff for me."

Nodding yes they start doing this unpleasant job. The other cowboys that aren't driving the wagons start helping them tie the bodies on the horses then make a long line of horses with dead bodies on them.

Glory swiftly runs over to Jake and ripping his shirt open sees the arrow wound is still bleeding. She starts unbuttoning her shirt then grabbing her knife she cuts the whole front of her chemise off then wadding it up, she presses it to stop the flow of blood freely flowing from his wound.

Grinning foolishly after seeing her beautiful naked breasts Jake weakly states, "It was worth gettin'shot!"

"Shut up, Jake. I've got to get the bleedin' stopped," Glory answers with a wan smile then anxiously calls, "Papa, I need ya!"

Joe rushes over and seeing Jake is bleeding, he kneels down across from Glory as she orders "Hold this Papa; I need to cut off some more."

Joe's eyes widen as he sees her naked young breast then watches her grip her knife and cut the chemise at the shoulders pulling it completely off handing it to him. She quickly rebuttons the shirt closed before turning around and calling out, "Anyone got any whiskey? We need some for Jake!"

Looking over at her Skinny calls out, "We got some in one of buckboards. I'll git it to you!"

Soon Glory is handed a bottle of liquor so looking at Jake she says, "Take a deep breath, Jake, this is gonna hurt." She nods to Joe, he raises the wad of silk, and Glory liberally pours the whiskey into the wound.

Jake gasps as tears come to his eyes as he yelps in pain.

"Sorry, honey, but I had to clean it out," Glory grimaces sadly then leaning over kisses him. Looking at the wound again she states, "Papa, we need to bandage him."

"Yep," Joe replies looking steadily at her to see what she will do.

Realizing he is going to let her take control of this she nods then standing up walks over to Beth Ann and Carrie Lynn ordering, "Girls, I need some help. Get me a petticoat from my clothes, please. We need some bandages for Jake."

Glory notices that Shorty has his arms around Beth Ann (since their papa had run over to help her) but she doesn't say anything about it.

Both stop their crying immediately and scramble to the big wagon with the feather mattresses in it to get the petticoat. Then rush over to Jake's side to bandage his chest.

Turning to the men Glory advises, "Okay, whoever has been shot or stabbed or is a hurtin' and needs attention, come over here or yell and I'll come over thar."

Noticing Brad and Jay just standing around she frowns at them saying, "What'cha gawkin' at. Hep me!"

Smiling they turn and follow her and soon she has poured whiskey on the cuts and scratches the injured men have received.

Glory calls out, "Beth Ann, bring a couple more petticoats over here and hep me bandage up these men."

Beth Ann and Carrie Lynn are wrapping cotton strips around Jake's chest so when Glory calls out Carrie Lynn says, "Go ahead. I can finish this."

Beth Ann grabs two more petticoats and soon, with Brad and Jay's help, all the cowboys are bandaged and ready to travel.

Glory reports to the pa's and old gents, "Ain't any bad wounds except Jake's and it ain't really bad he's just lost a lot of blood and is weak."

Walking up Shorty admits, "Guess I need some of your nursing skill Glory," and holds out his arm where a long cut is dripping blood.

Nodding yes Glory points to a nearby rock saying, "Sit over thar."

When Shorty sits down on it, she rips his shirt sleeve completely off advising, "This is gonna sting!" Then leaning down and looking into his beautiful eyes she softly says, "Remember when ya taunted me about gettin' a spankin' from Jake."

Then she pours the whiskey all down the cut causing Shorty to yell, "Owwww, ya got a mean streak in ya, Glory!"

"Yep! I do," Glory answers as she gently wipes the blood off his arm and with Beth Ann's help they quickly bandage it.

"Beth Ann, you have a soft touch. Thank you," Shorty states with a smile at her as he frowns at Glory again.

Blushing Beth Ann replies, "I am sorry you are injured because of us."

Shorty winks saying, "I gotta protect my girls, don't I?"

Glory rolls her eyes at his statement but notices that Beth Ann smiles happily at Shorty. "Humm...does she have a likin' for him?" Glory wonders as she watches them smiling at each other then thinks, "Naw, she is just like a little sister to him. Shorty is too set in his ways to like any girl."

Standing up she looks over at her grandpas asking, "Why don't we git Jake on the mattresses in the wagon and head on home."

"Jest waitin' for ya to say it is time," Pokey answers then calls the drivers to get to their wagons again.

Walking over Joe advises, "We shouldn't have any more trouble on the way home, seems me like, we got'em all."

Puzzled Skinny asks, "What made ya'll ride to meet us, Joe?"

Joe points to Zak before replying, "Zak was missin' his young'uns and rode over saying, "Let's go meet'em", so I said, "Okay" and here we are."

"Why did yar cowboys come to the rescue?" Zak asks looking at the cowboys drinking from their canteens and resting near the wagons in the shade.

Wondering why himself, Pokey calls over, "Boys come over here a minute."

They quickly comply then Pokey asks, "How did ya know we was needin' help?"

Matthew answers, "Davey got beat up real bad by a big Indian." He points to Golden Eagle lying dead not far away.

"Davey said the Indian had a big scar across his chest," Branden adds as they all look at the long ugly scar across Golden Eagles chest.

"This Indian cut Davey up something terrible, boss," Mike advises sadly.

"Yep, boss, he was covered with blood," Norman states sadly.

Skinny and Pokey look at each other stunned then Skinny quickly asks, "He didn't die, did he?"

"Big John said he would take good care of him. We rode out quick as a wink to warn you that they were gonna attack you," Jesse explains sadly but earnestly.

Concern flows all over Skinny and Pokey's faces as they turn to Joe and Zak then Skinny states, "We are gonna ride back to the ranch with the boys and see how Davey is doin' then we'll ride back home in a couple of days."

Smiling Jake softly mumbles, "They said home."

Beth Ann is kneeling beside him so she smiles happily at the word home then answers, "I'm really ready to go home, too."

Taking a shallow breath, Jake answers, "Me, too."

Jumping down from the wagon after shifting the mattresses around and making the mattresses as comfortable as possible, Glory asks, "Would six of ya'll lift Jake into the wagon for me, please."

Jake frowns stating, "I can walk."

"No, ya don't! Ya'll start it bleedin' again," Glory states firmly as he moves to sit up.

Beth Ann pushes him back down sternly saying, "Don't make it start bleeding again, Jake. We finally got it stopped."

Smiling weakly at her Jake answers, "Nag, nag, nag."

Both girls smile then help as six men pick Jake up and carry him to the wagon then Brad and Jay jump up into the wagon and lift him over to the mattress and lay him down.

Beads of sweat dot Jake's forehead even though he hasn't exerted himself at all.

Glory lifts him up a little saying, "Drink some of this whiskey, Jake, it will deaden the pain."

Jake takes a couple of drinks, gasps at the fire that shoots through his stomach, then closing his eyes falls into an exhausted sleep.

Comfort walks over and stands at the back of the wagon watching everyone around Jake. When Branden reaches for his reins to tie him to the wagon, he backs up and snorts at him.

Looking over Glory states, "He's okay. He won't leave Jake, he will follow us." Looking at her father she asks, "Papa, should I sew him up now or wait til we git home?"

Joe glances at Jake's white face before thoughtfully replying, "We'll be home soon. Let him rest up some. Yalla Moon will have some herbs that will help, I'll go git her as soon as we git home."

Zak is standing at the end of the wagon with Joe, watching his son and nods he agrees with Joe then adds, "Shorty can go get Yalla Moon and meet us at your ranch, Joe."

Concerned Glory looks over at Zak advising, "Shorty's got a bad cut on his arm, Zak. He will need some takin' care of, too."

"Stephie will take care of him, honey, and she won't take no lip from him either," Zak answers with a smile.

So the wagon train continues to Joe's ranch as Skinny and Pokey along with their cowboys (who had ridden over from the ranch) ride back to their ranch to check on Davey.

At nightfall Skinny and Pokey tiredly ride their horses into the yard of the ranch house then walk directly over to the bunk house to check on Davey.

Big John opens the door upon hearing the horses and walks out to meet them saying, "Glad to see the boys got to you in time, boss. Davey is alive. He got beat up real bad but I've stitched him up and gave him herbs to make him sleep. He's got two broke ribs and many cuts all over his face and chest. Some Indian took a knife to him real bad."

"That Indian is dead now," Pokey states angrily as they walk over to the bunk looking down at Davey restlessly sleeping in his bunk.

Wincing at seeing Davey's eyes almost swollen shut and the many stitched cuts all over his young face, Skinny kneels down beside the bunk saying, "Davey, we owe you our lives."

"Boss?" Dave stirs agitated hearing their voices asking, "Boss? Gotta save'em… Ambush… Gotta save'em." Tears run down his cheeks as he opens his eyes as much as he can and sees Skinny and Pokey then he moans, "Yar alive! I told where you were goin' boss. The pain was so bad. I told'em where ya'll were goin'. I'm so sorry. Real real sorry. I was a hurtin' so bad, boss." Tears fall like raindrops from the grief stricken swollen eyes as Davey begs for forgiveness.

"You did fine, son. You did just fine. We are so sorry you got beat up cause of us. You got nothing to be sorry for. Nobody got hurt bad and you saved our lives by warnin' us," Skinny answers as he takes Davey's bandaged hand squeezing it lightly.

Pokey has tears running down his leathered cheeks also as he leans over saying, "Son, ya done real good. Yar gonna get well real fast like. Big John's gonna feed ya good and soon ya'll be out checkin' cattle again."

Looking up hopefully at them Davey asks, "You ain't gonna fire me? I can stay?"

"We don't fire our sons, Davey. Your ours!" Skinny answers smiling down at the handsome young man.

Davey closes his eyes as his tears run freely then he mumbles sleepily, "Thank you, boss! Thank you." He falls back into an exhausted sleep so the old gents stand up and walk back towards the door.

They almost reach it when Big John softly but angrily says, "I stitched up twenty places that Indian cut young Davey."

Gulping Pokey turns around sadly repeating, "Twenty? Oh, my God!"

Skinny looks down at the ground thinking of the suffering Davey had suffered because of them and wearily requests, "Take good care of him, John."

Looking down at Davey Big John smiles agreeing, "I fully intend to."

NO PLACE LIKE HOME
Chapter 19

"Home is the best place of rest for the
soul and comfort for the body."

Glory is sitting beside Jake in the wagon watching him. Soon she slips down beside him and sleeps from exhaustion with her hand on Jake's arm in case he moves.

Zak looks in the wagon a little later seeing his son's black head leaning against Glory's white blonde head smiling at the picture they make. Looking over towards Joe he motions for him to look at their children.

Riding up beside him Joe looks in then smiling says, "They are a good looking couple. Ain't we gonna have some fine lookin' grandkids!"

Smiling a little tearfully Zak nods yes saying, "Yep."

They move away from the wagon to allow their children to rest more as Zak says, "I'm amazed at seein' all that Glory knows how to do. I can still see her flying outta that wagon, so fast like. She looked like an… angry angel…I could see determination written all over her face. Good Heart's taught her to give a mean look when she is fightin'."

Chuckling Joe explains, "Good Heart told her over and over that intimidation is half the fight. Ya gotta let'em know ya mean it when ya have to fight. Yeah, she larned it real good. Surprises me some when I see her fightin' like that cause she don't normally show a high temper. She is just stubborn sometimes. Her tender heart usually wins out with her."

"Yeah, she is somethin' special," Zak replies smiling as he looks back at the wagon. Then turning calls out, "Shorty, come over here a minute, son."

Shorty is riding between Beth Ann and Carrie Lynn (joking with them as they are still upset by the ambush) he nods to them then backs up his horse and moves over to his pa saying, "Yes, sir."

"I'd like you to ride home and tell yar ma about Jake. She will be fit to tie if'n she ain't there to see him for herself. Then stop at Good Hearts an ask Yalla Moon to come over to see about Jake. Ride easy and don't git that cut a bleedin' again, son. You can git there much faster than these wagons can, so take your time," Zak requests then instructs.

"Yes, sir, I'd planned on doin' that anyway since ma would give me grief just like you said if'n we didn't let her know. I'll take it easy," Shorty answers with a short salute. Walking his horse back to the girls he explains, "I'm gonna ride home and tell ma about Jake bein' hurt. It's only about four miles farther to Joe's. As slow as these wagons are a goin' I'll be there about the same time as ya'll are." Nodding again he moves to the side of the road to ride for home.

Calling after him Carrie Lynn says, "Ride easy, don't open that cut on your arm, Shorty!"

Raising his good arm he waves at them as he leaves in a swirl of red dust.

Late in the evening Joe, Zak and the wagon train drive into the yard at Joe's house. Stephie and Payton are standing at the door with Elizabeth waiting to see how Jake is doing.

Good Heart and Yellow Moon sit close by in the yard chairs also waiting for the wagons to arrive.

Stephie immediately asks, "Which wagon is Jake in?" so Joe points to the one that is pulling up right in front of the door.

As soon as it stops, Stephie and Elizabeth run to the back and start to crawl into it, when Glory reassures them explaining, "He is fine, just weak from loss of blood. I've been givin' him whiskey to deaden the pain and he is a little drunk now."

Opening his blurry eyes Jake teasingly asks, "Ma, ya look beautiful. What's that thang on your head?"

Reaching up to the top of her head Stephie finds a twig sticking out of her uncombed hair. Smiling and relaxing she answers, "It's a new hat I just bought Jake. I wore it just for you."

Jake's crooked grin makes her smile as he drunkenly says, "It looks right fine on ya, Ma." Taking a deep breath he closes his eyes and falls back asleep.

Jumping down from the wagon Glory turns to Joe explaining, "Papa, he is out again. Let's get'em moved into the house for the night. Mama, where are we gonna put him?"

Looking at little surprised at Glory's manner Elizabeth answers, "We can carry in a mattress and put him in the parlor for the night."

Nodding yes Joe, Zak and Good Heart move towards the wagon to get Jake out.

Shaking his head no Short mumbles, "Three of'em cain't carry that horse outta the wagon," so he climbs in to help.

Glory and two cowboys grab a mattress and quickly carry it into the parlor then Elizabeth quickly spreads a sheet over it before they lay Jake down on it. He never wakes up but moans a time or two.

Good Heart and Yellow Moon quickly start working on him. Stephie has more bandages and her needle ready to sew him up when it is time.

Good Heart cuts the strips of petticoat off of his ribs as Yellow Moon looks at the shallow cut then nodding as she smiles saying, "Not bad...just deep it just take a few days to heal." She quickly puts some herbs in the wound explaining, "This make it drain anything bad out." Looking at Stephie she states, "Wait on stitching him."

Stephie doesn't love stitching skin in the first place so nods okay and walks back into the kitchen to put her needle and thread away.

Jake moans softly then opening his eyes looks into Yellow Moon's lovely face asking, "You look real good. Good Heart takin' good care of ya?"

Yellow Moon lays her small hand on his whiskered cheek replying, "Yes, he always takes good care of me. Did ya take good care of Glory for us?"

"Yep, most of the time. She took good care of me, too. Kilt the outlaw who was close to killin' me. Saved my life, I was gettin' weaker and weaker," Jakes explains then looks over at Glory, who is sitting at his feet, and smiles lovingly at her.

"He near scared me to death when I saw that arra hit him in the chest and he fell like a rock from Comfort," Glory explains as she relives the horror of that scene.

"So that's the reason my head hurts so bad," Jake states softly then looking at his mother explains, "Comfort saved my life, Ma. He knelt down right in front of me until I told him to hide. He did real good."

"I will personally give him a bucket of grain for you," Stephie softly promises as a tear slips down her pale face.

Speaking up Beth Ann advises, "I already asked one of the cowboys to do that," then looking over towards the window smiles saying, "Look over at the window, Jake."

Painfully Jake turns his head around and looks over as Good Heart moves out of the way and there at the open window stands Jake's horse, Comfort. His bridle and saddle are gone (taken off by Shorty as Comfort doesn't allow many to touch him). His large brown eyes cautiously watch everyone in the room but continually return to Jake. Calling out softly Jake says, "Good boy. Go to bed now."

Comfort whinnies then backing up walks away secure in the knowledge that Jake is alright.

"Well, I'll be! Cain't believe a horse can love anyone like that," Joe states looking at the empty window.

Chuckling Zak explains, "We are used to it. Comfort would walk right into the house when he was just a pony until he...uh...made a mess and Stephie shooed him out after that. Jake has shared his food with him and slept with him for years. He might be a bit jealous of you, Glory."

"No problem, I'll just bed down right beside'em," Glory smilingly answers as she looks down at the love of her life.

Smiling Zak nods yes replying, "Yep, guess you would."

Frowning Yellow Moon looks at the jagged cut down Shorty's arm before saying, "Not bad just be sore for a time," she puts some herbs on it then mixes up some different herbs saying, "Drink this, Shorty."

Looking at the dark liquid then back at her Shorty takes a deep breath and quickly swallows the concoction. He rolls his eyes at the bad taste then grimacing chokes out, "Thank ya, Yalla Moon."

Smiling she pats him on the shoulder replying, "It makes you heal fast like."

"Good, I don't want no more of it," Shorty answers shuddering at the taste.

Everyone is exhausted so it isn't long until Zak, Shorty and Payton walk out the back door heading for home. Stephie grabs Shorty as he starts to leave saying, "You are staying here with me tonight. You can sleep right beside Jake. I'm going to keep an eye on you, too."

Frowning he answers, "Ma, I'm alright. It's just a little scratch."

Raising her eyebrows at him Stephie gives him a level look so he raises his hands up resigned stating, "Yes, ma." He turns and obediently sits back down at the table frustrated.

Good Heart and Yellow Moon walk out with them on their way home. Yellow Moon explains to Stephie, "If'n they get a fever, come right over and git me and I'll come right back."

Hugging her Stephie answers, "I will and thank you both for coming over."

Nodding yes (confirming her thank you) Good Heart chuckles stating, "Jake good man! He be fine. Shorty, too ornery, for anythang to happen to him." They nod goodbye as they walk across the pasture to their home.

Glory never leaves Jake's side but tiredly lies down beside him and is asleep fully dressed when Stephie and Elizabeth enter the room a short time later. Both smile resigned as Stephie states, "Guess she picked her bed for the night."

"Yes, she did. It won't be long until their home is built and they won't be at our homes at all," Elizabeth explains sadly then looking at Stephie states, "I've missed so much of her life. I don't know how I'll be able to make it up to her."

"Day by day, Elizabeth, that is all we can do," Stephie answers smiling down at their children.

Walking in Shorty chuckles saying, "Well ma, there goes my bed. Guess I can head home now, huh?"

"Not if you want to live, my son," Stephie declares raising her eye brows menacingly at him.

"Humm…thought you'd say that. Guess I'll go to the barn," he turns around and starts out the back door when Elizabeth says, "That won't be necessary. We will bring another mattress in for you and Stephie to sleep on."

She quickly walks to the kitchen door requesting another mattress so soon another mattress is being carried in by Randy McDee and Earl Coe (Joe's cowboys). Elizabeth spreads another clean sheet over the top of it so it is ready to be slept on.

Shorty (tiredly sighs) smiling slightly says, "Thank ya, Joe and Lizbeth," then lies down and is promptly snoring softly.

Carrie Lynn and Beth Ann are on another mattress lying on the floor in her new bedroom when Beth Ann yawning largely says, "The house is different. I'm so tired I can't seem to understand why. Good night, Carrie Lynn." She falls into an exhausted sleep.

Carrie mumbles, "Good night," and is asleep instantly exhausted from the terrors of the day.

Elizabeth is sitting at the kitchen table as Joe walks into the room restlessly walking around explaining the ambush and what had happened to them.

Shaking her head sadly Elizabeth explains, "Race hung around quite a bit. He probably was fath…uh…Edgar's son. He looked a lot like him. But fath…uh…Edgar never claimed him, called him a no account bum. I'm sorry he is dead though. He was older than me. It is a shame since they wanted a child so bad that Mother and Father didn't raise him."

"Probably yar ma wouldn't have him," Joe answers thoughtfully.

Shaking her head no Elizabeth answers, "No, I don't think Mother knew about him until he was a grown boy. She disliked him intensely because he was such a rough talking boy. She might have raised him if she'd had him as a child. I just don't know. Ready to go to bed, I'm really tired. No one seems to notice the changes we've made."

"They are too tired, just wait until morning, honey," Joe advises wiggling his eye brows at her they stand up to go to their bedroom.

Opening her eyes Beth Ann lays looking around the room as the rising sun shines in the open window beside her. Smiling she glances around the bare room thinking, "Where am I? This isn't the loft. Jake is in the parlor. The sun doesn't come into Mother and Papa's room like this and where is the furniture?" Slowly she sits up suddenly realizing, "Papa built a bedroom for me. Last night he carried this mattress (from the wagon) in here and Mother led us in here and helped us undress to our underclothes to sleep in since we were so tired. Papa built me a new room!" Joy fills her so much she almost burst out laughing and crying at the same time. Looking around the room she smiles and tears do come as she whispers, "I can get all my furniture from St. Louis in here. I can keep it all. Papa loves me enough to give me a room like this." She glances down at the smoothly sanded floor and runs her hand over it as tears flow in streams down her happy face as she repeats, "Papa did this for me... just for me."

Joe and Elizabeth wake to the sound of soft crying. Quickly Joe looks over at Elizabeth stunned and seeing she isn't crying softly asks, "Who is crying, honey?"

Listening more carefully and now concerned Elizabeth answers, "It sounds like Beth Ann? Do you think she hates her new room?"

Quickly pulling on his pants Joe answers, "I don't know but something is wrong."

Pulling on her robe she follows him out of their bedroom and down the hallway to Beth Ann's new room.

The door is open and Beth Ann is softly sobbing her heart out.

Arriving at the door Joe and Elizabeth immediately go to her. Kneeling down on the floor and pulling her into his arms Joe begs, "Honey, don'tcha cry. I'll change anythang ya don't like. We tried to make everythang the way ya'd want it. Hush honey. Don't cry like that, yar breakin' my heart."

Beth Ann looks up at him unable to talk as she is crying so hard.

Kneeling down beside her daughter Elizabeth promises, "Oh, honey, what did we do wrong? Is it too small? I didn't do any decorating. I want you to do it anyway that you want. Please tell us what is wrong."

Stuttering Beth Ann replies, "You...you... made it for me...just for me! You love me enough to build this for... me. It's....ppperfect! The floor is so ssssmooth and the windows. I love looking outside and hearing…uh…seeing everything. It's so…ppperfect! And you …dddid it for me!" Tears flow freely as she hugs and kisses both parents.

Relief spreads through Elizabeth and Joe as lightning spearing through the air in a thunder storm. Both take a deep breath then Joe asks (just to be sure), "So yar happy with yar new room?"

Smiling brilliantly at him Beth Ann answers, "It is perfect! More than I ever imagined and so big. I can have all my furniture here……" Trailing off she looks down and the bright happiness fades from her face as she mumbles, "That is very vain to be happy because I have a place for things and not be happy just to be here with my family." Looking down at her hands, she sighs sadly continuing, "I guess I still don't appreciate all that I have been given…that things still mean so much to me."

Smiling fondly at her Elizabeth sits down on the floor then reaching over she touches Beth Ann's hand explaining, "Family is very important to you, Beth Ann, because you haven't been shown a lot of love in your life and mainly that is my fault. My pride…anger…whatever… well, honey, it caused me to be a bad mother and I'm very sorry for that. Your father feels bad about not being here for you, too." Elizabeth lifts up Beth Ann's sad face before continuing, "Beth Ann no one is perfect and no one will ever be perfect. No one expects YOU to be perfect. We all treasure "things" me probably more than others as I love pretty things. For your father it is the land and cattle but NOW for both of us it is our family first!"

Joe lays his hands on Elizabeth's shoulders leaning her back into his chest before saying, "We don't wanna change ya, honey. YOU are special just the way ya are. Yar a wonderful girl with a loving heart, we just wanta make ya happy."

Smiling again Beth Ann jumps up hugging them both back and forth three or four times stating, "It is the most wonderful gift I've ever received!"

Relief spills through Joe and Elizabeth seeing the sunshine of happiness in their young daughter's face again.

Grinning Joe replies, "This is yar room but we are hopin' ya won't mind to share it with Glory til she gets married in a month or so. We gotta build her house and it'll take a little time to do it."

Standing up Beth Ann smiles throwing open her arms wide she twirls in circles giggling stating, "I'll share with three sisters if I need to."

"How about one best friend?" Carrie Lynn requests as she sees the happiness radiating from all three of them then continues, "This is Beth Ann's room? It is really nice and BIG. I share with Payton and our room isn't this big. But I remember the furniture we brought down from St. Louis so know it will be filled up real soon."

Kneeling down on the mattress again Beth Ann hugs Carrie Lynn saying, "Always and Forever, my best friend."

With her eyes sparkling happily Beth Ann advises, "Do we have some stories to tell you about St. Louis! You won't believe some of them."

Grinning Joe replies, "Let's start some breakfast and check on Jake then we have a life time to hear all yar stories."

Kissing Beth Ann's cheek her mother asks, "Come help me make biscuits we have a houseful to feed."

"Yes, Mother," Beth Ann agrees happily. The girls quickly dress giggling happily then visit the outhouse. Stopping at the water pump they wash their hands before joining Elizabeth in the kitchen.

Carrie Lynn asks, "I'm going to look in at Jake for just a minute, if that is okay?"

"Certainly. I just looked in on him and he was asleep and so is Glory," Elizabeth answers then smiling continues, "If we make a little more noise they will wake up pretty fast."

Both girls' eyes widen at this statement from Elizabeth then smiling they look at each other and start singing a song not overly loud but not quiet either. Elizabeth joins in with them singing the melody.

Walking in the door Joe winks at Beth Ann as she softly informs him, "We are quietly waking everyone up."

Grinning back Joe states, "Oh, I see. Well, let me hep ya." then he joins right in with their singing (which is loud enough now to wake the dead).

So Jake, Glory, Stephie and Shorty all wake up to a chorus of angels (well rather like angels singing loudly). Smiling Jake says, "I reckon it's time to get up since they are singing to us and I believe I smell fresh coffee. Shorty, will ya hep me up. I need to go outside for a few minutes."

Stephie and Glory rush over as Jake raises his hand in a stopping motion saying, "First things first ladies. Shorty and I are gonna take a walk then have some coffee afore we do anythang else."

Ruefully Glory smiles at Shorty before calling out, "Papa, we need ya."

Frowning at her Jake states, "Shorty is strong as an ox. He can hep me git up."

Shaking her head no, Glory replies, "Remember Shorty hurt his arm. He don't need to git it to bleedin' again. Papa will hep ya."

Walking in Joe hears what is being said so nodding pleasantly says, "Me big strong man can pick up tree….no trouble picking up a giant." Joe walks like his leg muscles are so big he can't walk straight and everyone laughs at his joke.

Quickly Shorty and Joe help Jake stand up then give him a minute for his dizziness to go away before walking with him to the outhouse and back.

Looking at Stephie, Glory challenges, "I'll race ya to the outhouse. Bet we can both get in and out afore they git Jake there."

Grinning Stephie runs out of the room ahead of Glory calling back, "Okay, you on."

Laughingly heartily Shorty explains, "Ma likes to win."

They all laugh at Glory's shocked face then Jake advises, "You already lost but ya'd better run fast and make her think you tried."

"Hump," is the only sound Glory makes as she races after her future mother-in-law.

Elizabeth and the younger girls have breakfast almost ready by the time everyone arrives at the table.

As soon as Jake and Shorty sit down, Stephie approaches saying, "Let me look at those hurts now."

Jake pulls back his shirt and she pulls the bandage down then smiling says, "It is pink and looks to be healing well." Turning to Shorty she looks at the long jazzed cut on his arm advising, "It looks better but you will not lift Jake anymore. See it has broken open a few places here and here and here."

Frowning Jake looks over seeing the long jagged cut down Shorty's arm stating, "Good Lord, Wesley. Why didn't you say it was that bad, that must really hurt. Why didn't you say no when I ask you to help me?"

Smiling Shorty replies, "Jake, you only call me Wesley when you are really upset. Don't be. I'm fine and I'm healing. I didn't get hurt like you did, this is just a scratch. A couple of days and it will be gone without a scar. You, boyo, are gonna have a scar to brag about all your life."

Successfully he diverts his big brother from dwelling on his injury by turning his thoughts back to his own injury. But not Glory… leaning over she gently lays her hand on his injured arm softly saying, "Sorry, Wesley," and they both know it is for more than helping Jake to the outhouse.

Winking at her Shorty softly replies, "No problem, Glory. I deserved it for being ornery to you."

Glory starts to say something instead she just sadly nods at him before turning her head to her father stating, "Papa, I see a lot of changes in the house."

"Yep, yar ma and I worked our tails off and Uncle Hank and his boys came and heped us then my cowboys did a lot of the work so we have been working steadily on it since ya'll left," Joe explains smiling happily at them.

Beth Ann's eyes widen as she asks, "Mother, what did you do?"

Smugly Elizabeth explains, "I helped sand the floors, hold up boards to be nailed, ran and fetched tools and supplies they needed and mainly did whatever needed to be done."

They all look at Joe questioningly as he walks over to Elizabeth hugging her proudly before explaining, "Lizbeth worked every day on the house with us. She was on her hands and knees sanding the floors so long I had to lift her up as she couldn't stand up cause her legs had gone to sleep and her knees hurt so bad. She worked very hard."

"But yar gonna have a baby, Ma. Ya shouldna done anythang to hurt yarself," Glory states worriedly.

Laughing Elizabeth explains, "I'm one of those lucky women who is healthier when I'm carrying a baby, than I am otherwise. I'm seldom sick to my stomach. I just tire quickly. So when I was tired I rested awhile then started in again when I felt better. It was a labor of love from me and your papa. We love you all very much."

Glory and Beth Ann walk over to her hugging her as Glory says, "Thank ya, Mama. We appreciate all yar hard work."

"Yes, thank you so much, Mother. It is beautiful and we will remember always that you helped make it perfect," Beth Ann exclaims as she kisses her mother's cheek.

With her eyes shining with happiness, Elizabeth answers, "You ain't seen nothin' yet after breakfast we will show you all the rooms we built on."

Clearing his throat Joe holds open his arms wiggling his fingers so giggling both daughters immediately run over to him hugging and kissing him also.

Everyone laughs at their humor then eats a wonderful breakfast of ham, eggs, biscuits and jelly.

After the dishes are washed, dried and put away (everyone joins in so all can see the room additions together) Elizabeth and Joe walk to the hallway where Joe states, "Let's start here."

Everyone excitedly walks down the hallway to the Parlor door. Opening it they notice immediately the furniture is gone except for the two mattresses on the floor.

Shaking her head as she slowly looks around Glory states, "I didn't even realize the furniture was gone until now. Guess I was too tired last night to notice."

Wonderingly they look around the room when Beth Ann states excitedly, "You added book shelves all across the North end of the room."

"Yep, we asked the grandpas to bring as many as they could fit in the wagons cause we are gonna be educated," Joe replies smiling happily at them all.

"We are gonna havta teach ya how to talk better so people knowd ya are educated," Elizabeth replies talking like Joe usually does.

Grinning down at her Joe concentrating hard replies, "We have a young lady who is going to be a teacher so I believe that would be a good idea." Everyone laughs with him as he pronounces each syllable correctly.

"You are doing great, Papa, and I'm so proud of you that you want to," Beth Ann exclaims hugging him joyfully.

Bowing from the waist Joe solemnly replies, "Thank you, my lady."

Glory explains, "We brought ya two sofas, a long rug, three chairs, two fancy bookcases and a couple little tables with lamps for this room."

"Remember the pretty mirror, too," Jake adds in smiling at them.

"Oh, yes, it's beautiful, Mama, you will love it," Glory adds happily.

Elizabeth smiles at hearing Glory say mama instead of the forced way she usually says ma. She looks at Joe to see if he realizes it and sees he is looking at her happily then nods yes to her.

Swallowing a lump in her throat she smilingly requests, "It sounds wonderful. Let's go see Sammy's room next." Out the door and into the narrow hallway they all walk to the first door on the right and this is Sammy's room.

Opening the door Joe walks in and everyone follows as Joe explains, "We built a lot of shelves on this West wall for books, toys and whatever he wants to display."

Walking forward Beth Ann explains, "We brought his bed, dresser, and chest of drawers, shift robe for his clothes, toy chest, books and desk from St. Louis. We have a large carpet for the middle of the room and a small one to put beside the bed from his old bedroom."

Nodding happily Joe states, "It sounds really nice. He's back at Minnie and Benny's again. They love havin' him and he loves stayin' over thar so we have let him do that. Why don't we put his furniture in then wait on arrangin' it until he gets back, I know he'll be excited about doin' it."

They walk back out the doorway and taking a step or two walk into Grandpa Pokey's bedroom. "This is Grandpa Pokey's bedroom. We know he and Grandpa Skinny will enjoy being close to Sammy and being close to each other too. So we put a door on each side of the room so Grandpa Pokey can go out either one.

"That was real clever of ya'll to do that and a great idea," Jake states as he looks at the large room then nods to Beth Ann to explain what they brought from St. Louis.

Smiling happily she explains, "We brought Grandpa Pokey a chest of drawers, clothes closet, a small dresser, two lamps, two rugs for around the bed, a night stand and we found a real nice trunk for him to use for anything he wants to keep here that won't fit anywhere else.

They nod yes then walking back to the hallway turn right to the next room which is Grandpa Skinny's bedroom. Joe opens the door explaining, "This is Grandpa Skinny's room. We made bed frames and brought down the mattresses from the loft for his and Grandpa Pokey's beds. Shorely could have used yar help Jake but Shorty did a real fine job. He and yar Pa came over a couple times and heped us out."

Jake nods answering, "Much obliged for the compliment Joe. We brought a chest of drawers, two lamps, a shift robe, and a dresser along for Grandpa Skinny's room. I'm gonna make three chairs for our grandpa's rooms and Rev Max's room cause I know they will wanta sit around and talk a lot. I'll go over to the City of John and pick up some good wood real soon. These ole fellas really like rockin' chairs and I do love make'em."

Joe smiles warmly at him saying, "Ya might wanna look at the wood left over in the barn. There are two stalls full and see if'n any will work out for ya. We are gonna have a lot of wood for yar house, too, so ya might wanna wait just a tad afore ya buy any."

Smiling happily Jake nods yes before replying, "Thank ya, Joe. I'll do that."

Elizabeth walks to the door saying, "Next ones are mine. Follow me." She leads them back to the hallway and taking a right opens the door on the right as she steps in explaining, "This is Uncle Max's room."

Everyone walks in as Glory exclaims, "How nice. Uncle Max will have a room all to himself where he can always know he has a place to belong." Turning and looking at her parents she explains, "I've wondered about him for years cause he ain't got no home of his own and he ain't no young'un anymore. I wondered what he would do when he got too old to ride around preachin'. This is a wonderful gift to give him. I'm so proud ya'll thought to do it." She hugs both of her parents and so does Beth Ann.

Smiling Jake wipes a tear from his eye saying, "Mighty nice of ya'll. He is a nice man and oughta have a nice place to settle in."

Glory explains, "We brung him a big bed, a chest of drawers, two rugs, a nice mirror, a chair and a small bookshelf."

Wiping a tear away also Elizabeth requests, "Let's go across the hallway and we'll show you another room."

Following her they all walk directly across the hallway to another room while Elizabeth continues, "This is your Grandmother Nona's room. It is right by the kitchen (where she will be happy) and right by the nursery (which should make her very happy) AND right beside Beth Ann's room (which will delight her)."

Everyone admires the large airy room with the large window looking out towards the garden.

"She will love it. We brought her a canopy bed with matching dresser, chest of drawers and shift robe, two chairs, two lamps, a small rug and a large one for this side of the room," Beth Ann explains then exclaims, "She will be delighted, absolutely delighted!"

Glory's eyes are shining like beacons as she replies, "She will say tutt …tutt…ya shouldna done it, but I'm shorely glad ya did." Everyone laughs at her accurate imitation of Nona.

"She might like to bring her furniture from town so don't let it hurt yar feelin's if'n she does," Joe reminds them all.

They all think about this a moment then shake their heads yes they understand.

Joe grabs Beth Ann's hand asking, "Should we go to yar room next or to Lizbeth and mine?" He knows she'll want everyone to see her room so isn't surprised when she immediately states, "Mine, please!"

Smiling happily they all troop out of Nona's room then to the left to Beth Ann's room then left again into her room. Joe explains, "We built'cha a big bookcase and made the room big enough for all yar furniture. Yar ma knew how much was in yar room so we figured this would be big enough for it all."

Looking around the large room Beth Ann exclaims, "Yes, everything will fit in just fine. It is so beautiful. The floor shines so pretty and is so smooth. Thank you for making this special for me." Her eyes sparkle like stars as she looks at the large room pointing out, "My canopy bed can go here in between the windows. The large rug can go right here in the middle of the room. The small bed rugs can go on each side of the bed like in St. Louis and my desk can sit under the window by my new bookshelves." She walks to the other side explaining, "My chest of drawers can go here by the door, my dresser across from the bed and my shift robe in the West corner by the other window so I can see the clothes by its light. This is wonderful! Absolutely wonderful." She touches the walls and looks at the lovely oil lamp hanging down in the middle of the room then wrapping her arms around herself she tries to contain her joy.

Joe curves his muscular tanned arm around his lovely wife's waist hugging her to his side as they all smile happily at seeing Beth Ann's joy flow through her as the sun that shines and warms everyone it touches.

Looking around Glory asks, "Mind if I camp out with ya for a time while mine and Jake's house is built?"

Laughing happily Beth Ann answers, "Anytime …you are always welcome big sister!"

The sisters smile at each other having a better understanding of each others personalities and their closeness has increased a hundred fold since they departed home over two months ago.

Smiling happily at them all, Elizabeth requests, "Let's go look at the nursery next." She and Joe lead the way out the door and down another small hallway to the first room on the left and walk into a long narrow room.

Everyone crowds in as Elizabeth laughingly explains the closeness of the room, "We decided to make this a small room as the baby will sleep in here but will be with us wherever we are the rest of the time."

Grinning Joe explains, "This room is ten foot wide and twelve feet long that ain't a small room but yar ma don't see it that way."

"Joe, ya ain't gonna believe this but we found two nursery sets in St. Louie. One for a girl and one for a boy," Jake explains still amazed.

Chuckling Joe answers, "I couldn't believe it when Lizbeth told me about it."

"We brought both seein' as Glory and I might be needin' one in the next year," Jake states with a smug smile.

Joe raises his eyebrows ruefully teasing, "Gettin' cocky ain't ya. Ya ain't even married yet."

Jake almost falls down when he bows humbly replying while trying not to laugh, "I shoulda said after askin' yar permission to marry Glory then in a year or so we'd be havin' a little one."

Joe nods yes while trying not to smile at Jake.

Glory elbows Jake loudly whispering "Good job thar Jake!"

Dramatically Jake loudly whispers back, "Thought for a minute I was gonna fall on my knees and be a beggin' for yar hand when I realized I was just gettin' a little light headed from standin' so long."

"Good Grief, Jake! Come over here and sit down," Stephie exclaims firmly as she and Shorty grab Jake and pull him into the kitchen to a chair then help him sit down.

Following them Glory smacks his arm saying, "Don'tcha do that again. Yar face is as white as a sheet."

Elizabeth rushes over with a glass of water contritely saying, "Jake, I am so sorry. I got carried away. I should have realized you should be lying down and resting."

Smiling weakly, Jake urges, "Don't bother with me. I'm fine just a little weak cause of the blood I lost. Nothin' to get upset about, just let me rest a coupla minutes and I'll be fine."

"That's all right. The only room left is mine and Joe's and it is practically empty just waiting for the furniture," Elizabeth answers soothingly.

Smiling at her parents Glory explains, "I worked in yar room Mother. I packed all yar things and brought'cha the furniture ya asked for. I have never seen so many clothes in all my life and all those bottles of stuff on yar dresser. Beth Ann explained some of'em to me but I was purely mystified with'em."

Smiling at Joe she explains to everyone, "I asked for my fath... Edgar's bedroom suite because it is much bigger than mine is and also because the bed is much longer, which is what Joe needs with his long legs. Mother Nona has my bedroom suite."

"Yep! We brought ya the canopied bed, chest of drawers, dresser and shift robe and yar desk. Oh, yes, the lamps and little tables, too, and two of those fancy little chairs and a small rug on each side of the bed and a big one for the middle of the room," Glory explains in detail as she counts them off on her fingers.

"Sounds like a lot of furniture, my love," Joe replies doubtfully.

"There will be plenty of room, my dear, we have the biggest room in the house," Elizabeth exclaims happily then continues, "We will need room for the cradle to be in there at night and a rocking chair to rock the baby in."

Nodding yes, Joe replies, "We will make it work; however, ya want it, honey."

Eyes glowing with happiness Elizabeth looks around the group of people sitting in HER kitchen in HER new house thinking, "They all fill me with love so overwhelming I don't know if I can stand it."

Thinking about how nice the house is Stephie thinks, "I could be jealous of all these things that they have, which are much nicer than what we have, but what we have is ours and we worked hard for it. Why would I be envious of theirs when I am happy with mine?"

"Jake I want you to lie down on the mattress in the parlor and rest awhile," Stephie advises her grown son.

Turning his head to the side and looking at her he consolingly replies, "Ma, I am not going back to bed. If'n Joe will walk with me out to one of the lawn chairs I made'em in the yard, I'll sit there and help with the unloadin'. Not liftin' anythang but I helped load those wagons so I know what goes where."

Joe looks at Jake thoughtfully then nodding firmly replies, "That I will do but you WILL NOT get outta that chair and do anythang. This is clearly understood, son?"

"Are ya gonna paddle me if'n I do, Pa?" Jake kiddingly asks.

"Right now, I could," Joe seriously answers with an uplifted eyebrow.

"Humm…Okay, you got my word on it," Jake answers looking steadily at Joe.

Nodding okay Joe and Glory walk with Jake outside to the reclining lawn chairs (Jake made them earlier in the year) and help him sit down.

Elizabeth picks up a pillow for his head and Stephie carries a large glass of tea for him as they settle him in the comfortable chair.

Frowning Jake grumbles, "I hate this laying around stuff!"

"If'n ya wasn't so smart you'd be a laying in yar grave right now so don'tcha give us a hard time today," Glory states without sympathy, then leaning down softly requests, "Ask mama to hep ya when ya need it so she will sit down and rest more. Okay?"

Jake is frowning but Glory's statement opens his eyes to what could have happened to him so sighing he takes her hand pulling her down beside his chair confiding, "That was an amazing thang, Glory. It suddenly occurred to us that those outlaws would gun me, Jay and Brad down first. So I told'em what I thought about it, first thang Jay did was to tell Brad to go watch out for our grandpas so he'd be killed and not Brad. Course Brad didn't want to and argued with him but Jay won out. Then, I believe, God gave me the thought about using the leather to protect ourselves with. Where else could that idea have come from? I know I ain't the smartest man around and I know I ain't stupid but God's truth, Glory, I don't know where that idea came from if'n it wasn't from an angel whispering in my ear."

Kneeling down beside his chair, Glory lays both of her hands on his whiskered cheeks replying, "Jake, I thought I'd die when I saw ya fall off of Comfort and not git up. My heart broke into a million pieces and I just wanted revenge so bad that, I'm ashamed to say, I coulda killed every one of'em outlaws and not cared. It scares me to think about it, cause I know how to, and that's the truth. Then when ya called out and said ya were alive my heart leapt in my body and I felt it would be worth livin' again cause without ya I don't have a life. I know God heped us, Jake, cause we are his young'uns. We believe and love him and he loves us so I believe God would send us an angel to save our lives. Remember Zak had a bad feelin' and wanted to meet us? God sent him that message that we'd need help and Papa and Shorty came, too. God whispered in their ears, too, that we needed'em and fast like. Then that poor cowboy, Davey, he got near beat to death cause of us, but, Jake, he made it back to send hep to us. We weren't meant to die yet. God was protectin' us. I believe that from my toes to my head. God loves us and watches over us everyday of our lives and we just don't realize how much til somethin' like this happens."

Tears are in their eyes and they don't realize everyone has stopped what they are doing and are listening to them talk. Looking intently at each other Jake replies, "Well then, my love, we will live lives worth savin' from now on. We will do all the good we can and hep everyone we can cause God gave us a great blessin' and we need to share it."

Smiling while wiping her tears away Glory replies, "I agree, my love, I agree."

Taking both of her hands Jake requests, "Let's thank God as one this time."

Smiling Glory nods yes as Jake starts praying: *"Lord, we are so grateful for your help and guidance with the outlaws. We are sorry for the dying of the ones who were trying to kill us and we ask for your forgiveness for atakin' the lives of those men. Lord, we thank you from the bottom of our hearts for savin' us and keepin' us together. We thank you for the safe trip to St. Louie and the safe ride back home. Please watch over our grandpas and help them during this rough time. Help us, Lord, to do your will in all we do. In Jesus Name I pray."*

Glory adds, *"Dear Lord, thank ya so much for savin' Jake's life. I know ya know how much I love'em and need'em in my life. I'll always be grateful to ya for savin' him. Thank ya for whisperin' in his ears on how to save us all. It worked so good and saved our lives and we appreciate yar love for us. I pledge to also do whatever I can to hep people in your name. Please watch over my mama and keep her and the baby healthy, Lord, and also if'n ya will please watch over Minnie and her babies. In your Son's blessed name, I pray. Amen."*

Joe, Elizabeth and Stephie look stunned for a moment when their children started talking now they all wipe tears away saying prayers of thanksgiving of their own.

"Dear Father in Heaven, thank ya from the bottom of my heart for savin' my young'uns and keepin' em in yar safe hands. Thank ya for sendin' the messages that they needed hep and please Lord, hep the young cowboy Davey to heal fast and bless all the men who ran to hep us when we needed it. We be mighty grateful for yar love and guidance. In yar Son's holy name I pray, Amen." Joe stands praying in the middle of the yard not caring what time of day or place he is in when he prays.

Stephie's tears fall freely as she also prays from the heart, *"Lord, you blessed me so much with Jake as a son. He has been a wonderful one. Father thank you so much for saving his life. He is such a wonderful young man and we all love him so much. Thank you …thank you…oh, Lord, thank you for saving our son. I, too, pledge to help others as much as I can and please whisper in my ear anytime you need me to do something for you that I don't see to do. I'm sorry for the taking of lives also but know you understand all and know all and I thank you for all these blessings. In Jesus' blessed name I pray. Amen."*

Elizabeth jumps when Carrie Lynn and Beth Ann touch her hands as Beth Ann whispers, "Will you pray with us Mother?"

Elizabeth smiles and hugs them both as she wraps her arms around them and they all bend their heads as each quietly prays thankful prayers for all the help they have been given on their trip to St. Louis and their safe arrival back home.

A little subdued they all smile at each other as Joe advises, "Let's git busy unloading these wagons. I'm gonna git my cowboys to hep us out. Jake will ya tell Lizbeth which wagon to start on while I'm gone."

Smiling Jake repeats from memory: "Each item has a piece of ribbon on it. Here are the ribbon colors and where they go. Green is for Joe and Elizabeth cause of Joe's eyes. There is a double red ribbon that is full of breakables for Joe and Elizabeth, too. It needs to be kept separate. Yalla is for Nona cause she likes that color. Red is for Beth Ann cause of her hair. White is for Sammy and his white hair. Blue is for Glory and me cause we like blue. Orange is for Carrie Lynn cause she likes that color. Pink is for Ma, Pa and my family cause Ma loves pink. Black and blue are the two ribbons for Minnie, Benny and Arty. Brown is for Good Heart and Yalla Moon and the trunk with two ribbons colors yalla and green are for Miss Ella and Hank. Grandpa Skinny's color is purple cause he loves sunsets. Grandpa Pokey's colors are two ribbons black and white cause that is all he sees. Then Rev Roy's is black like his suits."

"Wow that is something, did you come up with that all by yourself?" Shorty asks wonderingly.

"Yep, I was thinkin' one day while we were cleanin' out the store about how are we gonna tell what's in all these trunks without openin'em and, I guess, an little angel whispered in my ear to do it this way," Jake replies smiling at them all then continues, "When I loaded the wagons

I put as many of the same colored ribbons together as I could so which room are we gonna start on?"

UNLOADING THE WAGONS
Chapter 20

"Blessed are the bearers of kindness in all shapes and sizes."

Looking around Glory asks, "Do we start with the easiest or the hardest, Mama?"

Elizabeth thinks a moment before saying, "I'm sure my bedroom will be the hardest as it has more furniture. So let's set up our grandpa's and Mama's rooms first just in case they get here earlier than we think."

She raises her eyebrows questioningly and they all nod yes then Jake states, "Look for yalla, purple, black and black and white ribbons and it will be thars. Guess I'll just sit here and watch ya'll work." He tries to make a joke out of it but it is hard for him to sit there doing nothing when there is work to be done.

Glory pats him on the shoulder then they all walk towards the loaded wagons.

Beth Ann locates them first so with the cowboys help they quickly carry the furniture in with Elizabeth being the guide. She requests where to set it up and they do. Smiling happily Elizabeth laughs out loud as she can't contain the joy that fills her knowing the happiness it will bring her grandfathers and Uncle Max when they see their new bedrooms. She sets the lamps on the tables then fetching some rags dusts the furniture as it is brought into their rooms.

Joe and his cowboys carry the large items with Shorty and the girls carrying the smaller items.

Shorty gripes, "Cain't believe I'm doing baby work when I should be doing man's work."

Smiling Stephie replies, "You are lucky that you can do any of this. We don't want that wound to get infected. Son, when you go back outside please go talk to your brother for a few minutes and calm him down. I can tell he is getting all riled up just sitting there."

Shorty looks at her through narrowed eyes asking, "Mother, please do not try to manage me. I know when I'm tired and I know when to rest."

Raising her eyebrows at him she replies, "Alright, Shorty, do as you please. You are the one who calms Jake down the best. Let him get up and start to help and start bleeding all over the place then you will be doing his chores longer while he is recuperating."

Nodding yes Shorty mumbles as he walks towards Jake, "Don't know why I try! I cain't ever win with her."

Stephie stands watching as Shorty walks over and in a few minutes has Jake laughing and forgetting about sitting instead of working like the rest of them are doing. "Well, I do know my sons. Now they will both rest for a few minutes," she smugly says to herself.

Joe asks his men to start unloading Nona's bedroom furniture so Elizabeth follows them in and asks them to set it where she thinks her mother will like it to be. Joe can't keep his eyes off of Elizabeth and how she glows with happiness thinking, "A few months ago I never woulda thought she could ever be this happy. She frowned all the time. Was surly, sharp tongued, bitter and angry and now she is a pure delight to be around. Love sure can change people." Looking at Beth Ann's happy face Joe can't keep from smiling again to himself praying, "*Lord, how she has changed. She doesn't even look like the same little girl who was so hateful and angry when they arrived. Her looks have changed drastically. It is amazin' how losing thirty pounds took away that pudgy look. A little work has turned her arms and legs into muscular ones now. Her face is all cleared up from those spots cause she don't eat candy all the time like she used to. I believe she has changed as much inside as outside except…well…there is that insecurity…. she still has a big dose of it. Lord, please hep me take it away so she will know I will always love her and always have. Thank you, dear Lord, for the blessings ya've given me. In Jesus Name I pray. Amen.*"

Soon most of the furniture has been moved into the house and the rooms are filling up.

"Hey, Joe! Can ya come over here for a coupla minutes?" Jake calls out a little weakly.

Nodding yes he walks over to him replying, "Sure enough. What can I do for ya?"

Blushing he nods at Shorty sourly saying, "The little rat won't let me even go to the outhouse by myself. Would ya give me a shoulder to lean on, Joe? I drank too much tea."

"Shorely," Joe states nodding yes then quickly pulls Jake to his feet before Jake can push himself up and strain those chest muscles.

Jake nearly collapses when he is up on his feet. He grabs a hold of Joe's shoulders blinking rapidly trying to stop the dizziness.

Shorty is right beside Joe as he helps stand Jake on his feet. He looks concerned at Jake's weakness.

Joe is a little surprised that Jake is this weak so after Jake is able to stand better he walks with him over to the outhouse then motions for Shorty to come over then whispers, "Go get Yalla Moon for me. Jake ain't doin' as good as he shoulda."

"That is what I thought, too. I was just gonna do that. He is exhausted just sitting up. Maybe we could put him in one of the grandpa's rooms and let him sleep?" Shorty asks very concerned.

"Yeah, that is a good idea. Grab ole Pete over thar and have him hep me git Jake to bed. Tell yar Ma, too. She can argue with him some if'n she wants to," Joe answers with his crooked smile.

"Yes, sir," Shorty replies then hurries over to Pete then to his mother then lopes over to Good Heart's sod house to ask Yellow Moon to come over and check on Jake.

"Joe???? I cain't stand up?" Jake's wobbly voice is heard through the outhouse door.

Slowly opening the door Joe sees Jake is standing but shaking all over. Tightening his lips Joe reaches in and grabbing Jake's arms pulls him towards him then leaning down takes Jake's weight on his left shoulder lifting Jake's body across his shoulder as Jake passes out. Grunting from the dead weight Joe staggers a moment before getting his footing bellowing, "Pete! I need ya now!"

Ole Pete is a small man but strong as an ox so he hurries over to Joe's side helping support Jake as they walk towards the house.

Glory walks out of the house stopping short (then her mother walks right into the back of her) as she sees her pa carrying Jake. She runs right over to Joe and helps take some of Jake's weight off of him.

Jake is unconscious.

Elizabeth and Stephie stand unmoving shocked senseless when Joe orders, "Stephie, get Uncle Max's bed made down and ready to put

Jake in. Shorty is gettin' Yalla Moon now. Lizbeth put some water on to boil. Yalla Moon will probably make a poultice for Jake. Move outta my way, ladies. He is real heavy."

They jump out of their stupor and quickly comply with Joe's requests.

Together they manage to get Jake to Uncle Max's bed while Jake starts shivering with fever.

"I KNEW he should have stayed in bed today," Stephie states through clenched teeth, "He will now!"

Standing at the foot of the bed Glory worriedly looks at Jake replying, "Yes, madam, he will!" She and Elizabeth quickly pull Jake's boots off then Glory is shooed out of the room while Stephie, Elizabeth and Joe undress the unconscious young man.

Shorty rushes in with Yellow Moon a few minutes later as she says, "Fever! I need hot water for my herbs." Then she kneels down with her bowl of herbs and crushes them into pulp.

Elizabeth hurries in with some hot water in a tea kettle setting it down beside Yellow Moon on a dish towel.

Yellow Moon mixes the herbs with the hot water to look like a wad of wet grass then scooping them up with a wooden spoon she puts them in a piece of thin cotton material squeezing all the water she can out of it. Looking up at Joe she sadly orders, "Hold him down, Joe. This is gonna hurt." She turns to Stephie and Glory saying, "Hold his arms and legs down so he don't make his wound bleed again." Looking at the handsome young man she walks over to his right side looking at the angry red gash on his chest saying again, "Hold him good." She quickly opens the gash and pushes the little pouch of herbs inside of it as much as she can.

Jake's glazed eyes jerk open and he roars in delirium as the pain shoots through his body. Glory quickly straddles his body putting her hands on his shoulders she adds her weight to the others and holds him on the bed. Moments later Jake slumps back down relaxing.

Nodding yes Yellow Moon explains, "This is good. The herbs hurt for a few minutes then they ease his pain and he will sleep. He has infection now. We need a lot of water for him to drink and to sponge off his body as he sweats. We need broth for him to drink when he wakes. The first time is the hardest with the healing herbs, next time it be easier. I stay." She pulls a chair up beside the bed and starts singing to Jake.

Jake sleeps peacefully.

Stephie, Elizabeth and Glory take turns bathing Jake's body when he thrashes around talking. Joe and Elizabeth are with him during the night when they learn some unexpected news about Elizabeth.

Jake mumbles, "Gotta protect Lizbeth...gotta protect her... cain't let Edgar sell her like that...cain't let him do that to her....cain't let him send Glory and Beth Ann to France...they cain't marry them foreigners....no way they can have Glory...Beth Ann...too young....to understand.... how bad it would be...gotta sav'em....gotta sav'em ....give Joe the letters...gotta tell Joe about'em...show him the letters....grandpas got'em safe...cain't tell Lizbeth how bad they were...she's too good for them....oh, ma, it hurts...my head hurts...."

Joe and Elizabeth look at each other horrified at Jake's words then Jake continues mumbling, "Potter... cruel...beat women...wants Lizbeth...will beat her...hurt her...oh...cain't let her find out how bad... gotta warn Joe...gotta tell Joe...he beat his slaves...mean mean man!"

"Oh, my goodness, Joe! What did they find out in St. Louis?" Elizabeth asks horrified as Jake tosses his head back and forth in the fever.

Joe frowns as he thoughtfully replies, "He said Edgar sold you, Glory and Beth Ann to a foreigner. Potter liked to beat women ...planned on beating you. My gracious how bad were they?" Shocked they look at each other and Elizabeth fairly leaps into Joe's arms for reassurance. Joe holds her tightly saying, "We will have to wait til he is stronger to tell us or until our grandpas arrive. Seems me like they learned some bad thangs about Potter and Edgar."

Glory peeps in whispering, "Better quit that huggin' and kissin' while Jake is sick." She smiles happily at them continuing, "I'm wide awake I'll watch him while ya'll get some sleep."

Looking at Jake and remembering his delirium Joe replies, "Lizbeth go to bed and don'tcha worry about nuthin'. I'll be in in a few minutes." Then looking over at his lovely daughter Joe asks, "Did ya find out some bad thangs while ya'll were in St. Louie, Glory?"

"Bad? Oh, no, nothin' bad. It was sad for Beth Ann. She took it hard and so did the grandpas closin' the house and store. I thought it was fun even though it was a lot of hard work," Glory answers puzzled.

Taking a deep breath Joe relaxes some thinking, "If Glory knows anything about this she would tell me so they didn't tell her. Good." Joe looks again at his beautiful daughter thinking, "If they were gonna sell her she would bring a rich price with her beauty alone but she would never have been happy and would end up dying either by killing someone or someone killing her. *Thank you, Lord that ya didn't let that happen to her, Beth Ann and Lizbeth.*" Joe lowers his sorrowful eyes looking down at Jake wondered at the things he has found out and will be telling him in the near future....some seriously bad things.

During the quiet night Glory sponges off Jake's fevered body and can't resist running her hands over his muscular arms and chest as she smiles to herself thinking, "He's mine...all mine." She tenderly bathes his face, arms and legs and feels and sees the strength in them and tingles at the pleasure of being so close to him and being able to touch him as she wants.

Jake's fevered dreams are not of Franklin Potter or Edgar Hawkins the rest of the night but of Glory and their future together. His breathing calms, his temperature lowers and he rests.

Jake's fever breaks during the early morning as he wakes to find Glory sitting beside the bed (with a shawl over her shoulders) asleep in the chair. He looks out the window watching the sun rise and smiles at feeling good. Frowning slightly he remembers bits and pieces of his dreams but not the complete dreams. Tiredly he closes his eyes and falls back asleep.

Glory wakes hearing Yellow Moon's soft voice talking to Stephie in the hallway as they walk towards Jake's bed. Smiling she looks quickly at Jake noticing him watching her with clear eyes and all signs of fever gone.

"So lazybones you are finally going to wake up," Jake raspy voice mumbles as he watches her with loving eyes.

"Why didn't ya wake me up if'n ya was awake? Ya were asleep ever time I looked at ya," Glory states kneeling down beside his bed taking his right hand in hers then continues, "Are ya hungry? We've got some good chicken broth just waitin' for ya."

"Never wake a sleeping beauty without a kiss and, honey, I cain't move much atoll. I'm so weak I just waited patiently for ya to wake up and give me a kiss," Jake explains looking at her sleep tussled face thinking, "It won't be long till we will wake up every morning together."

Glory leans over and gives him a sweet good morning kiss just as Stephie and Yellow Moon open the door and walk in.

Walking closer to the bed Yellow Moon chuckles at seeing the blush cross both their faces and seeing Jake is alert states, "The fever is gone. I can tell by lookin'. Jake, ya stay in bed two days more or I will give ya medicine that taste bad to make ya sleep," Yellow Moon states sternly shaking her small red hand at him.

Jake lifts a shaking hand and taking her small hand raises it to his lips, kisses it, sincerely saying, "Yes, madam. Thank ya for savin' my life, Yalla Moon. I'm in yar debt."

Yellow Moon raises her eyebrows at him and frowns down at him replying, "I give medicine. Only The Spirit Above heals. Don't go givin' me thanks, you thank the One. He gives me herbs to use and I do what I can and ask for His healing. Don'tcha let Good Heart see ya holdin' my hand, Jake. He take yars off!" She smiles happily at the good looking young man then sadly explains, "Jake gotta do it again. It hurt but not so much this time."

Taking a deep breath Jake replies, "Ma will ya send Shorty in for a few minutes before Yalla Moon starts. I need'em."

Nodding yes Stephie answers, "I'll send him right in. Glory, come with me."

Glory leaves as requested thinking, "Like I didn't know it was time to leave the room. Hump!"

Shorty helps Jake with his bodily needs again then Yellow Moon walks back in and applies another batch of her herbs to Jake's wound and smiles to see that the gash has a natural color and is partially closed now.

Jake sucks in his breath and gasps at the pain the herbs cause.

Glory wipes the sweat from his brow then kisses it as the pain diminishes.

Yellow Moon explains, "Wound look better...long as herbs hurt ya got infection...when no hurt then no infection...be back later."

While the rest of the furniture is brought in and set up Jake sleeps peacefully and by evening is feeling much better.

Shorty's arm is healing quite well so he has helped with a lot of the unloading.

When Glory hands him the large piece of leather Jake was wearing when the arrow struck him, Shorty cringes at the blood on it then says, "I'm gonna wash this off so Ma never sees it. She don't need to."

"No, she don't," Glory states looking at the amount of blood on it. She looks at Shorty wonderingly saying, "God protected us, Shorty. He knew they were after us and He protected us from harm. Jake volunteered to ride in the front knowin' they would try to take him out first. That was really brave. But he'd better not do that again! I thought I'd die when he fell with that arra in his chest. It was the most hepless feeling imaginable."

Putting his arm around her shoulders Shorty replies, "I want to find that kind of love, Glory. I want to love a woman like that and I want to be loved like that. I hope you know how blessed you are."

Smiling Glory kisses his whiskered cheek replying, "I'm very blessed and I know it. Keep looking, Shorty, and God will send ya the right wife."

With Shorty's help Joe and his cowboys carry all the furniture and trunks and set them in the rooms they belong in except for some special ones that are left in the parlor to be opened at another time.

When Glory helps carry Sammy's trunks into his room and helps set up the furniture for him she smiles at Beth Ann saying, "Sammy is going to be real surprised when he sees all he has here...it will be fun to give him all the surprises we brung him."

"Yes, he will be happy to have many more toys and clothes," Beth Ann answers giggling.

Back at Skinny and Pokey's ranch they ask all the cowboys that are home one evening eating supper to quieten down they want to talk to them.

"Men we've had an eye opener this past month. Realized if we'd been killed you boys here would have been left out of our will. So we have changed our will and are gonna give ya'll all some land as an inheritance from us. We want you to think about what parcel of land ya'd like to have and pray about it a lot and when we git back from Joe's ranch then we will set it all up," Skinny explains to the stunned cowboys in the room.

Pokey continues blushing as little as he talks, "Yep we have thought about this a lot since all these bad thangs happened with Lora dyin' and we always planned on takin' care of you boys since yar ours more than anyone's and we...well we love ya all and we want ya to know it."

The cowboy sons just sit open mouthed not knowing what to say when Big John laughs a little saying, "Boys ya'll have been our boys since the day the bosses brought ya'll home to us. All of "Older" men feel like yar pa's too. We heped raise ya and watched ya grow up and we are right proud that the bosses are gonna help ya to have a place of yar own."

Skinny smiles at John softly saying, "John your our son, too. All our older boys are just as much our sons as the younger ones. We couldn't have done what we've done without all of you helping us. We count you all as our sons and all will inherit land and cattle."

John and the older cowboy's mouths drop open as they hadn't expected to be included in the inheritance. The room is so quiet a pin could be heard (if one was dropped) as they all are shocked then one by one they stand and walk over to Skinny and Pokey hugging them then they all start laughing happily at this wonderful news.

"Come over to the bunk house and let's look at the map," Pokey advises the men so they all walk together across the yard to the largest sleeping quarters of the cowboys.

Leading the way Skinny and Pokey walk over to the bunk house where the large map of their ranches is on one wall. "Study the map and think about where ya'd like to live and think hard about it and talk it over with each other, boys. Think about what ya'd like to do…raise cattle or horses or plant some fields. We know you all have desires of the heart that ya'd like to full fill so now is the time to think about them," Skinny advises them."

Still almost numb with surprise the cowboys nod yes.

"We gotta go over and check on Lizbeth and the young'uns so we will be gone for awhile so think hard boys and we will talk to all of ya when we return," Skinny advises and again the men all nod yes.

The next afternoon Pokey and Skinny ride in with their escort of cowboys.

Jake and Glory are sitting in the shade in the yard chairs talking while Jake rests. His color is good again and he is agreeably relaxing now after collapsing on Joe.

"What'cha doing lazin' around out here for?" Pokey teases them.

Smiling Glory replies, "This is the first time Jake has been out of bed since he collapsed day before yesterday. His fever is gone and he's gettin' well rested fast now."

"Ya took a fever, Jake! Sorry to hear that," Skinny replies sadly as he tiredly climbs down off his horse.

"How is yar wound healin'?" Pokey asks worried now.

"Real good. I'm doin' fine. Just ain't got no power to move about yet," Jake answers smiling at these beloved grandpas then asks, "How's Davey doing?"

"Up and around some. Got some infection like you did so we hung around til he was on his feet," Skinny answers frowning at the ground.

"Did you know that injun stuck him over twenty times with his knife torturin' him to tell'em where we'd gone to," Pokey angrily states.

"Broke some ribs, too," Skinny adds sadly.

"Glad to know that injun is dead," Jake states disgusted with that man.

"Yep, he was gonna kill us all and shorely tried to with you and almost got Beth Ann. Glory, you woulda kilt him if yar pa hadn't beat'cha to it," Pokey states a fact as he looks at his lovely granddaughter.

Nodding yes Glory sadly answers, "I was ready to."

"Well tell us what has gone on since ya'll left us," Skinny asks as he sits down in one of the comfortable wooden lawn chairs.

"Glory will hafta do that as I've slept most of the time," Jake jokes as he lovingly looks over at Glory.

"We unloaded most of the wagons but decided to wait until Jake could go with us afore we deliver the surprises to his family, Minnie, Benny and Arty, Grandma Nona, Aunt Ella and Uncle Hank and we can't forget Good Heart's trunk. We didn't let Mama open up all the trunks cause we wanted ya'll to be here to enjoy it with us. Now that yar here we can have a party and do it," Glory advises them with a smile.

Looking over at Jake she sternly advises, "Sorry, Jake, but yar gonna miss this fun part. Yar to stay here and rest."

Jake frowns then shrugging replies, "Only if you promise to come out and tell me all about it."

"Will do," Glory agrees then asks, "Grandpas wait just a minute while I get Mama and Papa before ya go in the house, okay?"

Puzzled they nod yes then sit back continue talking to Jake asking to see his wound and how it is healing. Smiling he gladly shows his now "famous" arrow scar.

Glory trots to the house and walking into the kitchen calling out, "Mama? Our grandpas are here."

Elizabeth and Beth Ann rush into the room with eyes glowing happily looking around then asks, "Where are they?"

"Outside with Jake. Where's Papa?" Glory asks looking out towards the barn.

"He just left to get some meat from the smoke house. I will get him," Beth Ann answers then rushes out the back door towards the smoke house.

Elizabeth's eyes sadly watch the door shut after Beth Ann rushes out before turning to Glory confiding, "She watches out where he is like he is going to go "puff" and disappear. I hate that I caused her to be so insecure."

Cocking her head to the side Glory replies, "She is young and will soon realize that Papa ain't goin' nowheres and relax about it. He won't and ya won't either so none of us have to worry about it anymore."

Putting her hands on Glory's shoulders, and as they are about the same height, they are eye to eye Elizabeth asks, "What insecurities have I left you with Glory?"

Glory looks her mother straight in the eyes asking, "Truthfully? Ya want to know?"

Gulping and straightening her shoulders Elizabeth replies, "Yes, please. I'd like to know."

Glory bites her lips for a moment then she truthfully replies, "No one will ever take my young'uns away from me. No one will ever make me leave'em either. I will always be here for'em no matter what. I'll never leave Jake and I'll be sure to keep him happy enough he will never leave me. Mother, I love ya and I'm comin' to trust ya but it will take time to do that."

Elizabeth blushes at the beginning of their woman's talk but is smiling at the end when she replies, "I'm very lucky you have forgiven me, Glory. I realize that. I love you and always have and, well, I will make it up to you somehow. I promise I will."

Smiling broadly at her Glory explains, "Mother, just bein' here makes up for it. Don'tcha worry none about anythang else ….just be here for us all." Then she leans over and kisses her mother's cheek before turning and walking out the kitchen door.

"I will be…that is a promise," Elizabeth states quietly as she watches her daughter walk out of the door.

"Yes, ya will be cause ya love'em all," Joe's voice comes from behind her.

Turning around she nods yes stating, "Our grandpas are here. Let's show them their rooms."

Happily Joe leans down kissing his wife's lovely cheek saying, "Yep, let's do." Turning he calls out, "Beth Ann, come on out."

From outside he hears her call back, "I am outside, Papa."

"I shoulda known that. She ain't gonna miss a minute of the surprises," Joe chuckles as he walks with Elizabeth out the kitchen door to the yard greeting their grandpas and cowboys.

Jake sits talking to Kevin and Josh then wonderingly asks, "Where's Brad and Jay? I thought they'd be with you."

"We made'em stay home as punishment for keepin' us in the dark about the ambush," Pokey states looking menacingly at the young people.

Glory spreads her long skirted legs then folding her arms across her chest lifts her chin up replying, "Grandpas I ain't a bit sorry for protectin' ya and keepin' ya alive. If'n ya got anythang to say about it. ..go ahead. I ain't afraid of ya'll."

Joe lowers his head (sucking in his lips to keep from smiling) at his brave and foolish daughter.

Elizabeth raises her eyebrows at the challenging note in Glory's voice then hides her smile as she knows nothing pleases her grandpas more than spirit.

Jake raises his eyebrows at her audacity then realizes, "She is takin' the blame for what I did," so says, "Now listen here, Glory, it was my idea to git'em back in the wagon. Don'tcha start takin' credit for my handiwork." He moves to stand up when Joe and Elizabeth lay their hands on his shoulders holding him down. Frowning he looks up at Joe as Joe winks at him smiling slightly.

Skinny and Pokey's eyes light up in humor looking at Glory. They decide to test this granddaughter they love and feel like they know fairly well after spending the last few months with her. So they walk closer to where she defiantly stands.

"Well, Pokey, just what kind of punishment should we give to Glory if'n she is the one who is to blame for our shame," Skinny sternly asks.

Glory's eyes lose their hostile look so laying her hands on his arm she earnestly replies, "Grandpa Skinny there was no shame thar."

"Ya took our pride down a coupla notches by makin' us hide in the wagon, girl," Pokey states sternly.

Glory looks at him through narrowed eyes unrepentantly saying, "Okay, if'n yar pride is hurt then I'll apologize for it, but I ain't gonna say I'm not glad yar alive and not dead like Jake coulda been."

Skinny and Pokey look at each other again then nodding say, "Looks like we are gonna have to punish her…now." They grab Glory and start tickling her.

Shocked she lets out a shrieking laugh then starts giggling helplessly as they unmercifully tickle her to the ground and have her rolling in the summer grass.

Everyone laughs to see such a sight, two older gentlemen kneeling down in the grass with Glory trapped between them, as they tickle her.

Finally with tears of laughter rolling down her cheeks she calls out, "I give up! I give up. No more!"

Laughter fills the air as everyone enjoys the excitement and laughter. Joe takes a couple of steps over then helps each grandfather up then leaning down takes Glory's hand pulling her on her feet.

Wiping dirt streaked tears from her face Glory laughingly states, "That was totally unexpected!"

"What'cha think we'd do when we both know ya could take us down in one move," Pokey replies wiping tears from his faded blue eyes.

"Yeah, I was looking at this hard red dirt wonderin' how I'd git up when you knocked me down," Skinny answers wiping happy tears from his eyes.

They all know Glory wouldn't have knocked them down like they are talking about so Glory looks at each of them so pursing her lips replies, "Humm…yar pretty ornery, ain't cha."

Both nod yes then Skinny replies firmly, "Yep and proud of it."

Everyone smiles as Joe requests, "Come on into the house and git some fresh coffee. We wanta show ya the house. Guess ya can see we built on some rooms while ya'll were in St. Louie."

"Yep, hard to miss seein' as it is twice the size it was before," Pokey replies with a smile.

"Guess you got a room big enough for all yar furniture, Beth Ann?" Skinny teases her with a smile.

"Oh, yes, grandpa it is really nice. I will enjoy showing it to you," Beth Ann's eyes glows with her happiness as she looks towards her room by the back door.

"Josh will you take our bed rolls down to the bunkhouse for us," Skinny requests to his young cowboy.

Joe leans in saying, "Why don'tcha have some coffee with us first, Josh and Kevin afore ya do that. Okay with ya grandpas?"

Puzzled both grandpas shake their heads yes as everyone walks into the kitchen.

Shaking the coffee pot Elizabeth offers, "I'll make some fresh coffee. Joe would you like to show them around for a few minutes, while I make it."

This is prearranged so Joe replies, "Oh, surely, come on and I'll give ya the tour."

Joe leads the way straight to Skinny's room and opening the door bows saying, "Welcome home, Grandpa Skinny. This is yar room."

Skinny looks around the well-furnished room stunned asking, "My room?"

"Yep! We want'cha here as often as ya'll come," Joe states firmly smiling at this kindhearted man.

Skinny and Pokey look at each other as Pokey states, "Well, I'll be."

Elizabeth slips in then walking over to the door to the front porch explains, "Joe put a door here so you three can sit out here and rock anytime you want to and come and go as you want. We thought about Sammy so planned that he will be right here besides you three so that he will feel triple loved all the time."

"Three of us?" Skinny asks puzzled.

"Yes, we have a bedroom for both of our grandpas and Uncle Max," Elizabeth answers smiling happily, "This is your second home now."

Jake's voice comes out of nowhere and they all jump when he drawls, "Remember in St. Louie when we insisted on bringin' so much furniture down here. Well this is part of the reason. The dresser, shift robe and chest of drawers plus the little table and lamps all came from St. Louie."

"Well, you shore fooled us. I'm purely amazed at yar kindness," Pokey states smiling happily at them.

"Well come across the hall and see yar room, Grandpa Pokey," Joe chuckles as he leads the way across the hallway then teasingly explains,

"We put ya in the middle Grandpa cause the young'uns said Grandpa Skinny snores like a bull frog roaring and ya don't."

"I take exception with that. I sound like a kitten purrin'. I'm shore I do," Skinny smilingly admits chuckling happily.

Pokey slaps him on the shoulder replying, "Ya lie like a dog, brother. Ya sound more like two frogs and a cat fighting when yar sleepin'."

Everyone roars at his humor then Jake explains, "The chest of drawers and shift robe came from St. Louie as well as the little table and lamp. Joe built yar bed and Grandpa Skinny's and he built'cha that big bookcase cause ya like to read so much."

Pokey looks around the large room then wiping a tear away says, "It reminds me of home already. Ma and Pa had a big nice house once and the Indians burnt it down and we just rebuilt that small one we have now. But this reminds me of ma's touches. She always made the rooms comfy and homey." He walks around touching the cloth under the lamp, the curtains on his big window and the bedspread which matches both just as Skinny's does.

"Wanta see Max's room now?" Joe asks realizing the two older gents are almost speechless they are so touched.

They walk down the hallway taking a right then another right into Max Roy's room. Chuckling Skinny suggests, "I'd better draw me a map or I'm gonna get lost it's so big now."

Pokey looks around the large room sincerely saying, "This is real nice, Joe and Lizbeth. He will be real touched at yar kindness."

Jake sits down on the bed he has been sleeping in then explains since Joe and Elizabeth are teary eyed at their grandpa's happiness, "This here bed is big enough for a tall one like Rev Roy and we brung him this dresser, rugs and desk, and the little table and lamp from St. Louie. Joe built the large clothes closet and the book case for his books.

"Mighty good of you, Joe and Lizbeth, mighty good of you," Skinny sincerely comments before adding, "Max ain't had a home since his ma and pa died. When Bonnie Jean died and he started roamin' he didn't want a home so he'd stay with us on occasion but kept saying he wouldn't "put us out" can ya imagine that? He ain't got nothin' but what he's a carryin' on his horse and if'n he had anythang someone needs more than him, he'd give it away at the drop of a hat. Amazin' what he has shared with others."

Smiling happily Elizabeth replies, "He has a home always and forever with us just like you do."

Nodding to Kevin and Josh, Joe adds, "And any and all of yar men are always welcome here, too."

The young men smile and nod thanks as Kevin replies, "Thank ya, Mr. Gray."

Glory takes the saddle bags and bed rolls that Kevin and Josh have been carrying with them laying them in her grandpa's new bedrooms. She smiles looking at the rooms thinking, "What a blessin' it will be to know they are safe and right here close to home. No one will git past our cowboys to harm Grandpa Pokey and they can relax and just enjoy life for a while." She smooths out the quilt on the bed thinking, "My own home…soon Jake and I will have our own home. Just me and Jake…" Smiling dreamily she puts her head back and stretching out her arms she gracefully twirls around the room.

Joe watches Glory take the saddle bags and when she doesn't come directly back he follows her just as she dreamily twirls around the room. Smiling at the picture she makes as her hair fans out around her and her skirt fans out like a bell Joe can't help but treasure this moment in time. After a few minutes she slows then stops, taking a deep breath she opens her eyes and smiles at seeing her father standing in the doorway watching her.

"Are ya happy, honey?" Joe asks smiling at his lovely daughter.

"Yes, more so than I can ever remember," Glory answers with a grateful sigh.

"Want to sit down after supper and draw up the plans for yar house? We need to finish it," Joe asks watching her face light up in happiness.

"Yes, sir! I'd love that," Glory answers with a radiant smile.

"Then get Jake to a chair and ya'll talk it out and after supper we will git some paper and we'll finish drawing it out like ya'll want it," Joe advises smiling.

Grinning happily Glory answers, "Yes, Sir!" and leaves to find Jake.

Holding hands and talking Jake and Glory slowly walk out to the lawn chairs then sit for a long time talking about what they want for their new home.

When Joe walks back into the kitchen he notices Pokey and Skinny sitting drinking coffee with Elizabeth and Stephie.

Stephie explains, "We are heading for home in a few minutes. We appreciate you letting Jake stay one more night. He should be feeling well enough to ride home tomorrow. Yellow Moon said his wound will heal very quickly now and I'll make sure he lays around for another couple of days."

"He is always welcome as you all are. So don't rush off if you feel you need to stay," Elizabeth advises her good friend.

"I miss my family and it's time for us to get back to work. I'm sure Zak is tired of doing all the chores and Shorty is now able to help out. We truly appreciate all the hospitality you have shown us," Stephie replies sincerely.

"We'll be coming over real soon with some surprises for ya'll," Pokey states with a wink at Stephie.

"Yeah, and as yar gonna be family to us real soon. I'm expectin' a hug and a kiss when you see what we brought you," Skinny advises smiling at the lovely Stephie.

Shaking her lovely blonde head and with her blue eyes sparkling Stephie asks, "Did you bring me something that sparkles? I love sparkly things."

"Maybe we did and maybe we didn't!" Pokey teases her then continues, "If'n we did….well…it'll cost ya another kiss on the cheek."

Stephie giggles like a school girl replying, "You shall have it then."

"Gonna hold you to it," Skinny replies as they watch Stephie and Shorty walk out the door to the stables to get their horses.

Beth Ann meets them in the yard talking a mile a minute about everything and the last they hear is Shorty teasing her about talking so primly.

Glancing at the grandpas, Joe asks, "Guess ya got a lot of papers for us from St. Louie?"

Skinny and Pokey abruptly sit back and the joy vanishes from their faces (as dew from the roses in sunlight) as they look sorrowfully at Elizabeth then Joe before Skinny answers, "Yep. Got a lot of papers for ya'll. Some disturbin' and some bad but mostly just papers that end the lives of Lora and Edgar and, I guess, Potter, too." He looks down at the table as he says this knowing how upsetting it will be for them to hear all the bad news that is coming.

"The suspense is killing me, Grandpas. What is the worst news?" Elizabeth asks puzzled.

"Make yarself comfortable and sit close. We don't want the young'uns to know any of this," Pokey advises sadly then leans up closer to them. They all lean towards each other to hear this news.

Skinny starts out, "First thing is we brought ya'll is a lot of money. We left some in the bank at St. Louie cause ...well...we'll explain that. Edgar's ledgers were heart breaking as he cheated everyone he could and especially the poorest ones. We asked Beth Ann to tally up the books and she was shocked by what she learned then she explained it to Glory and they did some of the most amazin' thangs. Ya'll be proud of their sharin' hearts. Beth Ann re-added all the accounts with the clerk there, Randy Ford's, help then we sent Randy out with these tallies and he collected most all of it. I'm sorry to say there is some we weren't able to get cause the people just didn't have it." Skinny stops sadly remembering the shock on Beth Ann's face.

"We don't want anyone to ...uh...go hungry or anything like that so we will be happy with whatever you collected," Elizabeth replies then asks, "That's not nearly all of it, is it?"

Shaking his head no Pokey continues the story, "No, honey, not by a long shot. We found Edgar had taken jewelry on account when people needed food and couldn't pay for it and, honey, we just didn't feel this was right. Glory did a fine thing one day that I'm happy to tell ya about. A very poor family came in to buy two cans of milk for their baby...very poor family their clothes were almost threadbare so Glory told'em that there was a sale goin' on and she sold'em six cans for the price Edgar would have sold one for then she asked Beth Ann how much they owed. Beth Ann checked then said it was about eight dollars and they agreed not to collect it. The man stammered what about his wife's ring, how much would it cost to get it back. It had belonged to his ma and now his wife. Glory said that was taken into consideration and found the ring and gave it to'em. Beth Ann said the couple cried when the young man gave the ring back to his wife and that he promised never to pawn it again. Jake and the girls had been goin' through everythin' and cleanin' out the shelves already so they became Santa Claus and loaded up a couple of boxes and Randy and Chris, the store clerks, delivered them to the family that night and put a note from Santa on them. That was Jake's idea. Those young'un really care about others. We're real proud of'em."

Joe and Elizabeth sit holding hands waiting for the bad news so this news makes them smile as Joe says, "That sounds fine to me. We told 'em to use their hearts, instead of their heads when it came to dealing with the problems they would find. I'm proud they used their hearts."

"Yes, we want to right any wrongs they did," Elizabeth smilingly confirms.

Cocking his head to the side Skinny advises, "You know those girls never complained about a thang the whole time. I'll never forget Beth Ann askin' us if'n they could get one more set of clothes to wear while they were there so they wouldn't have to wear just the two they brought with 'em and I wanta tell ya'll. Those young'uns worked...Jake and Carrie Lynn worked as hard as yar girls did. None are slackers. Each did the work of two people. I can tell you that I was mighty surprised with Beth Ann cause she never learned how to work and I didn't expect she would."

"Me, too, and you know somethin' else ...well....we know she is book smart but she's a very carin' girl, too. I've already seen that she goes with her heart more than her head most of the time then I noticed she watches and it's like seein' her atotalin' everythang up in her head then she nods to herself and gets busy doing it. Let me explain better. She and the girls looked over all the material and divided it up. Glory was getting bored so just Carrie Lynn and Beth Ann looked at all the thread, buttons and stuff. Both looked at each other then Beth Ann said, "Okay, buttons first...then thread..." those girls talked about what each material would probably be made into and they divided all the little thangs as even as they could. It was really amazin'," Pokey explains smiling at Elizabeth and Joe.

Elizabeth smiles at her grandpas replying, "She is like Joe. He does the same thing...sometimes it is amazing and other times it is irritating!" She giggles as Joe leans over and tickles her arm in retaliation of her words.

"Tell us the worst news?" Joe requests firmly tired of waiting.

Both old gents look at each other then Pokey nods for Skinny to tell them so taking a deep breath he states it plainly, "Edgar made bride contracts for Glory, Beth Ann and you, Elizabeth, to some foreigners from France."

Elizabeth gasps, "Bride contracts? The girls and ME? I'm married already they couldn't.....Oh, I'd be a widow, wouldn't I?"

Joe picks up her suddenly shaking hands softly saying, "It is over now, honey. Ya don't haveta worry about it."

Scratching his balding head Pokey hisses out his breath explaining, "Yar wrong there, Joe. The last letter was just a few months ago and they are plannin' on comin' to get Glory this fall and take Beth Ann at the same time to git her ready to be a lady."

Frowning Joe replies, "What about Lizbeth, if'n I was dead?"

"She would become…his mistress," Pokey answers sadly.

"NEVER! They know I'd never do that!" Elizabeth states firmly as her beautiful brown eyes spark angrily.

Reaching over Skinny takes her cold hand explaining, "Ya would have been forced to… first by Potter then by this lord."

"Forced?" Elizabeth asks her eyes round in shock as she asks, "They were going to beat me to make me do it?"

Skinny looks down at the table with his finger starting to draw lines on the table cloth while replying, "It seems that Franklin and Edgar enjoyed beatin' women and hurtin' em. There was a diary and it told a lot of things we wish we'd never read about their treatment of females."

Pokey looks down at his worn callused hands and frowning sorrowfully quietly continues, "We found clothes that Edgar wore to help Potter in forcing people off land Potter wanted to take back and we found out a whole lot about women who they abused and forced to…uh… do thangs they didn't want to do."

"Oh, my God, how horrible!" Elizabeth injects fanning her blushing face.

Joe's green eyes glitter like emeralds as he thinks about all the wicked things the two men did to others then he asks, "Can we hep any of these people? We'd rather do that than take their money."

Smiling a little Pokey explains more, "Marshal Garth Wheeler is in charge of some money we left in the St. Louie bank. It was Potter's Bank but his nephew is in charge now and he is a right fine young man. When he found out what his uncle was up to he was as horrified as we were so we joined together to help all those we could find to help. That is one of the reasons we left some money there. Most of the money from the mercantile is in one account. We found quite a bit of money hidden there and after seein' how he got it we didn't feel ya'll would really want it so we left it in the bank. Then we put the money from the sale of the house in another account in yar names so that ya'll can get it anytime you want to. We felt it was money from Lora."

Elizabeth and Joe look at each other then Elizabeth suggests, "Let's leave it all in there and see how many need to be helped. With all the things you brought back we won't need anything for a long time and I'd feel better about it. What do you think Joe?"

"I don't need any money from them. We have plenty of our own. If the young'uns need anythang we can give it to'em. I'd prefer it stay up there and hep those people out," Joe sad eyes look first at Elizabeth then over to the grandpas.

"We thought you'd feel that way when we told ya'll about it," Skinny answers, taking another deep breath, explains more. "We found letters from a foreigner who Edgar was gonna sell our land to. As soon as you and the girls were sent away then Edgar was gonna parcel our land out."

Joe squints at them thinking before asking, "You said ...you and the girls, what about Sammy? He would inherit, too."

"Ahhh... I don't believe Sammy would have lived to inherit anythang," Pokey sadly and softly admits, "There is no mention of him at all so that leads us to believe that with him alookin' so much like you, Joe, that he'da been killed."

Joe slams his fist down on the table making everything on it jump then he shoves his chair backwards stalking angrily around the room. Breathing deeply he thinks, and thinks as Elizabeth is thinking, about losing their precious son then he states, "I've got to go for a ride. I'll see ya'll later." He almost runs out of the room and over to the barn and in a few minutes he gallops out of the barn on Devil (his huge stallion).

Elizabeth hasn't moved as her mind is working furiously finally she lets out a deep breath and looking up at her grandfather's anxious eyes she takes another deep breath then sadly smiles saying, "Well, we are forewarned now and I can tell you both this WILL NOT happen. No one will destroy my family. No one! If they come then they will have a very rude reception." She looks at their sad faces so smiling crookedly she softly continues, "I know this was extremely hard on you telling us and hard on you finding this out. Jake knows doesn't he? He mumbled something when he was in a fever that Joe and I didn't understand but do now. We will be prepared grandpas, so don't worry about it anymore. WE will take care of these people if they show up."

Pokey and Skinny smile for the first time as Skinny replies, "I believe you will." A great weight seems to fall off their shoulders as they realize all will be well with their loved ones.

Joe rides hard for a couple of miles as his mind flies in all directions. "Steal my family! Take my girls away to another country! Take my wife to be someone's mistress…treat her like nothing…be mean to her! My lovely Lizbeth! No way is this gonna happen! How could anyone do that to innocent women and young'uns? *God, I cain't understand this…how could Edgar of all people do this…he raised Elizabeth and Beth Ann…how could he want money so bad he would sell them….Sell them!*" Tears of anger and frustration run through him as lightning striking through the air in a thunderstorm. After a while he slows down then dismounting starts walking and really thinking clearly, "*Okay, I understand what is going on, Lord. I cain't understand why…It is just too amazin' to believe they would do this. I will have to accept that they were low down varmints below anyone I've ever known to do this. I will accept the truth. I have to.*" Joe walks and thinks a long time while he prays his heart out not knowing or understanding the type of people these two men were. Grimly he raises his head and looking around realizes he turned around some time back and is almost to Good Heart's home. Smiling he looks up saying, "*Thank ya, Lord, for hepin' me keep my sanity during this ride. I was beyond it when I started out. Amen.*"

Good Heart watches Joe walking his horse towards them so strides out to meet him asking, "Joe, yar horse hurt?"

Joe tiredly shakes his head no then looking up at Good Heart replies, "No friend. I have another big problem and I've been wonderin' how to fix it. I don't know how I can fix it and that's my problem."

Seeing how tired and sweaty Joe is plus Good Heart can tell Joe has been crying which is very unusual, he motions toward a stand of trees inviting, "Come, sit and rest a spell and tell me yar problem, maybe I can hep."

Joe nods yes and is glad to sit down in the coolness under the large oak tree and rest a few minutes. He looks over at Good Heart explaining, "We found out today that Lizbeth's fath…the man who we thought was Lizbeth's father…arranged for Beth Ann and Glory to marry two men in France. It's another country across the Atlantic Ocean."

Good Heart looks shocked asking, "But why? There are men here that are good, no good reason to go over thar."

Sadly shaking his head Joe closes his eyes in pain explaining, "He was selling them."

"Slaves? Our Glory a slave! No, this cannot happen. They would kill her or she would kill'em," Good Heart states angrily then looking back at Joe he pleads, "Not Beth Ann....it would destroy her for this to happen to her."

Joe nods yes and looking at Good Heart explains more, "He was gonna sell Lizbeth, too."

Good Heart looks shocked at Joe then nodding his head yes, he replies, "They were gonna kill ya and tak'em all. What about Sammy?"

When Joe just shakes his head no Good Heart lets out a horrible yell of anger then jumps up stomping around and around trying to contain his horrible anger.

Watching him Joe smiles sadly seeing Good Heart go through the same emotions he has recently gone through.

Good Heart finally stops and taking a deep breath to calm himself he goes down on one knee and starts to silently pray. "No, this not happen to our family. We do not allow anyone to take our family from us! Those young'uns are mine, too. I will kill anyone who tries to take them from us," Good Heart vows with lips quivering as he stands up before Joe. Then kneeling down on one knee in front of Joe he looks him directly in the eyes continuing, "Ya'll have to stop'em, Joe. Kill'em if 'n ya have to but ya'll have to be meaner than they are. Ya have no choice! Do ya know this?"

Taking a deep breath Joe sadly nods yes saying, "Yes, my friend, I realize what I will have to do. I cain't let'em be taken and used like that. I won't let it happen."

"Nor will I. When they come for'em?" Good Heart asks grimly smiling now.

"I'm not sure. They said this fall. Glory will be married to Jake by then and Lizbeth will be big with child. I'm gonna read all the letters and find out all I can and I'll let'cha know. It's my blessin' that I have ya'll to hep me in times like these," Joe replies truthfully and reaching out they clasp fore arms in the Indian fashion as Good Heart pulls Joe to his feet.

"Friends...yes...Brothers...always," Good Heart replies firmly and hugs Joe before they turn towards their homes very troubled.

Joe slowly walks back to the barn and unsaddles his horse. He gives him a long rub down talking softly to him as he does it. He isn't surprised when he looks up and sees Elizabeth is standing behind him watching.

"What a shock we had today," she softly admits as she watches the calmness in Joe now compared to the way he was when he rode out.

"Yep, I apologize for rushing out like I did. I was about to explode and I had to git away by myself afore I did and it weren't none of ya'll's fault they did what they did. I've thought about it all and prayed about it till my mind has settled down and Lizbeth thars no way we are gonna allow that to happen," Joe turns looking at his lovely wife with tears in his eyes, he continues, "Lizbeth, you are my heart and soul. If I lost ya again, I couldn't go on. I cain't let that happen and I won't lose my young'uns…. none of 'em! Ya know I'm not a gun fighter but I will be if'n I have to be to protect my family. I want ya to start learnin' to shoot also. It might save yar life."

Elizabeth's beautiful face glows when Joe says she is his life and smiling she thinks, "He said me first then the children. He loves me that much. Well, that is something…to be loved so much." Her smile wobbles a little as she answers Joe's statement with a definite yes, "I will start learning immediately. If Beth Ann can do it then certainly I can do it. Samuel is my biggest concern. He is too young to shoot a gun but he is the most vulnerable."

"I'm gonna start teachin'em how to shoot also but I believe Beth Ann is the most vulnerable. She ain't a bit aggressive not that she cain't be bossy but she could be scarred for life by this. Also she loved Edgar and it will be a crushin' blow to larn he planned to do this ta her and we must tell the young'uns so they will be prepared for anythang that happens," Joe sadly admits.

"Yes, they need to be prepared. Joe…uh….Grandpa Skinny gave me Edgar's will and he left everything to me and Beth Ann. He really did hate you for spoiling their plans for me. He left Glory and Sammy completely out. I don't think we need to ever let them know this, do you?" Elizabeth asks sadly.

"No use to put that on'em. Let's just put it up with our other papers we need to keep and forget it. Lizbeth, I never wanted their money. Yar the only thing I ever wanted from'em," Joe confesses looking at Elizabeth intently.

Smiling Elizabeth wraps her arms around his waist replying, "I know, that is one of the reasons I've always loved you."

They hug treasuring this peaceful moment then holding hands walk back into the house. Joe hangs his hat on the hat rack beside the door then immediately walks to Skinny and Pokey's bedrooms and knocks on their doors. When they open their doors he states, "I apologize for running out like I did afore. I was too angry to think right for a while and I needed to git out and ride out my anger. I'm gonna tell ya right out that there ain't no way I'm gonna let this happen to my girls and my son. If'n I have to be mean I will be and I don't relish the idea but my girls will all be safe from harm that I can guarantee ya."

"If'n ya had shrugged it off we woulda been worried but seein' how it upset ya we knowd ya'd take it seriously and it should be," Pokey answers sadly.

Patting Joe's arm Skinny replies, "We will always be close by and will come at a moment's notice if'n you need us. We could even bring some of our boys over for a time to hep you out, if'n you need it."

"Thank ya. I'ma hopin' it won't come to that but it is nice to know anyhow," Joe replies smiling at them. He starts to turn around and go back towards the kitchen when he stops and looking back at the two older gents explains from the heart, "I never knew my grandparents. All of'em had died afore I was born. I want'cha to know that I treasure ya'll and want ya to always be at home here and feel comfortable to come and go here like ya want to. Ya'll never out stay yar welcome and when yar ready to stay here all the time that is fine by me and Lizbeth."

Both men are stunned for a moment even though they realize Joe has a big heart this is a wonderful surprise. Skinny nods yes replying, "Much obliged Joe. Much obliged. We feel comfortable here and appreciate your kindness."

Pokey's lips are a quivering so when he looks at Joe he just motions for him to come closer and they hug then Joe hugs Skinny before returning to the kitchen.

Sitting down at the table Joe tiredly admits then requests, "I'm plum tuckered out, Lizbeth. Let's have an early supper then go to bed. My brain has stopped workin' now."

When he looks over at her, she gives him a sassy look with a wink saying, "I'm very tired myself an early night would suit me just fine."

Joe can't help laughing heartily at his mischievous wife and feels more of the strain drain off his mind. Sighing he sits with his cup of coffee thinking about Glory and Jake's new home and what will be needed for it. He pulls some paper and a pencil over and starts doing some more sketching planning it out.

Jake falls asleep after his talk with Glory about their future home so after a few minutes Glory quietly rises and does the evening chores and when she notices her papa isn't there she milks the cow and takes the milk into the kitchen for her mother. Then while Jake continues sleeping, she quietly walks into Beth Ann's room and helps her arrange it like she wants it.

Beth Ann is glowing with happiness with having this beautiful room and she has worked most of the day putting books in the bookcase then filling her desk with everything she brought with her. She carries all the books that she feels the whole family will enjoy reading into the parlor filling up a large portion of that bookcase. She dreamily rubs the backs of some of her favorite books thinking, "I must be dreaming to be this happy. Joy fills my heart to overflowing. I know without a doubt that my papa loves me, my mama loves me and it is a wonderful feeling. My grandpas are so wonderful and kind to me. I have a wonderful big sister and then there is Samuel. He has turned out to be a blessing, too. This winter we will have a baby in the house. I don't know much about babies but I intend to learn and Grandma Nona will be here and I will get to be with her a lot. Everything is working out so well. Life is wonderful." Humming she works happily all morning long and into the late afternoon.

"With all the excitement Pokey, we forgot about the money we brought Joe and Elizabeth, it's still in the bottom of your trunk," Skinny states sitting up straight in his chair as they sit resting and talking in their rooms.

"My goodness! I completely forgot about it, too, since we got back. Let's take it to them now and git it off our minds," Pokey states rising and going to the trunk in question.

"Wonder who carried this trunk in? It is the heaviest one we had," Skinny asks chuckling.

"Probably Joe since Jake ain't lifting much right now," Pokey answers smiling at his brother.

Skinny and Pokey carry the heavy wooden box into the kitchen and set it on the kitchen table then Pokey says, "Forgot to give this here money we brung back to ya'll."

Joe looks at the large and heavy box then opening it (with the key Skinny hands him) he sees it is filled with coins in all denominations. He runs his hand through it then looking at it says to Elizabeth, "Here is yar dowry, honey," wondering what she is thinking.

Walking closer Elizabeth also runs her fingers through the gold and silver coins then smiling sadly replies, "Joe, I don't want it for me. Can we save it for the children's future? Maybe we can put it to good use some way. One thing I'd like to do is help out Minnie and Benny a little. Do you think we could say they were left a little inheritance...maybe a hundred dollars or something like that so they will have some money on hand?"

Joe's hesitant smile widens as he nods yes saying, "Yes, madam. I think that would be a very good idea." Picking up the heavy chest he takes it into their bedroom to store it.

Jake walks into the room just then and chuckling states, "They ain't gonna believe what we have brung'em. We brought'em some stuff from the store and house. Beth Ann and Glory picked out thangs for'em. They won't know which end is up for awhile. Maybe we could ride over tomorra and take it to'em?"

"Depends if'n yar are up to the ridin' cause we ain't gonna take the surprises over till ya can go and see their happiness," Joe teases his soon-to-be son.

"I feel fine. Wound don't hurt none now. I just get tuckered out and fall asleep. Think I slept all afternoon today," Jake explains puzzled a little.

"You heal while you are sleeping so that is very good," Elizabeth states smiling at her soon-to-be son.

"Then I should be as right as rain real soon," Jake admits smiling at them all.

Smiling Elizabeth explains, "We are going to have fried chicken, mashed potatoes and gravy with lots of biscuits for supper with a few other things like two apple pies and two peach pies that I baked this morning. Sound good?"

A happy chorus of "YES, MADAM!" echoes across the room.

Elizabeth happily pulls out her two biggest cast iron skillets to start frying the chickens in. She calls out, "Beth Ann and Glory, I need your help with supper." They walk right in pick up their aprons and quickly start peeling potatoes and making biscuits for supper.

A wonderfully cooked supper and good conversation make for a relaxed and happy family for the discussion of Jake and Glory's new home after the pie is eaten.

Joe pulls out his sketch of the house and they all look it over. Glory requests, "I wanta have two bedrooms cause sometimes Grandma Nona and my Grandpas are gonna come over an spend the night with us and when we have a baby then we'll already have a room ready for him."

Looking over at her Joe asks, "Him? How ya know it will be a boy?"

"It will be," Glory smartly answers back.

"Sounds good to me," Jake states smiling and winking at her.

They all gather closer and soon have a house, barn, smoke house, tool shed, hog shed, out house and chicken coop plans completely drawn up.

"First thang is gotta be the well. We need to get Uncle Hank out here and have him find the water for us," Joe states explaining, "He is amazin' he is right near ever time. I heard ya'll brought some goodies for 'em so when ya tak'em in to'em then we can see when he will have time to come out and look the land over."

"Good Heart is real good at that, too. We can ask him to look, too," Glory advises them.

"Sounds good to me," Jake answers smiling and nodding yes happily.

"What do you think about going over to Minnie and Benny's tomorrow to give them their surprises?" Elizabeth asks with a twinkle in her eyes.

Smiling happily everyone agrees this will be a happy event to attend. So an early night ends a long stressful day for some of them.

Jake sleeps over again in Max Roy's new bedroom thinking, "Soon, my beautiful Glory, we will have our own home."

THE SURPRISES
Chapter 21

*"A gift from the heart is worth more
than a bauble or a diamond."*

After breakfast the next morning Jake (with help from Joe and
his cowboys) makes sure all the correct trunks and boxes are loaded into
a wagon to take over to Minnie and Benny's farm.

Beth Ann and Glory are almost bouncing with joy because soon
they will see the happiness in Minnie, Benny and Arty's faces when they
receive the presents they chose for them.

Elizabeth is riding with Joe as he drives the wagon and all the
others are riding their horses. Josh and Kevin are riding behind Skinny
and Pokey and both young men are as excited as the others in bringing
such wonderful surprises.

"It is nice feeling like we belong to the Gray family. I'm really
enjoyin' this time over here. Sorry that Brad and Jay missed out as they
heped carry and guard over these trunks, too," Josh admits with a gleeful
look in his eyes.

"Yeah, it's a shame they are missin' this fun but we will tell'em
all about it when we get back. I'm enjoyin' the time here, too, and I really
like Jake, Glory and the little girls…they sure have treated us family like,"
Kevin states as he looks over at the Gray family.

The riders are riding slowly so Jake will have an easy time of it.
They plan to arrive mid-morning after the chores are done. Glory and
Beth Ann ride ahead the last mile to the farm to tell Minnie she has
company coming.

Riding into the yard they immediately see Sammy and he happily
runs toward them calling, "Glory! Beth Ann! You are home!"

Both girls jump down from their horses and run over to him
taking turns hugging him.

Then Glory picks him up swinging him in a circle laughing
happily with him then she warns, "Jake, got hurt so don't let'em pick ya
up and open up his wound."

Frowning Sammy asks, "How'd he get hurt?"

"An injun shot him in the chest with an arra," Glory explains seriously.

"And he lived? Wow!" Sammy exclaims eyes wide in surprise then asks, "Think he'll let me see it?"

"Boys!" Beth Ann laughingly states then asks, "What do you think? He is a man. He will want to show off his scar!"

"Scar! Wow!" Sammy exclaims dancing all around when the wagon pulls in surrounded by the riders. He immediately goes over to Jake stating, "Glory said an INDIAN shot you with an arrow!"

Jake chuckles along with everyone else as this is the most important news item to him. Nodding yes Jake slowly dismounts then squatting down replies, "Yep, I was and Glory and yar Pa saved my life. Later I'll tell ya all about it."

Shocked Minnie stands rooted to the spot when she hears Jake has been shot with an arrow then she rushes over (as fast as a heavily pregnant woman can rush) and taking his arm pulls him over to one of the lawn chairs (he made for them when they first moved in) and pushes him down into it. She runs her hand through Jake's crows black hair saying, "Jake, are ya shore yar feelin' well enough to ride over here?"

Benny and Arty come running up with a smile on their lips then hear Minnie's words so look worriedly at Jake.

Holding up his hands Jake replies, "I'm fine. I'ma healin' good and feelin' good. Thank you for carin'."

Elizabeth explains, "They arrived home three days ago but Jake wasn't able to ride until today and we didn't want him to be left out when we brought over the surprises from St. Louis."

Eyes blinking wildly, Minnie stutters, "Surprises? From St Louie?"

Giggling happily Beth Ann answers, "Oh, Minnie, we had so much fun going through everything in the store and there was so much we didn't need so we brought you some of it."

"You chose surprises for us'ns?" Benny asks very surprised.

Beth Ann's smile fades a little as she shyly answers, "Yes, we wanted to bring you some special things."

Stepping closer to Beth Ann Glory frowningly explains, "Yes, we decided on the way to St. Louie that we wanted to do somethang special for ya'll. Beth Ann feels bad cause of the way she treated ya'll for years and it was her idea to bring ya some nice thangs."

Benny mouth drops open then smiling broadly he replies, "Well, that is so nice of ya'll to remember us. Beth Ann, there ain't no need to be makin' up for anythang. We forgave ya when ya asked us and we don't hold no grudge against ya."

"It would make me feel better if you would accept the surprises we have brought you," Beth Ann begs wringing her hands as she waits for their answer.

Benny is speechless as he looks at this young girl, who has changed so dramatically in the past months, so he smiles and humbly replies, "We be very grateful to be remembered by ya'll and thankful to be yar friends."

Beth Ann's eyes light up as she answers, "Oh, thank you! You will love them!"

Minnie and Joe have been holding their breath but hadn't realized it so now they both let out a deep sigh in relief at Benny's words and smile at everyone around.

Puzzled Elizabeth looks at Benny then turning to Joe quietly asks, "I wonder if I have been forgiven, I did much more than Beth Ann could ever have done?"

"I believe you have been but if not then it will just take time," Joe whispers back.

Minnie notices the sadness that fills Joe and Elizabeth's faces and also that a lot of the happiness has left both young girl's faces after this talk. She glances over at her beloved husband's face knowing he is sorry for his words. Wonderingly she watches as Benny looks all around and does what he always does when he wishes he'd kept his thoughts to himself. He starts biting his lower lip thinking how to make it right. She watches as he closes his eyes knowing he is saying a prayer for guidance.

Arty and Sammy are pelleting Jake with questions about being wounded so when Benny moves away and stands silently praying no one really notices except Minnie.

Jake whispers to Sammy, "Your presents are at home. We didn't bring them over but you got some good ones."

"I'm real glad ya'll remembered Minnie, Benny and Arty. They are my family, too," Sammy whispers back.

Nodding yes, Jake smiles back at Sammy, as he ruffles his blonde hair.

Sadly Benny looks down praying, *"Lord, I really put my foot in it. I didn't mean to hurt Beth Ann's feelings. I knowd she has changed. I was just shocked for a minute. I didn't mean to be hurtful to her. How can I make it right? They have been so good to us'uns and here I go and say somethang stupid. Please give me the right words, Lord. I need'em bad."*

Minnie's mind is blank and concerned she watches everyone talking then looking over at a contrite Benny, she doesn't know how to make it right with everyone.

When Benny raises his head he smiles as he walks over to her asking, "Did ya bake that big ham this morning from the hog we slaughtered yesterday?"

"Yes, I did. It's a big one, too. There's enough to feed everyone here," Minnie answers smiling at him.

Benny nods then stepping over close to Beth Ann asks, "Sorry, I guess I'm not such a good host. Would ya'll like some tea and coffee? We'd like to have a party to celebrate ya'lls safe return. We got a big ham Minnie is baking in the oven right now and it won't take much to make a good dinner for ya'll. We's right proud ya'll rode over today."

Grinning Elizabeth replies, "I brought some potatoes and a pot of red beans and corn meal to make bread with. Ham would be wonderful. I'm going to steal your recipe Minnie for that crispy topping you put on your hams. It is delicious."

Glory and Jake smile at each other as Jake suggests, "Beth Ann, why don't we get the big barrel out first. Minnie might want to see it before we eat."

Beth Ann almost shimmers with happiness as she looks at her father asking, "Papa will you?"

"Yes, honey, I will. Kevin will ya hep me git it down. Maybe we can carry it right into the kitchen," Joe replies then asks the blonde haired blue eyes young cowboy.

Glory follows after them picking up a large heavy box she starts to carry it into the house when Josh takes it from her and hefts it upon his strong shoulders carrying it into the house where he sets it on the table.

Jake walks to the wagon and starts to pick up another box to carry in when Skinny and Pokey push him back as Pokey states, "We'll get it. This is the one ya want in now?"

"Yeah, it's the pots and pans," Jake whispers to them.

Minnie's eyes are sparkling with excitement as Joe takes a crow bar and pries the lid off of the wooden barrel then steps back so Beth Ann and Glory can start pulling the beautiful china dishes out of the saw dust setting them on the empty kitchen table.

"Oh, my Lord, look at these beautiful blue flowers all over the dishes," Minnie gasps as she picks up a plate then continues, "I ain't never seen these afore."

"They are brand new. We found them in the store and Beth Ann thought ya'd like'em," Glory answers smiling at her.

"Why I just loves'em, thank ya both for thinkin' of us," Minnie states happily reaching over she grabs first Beth Ann then Glory in a tight hug.

Jake motions for the large heavy box to be brought over and they set it on the table as he says, "These ain't new but we thought ya'd get some good use outta them," when Joe pries open the top of the wooden crate. Jake lifts out two skillets, a huge pot for stews and three sauce pans all cast iron with lids to fit.

Minnie's mouth drops open as she looks at the complete set of cookware then looking at Benny she moves her mouth but no words come out.

Smiling Benny jokes, "Well, this is one time Minnie is speechless. Let's all take a moment and enjoy it!"

Everyone laughs at his humor as he happily states, "This is one big wonderful surprise ya'll brung us. We be very proud that ya think enough of us to bring us these thangs all the way from St. Louie."

Smiling sweetly Beth Ann quietly replies, 'We love all of you."

Looking over at her Benny sees she is serious and smiling kindly at her explains, "We'uns always loved ya'll, too. Ya'll was like our young'uns in St. Louie in that we took care of ya."

Giggling Beth Ann replies, "If you had been my papa, Benny. I would have been a much nicer girl because you would have made me be."

Chuckling Benny hugs her saying, "Amen to that girl!" Everyone laughs and the last of the tension seems to vanish.

Glory walks in with a long rectangular box and when Benny opens it they find three large wooden spoons, three long handled metal spoons, two long handed metal forks and two metal spatulas to be used with the cast iron cookware. Then she delves deeper in the box bringing out a colander and the wooden masher that goes with it. Minnie lets out a squeal of joy saying, "Oh, now, I can make jelly outta those berries Arty and Sammy found out in the woods. They have so many little seeds that it's hard to git all of'em out. Oh, thank ya for being so thoughtful as to bring us these wonderful presents."

Jake chuckles saying, "This ain't all. We have some more just thought we could hep ya get these washed up to eat off of for dinner. With all of us we can hav'em washed and put up for ya real quick like.... but there is somethang else yar gonna need first. Kevin and Josh are a carryin' it in right now."

Kevin and Josh (Skinny & Pokey's young cowboys) stagger in carrying a large item with a blanket tied around it. They set it inside the large kitchen then pulling out a bowie knife Kevin cuts the rope one time and rerolls it then stepping back Glory and Beth Ann unwrap the blanket and Minnie and Benny eyes grow large as they recognize the lower half of the buffet from the Hawkins's kitchen. It is about eight feet long with six large drawers in the bottom of it. One drawer is a silverware drawer and the rest are used to store dish towels, table clothes and other items needed in the kitchen.

Minnie and Benny are speechless as they look at the lovely piece of furniture and tears run freely down Minnie's face as she looks over at the crude wooden shelf Benny had built for her to set her tin dishes on. Turning she smiles happily at them for their thoughtfulness.

Just then Skinny and Pokey carry in another large item and puzzled Minnie and Benny look at it. Glory quickly lays a blanket over the top of the buffet and nodding Skinny and Pokey set the large bundle on top of it. Pulling his knife back out Kevin cuts the rope holding the blanket on this item and gently pulls the rope off and rewinds it as he did the other one then helps Glory pull the blanket off the china cabinet that sits on top of the buffet. It is a little dusty so Beth Ann picks up a dish towel and starts wiping the dust off of the wooden doors as Minnie and Benny stand shocked and rooted to the spot.

Benny lays his hand over his open mouth and doesn't know what to say for a minute then he looks at Glory and Beth Ann asking, "Ya'll brought us the whole cabinet? Why'd ya'll do that?"

Smiling happily Beth Ann cockily answers, "Because you need it."

"But...but..," Benny can't form words to say then he looks warily over at Elizabeth who is smiling happily at him as she replies, "We hope you will enjoy all the surprises that the girls chose to bring you."

"Much obliged...much obliged," Benny replies looking at the dishes then the china cabinet and buffet.

Minnie plops down in a chair and starts fanning herself thinking and thinking about their good fortune and is still speechless.

Smiling Joe asks, "How about we set it up for ya'll then we can hep ya fill it up after the dishes git washed."

Benny jumps as if shot saying, "Thank ye kindly that would be nice."

Quickly the men move towards the china cabinet and buffet and Benny walks over with his hammer taking down the small shelf. Laying it to the side as they carry the buffet over first then set the china cabinet on top of it as it should be. It is not new furniture but it is in very good shape and looking at it Benny can't see a scratch or mark on it thinking, "Amazin'...just amazin' it came all the way from St. Louie without a scratch gettin' on it."

Putting her hands on her hips and rocking back and forth Glory asks, "Ready for the next surprise?"

Minnie just numbly nods yes as Benny and Arty's faces light up in pleasure.

Rubbing her hands together she asks her papa, "Will ya bring in the other trunk now please?"

Beth Ann and Jake start grinning broadly thinking about the beautiful lamp they have brought. Joe and Josh carry in the heavy trunk by its handles and carefully set it right inside the door close to the kitchen table.

Glory motions for Beth Ann to open it and give it out. She smiles happily at doing it then requests, "Jake, will you do the top layers, please?"

Jake nods yes eagerly opening the rounded top trunk taking out two Stetson cowboy hats and hands one to Benny then one to Arty. Both grin widely saying, "Thank ya."

Jake pulls out two plain straw bonnets and hands them to Minnie then laughing he reaches in and pulls out four very small bonnets for the twins.

Minnie bursts out crying again as she looks at the beautiful little white straw hats clutching them to her bosom saying, "Oh, how purdy. Beth Ann had some like these."

Jake pulls out a large and long paper wrapped parcel that he had fitted into the trunk himself and hands it to Benny saying, "From our grandpas to ya'll."

Benny smiles at Skinny and Pokey nodding to them then with Arty's help carefully unties the string holding it tightly together then pulling the paper off sees a lot of leather in long strips wound in almost a circle for use in bridles and saddle reins. Benny's mouth drops open and he blinks rapidly knowing this is exactly what he needs. He looks up at them but can't do more than nod his thanks as he gulps down the rising tears.

Looking over Minnie bursts into tears again saying, "This is too much! We ain't got nothin' to repay ya'll for all these fine thangs."

Kneeling down beside her chair Joe replies, "Ya don't owe us anythang, Minnie and Benny. This is extra stuff we don't got no use for and we just want to share some with ya."

Elizabeth lays her hand on Benny's shoulder so he turns around then she says, "We don't want anything in return except your continued friendship. When one has abundance it should be shared."

Benny does something he never thought he'd do. He hugs Elizabeth and kisses her cheek humbly saying, "Missy...Lizbeth, yar bein' too kind to us'ns."

"No one can be too kind to a friend and your family has always treated my family like friends even when we didn't treat you kindly. We regret that very much and hope this will in some way make up for those hard times," Elizabeth explains wiping a tear away.

Beth Ann never moves even though she wipes a tear away a few times as she avidly watches what is going on. Turning to her Benny hesitantly asks, "Beth Ann ...will ya forgive me for doubtin' ya?" He opens his arms and Beth Ann rushes into them and hugs him as tightly as he hugs her. He chuckles then throwing back his head says, "Lord Almighty! We are so blessed!"

Everyone laughs with him as they have seldom seen him boisterous and loud (being brought up a slave that wasn't allowed).

Grinning happily Beth Ann quickly walks back to the trunk and starts pulling out bolts of material and a sewing box with Minnie written on the lid. She hands the sewing box to Minnie explaining, "My grandpas made this for you."

Smiling happily Minnie looks up at them saying, "Thank ye very much for the pretty box." She looks at the decorations on the tin lid which has tiny little holes in it spelling out her name and the little etching done in each corner. Opening it she gasps for inside is a pair of silver sewing scissors, needles, thread, buttons and a large pair of shears. "Oh, my, oh my, look at all these pretties and look they match the material. Now who would go to so much trouble to match up all these pretty thangs?" She looks at Beth Ann as Jake and Glory say at the same time, "Beth Ann!" Minnie knows that Beth Ann would have the patience and would take the time to do something so thoughtful. "Thank ya, Beth Ann, for yar thoughtfulness. Yar a sweet girl to remember me and pick out all these wonderful surprises for us all," Minnie says from the heart.

"You are all very welcome. Glory, Carrie Lynn, Jake and I had a lot of fun thinking of things we thought you would enjoy and this one is very special and Glory is going to give it to you," Beth Ann explains then steps back as Glory leans into the trunk picking up the beautiful orange lamp with the crystals on it. They had wrapped it over and over in white cotton material so it wouldn't get broken so she carefully sets it on the table saying, "This is something very special for ya'll. It is very breakable. Here, Minnie, you open it."

Minnie's hands tremble as she carefully takes off the first layer of material unwrapping it around and around laughing she says, "Guess I got some more diaper material right here."

Jake reaches into the trunk and lifts out the mantle clock holding it ready to give to Benny.

When Minnie unwraps the first piece (which is the globe) she lets out a sigh of joy as it fairly sparkles in the light. Then comes the bottom (which is a bright orange) and inside she sees something wrapped up so taking it out she sees the dozen little crystal that will hang and sparkle so brightly. "Ain't it purdy!" Minnie softly speaks as she watches the light dancing off of it.

"I've never seen anythang so purdy in my whole life," Arty states with his eyes glued to the beautiful lamp.

"Me, either," Benny agrees staring at the lovely lamp.

Jake hands Joe the package he is holding whispering, "It's a mantle clock…ever family needs one."

Joe whispers back, "You can give it to'em."

"We'd like you to present it to them with some wise words," Jake whispers back with a smile and a nod.

"Wise words...humm...okay," Joe thinks a minute then leaning over hands the bundle to Benny saying, "This here is something extra special for ya'll that the young'uns chose to remind ya that everythang has a time and a place for what happens to us'ns."

Puzzled Benny looks down at the wrapped item then gently laying it on the table starts unwrapping it. When he sees the gleaming wood on the back of it he stops, caresses it, saying, "Nice wood." Then he unwraps it some more seeing the shape of it, he looks closely as he turns it over and his mouth falls open as he sees the ornate gold filigree all over the front of it. He and Minnie look stunned then Arty says, "Oh, my goodness! It is so purdy. It's a clock and there is a key to wind it up."

"Oh, this is nice. So vary nice. Thank ya'll so much for a thinkin' about us'ns. I don't know what to say," Benny's smiling face is a joy to behold as he looks from face to face then carefully laying the clock down starts shaking hands with everyone even Skinny's cowboys. He hugs Glory and Beth Ann again and kisses their cheeks for thinking of them.

Hiding a smile Pokey nonchantly asks, "Don't reckon Arty is interested in what I brung for ya, are ya?" He looks down at this fingernails just waiting for Arty to reply.

Arty's head pops up as he breathlessly asks, "Ya brought me somethan'?"

"Yep, Skinny and I thought you'd like these. You and Sammy boy can have a lot of fun playin' with 'em," Pokey hands Arty a heavy bag.

Smiling brightly Arty slowly unties the bag pouring colorful marbles out of it into his hand....probably twenty marbles are in the bag, "Marbles...wow...I seen lots of boys playin' with 'em but I ain't never had any of my own. Thank ya so much for thinkin' of me." His beautiful eyes shine brightly as he turns to Sammy saying, "I got some marbles of my own now!"

"Real pretty ones, too, Arty," Sammy states as he looks at the marbles.

"That ain't the only thang. We brought ya somethan' that all boys like real well and shows yar becomin' a man," Skinny adds hiding a smile.

"What? What? Can I have it now?" Arty begs with his beautiful brown eyes sparkling happily.

"Yep, ya can," Pokey answers reaching into the trunk pulling out a long narrow bundle handing it to Arty.

Arty fumbles with the string but no one helps him as they realize Arty wants to do this on his own. After a minute he unties the largest knot and jerking the string off he quickly unwraps a rifle.

"A gun! A real rifle for me?" Arty squeals and his voice breaks but this time he doesn't care. He hugs the rifle to his chest hesitantly asking again, "For me yar sure?"

Nodding yes, Pokey lays his hands on Arty's shoulder as he looks him in the eyes replying, "Son, this is a weapon and not a toy. If'n yar pa don't mind, I'd like to teach cha to shoot. I've had a lot of practice and I'm pretty good at it. Son, a gun is for shootin' food for the table and for protection only. Promise me ya'll be very careful with it cause it can kill and maim real easy."

Arty listens intently to all Pokey says then putting his hand over his heart he looks Pokey and then Skinny in the eyes replying, "I promise I'll be very careful like and I will think about what I'm gonna shoot before I use my gun."

Skinny pats his shoulder saying, "Good boy, there is nothing more important than bein' responsible with a weapon." He turns around and picks up ammunition from Jake then sets six boxes of shells on the table then looking at Benny he thoughtfully says, "I'm sorry if'n we shoulda asked you first Benny. I just realized maybe you didn't want your boy to learn to shoot a gun yet."

"I appreciate that, sir, but this is real important an Minnie and I'ze been talkin' about it quite a bit cause Arty be her only protection sometimes when I'm in the fields and away from the house for a time. It'll make me feel much better knowin' he can protect'em both," Benny seriously explains shaking hands with both men again.

Grinning cockily Pokey asks Benny, "Guess ya thought we didn't bring ya anythang?" He pulls another gun out of the trunk handing it to Benny and setting more boxes of ammunition on the table then Jake picks up a bundle and opening it lays a hand gun and holster on the table along with shells for it.

Benny's eyes almost jump out of his head as he looks at the expensive rifle and hand gun. His mouth works but no words come out. Benny looks at each one of the men but can't put two words together to say thanks. With his mind racing he thinks, "How can I pay for these guns. I ain't got no money. But we need'em so what do I do?"

Smiling Joe explains, "Know ya'll will need meat for the winter and ya need a good gun to git it and, Benny, there be a lot of dangers out thar when ya'll need a pistol and a belt to keep it in. A rattle snake can bite ya real fast like and a coyote can jump ya real quick. It's best to be prepared for ever thang that can happen. We knowd ya don't know how to use'em yet so anytime ya got some time ride over or we'll ride over and teach ya how to use'em."

Smiling at the speechless Benny Skinny asks, "Benny, I chose you a plain gun belt for a reason. I like workin' with leather and I was wonderin' this winter when we have spare time could I teach you how to make fancy designs on leather for your gun belt and maybe a belly wearin' belt?"

"Could I have a fancy belt with my name on it?" Arty asks smiling happily.

"Yes, sir. I know how to do that, if'n ya'd like to know how I can teach ya'll," Skinny replies rubbing his hand across Arty's slender shoulders.

Benny put both hands around Skinny's hand shaking it hard as he replies, "That is somethang I'd really like to larn. We could maybe make a livin' makin'em for other folks, too."

"I hadn't thought of that but yes, ya could," Pokey replies nodding his head yes.

Fanning herself rapidly, Minnie exclaims, "I don't know if'n I can take any more surprises, these has taken my breath away!"

Jake smiles lovingly at them replying, "Just a couple more." He reaches down into the trunk bringing out the new pants and boots setting them on the table along with some new gloves and shoes. When he sets out some baby shoes and little girls shoes Minnie's tears start up all over again.

Benny looks at the big stacks exclaiming, "Well, I'll be.....I'll be... this is better than any Christmas I'ze ever seen."

Arty laughs happily replying, "Pa, we only git one present at Christmas...this is more than all the Christmases I'ze ever had!"

Beth Ann nods mumbling, "That is what I wanted." She looks over at Joe and sees he is watching her so winking at him she nods yes, "I have done what I needed to do to make amends."

Joe reads her mind easily and smiling happily at her knows she will be able to put all the memories of the bad things she has done to them in the past because now she has made amends.

Glory reaches into the very bottom of the trunk pulling out a heavy bundle and lays it with a thump on the table in front of Minnie saying, "We found a set of silverware that has a flower matching the little blue flowers on the china. So we knew they belonged together."

Benny unrolls the heavy bundle and counts a setting for twelve including serving spoons, forks and in the very middle two little sets of forks and spoons for small children. Open mouthed in shock they look first at Glory then Beth Ann as Jake explains, "Glory and I bought ya'll the baby sets. We'd never seen any afore and thought that you otta have some for yar babies."

"What….how…uh…thank ya so much! I'ze outta words to say thank ya enough for all these wonderful thangs ya'll brought us. We'll take good care of 'em and will always treasure'em. Thank ya…thank ya," Benny gratefully states as he and Minnie hug each other joyfully.

Skinny and Pokey each reach down into the trunk pulling out two small bundles and each hands them to Arty. Smiling happily at receiving more presents from them, he carefully opens each and crows with laughter when he sees a sling shot (a bigger and better one than Sammy has) and about a dozen silver soldiers. He literally plops down in a kitchen chair. His mouth hanging open as he looks at the soldiers seeing they are so finely etched that he can see the expressions on their faces. Smiling happily he looks at the two older gents saying, "I reckon I'm the luckiest boy in the world cause ya'll sure has been good to me."

Skinny rubs his woolly head replying, "Cause yar a good boy and you care about others. We think yar a very special young man."

Arty (almost tearfully) looks at all the people around the table saying from his heart, "I'ze never knowd there be good folks like ya'll in the world. I'ze never met anyone like ya'll in St. Louie. No one cared about us'uns much there but here we be people and bein' free people is so much better than bein' servants to someone else. I don't haveta remember to say Yes, Sir, and No, sir, or duck to miss bein' hit for nuthin'. Ya'll cain't know how good it feels to be free and have friends like ya'll in our lives."

Everyone is speechless for a minute then Glory kneels down in front of him taking his callused hands she explains, "Arty, I'm right sorry ya'll were treated that way in St. Louie. It would be very hard for me if'n I was treated that way. But ya know what I think?"

Arty shakes his head no wonderingly.

"If'n ya hadn't gone through that in St. Louie ya wouldn't appreciate all ya have now and ya wouldn't understand someone else that has gone through what ya'll has. Maybe God needs ya to help someone that will come into yar life who has been through what ya'll's been through. The Bible says everythang happens for a reason and we don't know why but God knows why and HE does it or allows it for a reason. One reason that I sees is Sammy. Cuz of ya'll Sammy had a better life. Sammy became yar brother in St. Louie. So if'n ya can remember it was for a purpose....God's purpose then maybe ya won't feel mad or angry about it."

Arty lays his hand on Glory's beautiful cheek replying, "Ya got a good heart, Glory. I sees what yar saying and I'm gonna remember it and I'ze gonna pray about it. Yar right about Sammy boy, I'ze loves him like my brother and I'ze be real sad not to have him in my life."

The stricken look fades from everyone's faces as they watch Glory's intent face and hear her words and Arty's answers sooth the hearts of all who hear it knowing that healing is on the way for him and his family.

Quickly the girls start washing Minnie's new dishes, silverware, pots and pans and handing Minnie a wet cloth she washes the lovely lamp globe and base then Benny sets it on the mantel beside their new clock. Joe shows Benny how to wind it and set it so faintly the tick tick tick of the clock sounds in the room. Soon a delicious meal is set on the table and everyone gathers around the table for the blessing which Benny gives: "*Lord, we are so blessed today. I cain't find all the right words to thank ya for bringin' us to such wonderful folks. They have blessed our lives beyond words. Thank ye, Lord, for the blessings yar has sent to us and bless all those who brung'em to us'uns. Lord, please hep us to show'em just how much we appreciate all their kindnesses to us'ns. We humbly ask yar continued blessings on all of 'em. In your Son's Blessed Name we pray, Amen.*"

"Amen," is heard around the room then the feast begins.

After the meal is over Elizabeth and the girls start washing the dishes and cleaning up the kitchen while Minnie sits and rests.

Joe walks over to Benny asking, "Could I talk to ya a few minutes outside, Benny?"

Smiling happily Benny replies, "Certainly, Big Joe." They walk out towards the barn as Joe starts explaining, "When Lizbeth's folks died they realized they hadn't treated ya'll in a good way. They left ya'll a small amount of money to hep ya start yar life." Joe hands Benny a pouch of money, it is pretty heavy as it holds five twenty dollar coins in it.

Benny's eyebrows raise and he starts to say something when Joe smilingly requests, "Please just take it and know we want'cha to have it. There is something else I'd like to tell ya about that is kinda hard to explain. But bein' our friends I might be a callin' on ya to help me outta a hard time that maybe comin'."

"We's do anythang we can to hep out, Big Joe. Yous always been more than fair to us'uns," Benny replies quickly.

Taking a deep breath and turning to look Benny in the eyes Joe explains, "Benny, I've never done anythang to expect ya to hep me when I need it. I only did what I consider right. Don'tcha feel ya'll owe us anythang, cause ya don't. What we gave ya is freely a gift and nothin' more. I'm not a man to expect somethang back for a kindness. Do ya understand what I'ma tryin' to say?"

"Sure Joe. Yar not a man with strings attached to yar good deeds. What is a worryin' ya?" Benny asks concerned as he sees the distress on Joe's face.

"It seems that Edgar had bride contract on my girls and Elizabeth. He planned to send'em to France this fall. Those people may come to git my girls and I need everyone to be alert for me and I'ma askin' ya to hep me keep my family together," Joe explains sadly.

"France, that's in Europe, Beth Ann showed me on a map one time? Bride contracts? Ya said Elizabeth, too? He was gonna send her to a man in France? The girls? Glory wouldn't do that ever! She loves Jake with all her heart...we all can see that. Beth Ann???? No...no...that would kill her heart and break her wonderful spirit. Joe, we won't let this happen to our girls! No way will this happen. Ya'll can count on all of us to be here and hep anyway we can," Benny states furious as he walks around the hay in the barn. He shakes his head no and looking at Joe states, "Edgar Hawkins be a mean man. He done thangs that were real bad. I knowd about some but nuthin' I could do about'em. He liked doing it which is even badder in my book. I'ze never thought he'd do this though! He loved Lizbeth at least he acted like it all the time. He watched her like a hawk always a thinkin' look on his face but I'ze never thought he'd do somethang like this to her. Lizbeth know this?"

"Yes, she does and we appreciate yar hep in this. We got some time to plan what to do and don't tell Minnie til the babies are born. She will feel hepless now and worry when she don't need to. I probably shoulda waited to ask ya but it lays heavy on my heart right now," Joe explains thoughtfully.

"Friends hep whenever they's can. We be always friends, Big Joe! Ya changed our lives from bein' hopeless to bein' hopeful and free. Nothin' ya could ever ask us would we'uns be unwillin' to hep ya with," Benny states from his heart.

"Thank ya," Joe states as he claps Benny on the shoulder.

Suddenly Benny looks up sharply at Joe asking, "What about Sammy boy? Ya didn't mention what theys planned to do with him?"

Joe's lips thin and anguish fills his eyes as he looks down then taking a deep breath he quietly replies, "We figure they planned on killin' him. There weren't any plans written down about his future."

Immediately tears fill Benny's eyes as he stares horrified at Joe then angrily he wipes them away saying, "No one better hurt our Sammy boy. No one! We won't let that happen!" Gulping down the tears that are threatening to fall Benny's lips quiver with the effort then shaking his head no again he softly swears, "We ain't neva gonna let that happen. Neva."

Joe gulps down his own sudden tears before replying, "No, we won't let that happen." Then he continues, "Lizbeth is the only one that knows about this right now. We are gonna tell the girls about them comin' but never tellin' Sammy about what they woulda done to him. Don't tell Arty anythang yet either, okay? He don't need to worry about it. Nothin' we can do about it until these gents arrive."

"We be prepared to hep at any time, Joe. Anythang to keep'em all safe, we will do," Benny promises as an oath.

Joe nods yes then his eyes light up as he jokingly explains, "I have one more surprise for ya, Benny. But it will cost ya a couple of dollars. But it is somethang that they say ever woman wants, if'n ya want one."

Taking a steadying breath and chuckling Benny replies, "Okay, what'cha got Joe?"

Joe pulls a small pouch out of his pocket then opening it says, "For two dollars ya can pick out a weddin' band for Minnie. They ain't never been worn and I noticed Minnie don't wear one. So if'n yar interested then ya can choose the one ya like."

"A weddin' ring! We never had no money for one if'n Minnie even be allowed to wear one. Let's see it be fourteen years this Summer since we got hitched. Minnie like one real well. But I don't know what size she wear and her hands be all swollen up right now so don't know what I should do," Benny explains as he looks at the shiny bands in Joe's hand. All are gold bands, some have etchings on them. Benny picks up one that has birds circling around it. He looks at it closely then asks, "She like this real well but don't know what to say Joe. What should I do?"

"Think about it and when yar ready the rings will be at my house and ya'll can choose whichever one ya like," Joe answers slipping the rings back into the pouch then back into his vest pocket.

Benny thinks a few minutes before explaining, "I'ze do wanna git her one. It will make me feel proud to do that. Be nice for Minnie to see'em and pick out the one she likes best, too."

"If'n ya want Minnie to pick it out after the babies come and her swellin' down then just tell me and ya'll can choose whichever one ya like," Joe explains again smiling at his good friend.

"Thank ya very much, Joe. We appreciate ya," Benny repeats as they walk back towards the house.

Walking back into the house Joe advises, "We'd better be gettin' back home now. Sammy git yar clothes and horse ready, son."

Sammy hasn't left Glory and Beth Ann's sides since they have arrived, even helping with the dish drying. He never stops talking to them and asking question after question. He nods yes and after hugging Minnie, Benny and Arty he gathers his small bundle of clothing before saddling his horse and is ready to head home with his family.

"Glory, did you bring me lots of surprises from St. Louis?" Sammy asks his small face full of pleasure.

"Yep! We shorely did," Glory chuckles answering him then nudging him says, "I'd race ya home but I cain't give ya nothing til everyone gets there so go pester Jake and Beth Ann about it, cause I'm not a tellin' ya nuthin' else."

"Humppp," Sammy mumbles with a pout.

She laughs delightedly at his pout so consolingly explains, "We brought ya some candy. Bet Mama will let'cha have some tonight."

"Yee haw!" Sammy cries out and rides over to Beth Ann and Jake trying to wheedle information out of them.

Laughing they give him very little (but teasing) on the ride home.

Sammy arrives home from his "vacation" at Minnie and Benny's full of anticipation of all the presents he will be receiving. He is a little more tan than before due to helping Benny in the field planting, toting rocks out of the field, hoeing, helping paint and running errands back and forth to the house. He feels wanted and that is the best reason of all to be happy.

The Gray family and Jake ride slowly back to the Rocking J Ranch tired but so happy to have given Minnie, Benny and Arty such wonderful surprises.

Riding into the yard Earl walks out of the barn asking, "How about I take your horses for you? You all looked tired out."

Smiling gratefully Elizabeth answers, "Yes, we are and we appreciate your kindness, Earl. We are all very tired." Everyone isn't as tired as she is but they are not going to have a baby so they just smile and thank Earl as he takes the horses into the corral then drives the wagon to the side of the barn and parks it.

Sammy rushes into the house saying, "Can I see my surprises now? Please please!"

Joe and Elizabeth smile at each other and tell Beth Ann and Glory, "Take him to his room please girls."

Sammy has been back to the house but not since it was completed so he looks expectantly at Joe asking, "My room? I have a room all to myself?" He looks up towards the ladder that goes up into the little attic loft and frowns.

Glory takes his hand leading him down the hallway to his room saying, "This way little man....you have a big room now!"

Surprised he looks over at Beth Ann (who is smiling happily at him) as she follows them.

Walking into his new room he just stands and stares at the big room with HIS bedroom furniture from St. Louis all set up in it. "Wow! Lookee at this, I never expected this!" Sammy states as he touches the bed, dresser and desk then looks up at the wall of shelves Joe had built on one wall. His mouth just hangs open in surprise as he looks at every little thing in the room. Tears come to his eyes as he realizes he no longer has a home in St. Louis and he thinks on this for a minute realizing, "I wasn't happy there so why am I sad now?" Blinking he looks at the nice wooden floor and the rugs covering it then taking a deep breath he says, "It is better than I ever thought it would be. This is home....my own home now. I didn't realize I missed some of my things but I did and it feels real good having them. Thank you for bringing them to me." Still a little teary eyed he remembers his Grandmother Lora telling him, "Take care of what you have Samuel...it maybe all you ever get." Nodding yes at the memory Sammy vows to take good care of this gift of furniture. Turning around he looks at Joe and Elizabeth explaining, "I never thought about having my own bedroom until I was at Minnie and Benny's and they don't have much...well...not as much as we have and I thought how unfair it is that I have so much and they don't and when I told Minnie she said, "Sammy, we gots what we needs and we be happy with what we's got. We will get better when we needs it so don'tcha worry none about us'uns." I have thought about that a lot, Papa and Mother. I'm real lucky to have you. Thank you for taking such good care of me all my life. I'm sorry I'm a trial somedays and I will try to be better."

Shocked at this grown up speech Elizabeth doesn't know how to answer so just looks at Joe who is smiling happily at Sammy.

"Sammy ya have a good heart in ya. Ya care about others and that is a great way to be. Minnie and Benny are sorta just startin' out. It will take them awhile afore they have nicer thangs and sometimes it is real nice to get those nice thangs for yarself. I don't know if Benny knows how to build with wood like I do or Jake does but we will be here to hep'em larn when they are ready to. That is what friends and family do...they hep each other...just like ya hepped them these past days. Sammy yar old enough to larn how to make beautiful thangs, too. Sometimes it just takes time to get all the nice thangs ya'd like to have.

"Don't forget Sammy boy, Pokey and I know how to build things too and we will be around to teach you thangs you want to know how to do," Skinny adds smiling down at his great grandson.

"I am a lucky boy. I realized that when ya'll were gone because I missed my sisters and Jake and I never had a grandpa I could talk to before and have fun with so I wanted to remember to tell ya'll that I really missed both of you, too, and I'm glad you are gonna live here with us because you are really fun to be around. It is nice to know I'm loved so much," Sammy seriously states as he looks around the room at his family.

Beth Ann and Elizabeth look sadly down at the floor for a minute as this truth hits them in the face....how unloved Sammy felt in St. Louis...both don't know what to say when they feel Sammy's hand reach for both of theirs and he smiles at them and winks so much like Joe that they can't keep from smiling weakly back at him. He nods yes that all is okay now. Both take a deep breath still feeling bad but not quite so much.

Clearing his voice Jake asks, "Want to see the presents we brought you?"

"I shorely do!" Sammy states jumping up and down happily.

"We brought ya everythang ya asked for from yar room," Glory clears her voice starting when Beth Ann interrupts with, "And no short pants!"

Everyone laughs as Sammy mimes wiping sweat off his brow and laughs with them.

Opening the trunk Jake pulls out two Stetsons – one black and one white handing them to Sammy who looks at Joe stating, "I look more like you now, Papa!"

Nodding yes, Joe agrees, "Yes, ya do, son."

Then Jake reaches back into the trunk picking up some wrapped boxes and hands them to Sammy.

Smiling happily Sammy lays them on the bed and rips them open seeing new board games to play saying, "Oh, I wanted this game. Thank you, Beth Ann, you knew I wanted these." Then he hugs her for remembering.

Next Glory hands him new books from the mercantile about birds, animals and story books. Sammy laughs happily and carries them over to his bookcase in the wall and immediately puts them there.

Reaching farther down into the trunk Jake hands Beth Ann and Glory stacks of pants, shirts, long johns, socks and shoes including two pair of cowboy boots...one for now and one to grow into.

"These are from the mercantile, Sammy. Jake picked out ones he thought you would like," Beth Ann explains smiling at his happiness.

Looking up at Jake, Sammy smiles saying, "Thank ya Jake. I appreciate you choosing such nice ones for me and thank ya for remembering Benny and Arty...they needed them, too."

Jake lays his hand on Sammy's shoulder and looking him seriously in the eyes explains, "Sammy ....you know this world we live in can be a hard place to be sometimes....guess maybe you know that and have now seen a different world to live in...I think yar blessed cause you got to see both ways of living and so did Arty. I think you and Arty are gonna be real fine men when you grow up because of it."

"We's already talked about it and we ain't gonna let others beat up on the ones that can't fight back...we are gonna be tough men like you and Papa and Grandpa's Skinny and Pokey but we are gonna be nice, too," Sammy explains shaking his head yes he understands.

Pokey leans down explaining, "Sammy I've seen many bad men and lots of men have done bad things cause they didn't have a loving family in their lives. You are real lucky cause ya have a big loving family and so does Arty and if he had doubts before about being loved he shouldn't now. It all comes down to choices we make in our lives....just pray about those choices when they come up and do what God tells ya to do and ya'll be fine."

Sammy seriously listens then shaking his head yes states, "Papa told me about that not long ago, ya know, think about what I'm going to do and I am trying real hard to do that."

"I think yar doing real good, son," Joe states patting his shoulder before continuing, "And that is what happens when ya listen with yar heart instead of yar head."

Chuckling Skinny asks, "Still got you some more presents, Sammy boy. Are you ready for another one?"

"I'm always ready for another present," Sammy states smiling widely.

They all laugh at this true statement...who isn't.

Pokey exaggerates reaching into the trunk and pulling out nothing and handing it to Sammy.

Sammy raises his eyebrows at him curiously then reaches out his hands for something invisible.

Pokey chuckles and drops a small wooden whistle onto Sammy hand. It is very small and carved beautifully.

Curiously Sammy puts it to his mouth and gives a little toot on it. It is wooden so it gives out a hollow echoing sound.

Both of the girls look at the whistle and frowning Glory asks, "Grandpa I never saw this at the store...where were they?"

"I didn't either," Beth Ann admits looking again at the toy.

"That's cause I took'em all and hid'em in my pocket so I could surprise ya'll with'em," Pokey chuckles as he hands each person a small whistle on a string.

Each person toots their whistle amazed that they all sound different. Smiling each one says thank you and puts their new toys in their pockets.

Sammy looks at his and then at Grandpa Pokey stating, "This here whistle could save my life if I was hurt and ya'll were looking for me and couldn't find me."

Skinny answers ruefully back, "Yes, sir, that could happen and it could spook the cattle and horses into stampeding so watch when you use it, son."

"Oh," Beth Ann and Sammy say looking at each other.

"I guess this is one of those presents to be careful with," Sammy explains nodding his head yes.

Jake laughs a little saying, "That's true and so it is with these two toys we brought back for you." So saying he pulls out two long bundles handing them to Sammy.

Smiling happily Sammy lays them carefully on the bed untying the string from around them. Inside the first package are two wooden swords with elaborate carving on them.

Silently Jake hands Joe two small packages and nods yes to him that this is something Joe has requested.

"We brung ya two swords so ya could play fight with someone else," Glory explains smiling down at Sammy.

With his eyes huge he smiles saying, "Arty and I can have a bunch of fun being soldiers and fighting each other. Thank you for the swords." Then turning towards the second wrapped package he pulls the string holding it and sees a wooden rifle...it also has beautifully detailed carving on it.

"This is a play rifle so you can get used to carrying one around when you are old enough to have a real one," Jake explains smiling happily at Sammy's happy face.

"My first rifle and it is so purdy. I will take good care of it, too," Sammy promises as he runs his hands up and down the stock of the gun.

"Just a few more presents then ya can play with yar toys, Sammy. I wanted ya to have somethang I always wanted as a boy. So I asked Jake to find ya some," Joe explains as he hands Sammy two wrapped packages. Sammy's eyes light up happily at getting more presents.

Inside the first package is a bag which makes a funny sound when Sammy shakes it softly then he smiles as he states, "Marbles! I bet it has marbles in it." Opening it he pours out a handful of multicolored large marbles on his bed and everyone looks at the bright colors and exclaims on how pretty they are.

"I never had any marbles, son, so if you know how to play I'd like to larn too so we can play together," Joe explains with an inquiring look.

"I know how to play, Papa, I just never had anyone to play with. They wouldn't let me go outside and play in the dirt like I needed to so I know how to shoot them and know the rules but just haven't played much," Sammy explains with joy in his eyes.

"Well since Shorty and I had some marbles when we were young'uns I bet we could take ya'll on someday when Joe gets good at it," Jake teases as he elbows Joe in the ribs.

"Might make it a tournament then...Skinny and I raised us a bunch of boys and they all played marbles...we saw to it they had'em and we taught'em how to play so guess maybe we "might" be the best ones around here," Pokey states breathing on his fingernails and buffing them on his shirt.

Everyone laughs at his teasing as Sammy states, "That would be fun!"

So a marble tournament will be played in the near future.

"I have one more for you son," Joe announces handing Sammy the second bag Jake had handed him.

Sammy smiles happily as he opens it and finds it full of small marbles. Cocking his head to the side he looks at Joe curiously.

"When I was cowboyin' around one ranch had this game called Chinese marbles that uses colored marbles or pegs with it. I can make the board but I didn't have any marbles so I asked Jake to find at least six marbles in different colors cause six people can play this game of marbles or one or two and I think it will be a fun time playin' it again," Joe explains with excitement in his eyes.

"What a good idea, Joe. I would like to learn how to play," Elizabeth states smiling up at her handsome husband.

"Me, too," is echoed around the room.

Looking at all his presents Sammy states, "Thank you all for being so good to me. I love the presents and Mother I will take care of them and put them up so nobody falls over them. I am growing up fast so I will be responsible with them. Thank you for remembering me. I love ya'll."

Everyone hugs him and tells him how happy they were to bring him presents when Skinny and Pokey remember Beth Ann's surprise they brought her.

Skinny clears his voice saying, "Pokey and I found out that Lora had bought a birthday present for Beth Ann's 13th birthday. We know that ain't until January 14th but thought she should enjoy having it now instead of waiting so long to get it. What do ya say Joe? Can we give it to her now?"

Of course they had already told Joe and Elizabeth about the small piano because it is in a crate in the barn so Joe takes a deep breath looking down at his wide eyed daughter hopefully looking up at him so smiling says, "I think that would be a good idea, grandpas, she will treasure it knowin' her Grandma Lora wanted her to have it."

Jiggling in place Beth Ann can't wait to see what her present is so just giggles happily.

"Let's go out to the barn and open it in there so there won't be anything to mess up my floors," Elizabeth advises so they all walk out to the barn where Joe removes a tarp from a large crate.

Beth Ann looks at the large crate curiously not knowing what it can be. "Humm…what would Grandmother have wanted me to have?" she wonders as Joe and Jake take pry bars and start dismantling the crate. When she sees the gleaning wood on the back of the piano she lets out a cry of happiness stating, "It is a piano! Grandmother said she would get me one when I was older!" Jumping up and down she cries happy tears at receiving such a nice present. Turning to her mother she invites, "You can play on it too, Mother. You play beautifully."

"Thank you, Beth Ann. I'm sure we will enjoy having such a wonderful gift at the house. I even know how to tune one, when this one needs it. Father…uh…Edgar made me learn when I was young so he wouldn't have to pay someone to tune the one we had at hom….in St. Louis. What happened to one we had in St. Louis?" Elizabeth explains then asks curiously.

"We gave it to the Baptist Church cause theirs was fallin' apart," Glory advises as she explains then continues, "We gave it in memory of Grandmother and Edgar."

"That was a very nice thing to do…Mother would have appreciated your thinking of her," Elizabeth states hugging both girls for their thoughtfulness.

"We told'em they should sell it to the church or even the theater but their kind hearts told'em differently," Skinny advises with pride.

"It was the right thing to do," Beth Ann quietly states as she admires the small piano. Beth Ann asks, "Shall we put it in the parlor, Papa? That way everyone can see it and enjoy the music when it is played."

Looking at Elizabeth (who nods yes) Joe agrees, "Sounds good to me."

Looking around Jake says, "Glory don't forget to get the little chair out of the other crate."

Looking around they see another much smaller crate with Beth Ann written on it, Glory pries open the top and picking up the small seat carries it into the house to set in front of the piano.

Looking at the piano Joe asks, "Jake and grandpas do ya think we can carry this into the house by ourselves?"

"Jake and Randy Ford loaded it in St. Louie…don't think it is too heavy," Skinny advises as they all reach down and pick up a corner then easily carry it inside the house.

Beth Ann stops at the door of the barn and silently prays, "*Dear Lord how lucky I feel to be here and know I am loved so much by everyone. Even though Grandmother and Grandfather Hawkins aren't here anymore please tell them thank you for remembering me. I did love them, Lord. I know they did wrong but it doesn't take away all the good they did for me. I don't understand why they did some things they did but hope you will remember they did lots of nice things for us. Thank you for all the blessings you have given me and help me to always be thankful for your wonderful blessings. In Jesus Name I Pray. Amen.*"

MIRACLES OF BIRTH
Chapter 22

"God grants us blessings for life in the birth of a child."

Waking Minnie feels different so smiling thinks, "Maybe today my babies will be born. *Please dear Lord, let'em be all right."* Minnie sits up slowly in bed noticing (as usual) that Benny is already up and gone. Smiling she says to herself, "Okay, this is gonna be easy this time. No problems and nothin' will go wrong. *Please Lord no problems this time I'ze been real careful like and not done anythang to lose these precious babies. Please give me the strength and will power to give birth easy this time. Thank ya, Lord. Amen."*

Looking in Arty's room Minnie notices he is gone also so taking a deep breath she smiles as her eyes light up happily as she states out loud, "Today I'll have my babies!" She hums as she fixes breakfast for her men and when they walk in they see her good mood so Benny asks, "What's makin' ya so happy today Minnie?"

"Today our babies will be born. Labor has started," Minnie replies happily.

Blood drains from Benny's smiling face as he jumps up saying, "Sit down, Minnie. Take it easy. How fast ya think these babies be?"

"It's early yet. Labor just started a little while ago. I be fine and so will these precious babies. Don'tcha go a worrin' about us, we be all right," Minnie happily replies.

Benny and Arty look at each other and Benny remembers the last two times when Minnie lost the babies and how she had been in such pain before they were stillborn so narrowing his eyes he looks at Arty nodding yes. This unspoken signal is something they had decided on earlier, so as soon as breakfast is over Arty saddles his horse and heads over to Joe's house.

Riding up into the yard he calls out, "Lizbeth! Big Joe!"

Elizabeth immediately walks out of the kitchen wiping her hands off asking, "Arty is somethin' wrong?"

"Ma said the babies are a comin' today. She seems to be doin' good but we'd feel better if'n ya would come over," Arty asks with an anxious face.

"I'll be right over. Are you going to ask Yellow Moon to come, too?" Elizabeth questions hopefully.

"Yes, madam. Yalla Moon asked me to come and git her as soon as ma's labor started," Arty replies then tipping his hat he rides towards Good Heart's home.

When Good Heart sees Arty waving his hat he calls to his wife, Yellow Moon, saying, "Minnie needs ya."

Yellow Moon picks up her medicine pouch walking out just as Arty arrives ready to ask her to come.

"Is Minnie hurtin' bad?" Yellow Moon quickly asks Arty.

"No, madam, it's just startin'," Arty replies anxiously.

Yellow Moon pats his leg replying, "A birthin' takes time. Don'tcha worry so. I'll get my horse and be right over."

She turns to her children requesting they watch the baby while she is gone then Good Heart gives her a leg up on her painted mustang and she follows Arty out of the yard. They meet Beth Ann, Glory and Elizabeth at their ranch in the yard waiting for them. Yellow Moon softly advises, "No need for all to come. It will be some time before babies come."

Blushing Beth Ann requests, "I need to help, if I can."

Yellow Moon nods at Beth Ann saying, "Being there will help. Let's go."

Quickly they ride over to Minnie and Benny's just as Minnie is changing the bed making it ready to have the babies. Elizabeth and Glory immediately take over this chore with Glory asking, "What is all this paddin' needed for?"

Elizabeth explains, "There is water that breaks before the baby comes and then there is the afterbirth after the baby comes. We need to protect the mattress from all this."

Nodding yes Glory replies, "Of course, I remember, I've seen cows and horses birthin', just forgot for a minute."

Putting her hand on Glory's shoulder she asks, "Glory it would be good for you to see how a child is born. It is different from animals in a lot of ways. Would you like for me to ask Minnie if you can stay in the room when the babies are born?"

Looking at her mother intently before replying Glory states, "It would be a good idea. I might be able to help ya when ya have my brother or sister."

Now Elizabeth blushes replying, "You never know it could happen that way."

When asked, Minnie immediately answers, "Of course, I'd be right proud for ya to hep me with the babies especially since there be two to take care of."

Yellow Moon explains in detail what to do to Glory and Beth Ann listens intently (even though she isn't supposed to) thinking, "I remember bringing a book about doctoring with us from St. Louis. I'm going to read all about babies before Mother's time comes. She might need my help."

Elizabeth also talks to her girls explaining about what will be happening as she has had three children and knows the routine well.

Soon Stephie rides in with Carrie Lynn beside her and they knock on the door where they are eagerly greeted. Stephie advises, "Joe promised to let us know as soon as you heard Minnie is in labor so we could help, too."

"I thank ya for comin' to hep me," Minnie states as she hugs them.

Minnie's pains are getting harder now so they all take turns walking her around the house.

Stephie has thoughtfully brought a sack of red beans so she starts cooking red beans with ham hock in it for later as they all take turns helping out where they are needed.

Benny and Arty walk in numerous times while trying to do their chores. Beth Ann and Carrie Lynn make sandwiches for the noon meal and eat the cookies that Beth Ann had brought with her for dessert.

At three in the afternoon Minnie's labor is in full force and after her water breaks she is weakly put to bed for the remainder of the labor. Glory and Beth Ann take turns sponging off her face as the pains come closer together.

Carrie Lynn boils the required water and helps Arty fill a couple of tubs full of cold water to put the bed sheets in after the birth. Elizabeth shows the girls how to have a little dishpan ready to mix warm water in to bathe the babies after they are born and to dress them quickly to keep them from getting chilled.

Yellow Moon looks Minnie in the face saying, "I stay with you the whole time. Lizbeth and Stephie take care of yar babies. Everythang be fine. Don'tcha worry none. Okay?"

Smiling weakly Minnie replies, "I trust ya'll."

When the pains are very close together Elizabeth advises, "Beth Ann and Carrie Lynn it is time to leave the room. Minnie needs her privacy now."

Both plead to stay but their mothers say no that they are too young right now to experience this. Glory stays and helps where she is needed and learns a lot about birthin' a baby.

Arty and Benny walk the floor in the kitchen now going around and around the kitchen table as they listen for every little noise in the bedroom. Benny walks to the bedroom door many times, talks to Minnie a few minutes then is shooed out a number of times. Yellow Moon assures him that all is going well and not to worry.

Carrie Lynn and Beth Ann are so nervous that they start making cornbread for supper then two pies to celebrate the births of the babies. Benny encourages them to make cream pies as Minnie loves them so they spend a lot of time decorating the crust and fixing the evening meal.

Minnie's labor is hard as she gasps, "Cain't believe how hard it is to have the babies when it is so easy acarrin'em."

Yellow Moon soothes her and talks softly to her and soon the first baby is being born. Yellow Moon and Elizabeth encourage her to push a little harder and Minnie does then the head appears and Glory watches in awe as Yellow Moon cups the head and cleans out the mouth. Minnie gives another push and out the little body comes and starts a wailing.

All laugh as they hear Benny shout *"Amen, Lord, Amen,"* from the kitchen.

Yellow Moon motions for Glory to tell Minnie, "Ya have a beautiful little girl, Minnie!" Glory glows with happiness at the beautiful baby.

Yellow Moon and Elizabeth tie the knot in the umbilical cord then Stephie quickly wraps the baby in a soft cloth and shows the beautiful little girl to Minnie.

Minnie tenderly touches her face as the baby's cries fill the air.

The second baby is on her way out quickly and a minute later out pops her little head then with another push her tiny body lands in Yellow Moon's hands. She quickly cleans this baby's mouth out and soon the wail of the second baby is heard through the house.

Benny and Arty do a dance with Carrie Lynn and Beth Ann in the kitchen as they all laugh happily at hearing the babies cry.

The second time Glory ties the cord with string and Elizabeth wraps the infant in a blanket and takes her to Minnie to see.

"You are blessed with another daughter," Elizabeth happily states.

Minnie smiles happily at the baby as tears flow down her sweaty face she asks, "They both look healthy, don't they?"

"Yes, they both look very healthy," Elizabeth reassures her.

Benny and Arty watch as Stephie bathes the first little girl and after she is bathed, diapered and put in Benny's arms they head back towards the bedroom.

Walking out Elizabeth shows Benny his second daughter requesting, "Wait just a few minutes more. The afterbirth hasn't come yet."

Glory walks towards the door to follow her mother when Yellow Moon requests, "Glory, stay and help." She shows her how to rub the stomach to get the afterbirth to break free and flow out. Minnie groans at the process but doesn't say a word then the afterbirth gushes out and Yellow Moon tiredly says, "Minnie, all is right. No problems."

Minnie chuckles tiredly saying, "*Thank ya, Lord. Thank ya so much!*" Tears of happiness flow down her tired face as Glory and Yellow Moon start cleaning her and the bed up. The sheets are removed and put into cold water to keep them from staining. A fresh night gown is put on Minnie after she is bathed and the bed remade. Sitting down on the bed beside Minnie, Yellow Moon explains then asks, "Friend, ya did good. Ya don't have no tearin' so ya'll heal fast. Ready for Benny and the babies to come in?"

Minnie pulls her friend's face down kissing both of Yellow Moon's cheeks saying from the heart, "Thank ya so much Yalla Moon. Havin' ya here heped me a bunch, I weren't so worried this time. I treasure ya and I thank ya from the bottom of my heart for takin' care of me and the babies today."

Smiling happily at her Yellow Moon leans forward kissing her friends forehead before replying, "We prayed all the time that ya and the papooses be healthy. God answered our prayers. Yar most welcome."

Exhausted Yellow Moon walks out of the room and into the kitchen then sinks wearily into a chair with Glory following. Stephie and Elizabeth are sitting already exhausted from the stress and tensions of the day.

Benny carries one baby and Arty follows with the second baby as they walk into the bedroom to Minnie.

Beth Ann sets a large glass of tea in front of each of them along with a bowl of beans and cornbread so tiredly all the women eat.

Looking at the exhausted women sitting at the table Glory asks, "Was this a hard labor?"

"*Thank God, it wasn't,*" Elizabeth answers truthfully as she looks at the sweat tangled hair around Glory's young face. Then she explains, "Before when Minnie went into hard labor something happened and the baby died before it was born. I don't know why but it happened twice so we were worried it might happen again. Minnie didn't have easy labor then."

"So you were there when she lost the other babies?" Glory asks curiously.

Shaking her head no Elizabeth answers, "I'm sorry to say that I was talked out of helping Minnie during labor. Mother didn't think it was seemly for a white woman to help a colored woman in labor. Sad thing is she insisted Minnie help me when I was in labor with Sammy. I never saw the difference. I did have a colored midwife there for Minnie both times but the babies died anyway."

"Well she had five white women and a red woman to help her today. Maybe that will make up some for the past," Carrie Lynn explains cheerfully. They all look around agreeing as they smile at each other.

Benny and Arty hand the babies to Minnie as they look at the beautiful baby girls. "They look just alike," Arty states looking from baby to baby.

"They do right now but they will change some every day. Which one was born first?" Minnie asks looking at the babies.

Benny picks up the foot of one of them explaining, "This one. Stephie tied a red ribbon on her ankle so we'd be able to tell which one came first."

"That was real smart of her," Minnie answers with a tired smile then asks, "What we gonna name'em?"

"We talked about a lot of names but I like Catie and Connie the best," Benny replies admiring his small daughters.

"Me, too, ma. They sound right," Arty replies as he runs a finger over the tiny foot of one of the babies.

"I'm right fond of those names, too. What about their middle names?" Minnie asks her men.

"Middle names? We ain't got no middle names?" Arty questions before asking, "Do we?"

"Never thought about it much afore but now I think we otta have middle names and the babies should be given'em now they's born," Minnie answers seriously.

"Okay, what names ya thinkin' about?" Benny asks smiling happily as he takes one baby touching her small hand and feels it squeeze his heart with joy.

"Well I'ze been thinkin' about it a lot. We could have Ann for Beth Ann and Lizbeth. We could use Stephie's middle name of ..." Minnie starts when Benny interrupts saying, "These are our babies let's name'em after our family. What middle name would ya chose for yarself, Minnie?"

Blushing Minnie answers, "Mammy's name was Annan. So I thought I'd take Ann as my middle name and Connie's middle name. Then I thought about yar Mammy Benny and her name was Lyna so I thought maybe Catie Lynn for our second girl."

Benny thinks a minute before answering, "Connie Ann and Catie Lynn. Sounds real purdy to me what'cha think Arty?"

Arty thinks a minute or two before replying, "I like those names and I've been thinking about my middle name and I'd like to have Benjamin as my middle name after pa. Arthur Benjamin Freed."

Benny smiles brilliantly at him saying, "I'd be right proud to share my name with my son. What middle name can I have? Have ya thought about any for me?"

Smiling Arty replies, "Gramp's name was Buckley. Ya could use that or just Buck."

Looking down Benny sadly shakes his head no explaining, "Buck is what a colored man is called by white people. I don't like that, pa never liked it either. Our people called him Burk at home. I think Benjamin Burk Freed would be a good name. What'cha think?"

They all look at each other and smiling happily shake their heads yes then Benny states, "Catie Lynn and Connie Ann Freed this is yar Ma Minnie Ann Freed and yar Pa Benjamin Burk Freed and yar big brother Arthur Benjamin Freed. Welcome to the family."

BRINGING JOY TO ALL
Chapter 23

"Find the joy in giving to be more than the joy of receiving."

A few days later after returning home from Minnie and Benny's home Elizabeth sits drinking coffee with her family when Glory asks, "Mother we haven't given ya all the surprises we brought ya from St. Louie. How about we do it now?"

Elizabeth's eyes light up as she smiles happily at them replying, "Oh, yes! That would be wonderful. I've been dying to look into the trunks that you brought back, but I haven't, even though it has been a trial not to."

Pokey and Skinny smile happily at seeing the joy fill all the faces around the table so Pokey replies, "Been kinda like Christmas with gettin' presents like this."

Nodding yes Skinny adds, "Did we tell ya'll that they brought us some surprises too?"

Joe and Elizabeth smile back at them before Elizabeth replies, "They have talked non-stop since getting home and, yes, they told us how much they enjoyed planning some surprises for you two."

"We got more presents that day than we ever got in our lives. Gonna be a memory I'll cherish all my life," Skinny admits smiling at the young people.

Happily Joe answers "Then it was worth the effort, wasn't it young'uns."

Both daughters answer, "Yes, sir!"

Quickly they walk into the parlor where the trunks are sitting waiting to be unloaded. Both of the girls look at each other then walk to the one with the crystal lamp in it and open this trunk first.

Glory sighs saying, "Wish Jake and Carrie Lynn were here to see yar joy in what we brung ya but ya'll can tell'em later." She lifts the lid taking out two Stetsons for Joe handing them to him.

Laughing Joe asks, "How did ya know I needed these?"

Beth Ann wittily answers, "Just by looking at the one you wear all the time."

Chuckling Joe nods yes saying to everyone, "Thank ya."

Beth Ann reaches in and pulls out two pair of boots from the side of the trunk and three readymade shirts and hands them to Joe.

"Well, this is like Christmas. Thank ya again," Joe states delighted with the clothing.

"Mother, this is for ya," Glory states as she picks up a large bundle out of the trunk then kneeling down in front of her mother holds it while Elizabeth starts unwrapping it.

Elizabeth face is animated with joy as she carefully unwraps the crystal lamp. When the globe is uncovered the brilliant green seems to cast a glow into the whole room as Elizabeth raises it saying, "I've never seen anything like it." She carefully hands it to Joe who wonderingly looks at it before setting it down on one of the little end tables as Elizabeth unwraps the rest of it. Layers of white cotton litter the floor in front of her as she reveals the green base of the lamp and sees the small wrapped bundle inside the base. Reaching in she pulls it out unwrapping the sparkling crystals that will hang all around the base of the globe. Elizabeth gasps as she sees the way the light sparkles off the crystals casting rainbows all around the room.

Sammy's eyes are glued to the beautiful lamp as he tentatively reaches a finger out to touch it waiting for someone to say no but no one does. It is so lovely that it just invites people to touch it.

"Glory chose the color for you, Mother. Green since Sammy's and Papa's eyes are green," Beth Ann softly advises into the silence (including Sammy in the surprise, too).

Carefully handing Joe the base and crystals Elizabeth stands and hugs first Glory then Beth Ann saying, "Thank you so much for thinking of me. It is a lovely present. I know I will cherish mine just as Minnie cherishes hers."

"We have a pink one for Stephie and a blue one for our home," Glory explains happily.

"It was a good idea to share'em so each will be treasured. That was a very thoughtful thang to do," Joe states pleased with his daughters' thoughtfulness.

"Stephie will scream when she sees hers," Elizabeth states with a giggle as she looks again at the lovely lamp.

Chuckling Glory replies, "She will probably jump up and down in joy. May we take theirs over to them after our chores are done?"

"Yes, spread the joy around," Joe agrees smiling at his lovely girls.

The girls start pulling out more surprises and soon Elizabeth and Joe are overwhelmed with the gifts given to them. New clothes, hats, shoes are given then Glory explains, "Papa, this is something special for ya. Miss Ella may have to fix it up for ya but here it is." She pulls out a black suit and a white lawn shirt to go with it as Beth Ann picks up two small boxes.

Smiling Joe looks at the suit saying, "That is a fine suit, Glory. What am I gonna need a suit for?" He winks at Beth Ann as he asks this.

"Might be just for church but I'ma hopin' it'll be for my weddin'," Glory jokes back.

"Hummm...guess it will work real well for that," Joe thoughtfully says then bursts out laughing at Glory's sad expression. He picks her up with the suit and gives her a smacking kiss on the cheek saying, "Thank ya for thinkin' of me darlin's."

"These go with it," Beth Ann states biting her lip to keep from smiling as Joe raises his eyebrows taking the two small boxes.

"Did ya bring me a belt buckle in here?" Joe teases as he takes the boxes then opening one he sucks in his breath at seeing a gold finely etched pocket watch that says, "To our Papa" opening it he smiles at seeing a picture of Elizabeth in a tiny frame with a clock face on the other side.

"This is very special and I will always treasure it," Joe softly states from the heart as he kisses each girl's cheek again as he hugs them. Handing the watch to Elizabeth he opens the second box and it contains a set of gold cuff links with G engraved on them. His mouth opens and closes as he looks at them then asks, "How did you get these engraved and how did ya get the writing on the watch?"

"Anything is possible in St. Louis, Papa. I know a jeweler there and he did a rush job for us," Beth Ann explains happily then continues; "We started to put JG on the cufflinks but knew you wouldn't wear them much so just put a G on them so Sammy could use them later."

"Thoughtful and smart! How have I gotten so lucky to have such wonderful daughters?" Joe asks happily looking at his girls.

Looking closely at both items Sammy asks, "Where did you get the picture of mother?"

"Grandfather had a couple of pictures of Mother in his desk so I took this one and we cut it down to fit inside the watch," Beth Ann explains happily.

Joe quickly looks down at the picture as he thinks, "Wonder if he sent one like this to that foreigner? Does he know what Lizbeth looks like?"

"Were...there any other pictures of me in his desk?" Elizabeth faintly asks.

"Yes, we found some good ones of me and you and a sketch of Glory but it didn't look much like her. It showed dark hair and her face wasn't nearly so pretty," Beth Ann innocently answers.

Joe looks over at the grandfathers and they nod yes as Skinny explains, "We brought all of'em to ya with the papers we brought."

Joe nods yes then looking at Elizabeth sadly smiles saying to the girls, "Thank you." Then he thinks, "So those men know what Elizabeth and Beth Ann look like. No way we can change that now, we will just deal with it."

The girls give out more gifts to their parents and Sammy and the happiness it brings the girls makes it a richer surprise to their parents. When Glory hands Joe a small box she smiling says, "This is somethan' I thought you'd like to give to our cowboys."

Opening the box Joe finds it is full of pen knives. Picking one up he says, "I've heard about these little knives but never seen one afore." He lifts one up and sees it is about the size of one of his long fingers then continues, "Thank ya for remembering the men." He lays the small box aside as Beth Ann hands him a large bundle well wrapped in white cloths and smiling happily at him explains, "I know this is something you don't need but it is so beautiful that I wanted you to have it, if you want it."

Joe carefully unties the string holding the material to it seeing a large wooden mantle clock. Large numbers show the time and the case is a golden brown which matches the furniture in the parlor. Before Joe can make a comment on it Beth Ann kneels down in front of him earnestly explaining, "When we saw these mantle clocks we knew we wanted to bring some home. Glory chose one for her new home and Papa we gave the prettiest one to Minnie and Benny because we knew it would be something they will treasure always. Papa to us it is a clock but to them it will be something very special. Glory said the clock in the kitchen was your mother's and that makes it special so it wasn't as important for this one to be that special." She ends her explanation with a hopeful look.

Putting his large hand under her chin and looking into her earnest eyes Joe replies, "Anythang ya give with a lovin' heart is to be treasured.

Ya showed a lovin' and carin' heart by givin' one to Minnie and Benny and yar right they will always treasure it cause it is real purdy but they will treasure it cause ya gave it to'em also. Yar ma and I will treasure this one cause ya put such love in choosin' it for us. Thank ya, honey, for bein' so thoughtful." Joe kisses her cheek then motions for Glory to come over and he kisses her cheek also.

Looking at the clock Elizabeth exclaims, "It is perfect for this room. I couldn't have chosen a better one, thank you, girls."

Beth Ann and Glory smile at each other as Beth Ann takes a deep breath of relief thinking, "I was worried they wouldn't like it but they do."

Walking over to another trunk Glory advises, "Grandpas this is the one ya said ya wanted to give mama."

They look at each other then glancing back at the young'uns Skinny asks, "This is a private one for yar ma and pa. Would you mind goin' into the kitchen while we give it to them?"

The girls look confused as they don't understand why they can't see what is in the trunk but all three obey and leave the room.

Elizabeth gives Joe a puzzled look then looking at her grandfather's asks, "What could be in there that the children shouldn't see?"

Pokey smirks replying, "We'll show ya." They unlock and open the trunk and start pulling out all the women's clothing they had found hidden in the box in the mercantile.

Joe and Elizabeth's eyes are round as saucers as they look at the flimsy and very sexy clothing that is being handed to them. When knee boots with very high heels are brought out Elizabeth gasps saying, "Those would kill my feet!"

Skinny gives her a rueful look before replying, "I don't think the intention is that ya'd be wearin'em long," and chuckles at her blushing face.

Joe's face is rosy; too, as he picks up some of the intimate items and holds them up then looking at Elizabeth he gives her his crooked smile saying, "Well, this is interesting. How did ya come up with these?"

"We found'em in a locked cabinet in the mercantile along with these boxes of rings and watches, the girls chose one watch to give ya and these are the other ones," Skinny explains.

They hand Joe and Elizabeth the three boxes of jewelry then sit back down as Pokey explains, "This box and another box were hidden in a cabinet in the back of the mercantile like Skinny said. The other box was full of black clothes that would fit Edgar and we believe they were used to burn out farmers and do evil deeds. We left all that with Marshal Wheeler. Now the box these were in was full of paddles, whips and other thangs I don't even want to think about. It seems Edgar was into pain and hurtin' others. These clothes don't look like theys been worn and since they belong to ya'll we decided to bring'em to ya. Didn't think ya'd want us to bring the paddles as ya ain't too fond of'em," he ends with a hopeful joke.

Elizabeth gulps blinking rapidly at this news then looking at Joe softly exclaims, "I didn't know him at all. I thought I did...but, I never knew or imagined he was into hurting women like he and Franklin did. He never hurt Mother that I know of. He slapped her a few times but only a few times that I saw. He slapped me a number of times so I guess I got off easy."

"He knew ya would have come back to me if'n he'd beat ya and they didn't want that," Joe answers smiling wanly at her.

Elizabeth mouth drops open as she admits, "Yes, you are right. How sad to realize how little I knew him." She looks at all the fancy clothes then smiling at Joe asks, "Well, darlin', do ya think we could use some of these purdy thangs here?"

Laughing at her use of slang Joe replies, "Why not, some are right nice."

Skinny clears his throat explaining, "Jake got an eye full when he opened the box. It might be nice if'n ya gave Glory some too. Better show her how to wear'em, too."

Joe and Elizabeth look shocked for a minutes then looking at each other burst out laughing when Elizabeth asks, "MEEE??? Let's gather these up and take them to the bedroom, Joe. Then ask the children to come back in."

Quickly they gather up all the items and it is quite a lot so Pokey says, "Why don't we give ya the gift that Lora had bought for ya then maybe ya'll could put these clothes back into the trunk and keep'em there."

Looking at the large pile Joe agrees, "Sounds good to me."

As Pokey and Skinny bring out each set of the party dishes, Joe and Elizabeth are staggered by the beauty and the many different colored sets of dishes. They are lovely with each having a rainbow tint to the bright colors.

Tearfully Elizabeth explains, "Mother always wanted to be the perfect hostess and have exactly the right things for every occasion. I will treasure these and later share them with the girls when they have their own homes. They are really lovely. We could use them for Glory's wedding reception, if we want to."

"Whatever ya want, we will do," Joe answers smiling at her happiness.

Skinny lifts out three bundles from the trunk laying them to the side then he returns all the women's clothing to the trunk before firmly closing the lid.

Elizabeth stands beside the party sets admiring them when the children walked back in…curious, of course. Seeing the beautiful dishes they all walk over to look at them as Pokey and Joe carry the trunk out of the room and down to Joe and Elizabeth's bedroom. Joe stands looking at the large bedroom before advising, "Let's put it behind the dressing screen. It will be less noticeable there. Thanks for hepin' me carry it in here."

Pokey looks around the large neat room as he says, "This be a fine room ya have now. It must be over twice as big as the old one."

"More like three times as big," Joe chuckles explaining, "Lizbeth hated having to squeeze around the bed. Now look at this huge bed, it is certainly big enough for my long legs. It's real nice."

Pokey nods yes then looking down at Joe's booted feet teasingly says, "Guess ya can get yar BIG feet under the covers now. Ya do have some big feet thar son!"

Joe lifts up one foot and looking at it chuckles answering, "Yep, I do. Look at Jake's when he is over here. His feet are much bigger, Glory can use his old boots to plant flowers in when he wears'em out."

They both chuckle as they walk back to the parlor just as Glory and Beth hand Sammy one of the bundles to give to their mother. Smiling happily he hands one to her saying, "Happy Birthday early Mother."

Taking the bundle she carefully unwraps a lovely music box… it has a small blonde boy holding a puppy painted on the top. Elizabeth lets out a gasp saying, "It looks like you Sammy! Isn't it lovely?" She turns the little key on the bottom and tinkling music floats through the air. She hugs Sammy saying, "Thank you so much for the lovely present, honey, it is wonderful." She kisses his cheek and he hugs her back glad that she is happy with the present he had asked Beth Ann to find for her.

Smiling he explains, "I asked Beth Ann to find you a beautiful music box while she was up there. I know you really like them."

"I certainly do and thank you for remembering me," Elizabeth gratefully says as she hugs him again for his thoughtfulness.

Sammy looks over at Glory and Beth Ann winking at them happily.

Beth Ann hands Elizabeth the next bundle saying, "This is from me."

Opening it Elizabeth eyes light up at seeing a beautiful dancing ballerina on the top of the music box. The lovely ballerina has red hair and is smiling brightly.

"I chose this one because I like the tune but mostly because I'm so happy now that I find I am smiling all the time," Beth Ann explains happily.

"It is lovely, honey, and nothing makes me happier than knowing you are happy. Thank you for a lovely present," Elizabeth states sincerely then leaning over kisses Beth Ann's cheek after giving her a hug.

Thoughtfully Glory hands her bundle to their mother and watches as her eyes light up as she opens the third present.

Elizabeth bursts out laughing when she opens the third seeing a blonde headed man riding a large black horse with a blonde haired little girl sitting behind him holding on. Elizabeth declares, "I imagine this happened quite often with you and your papa, Glory. It is perfect. I shall treasure it and your thoughtfulness."

Glory smiles knowing she has made a point and also shown she has a sense of humor with her gift and is pleased that Elizabeth sees it for that.

Standing Elizabeth kisses her then hugging her whispers, "I understand." Then looking around the parlor asks, "Where can I set these to show them off the best?"

Everyone makes suggestions so soon a special place is selected for each music box. Elizabeth looks around the parlor and smiling asks, "Isn't this room nice. It is exactly what I always wanted lovely and homey comfortable and soothing. Thank you everyone for making it so."

Soon all three young people leave in a wagon with Sammy and Glory driving and Beth Ann riding her horse beside the wagon and listening on how to drive a wagon as they head over to Zak's home with the surprises for them loaded in the back. Pokey and Skinny are riding beside the wagon talking and giving helpful but unnecessary instructions to Sammy about driving the wagon. Glory has driven wagons for years so knows how to do it and knows this is the best route to travel to the Ewing's ranch.

They reach Zak's ranch and it is much smaller than Joe's and he has only one cowboy who works for him. Michael Dean grew up with Zak and after his family grew up and moved away then he became a widower he looked up Zak and moved here to work for him. Old but able Gramps is a wizard at fixing things and knows what to do before he is even asked. Gramps (Don Ewing) and Granny Joy Ann live in a small house behind the ranch house. They are Zak's parents who moved to live with them when Payton was born and Stephie was sick for quite some time.

Stephie and Granny Jo have just finished making lye soap so are sitting in chairs under a large tree cooling off when they see the wagon coming up the drive.

Looking down at her oldest dress Stephie jumps up saying, "I'm going to change clothes, I'm filthy. Please entertain them while I'm gone, Ma."

Granny Jo looks down at her stained and dirty clothes saying to herself, "A little hard work gets ya dirty so don't reckon I care if'n I'm dirty or not for unexpected company." She smiles when she sees Glory and they both wave to each other.

Stephie advises the girls that Glory and family are driving up so Carrie Lynn quickly tidies up then walks out to the arriving wagon.

Beth Ann rides right up to Carrie Lynn, dismounting she hugs her best friend then looks over at Joy Ann smilingly saying, "Good afternoon Granny Jo, it is wonderful to see you today."

"What nice manners you have, Beth Ann. It's always a pleasure to see you," she gracefully replies. She looks at Glory whispering, "Are you ever gonna talk that purdy?"

Raising her eyes brows thoughtfully Glory replies, "Probably not," then smiles as they both chuckle. Looking around Glory asks, "Is Jake around? Where are the men?"

"Looking over the stock," Granny Jo answers then looking up at the sun continues, "Bet they will be home in just a little while. It's about eatin' time. I tole Stephie I'd make dumplings to go with the chicken broth she's got simmering so guess I'd better git started on it. See ya, honey."

Granny Jo walks into the house as Stephie walks out looking clean and smelling of perfume. She walks over hugging Glory and Beth Ann then invites them all to come sit on the large porch and have a cool drink.

"It's a good thang that Jake likes to make chairs or else we'd all be a sittin' on the ground," Pokey states as he gratefully accepts a glass of tea.

"Yes, these are the first ones he made. He has gotten better with time but these still mean a lot to us and are in good condition so we continue to use them," Stephie explains as she rubs the smooth arm of the wooden chair she is sitting in.

"We'll he does a fine job makin'em," Skinny states positively as he also rubs the smooth finish on the chair he is sitting in.

Leaning forward Glory explains, "We brought ya'll some surprises from St. Louie but reckon we need to wait til everyone gits here to give'em to ya."

Laughing Stephie replies, "Now that is not nice to say I'm bringing you a present then not give it right to me."

Beth Ann raises her hand over her eyes (shading them) replying, "I think I see them coming now so you won't have to wait long."

The men ride straight to the barn, unsaddle their horses, and let them loose in the corral to run around while they eat.

All five stop at the water stand taking turns washing their hands and faces of the red dirt covering them.

"Ma is making chicken and dumplings right now. Do you want to eat first or get our surprises first?" Stephie asks the men with excitement in her lovely blue eyes.

Gramps laughingly replies, "Know what Stephie wants to do.... get a present. Ma, how long til the dumplings be done?" he calls into the house.

"They's made but not cooked yet. Wanna see the presents the young'uns brought first or eat first?" Granny Jo calls back.

Smiling at his lovely wife Zak answers, "Wait on cookin' the dumplings, ma, I don't think Stephie can wait on gettin' a present."

Stephie jumps up and hugs Zak and his pa then sitting back down calmly states, "Okay, bring on the presents." Everyone laughs as Jake climbs into the back of the wagon with Glory as they open the first trunk.

"Beth Ann, Carrie Lynn and grandpa's will ya hand the presents out for us?" Jake requests. All four eagerly nod yes.

Jake pulls out Stetsons for all the men. He sets his in the top of the trunk then hands the rest to Pokey to hand out.

"We thought ya'd like to have a new hat and we have a plenty of 'em," Skinny says as he hands each man one.

"Why thank ya for thinkin' about us. We appreciate it," Zak replies happily looking at the new hat.

When Beth Ann hands Michael Dean a Stetson he is startled saying, "Well this is right nice of ya. I weren't expectin' any presents. I'm just the hired hand."

"Michael you've been family since you were a little one...don'tcha ever let me hear you say different," Granny Jo states firmly.

Blushing and smiling at the same time, Michael answers, "Yes, madam."

"Ain't had a new hat in five years knowd it was time to be gettin' rid of this old one," Gramps states chuckling happily.

Surprised Shorty looks around saying, "This is real nice. I appreciate it."

Next Glory hands shirts down to Carrie Lynn and she hands them out.

She sets them on the porch in stacks – two shirts for each man then goes back to help more. The men look at the shirts and their eyes round in surprise when Jake hands new pants down to Beth Ann and Skinny walks over and sets the pile of pants beside the shirts.

The men look at each other in surprise when boots, socks and long johns are placed in rows beside the other clothes.

Zak starts to rise up in protest when Granny Jo lays her hand over his whispering, "Don't kill their joy in bringing us surprises. See how happy all of 'em are doin' this."

Zak looks at the glowing faces of his daughter and son then at Beth Ann's and Glory's then over at the grandpa's faces and they all are smiling with joy jumping out for anyone to see. Their eyes are bright and happy with the giving. Sitting back he looks over at Stephie as she smiles happily at him for not saying something to break the happy mood.

When a very long wrapped package is pulled out of the trunk Zak puzzles what it can be. He is watching Jake when Jake looks over at him and pure joy leaps from Jake's eyes as he softly asks Pokey, "Please hand this to my pa for me."

Pokey smiles happily and taking the leather hands it gently to Zak saying, "Ya got a good son there Zak. We got some stories to tell ya about him someday."

Zak nods his head yes he would like to hear the stories as he takes the cumbersome bundle and starts unwrapping it. When the material drops away he looks astonished at all the leather in his hands because it is not cheap to buy leather. Looking up sharply at Jake he starts to ask a question when Pokey steps forward explaining, "Just in case yar thinkin' what are we gonna owe on this. The answer is nothing. Jake saved our lives on the trip. Ya don't owe us nothin' so don't insult us by offerin'."

Zak's mouth opens and closes a couple of times then looking down he blinks a few times before softly saying, "Much obliged. This is overwhelmin'."

Opening the second trunk Glory starts on the female things. She hands two wrapped packages to Beth Ann and Carrie Lynn then standing up Glory explains to everyone, "Jake was real smart when we was wrappin' all these presents cause he used colored ribbon on each trunk to tell us who it goes to or else we'da had to open ever trunk to see who it belonged to. He is a right smart man."

Jake clucks her under the chin blushing and smiling at his lovely lady.

Stephie smiles replying, "He is good at surprises. So is Carrie Lynn. They didn't tell us they had brought all these wonderful things to us."

Beth Ann giggles as she replies, "You ain't seen nothin' yet!"

Everyone chuckles at her humor when Carrie Lynn hands her mother the bundle she is carrying she kisses her cheek saying, "For a beautiful mother."

Blushing Stephie carefully opens the present seeing the lovely silver hair brush, comb and mirror set.

"Oh, my, oh, my, this is beautiful. My old wooden set is about worn out. Thank you very much," Stephie exclaims happily.

Payton opens hers then smiling glumly says, "Thank you very much."

"I don't wanna brush my hair at all and now I get this! Yuk! Where's the toys," she thinks as she smiles a sickly smile at Beth Ann.

Carrie Lynn smiles happily as she opens her comb and brush set, then hugs and kisses the grandpas again for giving it to her. They smile happily at her knowing how much she had wanted it.

Next Glory and Jake hand down dresses, petticoats, material and two sewing boxes with Joy Ann on one and Stephie on the other.

Granny Jo hadn't expected anything so is pleasantly surprised when Carrie Lynn hands her a wrapped bundle. Opening it she smiles at the lovely tin top with her name on it. Happily she opens it seeing needles, thread, buttons, pins and a pair of silver scissors in the box. Looking up she says, "This is the nicest sewing box I've ever seen. Thank ya so much for thinkin' of me."

Beth Ann's face glows with happiness as she explains, "My grandpas made the top and wrote your names and Carrie Lynn, Glory and I filled up the boxes for you."

Leaning down Glory advises, "Truthfully Carrie and Bethy did it. I don't know how to sew and what to use but I picked out colors." She giggles happily as Stephie looks down into the lovely box saying, "It is so lovely. Thank you so much for thinking of us." Setting the box down she stands and kisses both grandpa's cheeks and hugs them.

Pokey chuckles saying, "That is one hug just wait til you see the …uh…prettiest little thang you've ever seen. Then I git another hug and kiss."

Smiling happily, Stephie nods yes, saying, "You shall have it, too."

Smiling happily Jake looks at his mother then whispers to Glory to take this one to his mother. Glory jumps down taking the large heavily bundled present over to Stephie laying it tenderly on her lap. Her eyes are full of joy and so are everyone elses who know of the special joy this little crystal lamp will give Stephie. They all crowd around as Stephie carefully opens the lamp layer by layer. Cotton material falls off her lap onto the porch as she unwraps it. Soon the pink globe appears and sparkles in the light. Stephie gasps and carefully finishes unwrapping it. "Oh, my dears, it is lovely….so lovely…" She carefully hands the globe to Zak who holds it up to the afternoon light as rainbows dance off of it.

Smiling Zak looks happily at Jake winking at him nodding yes saying, "Well done!"

Stephie unwraps the base of the pink lamp exclaiming, "It is beautiful...more beautiful than anything I've ever seen."

Carrie Lynn hides her smile as she requests, "Look inside the base, Mama."

Turning the base around a little Stephie notices a small bundle and pulling it out she hands the base to Shorty and starts unrolling the crystals that hang from the globe then lets out a scream of joy as the sunshine sends rainbows dancing all over the porch.

Stephie dances in her chair in happiness then standing up she leaps into Jake's strong arms hugging and kissing him at the same time. He swings her in a circle as she cries in her happiness of the lovely gift.

When he sets her on her feet she immediately walks to her daughter and Beth Ann hugging them and giving them each a loud smacking kiss on their cheeks.

Standing with her arms folded across her chest Glory states, "I heped!"

Laughing delightfully Stephie grabs her, hugging tightly they swing around in a circle, as they both laugh happily.

Stopping for breath Stephie looks at the two old gents saying, "You two are just wonderful. Thank you...thank you...thank you for all the lovely presents and for taking care of my young'uns on the trip...for allowing them to go...for thinking of us and bringing such wonderful presents back to us."

She hugs and kisses each one half a dozen times more before Zak literally pulls her away helping her sit back down in her chair with the lovely lamp being set in her lap.

Shorty has attached all the little crystals to the pink lamp so now it shines like a beacon and Stephie sits looking at the lovely lamp oblivious to anything around her.

Laughing Zak advises, "We won't get anything outta her for some time as the sparkles have won out."

Beth Ann's smile is the biggest one as she watches the joy they have brought to everyone then looking at Payton realizes she hasn't gotten all her presents yet so quietly asks, "Payton, I brought you some things that were mine that I hope you will like." They walk over to the wagon and climbing up into the back to the first trunk Beth Ann leans down then pulls out a beautiful china doll.

Forcing a smile Payton says, "Thank you, Beth Ann, she is very pretty." But she thinks, "I don't like dolls. I don't play with dolls!"

Carrie Lynn had explained this to Beth Ann but she still wanted to give her one of own dolls so now Beth Ann grinning happily says, "Maybe you will like these better."

Leaning down she picks up a wooden horse with a leather bridle and saddle with a man sitting on top of it then opening a small wooden barn she shows Payton farm animals with tiny chickens and ducks.

Payton's eyes round in surprise and laughing she claps her hands saying, "Oh, this is wonderful. My own farm. There are all kinds of animals here. Oh, lookee here! There is a mother and children to go with the pa. This is the best present ever! Thank you, Beth Ann!"

Folding her arms across her chest Glory stands at the end of the wagon tapping her foot as she says, "Just Beth Ann. I believe Jake and I had a hand in gettin' that for ya."

Laughing gleefully, the usually somber Payton, literally jumps into Glory's arms hugging her then kissing her cheek repeatedly.

Glory hugs her back before saying, "How much do ya weigh now Payton! Yar gettin' real heavy."

Jake plucks his youngest sister out of Glory's arms as she wraps both hands around his neck kissing him repeatedly saying, "Thank ya Jake! I love it!"

Jake kisses her back then whispering softly advises, "Kiss yar sister then the grandpas, honey."

Payton runs over to Carrie Lynn hugging her and standing on tip toes kisses her cheek then she runs over the grandpas seriously asking, "Are ya'll my grandpas, too?"

Skinny's smile almost breaks his face as he happily replies, "If'n ya want us to be we be honored."

"Good!" Payton replies as they pick up the tiny little eight year old girl and hug and kiss her right back.

Payton looks over at Sammy as he is smiling watching everyone being so happy then walks over to him snidely asking, "Did you help? Do I need to thank you, too?"

Sammy wants to give her a shove for her ornerness but knows that would be wrong so just looks down at her from his superior six inch taller height saying, "Nope and I certainly don't want'cha to ever thank me for anythang."

"Don't worry that is somethang I never want to do," Payton snarls back at him then giving her head a toss walks away from him.

"Girls! Don't know why they are so irritating," Sammy mutters to himself.

"This last trunk is full of thangs for Carrie Lynn a payin' her for all her hard work on the road and in St. Louie. She was a hard workin' young lady and she was an angel on the trip. Not one time did she cause us any worry....well except being kidnapped by the Indian braves...but that weren't her fault," Skinny explains as Shorty and Jake carry the trunk into the house and set it in Carrie Lynn's room.

The Ewing's think this is all so everyone starts shaking hands and saying over and over thank you so much for all the wonderful presents.

When Pokey states, "The young'uns brought ya'll most of the presents. They have given ya theirs but we brought a few more thangs for ya'll. In case ya'll don't know Jake and Carrie Lynn hepped out all along the way. We had to go to St. Louie to do a real hard thang cleaning out the store and house. They were a great help. They never complained. They did more than we could have asked of'em. Then Jake saved our lives during the ambush. This is a small repayment for all of that." He walks over to the last long trunk opening it starts laying pistols and two rifles out on the floor of the wagon then ammunition beside the guns. He lays out five sets of holsters...all plain ones...and a very small gun and holster for Carrie Lynn. Pokey explains, "We started teachin' Carrie Lynn how to shoot and she needs more lessons. She had to use one of our pistols and they were too big for her so we found one just her size at the store. The holsters are plain. We didn't have any time to decorate'em for ya'll. That is something Skinny is really good at. I'm passable but he is really good." Pokey looks over at Skinny nodding for him to continue.

"We are hopin' this winter when it's real slow maybe we could show ya'll how we do it and hep ya decorate yar own gun belt. It is a joy for us to do it. I tole Benny that I'd teach'em how and I'd be proud..... we'd be proud to teach ya'll what we know about it too," Skinny explains hopefully.

Zak, Don, Michael and Shorty all stare in amazement at the guns laying there and when Zak opens his mouth to say something, Pokey explains again, "Jake saved our lives and we pay our debts. There ain't no way we are gonna take any money for our gifts to ya'll. So don't insult us by asking."

Zak shuts his mouth looking bewildered at Skinny and Pokey and doesn't know what to say.

Narrowing his eyes as he looks at the two old gents Shorty asks, "Well if my brother and sisters call ya grandpa that must mean ya'll are mine too?"

Skinny hides a grin as he teasing asks, "That is right, Shorty. But don'tcha think we otta know yar full name grandson?"

Biting his lips Shorty smiles a big wide smile holding out his hand replying, "Wesley Ray Ewing, grandpas."

Smiling Skinny and Pokey shake hands then hug the tall good looking young man.

Then Pokey asks, "Why are ya called Shorty? Yar near as tall as yar Pa and taller than yar grandpa over thar?"

Shorty leans against the wagon as he lazily replies, "Well its cause of that big gallut standing over there. Jake was a big baby and just kept gettin' bigger and bigger and he ain't stopped yet. Me, I was normal size and ma said, "Thank God for that!" So with him bein' so big I looked small and short so they started callin' me Shorty and it stuck. But when I turn sixteen soon and go out on my own I'm gonna be called Wesley Ewing not Shorty anymore." He states the last sentence strongly looking around at his family rather defiantly.

Slapping him on the shoulder Pokey seriously asks, "Heard tell that this fall one of the deputys in the City of John is gonna retire. If'n ya want me to put in a good word for ya, I will."

"I'm gonna be a Sheriff or Marshal someday but I know I gotta start out as a deputy so that will be real fine by me. Thanks, grandpa," Shorty explains with a crooked smile.

Skinny lays his hand on Shorty's shoulder asking, "Why do you want to be a deputy, a sheriff or a marshal, son?"

Straightening up his shoulders Shorty explains with a piercing look, "To stop the mean ones from hurtin' the innocent ones. I can't stand a bully so I plan on makin' it my life's work to stop'em." Then looking over at his parents he sighs saying, "I'm sorry, Ma and Pa, but I'm gonna do it."

Sadly shaking his head Zak answers, "Yep, we knowd it son. You have been planning it for a long time."

Pokey looks at Zak as Shorty thoughtfully walks away explaining, "There are three deputies in the City of John. He will start out low and haveta work his way up but he can do it and learn a lot on the way up. Right off he will just be a runnin' here and there doing errands. He might decide to quit but he will learn a lot over thar and the Sheriff's a good man. Ya cain't ask for more than that."

Nodding yes Stephie sighs, "I'd just rather he stayed a little boy longer."

"He is a man and in some ways has been for longer than Jake has. Shorty is a thinker and he ponders out problems a long time before he acts....usually...he doesn't normally go off halfcocked like Jake used to," Zak explains watching his youngest son talk to Glory.

They stay for chicken and dumplings then head back to the ranch before sunset.

Early the next morning Glory and Beth Ann drive the wagon over to Good Heart's home with all their surprises for them.

Good Heart walks over to the wagon when they stop welcoming them with, "Good to see ya'll...need some help?"

Giggling Beth Ann replies, "Yes, I guess we do. We are bringing your family some presents from St. Louis."

"Presents? What kind of presents?" Good Heart asks puzzled.

"Well ya know we went to St. Louie to close down our grandpa and grandma Hawkins' house and they owned a store, too. There was so much we didn't need so we chose somethangs to bring to people we love and that is ya'll," Glory explains smiling happily.

Blinking rapidly at his lovely wife, Yellow Moon, Good Heart opens his mouth but can't think what to answer.

"You will accept our presents won't you?" Beth Ann asks suddenly afraid they will have too much pride to do so.

Glory's face blushes bright red in confusion and hurt looking at Good Heart when Yellow Moon elbows him in the ribs before asking, "Ya'll chose some thangs just for us?"

"Yes, madam," Glory answers fighting tears at this turnaround.

Yellow Moon smiles her beautiful smile explaining, "We don't receive many presents, young'uns, please forgive us. We be right proud to accept yar presents, won't we Good Heart."

Good Hearts swallows nodding yes.

Taking a deep breath Glory explains again, "We brought ya'll thangs…special thangs…that we thought ya'd all like. We hope ya will. Will ya ask the young'uns to come over to the wagon, too?"

Good Heart nods yes and calls his children over.

Both girls open the biggest trunk that Beth Ann is standing in front of and pull out a large rug saying, "This will cover the floor in your house and keep you warmer in the winter."

Yellow Moon smiles happily at them saying, "It be very warm, thank ya."

Beth Ann smiles beautifully as she lifts out clothing saying, "We guessed on sizes but thought these might fit you." She lays out pants, shirts, socks, long johns and boots for everyone.

Good Heart and Yellow Moon are shocked at the large stack of clothing for everyone that is given. Yellow Moon looks at Good Heart to see what he is thinking and is surprised to see a tear (quickly wiped away) in his eyes at this bounty.

Glory is in the second trunk now and pulling out wrapped packages with names written on them. Her eyes are shining with the love of giving to her second family. She hands the first to Good Heart so nodding yes he takes it and opening it sees two clay pipes and tobacco.

His beautiful eyes light up happily as he says, "Thank ya, girls."

Next Glory hands Yellow Moon a large package which she smiles taking then her mouth drops open when she sees it is yards of material for clothing for her family. Inside the large package is a smaller package with thread, needles, pins and a pair of silver scissors. Amazed at the lovely gift Yellow Moon says thank you then hugs each of the girls for the presents.

Glory explains, "Beth Ann chose those for you, Yalla Moon."

Beth Ann hugs Yellow Moon saying, "I wanted to bring you something special and talking about special Glory has something really special from us."

Glory then jumps down from the back of the wagon with a cotton wrapped present walks over to Yellow Moon saying, "This is something real special we wanted you to have."

Yellow Moon takes the present and starts unwrapping it. When she sees it is a pretty box she smiles at Glory saying, "Thank ya."

Glory smiles at her and taking the box turns it over and turns the key a few times and music plays.

Yellow Moon's eyes are riveted to the lovey music box as it tinkles out a lovely melody. She looks it all over to see where the sound is coming from until Beth Ann opens part of it and they see how it works.

"Music in a box...how wonderful," Good Heart says as he gives each of the girls a big hug.

Yellow Moon has tears in her eyes as she again hugs the girls saying, "Thank ya, young'uns. I love ya'll."

Next each of the children are handed a wrapped package from Glory and Beth Ann. When Running Bear sees the knife, marbles and play sword that he is given he laughs out loud (which is unusual for him) saying, "Thank ya for the presents. We don't give or receive them often so this makes this a special time for us. Thank ya'll"

Beth Ann explains, "Sammy and Arty have received play swords so we thought you would enjoy playing with them and the marbles are a game that boys play all the time and our grandpas are going to teach everyone how to play them. Then we are going to have lots of games together.

Jumping Rabbit is also thrilled to receive marbles, knife and a play sword as presents for him saying, "I thank you for the knife...it is a nice one and I will always use it. I will remember your kindness in thinking of me and will enjoy learning to play this game of marbles."

Glory wipes a tear away explaining, "Ya'll heped save me. Ya'll watched over us all to keep us safe and if Good Heart hadn't been there when I was kidnapped and kept me feelin' safe and knowin' I was safe with him there...well, it means more than I can ever say thank ya for."

Good Heart clears his throat saying, "No need to repay us for keepin' our daughter and sister safe from harm but we thank ya for the rememberin' of us'uns."

When Beth Ann hands the girls (Smooth Waters and Morning Sun) their large bulky packages they exclaim happily receiving cloth dolls with black braided hair and beautiful calico dresses first then see there are two changes of clothing for the dolls and a set of tin play dishes for the girls to share.

"Glory pulls a large wooden box out of the bottom of her trunk explaining, "Running Bear and Jumping Rabbit this is mainly for you boys cause we thought ya'd enjoy playing with it but the girls may, too." She hands it to the boys and they start untying the string holding it together. Everyone watches as they open it and see inside a complete wooden train set with authentic engine, cab, cars and caboose.

Running Bear asks, "This be a train, right? We ain't never seen one but will one of these days."

"Yes, it is. Someday there will be train coming close to us but not yet," Beth Ann explains as she smiles at the wonder in their eyes.

Glory and Beth Ann are smiling happily as they nod to each other and start unloading the rest of Beth Ann's trunk. They set out flour, sugar, tea, canned fruit and milk then a new set of tin dishes and a few pieces of cast iron cookware. The last in the trunk is a set of silverware and a colander and wooden masher. Yellow Moon looks at it questioningly so Glory explains, "This is what we use to make jelly from fruit. After you wash the fruit and cook it soft then you put it in here and using this wooden masher you squeeze all the juice out then boil the juice until it thickens for jelly." After explaining what the colander is Yellow Moon is very happy to have it.

Turning to the last wrapped box Glory smiles brightly explaining, "Our grandpas sent ya'll these." Opening the long rectangular box she lifts out two rifles and ammunition then hands each of the children a small wrapped package.

Good Heart's face is pure shock as he looks at the expensive rifles being "GIVEN" to them. Concern lines his face as he wonders why they would give him such expensive gifts when Glory explains, "Good Heart my grandpas want to thank you for teaching me how to take care of myself and these rifles come from the store. We want to share'em with ya, will ya accept'em?"

Good Heart has a lot of pride and he doesn't know what to say for a minute so he prays a short prayer and feels the answer comes right back that these gifts make the debt smaller to Glory's family so it is all right to accept these expensive gifts. So he says, "Child of my heart...no one needs to repay me for taking care of my daughter. I accept the presents with love from ya and yars. Know, my child, love can never be repaid."

"Oh, Good Heart you are like my pa in so many ways and now with Beth Ann and Sammy and even Arty ya've taken us all into yar heart and we're so grateful that ya have because we love all of ya'll," Glory states wiping a few tears away as Good Heart hugs her lifting her off the ground he swings her around laughing. Then turning to Beth Ann he does the same thing laughing happily.

Two very happy girls return home well satisfied they have accomplished their goal in the presents given to Good Heart and family.

After chores the next morning Jake rides over then along with Skinny and Pokey escort Beth Ann and Glory into the City of Roy to deliver their surprises to Miss Ella, Hank and especially to Grandma Nona.

Arriving at the livery Jake hops down then helps both girls down before they can climb down calling out, "Hank, are ya in thar?"

"Yeah, come on in," Hank bellows from one of the back stalls. They quickly enter finding Hank shoeing a horse. He is talking softly to the young stallion to keep him quiet while he finishes shoeing it.

Jake and Glory smile as they see the care and love that Hank gives to his animals as he helps them.

Hank finishes a few minutes later then leads the newly shod horse into the corral to run around. Smiling he asks, "What'cha doin' in town today? Pickin' up supplies?"

Smiling happily Glory answers, "Not today we are deliverin' surprises, Uncle Hank."

Hank wiggles his eyebrows asking, "What kind of surprises ya got?"

Glory pulls a large Stetson from behind her back handing it to him saying, "Surprise!"

Hank looks at the large black hat and a big smile fills his face as he asks, "Ya brought somethang for me? It looks big enough."

"It is the biggest one we could find!" Jake answers smiling at the huge man (with the heart of a kitten).

Looking at the shiny black hat Hank says, "This be real fine. Thank ya for a thinkin' about me. When we gonna start on yar house? Knowd ya'll are gettin' hitched sometime soon."

"We gotta dig a well first and we're wonderin' when would be a good time for you to come out?" Jake answers seriously.

"First of next week fit me just fine," Hank replies smiling at the good looking young couple. He looks over at Beth Ann asking, "Yar surely quiet, Bethy, somethang wrong, honey?"

"No...uh...I was wondering, Uncle Hank, uh.....it is really nothing....how did you learn to shoe horses?" Beth Ann hesitantly asks.

"My pa taught me. My Uncle Donny was a good blacksmith and so was my pa so they taught me and I've taught my boys," Hank explains smiling as Beth Ann looks thoughtfully at him.

"Thanks, I just wondered. Some day may I write down all your family's names so that I will remember them?" Beth Ann requests hesitantly.

"Well I'd be right proud for ya to do that. It just goes by us tellin' our young'uns and it would be a pleasure to have ya write it down for us," Hank answers pleased with her question.

They walk slowly to the door as Beth Ann quizzes him some more, "What was Uncle Donny's wife's name and their children?"

"Uncle Donny's wife was Sarah and their young'uns were: Clayton, Jed and Jessie. They're all dead. There was a big fire in town one day and Donny and Clayton did their best to save everyone but couldn't then they died from their burns a day or so later. Real sad."

"I'm sorry to bring up sad memories. I was just curious," Beth Ann states as she lays her small hand on top of his large one.

"No cause to be sorry, Uncle Donny was a great fellow. He taught me a lot about life and how to live it. Great sense of humor, always a jokin' around with everyone, I miss him lots," Hank explains smiling at this young girl so dear to his heart.

Glory and Beth Ann hug him then Jake drives the wagon on down to Hank's wife (Miss Ella's) dress shop. Picking up a trunk Jake carries it inside and sets it right in the middle of the floor.

Not seeing Miss Ella, Glory walks into the back calling, "Aunt Ella? Are ya home?"

Smiling Beth Ann whispers to Jake, "I can hardly wait to see her face when she sees the clothing we brought her."

"Yeap, she will be surprised," Jake answers as he happily smiles down at her.

Ella walks into the room and seeing the trunk walks around it to hug each of the young people before asking, "Did ya bring a bunch of material in for me to sew on? That's a big trunk!"

Beth Ann replies with a smile, "It is material but not for clothes to make for us. It's our gift to you."

"For me? Why ever for me?" Ella inquires surprised.

"Our grandmother Lora and ya are about the same size and so if ya will accept'em ya can have a new wardrobe full of her clothes," Glory explains as Jake opens the trunk.

Ella looks into the trunk then gasps at the beautiful clothes inside. Hesitantly she picks up dress after dress then looking at them says, "Lordy, she was the same size as me! We coulda been twins."

Jake shakes his head no saying, "Nope, yar much prettier than she was."

Slapping his arm playfully and blushing slightly Ella says, "Don't be charmin' me, Jake Ewing, I knowd I ain't no spring chicken anymore."

Turning her around and looking into her soft brown eyes Jake seriously states, "Yar beautiful all the way through Miss Ella. There ain't an ugly or mean bone in ya."

Ella looks up at the handsome young man as a tear comes into her eyes as she chuckles replying, "Ya shorely do know how to make a woman's heart beat faster, young Jake, better save it for Glory here she be the one yar gonna haveta stay in good with."

Jake gives Glory an adoring look before replying, "I got plenty to share with ya, Miss Ella."

Beth Ann and Glory lift out the rest of the dresses, bloomers and night gowns laying them on one of the tables in the room then Beth Ann picks up the sewing box that Skinny and Pokey had made for Miss Ella and hands it to her.

Ella smiles brightly when she sees her name spelled out on the lid of the box, she runs her fingers over the details of the box with the tin top with all the little holes spelling Ella out on it. "This is right purdy and the designs are so nicely done. Who made this for me?" Ella asks as she looks at the pretty box.

"Our grandpas made it...they made one for each of us and we didn't even know it until we opened up the trunks and saw'em. Look inside," Glory explains then requests.

Ella lifts the lid and her eyes widen as she sees needles, thread, buttons and a pair of silver scissors inside the box. She smiles happily saying, "This be worth its weight in gold to me. I will think about their kindness and yars every time I use these. Thank ya for rememberin' me." She hugs each one of them thanking them for being so kind.

Next stop is Nona's Café and just in time to help for dinner. Nona walks out of the kitchen door after they walk in making the little bell on the door ring out. She hugs all three of them saying, "Good to have my young'uns home. No problems on the trip?"

"We will tell you all about it over lunch," Beth Ann answers with sparkling eyes asks, "We brought you some surprises all the way from St. Louis. Would you like to see them?"

"I'd love to, honey, but I will have folks walking in to eat any minute. So let's wait til after dinner and we can sit and talk for a spell then too," Nona replies as six people walk in to eat.

Quickly she tells them the specials of the day as the girls help out by carrying the plates to the tables. Jake fills glasses and coffee mugs and helps out wherever he is needed. After an hour the café is empty again so they all sit down to eat.

As soon as they finish Beth Ann asks, "Can we bring in your surprises and then do the dishes Grandma?"

Nona hugs her youngest granddaughter and her joy fills her as she replies, "I'm just a quivering to see'em. Bring'em in, Jake!"

Joyfully the young people lead Nona back to the kitchen and she sees a trunk and two crates sitting just inside the back door.

Nona stops and just stares at them stunned.

Jake walks over to one of the large crates and starts pulling out all the cookware and utensils.

Nona's eyes almost bug out of her face as she looks at the new set of cookware. Almost speechless she asks, "But where did you get these? How? Why...I..uh...don't know what to say?"

Cockily Glory replies, "Thanks will do."

Nona raises her eyebrows at her then takes the large kettle that Jake hands her looks at it saying, "These are nice....really nice.... thank you."

All three young people pick up the cookware and set it to the side as Jake walks over to the second crate and starts handing the china out of it. Nona looks at the pretty yellow flowers on heavy china dishes and lets out a gasp of surprise and joy. "How lovely they are? You chose these for me? But why? I don't mean to be unappreciative but why?"

"Cause we love ya and want to share some pretty thangs with ya, that's why?" Glory pertly answers for all of them.

Jake relaxes against the nearest cabinet, crossing one booted foot over the other then crossing his arms over his massive chest yawns stating, "Well, IF we have to be truthful...it is apparent that yar a wonderful cook...my future grandma...our dearest friend and a joy to be around... uh...shall I continue? But mostly we just wanted to do something nice for ya!"

Beth Ann claps her hands laughing as she replies, "You are the best grandma we could ever have and we wanted to bring you some nice things to say we love you!"

Nona smiles happily then looking over at Glory (who is biting her lips) says, "It was all their idea I just came for the ride!" Then she bursts out laughing at Nona's shocked expression.

Nona grabs her and hugs her then gives her a swat on the bottom for her sassiness then hugs the other two.

After all the dishes are set out on the cooking table ready to be washed and the scattered sawdust swept out the back door Jake and Glory carry the trunk closer to the other table as Beth Ann brings a chair over and urges Nona to sit down in it. Puzzled she does as she is asked.

Beth Ann pulls out the new store bought dress they had chosen for Nona.

Nona looks at the lovely dress saying, "Oh, this is so pretty. It is absolutely beautiful, thank you for thinking of me." Nona fingers the lovely cotton dress with lace at the neck and wrists thinking, "This is made for a queen. The color is beautiful in between the colors of flowers – lilac and violets. I normally don't wear this color because it clashes with my red hair but it doesn't seem to at all. It is lovely just lovely."

Next a large bundle is lifted out and carefully handed to Nona to open. Jake and Glory kneel down in front of her balancing the large bundle. Beth Ann is standing right beside Nona's chair as she starts unwrapping the layers of cotton surrounding the lovely yellow lamp that is hidden from view at the moment.

"My goodness...whatever could this be?" Nona quietly queries as she unwraps layer after layer then suddenly the bright yellow of the globe shines through the last layer of cotton and Nona smiles at her favorite color. "My what a beautiful color...sunshine in glass...yellow always makes me feel good," Nona explains as she lifts the globe up to look at it. Jake is holding the base and Glory is picking up all the cotton lying on the floor.

Smiling happily Beth Ann replies, "We knew it had to come to you when we saw how beautiful it is."

Dazed Nona hands the globe to Beth Ann then starts unwrapping the base of the lamp. When the bright yellow base is exposed Nona just leans back thinking, "*Thank you, Lord, for such a beautiful present.*"

Glory advises, "Look inside the bottom."

Looking inside Nona notices the wrapped crystals and slowly opens the little bundle seeing the crystals sparkle in the light.

Chuckling Nona states, "I've never seen such a beautiful lamp. It is absolutely beautiful. Thank you for thinking of me and bringing it to me. I can see you did a fine job of wrapping it to keep it from getting broken and it came all the way from St. Louie. Thank you, young'uns." She hugs and kisses each one of them two or three times.

"We want you to feel special just like you make each one of us feel special," Beth Ann softly explains with her eyes sparkling and her cheeks rosy.

"That ain't no problem cause you are all three my young'uns, too. I share ya with the others but you are MINE!" Nona declares as tears run rivers down her lovely blushing face. Sniffing she continues, "I'm trying very hard to talk correctly so you won't be ashamed of your grandma, Beth Ann, and here I go back to talking like country folk again."

Laying her hand on her grandmother's shoulder and looking her in the eyes Beth Ann replies, "I will NEVER be ashamed of you, Grandma. You mean a lot to me, too."

Two hours later the three young people head back home with an empty wagon and a heart full of joy. They don't rush the trip just enjoy the ride talking about all the surprises they have given out to everyone since their return.

Beth Ann nods yes and sighing exclaims, "I've never been so happy in all my life as I have been this last couple of months. The adventures we have had...I'll remember them always. The way the boys looked at me and even said I looked beautiful. How nice Randy and Chris from Grandpa Edg...uh...the Hawkins's Mercantile were. The people we helped with food and clothing. Getting to be Santa Claus for those little children and knowing that baby will have plenty of canned milk. This has been the most wonderful days of my life."

Smiling back Glory answers, "Gettin' kidnapped by Indians was an adventure and even though you and Carrie Lynn had a bad scare it all came out good. We were able to help Gray Bear and Morning Lark find their love then we had the adventure of the ambush. I don't wanna a repeat of that but I can see God's hand in it. I appreciate more what Good Heart taught me and I know now I can do what I have to do when forced to. Being away from home was good for me, too, cause I know I'm ready to git married and live with Jake and it will be fine just visitin' now and then."

Jake smiles hugging Glory to his side saying, "It was good to see a big city and Beth Ann I appreciate all the educatin' you gave me afore we got there. It was nice to eat in a fancy hotel and say I have eaten at Johanna's Café. It was real nice and good. We will enjoy chicken pot pies and remember her. Bein' with the grandpas and learnin' from'em and seein' where they live and all they have done, it amazes me. I'll always be grateful that God whispered in my ear about how to use that leather to save our lives. I'm so grateful for all these wonderful blessin's we have been given. Let's all say some prayers of thanksgiving this last mile. Okay?"

Both girls nod yes and silently they all give thanks for all the blessings they have received.

The End

Don't miss the next story – Heart of My Heart – when Glory and Jake get married, Elizabeth has her baby and the foreigners arrive for their brides.

Go with God Always

Inspirational Thoughts

Trust God to be with you in everything, everywhere and in all ways throughout your life and He will be.

A promise is an oath of trust...never to be broken and never to be treated lightly.

Helping others to their greatest heights will take you to your own.

Inspire others to greatness by doing your best.

Insecurities arise from thoughtless words.

De-stress today and pray as you play.

No one can make you happy but yourself.

Never trying will lead to never succeeding.

Always insisting on your way paves a rocky road.

For unto you is given the power and the majesty
to do all things in Jesus name.

Fill your days with the work of your heart and it will be filled with joy.

You cannot achieve your goals if YOU never start them.

Close to thee is where God wants to be.

To forgive you must forget and to forget you must forgive.

All your pathways will not be clear but remember God created
the grass and the lawn mower.

Faith is a button, God is the thread and you are the needle…sew
forth in all directions.
Homeward bound is where the heart is found.

Traffic is a flow of people…direct them to God's highway.

When you want friends of the same feather, find your flock
and fly together.

Every challenge has the potential for great success.

Compose yourself as if you are the greatest gift anyone can receive.

The ending of a life is the beginning of another.

When your heart is breaking KNOW who holds it.

A change of heart can mean a change in direction not a stop sign.

Working hard will accomplish much but working for the Lord
will accomplish miracles.

Make your life a composition full of rich melodies and
completed symphonies.

Believe in your success and it will follow you wherever you go.

Aggravations can lead to inspirations.

Friends are soulmates through time and space.

The way to have peace is to give peace.

Let the music of your soul reach out and touch the hearts
of those around you.

To love beyond all is to have it all.

Heaven is just a breath away.

From me to THEE to eternity.

Getting a blessing from a lesson is sometimes the lesson.

Smile when you greet people let the SONshine through you.

Generosity is a blessing sent by God and delivered by angels.

The plane of your mind depends upon the soaring
you are contemplating doing.

Failure is only an option when you decide to accept it.

Sorrow pulls you down so reach up and let
God lift you to higher ground.

All things are possible when God is in control.

You are a priceless treasure to God...your value is beyond counting
and the price has been paid.

Small changes can become great strides.

Happiness happens moment by moment.

Friends far and near are ever dear.

Health doesn't just happen it is a work in progress.

When low in spirit get high on God.